best ever book of
paper fun & amazing origami

best ever book of

paper fun & amazing origami

Paul Jackson & Angela A'Court
with Marion Elliot

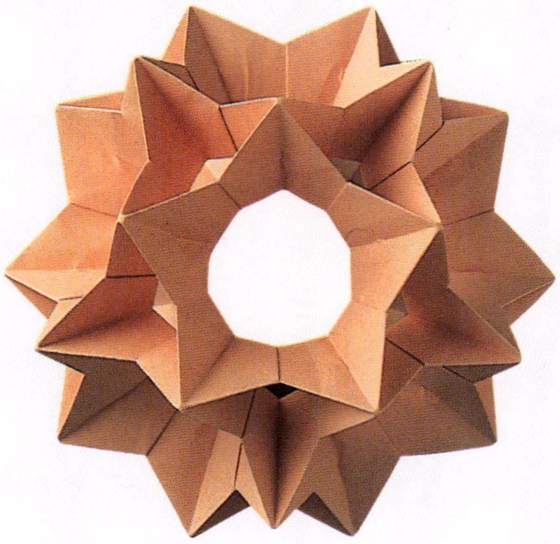

HERMES HOUSE

PUBLISHER'S NOTE

No occupation is gentler than papercraft, but some general points should be remembered for safety and care of the environment.

Always choose non-toxic materials whenever possible: for example, PVA strong clear glue, non-toxic varnishes and poster paints.

Craft knives, scissors and all cutting implements should be used with care. Children love papercrafts, but should only be allowed to use sharp tools under supervision.

Always use a cutting board or cutting mat to avoid damage to household surfaces (it is also safer to cut onto a firm, hard surface).

Protect surfaces from paint, glue and varnish splashes by laying down old newspapers.

This edition is published by Hermes House

Hermes House is an imprint of Anness Publishing Ltd
Hermes House, 88–89 Blackfriars Road, London SE1 8HA
tel. 020 7401 2077; fax 020 7633 9499; info@anness.com

Published in the USA by Hermes House, Anness Publishing Inc.
27 West 20th Street, New York, NY 10011; fax 212 807 6813

A CIP catalogue record for this book is available from the British Library.

Publisher: Joanna Lorenz
Project Editor: Penelope Cream
Art Director: Peter Bridgewater
Designer: Michael Morey
Photographer: Martin Morris
Illustrator: Lorraine Harrison

Printed and bound in China
1 3 5 7 9 10 8 6 4 2

CONTENTS

WINSOR & NEWTON
DESIGNERS
GOUACHE
ROSE
TYRIEN

INTRODUCTION

Paper is everywhere: our lives would be impossible without wrappings, letters, magazines, cards, packaging, leaflets, posters, newspapers and notepads. It is one of the most inexpensive and readily available of materials, yet it is commonly neglected as a craft, art and hobby medium. With know-how, imagination and enthusiasm, papercraft skills, origami techniques and papier-mâché artistry can transform this simple, functional and cost-effective material into fantastic gifts, wonderful shapes, delightful stationery and beautiful objects, such as toys, bags, jewellery and boxes.

Decorative Papercrafts

NATTY NAPKINS

Here is a very quick way to add your own style to ordinary napkins and add a sparkle to the tone of your meal! Even a squiggle, a dot, or a circle can transform the napkin. Try experimenting with different shapes, and perhaps give everybody their own design.

YOU WILL NEED

Plain coloured paper napkins
Pen
Gold and silver metallic pens

1 For a Christmas feel use a plain red napkin and lightly mark out a holly leaf and berry sprig in pen.

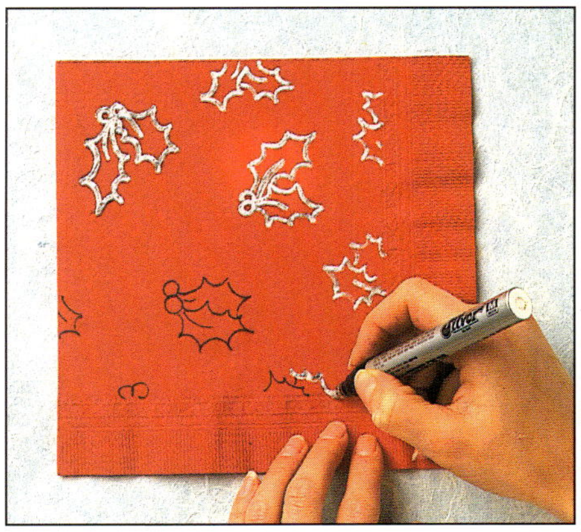

2 Then take a silver metallic pen with a medium nib and carefully trace over the pen lines.

3 For a Hallowe'en evening take a black napkin and draw gold stars and half moons with a gold pen.

TWO-TONE GIFTWRAP

Here is another way to make your own wrapping paper, this time using two layers of co-ordinating crêpe paper.

YOU WILL NEED

Crêpe paper in two contrasting colours
Glue

1 First work out how much paper you will need in order to cover the gift. Now cut a piece of paper to this size in each of your two chosen colours. Decide which colour will be on top and pleat it lengthwise.

2 Now cut circles out through all the layers along both sides of the pleat.

3 Open up the top paper and glue it onto the bottom. It is exciting to see how the colour of the bottom layer shows through. If you want a really elaborate design, add cut-out pieces in a further colour, leaving openings large enough to reveal the colours beneath. Now wrap your gift up in the two-tone dotty paper.

BAROQUE BAUBLES

We have used a polystyrene ball for this decoration. They can be found, in a range of sizes, in craft shops and are used for making dolls' heads.

YOU WILL NEED

Polystyrene ball
Gouache paint
Gold doily
Glue
Brass paper fastener
Gold thread

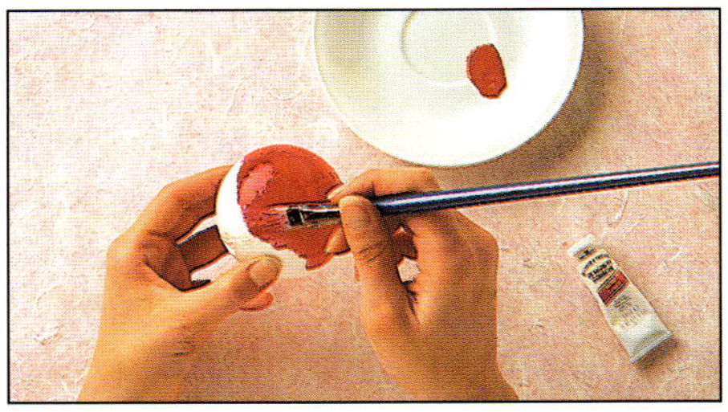

1 First of all, paint the bauble with some gouache in a suitable colour.

2 When the paint has dried, cut out pieces from a doily. Decide how they are to be arranged on the bauble and glue them into position.

3 Cut out a further motif from the doily and take a brass paper fastener and push it through the centre. Now push this into the top of the ball.

4 Taking some gold thread, wrap it around the brass fastener so that it is ready to be hung on the Christmas tree.

ORIENTAL FAN

Here is an easy way to make a beautiful fan to cool yourself on a hot summer's day. This fan is loosely designed on a Japanese fan and so we have made it with Japanese rice paper.

YOU WILL NEED

Thin card
Craft knife
Glue
Double-sided tape
Rice paper or tissue paper

1 Cut out an oval piece of thin card. Make sure that the card is not too thick so that it is flexible for fanning. Cut out the bottom area of the fan with a craft knife.

2 Next cut thin strips of card and lining them up at the base, stick them on both sides of the fan so that they follow the cut out lines.

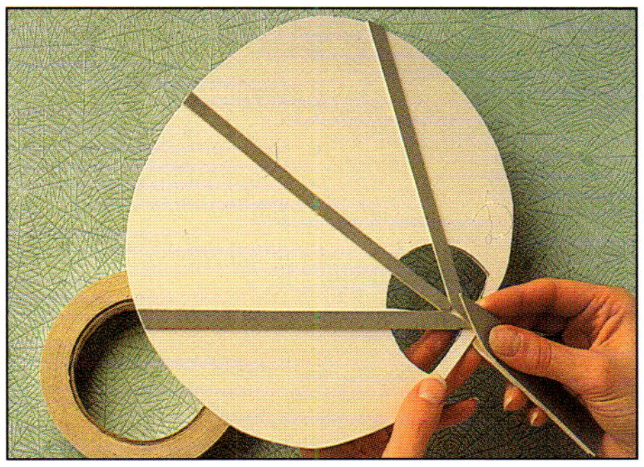

3 To make the handle, cut out two strips of thicker card measuring 14 × 1½ cm (5½ × ½ in). Taper the ends and stick double-sided tape onto both pieces. Attach them to either side of the base part of the fan.

4 Now cover the fan in rice paper by gluing round the edge and along the struts. We have used a different colour paper on either side for variety. If you cannot find rice paper, use tissue paper instead. Trim the edges with scissors.

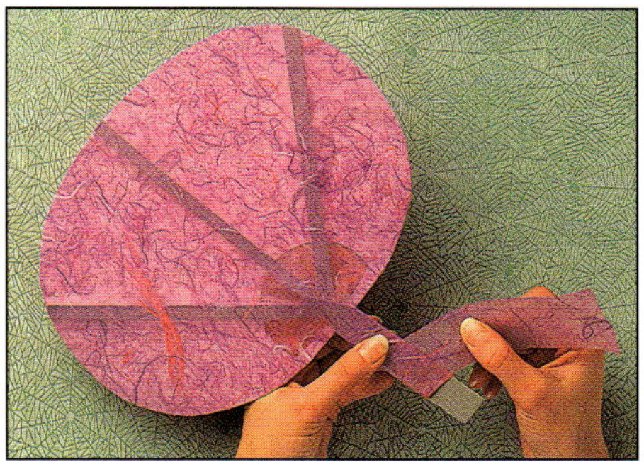

5 Cover the handle by wrapping it with a long strip of rice paper and gluing it at the bottom.

WELL-DRESSED NAPKIN

Here is a quick and simple way to dress up a napkin using coloured card. You can make the holder in contrasting or a toning coloured card to suit the setting.

YOU WILL NEED

Paper napkins
Thin card in two contrasting colours
Glue

1 First cut a square of card to the same size as the folded napkin.

2 Fold the card diagonally with the front fold halfway up. Cut a triangle in contrasting coloured card slightly smaller than the front triangle. Cut out a zigzag edge along two sides.

3 Now fold the napkin in half and place it into the napkin holder. Why not experiment with different designs on the front, or leave it plain and glue on a cut out motif from a magazine.

GIFT BOX

Here is an easy and stylish way to present an awkwardly-shaped gift. It also makes a lovely box to use afterwards to keep things in.

YOU WILL NEED

Empty shoe box with lid
Patterned and plain wrapping paper
Glue
Tissue paper

1 Wrap the outside of the box in the patterned paper.

2 Now line the inside of the box with plain paper.

3 Cover the lid of the box on the top and inside in the plain paper. Take some tissue paper in a co-ordinating colour, softly scrunch it up and arrange it in the bottom of the box. Place the gift inside and put the lid on.

4 As a further decoration, enhance the top by attaching paper strips cut from the patterned paper to suggest ribbons.

CLASSIC LINES

If you want to write a letter in a hurry, but still want it to be stylish, here are a couple of quick ways to make some beautiful writing paper. You will need some lightly coloured wrapping paper in a classical design.

YOU WILL NEED

Pale wrapping paper
Tracing paper
Glue
Sheet of white paper

1 Cut out a rectangle of wrapping paper to the size of writing paper, and cut a piece of tracing paper to the same size. Stick the tracing paper on top of the wrapping paper, smoothing out any bubbles. Use a black felt-tip pen to write your letter so that it shows up clearly.

2 If you have a bit more time you could select one particular motif from the paper and cut this out.

3 Glue the motif to a sheet of white paper.

4 As before, glue a sheet of tracing paper on top to give an elegant double layer. You could make a collection of writing paper by cutting out different motifs from one sheet of wrapping paper.

PAINT AND PAPER

Have fun turning an ordinary piece of black paper into bright and jazzy wrapping paper. You could of course vary the colour of the paper and paints.

YOU WILL NEED

Plain paper
Paints

2 Add more colours as you wish until the paper is brightly decorated.

1 Take a piece of black paper large enough to cover your present. Now choose the paint colours you are going to use. This example uses fuchsia pink, orange and gold paints to contrast with the black background. After preparing the paint on a saucer, decorate the paper with random 'blobs', working with one colour at a time.

3 For a more regular painted pattern, the present can be wrapped first and then, following the shape of the gift, painted with wavy lines.

TWELFTH KNIGHT

Whether entertaining the Knights of the Round Table or just arranging a boys' party, these heraldic place mats will certainly set the tone.

YOU WILL NEED

Silver, purple and orange card
Glue

1 Place mat To make this heraldic place mat, trace out a shield shape onto silver card and cut it out. It should have a width and length of about 25 cm (10 in). Cut six strips of purple card measuring 2 × 27 cm (¾ × 11 in). Glue and place two strips to form a cross on the shield and trim at the edges.

2 Cut out eight wavy lines in orange card and five dots in purple card. Using the template, scaled to the size required, draw and cut out the fleur-de-lys shape.

3 Following the design in the photograph, arrange all the shapes onto your card and glue them into place one by one.

4 Napkin holder Take a piece of purple card 22 × 5 cm (9 × 2 in). Join the short ends together and glue. Cut out a small silver shield in card and an orange fleur-de-lys. Glue together and then glue onto the napkin holder.

5 Name place card To complete the heraldic theme, make up a name place. Cut a piece of silver card 9 × 10 cm (3½ × 4 in) and fold it lengthways down the centre. Cut out a smaller fleur-de-lys shape 4 cm (1½ in) high in purple card and glue it onto the silver card. Add the orange band.

ELEGANT ENVELOPES

Finding the right size and style of envelope to match your home-made stationery can be a problem, so why not make your own?

YOU WILL NEED

Coloured card
Glue
Contrasting coloured card

1 Measure out the size that you require by placing your card onto a piece of coloured card. It must be twice as long plus 3 cm (1 in), and as wide plus 6 cm (2 in). For a pointed flap you will need an extra 10 cm (4 in) on the length.

2 Cut off the excess corners and then fold up the bottom and sides and stick them down.

3 Cut out a motif to stick on the back flap in a different colour. If the envelope has a pointed flap you might like to make this a contrasting colour by cutting out a triangle to the same size and gluing it to the back flap.

IT'S A CRACKER

Sometimes a gift has such an obvious shape that even when it has been wrapped up it is immediately recognizable. Here is a fun way to disguise the shape by dressing it up as a cracker.

YOU WILL NEED

Cardboard tube
Wrapping paper
Double-sided tape
Ribbon

1 Place your gift inside the cardboard tube and cut a piece of wrapping paper so that it extends about 10 cm (4 in) at either end. Roll the paper around and secure it with tape. For a really professional look double-sided tape should be used.

2 Now cut two lengths of ribbon and tie at each end of the tube. Trim the ribbon ends. For a more colourful effect you could use several colours of ribbon.

3 Holding the cracker in one hand, cut a zigzag design at the end and then turn around and repeat with the other end.

STENCILLING

Stencilling is a very popular craft and a huge variety of effects can be achieved. Stencilled patterns can be combined with other decorative techniques such as speckling or batik effects using wax crayons. Either a stencilling brush or a sponge can be used to apply the paint through the stencil; a brush will give a stippled effect, and a sponge a solid, denser result.

YOU WILL NEED

Stencilling card
Craft knife
Paper
Assortment of paints
Piece of sponge
Stencil brush

1 Draw a design onto the stencilling card and cut it out carefully using a craft knife.

2 Lay a piece of paper onto a flat surface and place the stencil on top over the intended position of the design. Mix the paint until it is quite sticky in consistency; take up a fair amount of paint using the sponge and carefully dab it over the pattern in the stencilling card. Take care not to let the paint become too thin as it will seep under the edges of the stencil, giving a blurred design.

3 To use a stencil brush, lay a sheet of paper down on a flat surface and place the stencil on top. Load the brush with fairly thick paint and press it gently over the stencil, covering the paper beneath. Again, make sure the paint is not too thin. Dab paint over the stencil so that a mottled effect is achieved.

RIBBON PLAITS AND CURLS

There are many different effects that can be achieved by mixing and matching coloured ribbons. They can be plaited or twisted and grouped into colours to cascade down a wrapped present.

YOU WILL NEED

Assortment of ribbons
Double-sided tape
Felt-tip pens
Gold metallic pen

1 One of the most straightforward ways to use ribbon is to curl it. This effect is achieved by pulling the ribbon through closed scissors to make it twist and fall into natural ringlets. Try doing this to different lengths and colours of ribbons and then attach a bunch of curls to your present.

2 Another effective way to use ribbon is to plait it, using at least three different colours. Tape the ribbon ends together and plait to the required length. Secure and cut the ribbon ends.

3 In this example a whole medley of ribbons in different colours and widths is plaited together in order to create a riot of colour. Tape and cut ribbon ends.

4 To give ribbon an individual look, decorate it by drawing a design taken from the wrapping paper with a felt-tip or metallic pen.

TAG TIME

Make your own gift tags for a personal touch as well as to save money. Used greetings cards can often be cut down and made into brand new gift tags. Another idea is to take a motif from the wrapping paper used to cover your present.

YOU WILL NEED

Wrapping paper or greetings cards
Glue
Thin card
Ribbon

1 When you have wrapped the present, cut out a suitable motif from the spare paper. Glue the motif onto some thin card in a co-ordinating colour.

2 Following the shape of the motif cut around the design so that the card forms a border.

3 Now punch a hole in the card with a scissor blade and thread a ribbon through the hole. Write a message on the tag and attach it to the present.

STRAIGHT-SIDED BOX

This pretty box is made in two parts; each half can be in a different colour to create a contrast effect. It is assembled using a clever interlocking action.

YOU WILL NEED

Thin card in two different colours
Craft knife
Glue

1 Both halves are made in the same way. Scale up the template for the two halves of the box to the size required and transfer to the coloured card. Cut out the pieces with a craft knife. Fold in and glue the side tabs.

2 To assemble the box, interlock the two halves by first tucking each tongue beneath the shallow edge on all sides of the box. Push the halves together to close the box.

BATIK EFFECTS

Lovely batik-like effects can be achieved on paper with wax crayons and thin paint. Designers' inks, which have very intense colours, can be used for striking results.

YOU WILL NEED

White and coloured paper
Wax crayons
Assorted poster or gouache paints, or designers' inks
Clear wax candle

1 Draw a design onto white paper with wax crayons, using either a single colour or a variety. Load a paint brush with thin paint or diluted ink and brush it over the wax. Two coats of paint can be applied to achieve a stronger colour layer where required.

2 To create a multi-coloured effect where the base colour of the paper will show through, use a clear wax candle to draw the design onto coloured paper. Paint over the wax marks with one colour and leave to dry. Next, make more wax marks and paint over the paper again with a second colour so that the second set of designs will take on the colour of the first layer of paint.

ABSTRACT STATIONERY

Every piece of writing paper will be different using this technique of tearing and gluing paper to create an abstract design.

YOU WILL NEED

Craft knife
Writing paper
Card in two contrasting colours
Glue

1 Using a craft knife, cut a small rectangle at the top of the writing paper, in the centre. Next, choose two pieces of different colour card just large enough to cover the opening, and tear one in half.

2 Glue one of the torn halves onto the other whole rectangle.

3 Glue this onto the back of the letter-head.

4 Instead of using a plain card, a favourite patterned wrapping paper can be put behind the opening. Different shaped openings can be cut for the effect you like. In this step some paper is glued on to card and then slotted in and glued so that it breaks up the top line of the paper.

5 Of course the plain and patterned papers can be mixed.

centimetres
2
3
4
5
6
7
8
9
10
11
12
13
14
15
16
17
18
19
20
21
22

SPECKLING EFFECTS

Speckling produces a variety of results depending on how the paint is applied, and on how sharply the brush is shaken. Gentle taps produce fine marks, rather like freckles. More boisterous movements can produce a more startling effect.

YOU WILL NEED

A selection of papers
Assorted poster or gouache paints
Length of wood or other object to tap brush against
Nail brush
Stiff cardboard

1 Lay the sheet of paper to be speckled on a flat surface. Mix the paint to a fairly thin consistency and load a paint brush with it. Hold the length of wood over the paper and bring the brush down on the wood, tapping along its length over the paper to produce a speckled effect.

2 More than one colour of speckling can be applied; colours that tone in with the first layer of paint or even those which contrast sharply with it can look very effective. To obtain a fine spray of speckles dip a nail brush in thin paint and position it over the paper, holding it with the bristles uppermost. Pull a strip of cardboard over the bristles (taking care to pull it *towards* your body so that you do not splash yourself with paint), moving the brush around the paper to create an even coating of paint.

CURVY-EDGED BOX

This unusual box is almost as pretty in two halves as it is when assembled. To get the maximum effect choose two contrasting or complementary colours for the two halves so that the pattern of the curves stands out.

YOU WILL NEED

Thin card in two different colours
Craft knife
Glue

1 Scale up the template to the size required and transfer the pattern twice to a piece of card, once for each half of the box. Cut out the patterns using a craft knife, taking extra care around the curves. Both halves are made in the same way: fold and glue each tab beneath the semi-circles to form the sides.

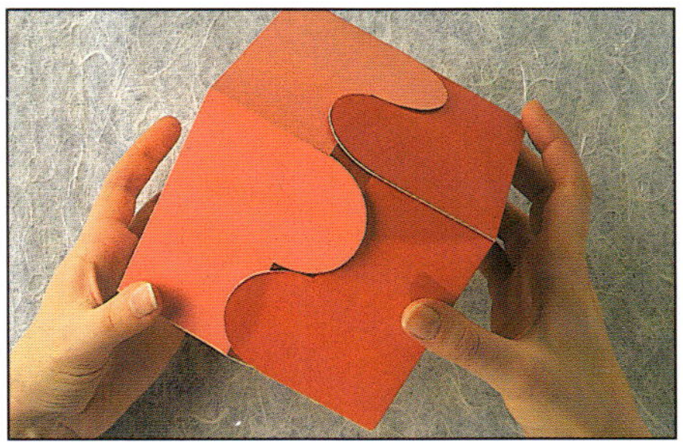

2 Repeat the process with the other half, gluing each side firmly.

3 To assemble the box, interlock the two halves, making sure each semi-circle overlaps on the outside of the box.

QUILLS AND COILS

Quilling is a traditional way of rolling strips of coloured paper and then squeezing them into different shapes; they are used here to decorate cards.

YOU WILL NEED

Coloured paper
Glue
Contrasting coloured card
Hole punch
Ribbon

1 To make up the individual quills, cut strips of coloured paper 7 × 25 cm ($2\frac{3}{4}$ × 10 in). Starting with one end, roll the paper up.

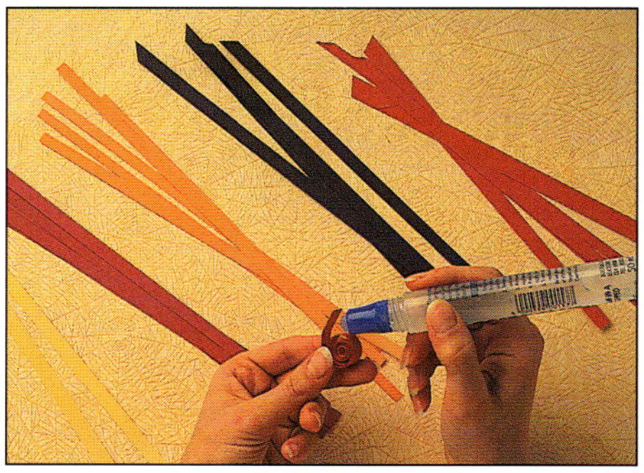

2 When you have rolled it completely, let it uncoil slightly and glue the end to hold it.

3 Once the strip has been coiled and glued it can be shaped into one of the many traditional quill styles, such as the triangle, or the pear, or the scroll or the eye.

4 Take a piece of folded card in a good background colour and arrange the quills into a pattern. Punch a hole with a hole punch and thread a ribbon through to make an original and delightful miniature card or gift tag.

BOOKLET CARD

Just a small piece of wrapping paper from your gift is enough to make this booklet card or gift tag. Secure with embroidery thread to match.

YOU WILL NEED

White card
Wrapping paper
Glue
Ruler
Craft knife
Writing paper
Needle
Embroidery thread

1 Take a piece of white card 28 × 7 cm (11 × 2¾ in) and cut out a piece of wrapping paper the same size. Glue this paper onto the card.

2 On the reverse, lightly score a line at the centre using a ruler and craft knife, and fold in two to make the outer card.

3 Then cut a piece of white writing paper so that it is just smaller than the card and fold this in two.

4 With a needle and some embroidery thread to match the wrapping paper, sew the two layers together with one stitch, and tie the threads into a knot to secure the booklet.

THIS LITTLE PIGGY

Great for children's parties or for a more adult gathering, this piggy place setting will bring oinks of delight! Choose bright pink, or a pale pink for a Miss Piggy.

YOU WILL NEED

Circular plate
Pink, green and blue card
Glue
Craft knife
Felt-tip pen

1 Place mat
Using a plate as a template, mark and cut out a circle about 24 cm (10 in) in diameter in pink card, remembering to include two ear shapes.

2 Using green and blue card, cut out and glue all the features of the face into position.

3 Then attach the curly tail to the right-hand side in order to give the finishing touch to your pig place mat.

4 Name place card
To make up the name card, take a piece of green card measuring 9 cm (3½ in) square. Draw a line down the centre and around the top half of the pig's head and ears. Score along the head and ears only and then gently fold, and the pig's head will stand up.

5 Glue the piggy's features as before onto a piece of pink card and then attach the finished face on to the folded card. Add the curly tail.

6 Napkin holder
Take a strip of pink card measuring 22 × 5 cm (8½ × 2 in) and glue the ends together.

Before the glue has dried, slip a green curly tail card under the join and hold firmly until it is dry.

TIGER STRIPES AND HOPPING FROGS

Here are some ideas for making writing paper with an animal theme. You can use these ideas to design original writing paper, based on your favourite animal.

YOU WILL NEED

Orange, black, blue and green paper
Glue
Writing paper

1 To make a jungle theme take a piece of orange paper and cut out 'stripey' shapes from a piece of black paper.

2 Arrange the tiger stripes down one side of the paper and glue them into position.
To add colour to a sheet of white writing paper you can also cut out an abstract squiggle and glue it onto the right hand side.

3 For a fishy theme cut out shapes of watery ripples and a swimming fish from blue paper and then stick them at the top and bottom of the page.

4 This hopping frog theme is made by cutting out a frog shape in green paper and fixing it to the top of the page. You will then need to cut out and glue small squares of green paper to represent its hop!

PAPER-MAKING

Paper-making is an ancient art form, practised for many centuries since the process was first discovered by the Chinese. It can be very satisfying to make your own paper. If you want to make paper of writing quality, dissolve two teaspoons of size powder in a pint of warm water and add it to your pulp. It is possible to produce many interesting effects in your paper. Small pieces of coloured paper can be added to the pulp to give a speckled effect; this can also be achieved by adding organic material such as tea leaves, seeds, hair, leaves and flower petals. It is also possible to colour and perfume your paper by adding waterproof ink or a few drops of scent to the pulp.

YOU WILL NEED

Waste paper
Blender or liquidizer
Fine sieve
Rectangular bowl
Kitchen cloths (one for each piece of paper to be made) or towelling
Newspaper
Paper-making frame (deckle and mould)
Two wooden boards

MAKING PULP

To make paper pulp, tear up waste paper into small pieces. The lighter the colour of waste paper used, the paler the result; newspaper will produce a greyish paper. Old computer printout paper is good. Place the torn paper in a bucket of warm water and let it soak overnight. To reduce the paper to a pulp, squeeze out as much water as possible, and place a small handful of the mushy paper into a blender or liquidizer, covering it with two parts of water. Blend the paper and water together for a few seconds at a time. Add more water if the pulp is too thick for the blender to rotate freely.

1 When you have pulped all the soaked paper, drain it through a fine sieve, and place three or four handfuls in the rectangular bowl. Cover the pulp with warm water. You will need roughly three parts of water to one part pulp.

Before you start to make your paper, prepare a 'couching mound'. This is a small pile of wet material such as kitchen cloths or towelling, cut or folded to the same size as the frame and placed on top of a thick wedge of newspaper. The pulp is transferred from the mould onto this mound to dry.

2 Take your paper-making frame. The mesh-covered frame is called the mould, and the open frame is the deckle. Position the mould mesh-side up, and place the deckle on top of it.

3 Put the frame into the far end of the bowl, with the deckle facing you.

4 Next, submerge the frame in the pulp.

5 Pull the frame gently towards you, while holding on to keep it tightly closed and completely submerged. Lift the frame from the bowl, keeping it horizontal. Let the frame rest on the side of the bowl for a minute to drain, and then remove the deckle.

6 Stand the mould on its short side and lower it onto the couching mound, pressing it down firmly. Then lift the bottom edge off the couching cloth, and remove the frame. The pulp will stick to the cloth. Cover the pulp with an opened-out kitchen cloth, and continue couching sheets of paper, covering each new piece with another kitchen cloth.

7 When you have used all the pulp, or feel that you have made enough paper, cover the last piece with a kitchen cloth, and transfer the pile of cloths containing your paper on its couching mound and pile of newspaper onto one of the wooden boards. The board should be placed on a surface that is easy to mop dry as a great deal of water will come out of the paper.

Place the second board on top of the pile, and then stand or lean heavily on it to press the paper flat. Press on the paper for a couple of minutes.

Remove the pile of cloths from the newspaper, then gently lift the top cloth, uncovering the last piece of paper that you made, and lay it out, still on its cloth, on a flat surface to dry. Do the same with every piece of paper. The sheets may take two days to dry properly. To remove the paper from its drying cloth, slip a blunt knife under its edge and gently separate the two.

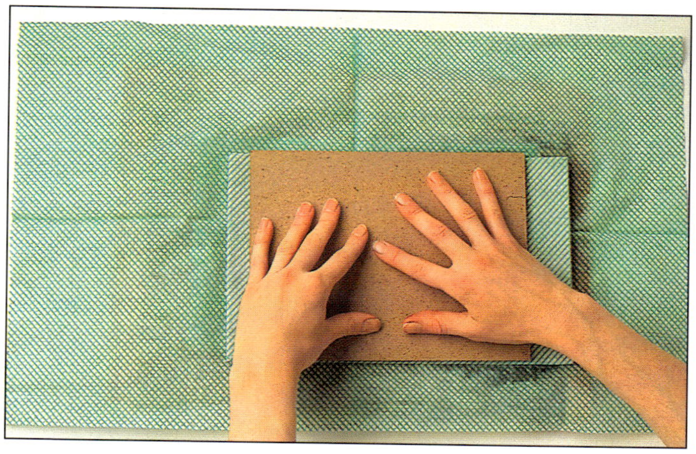

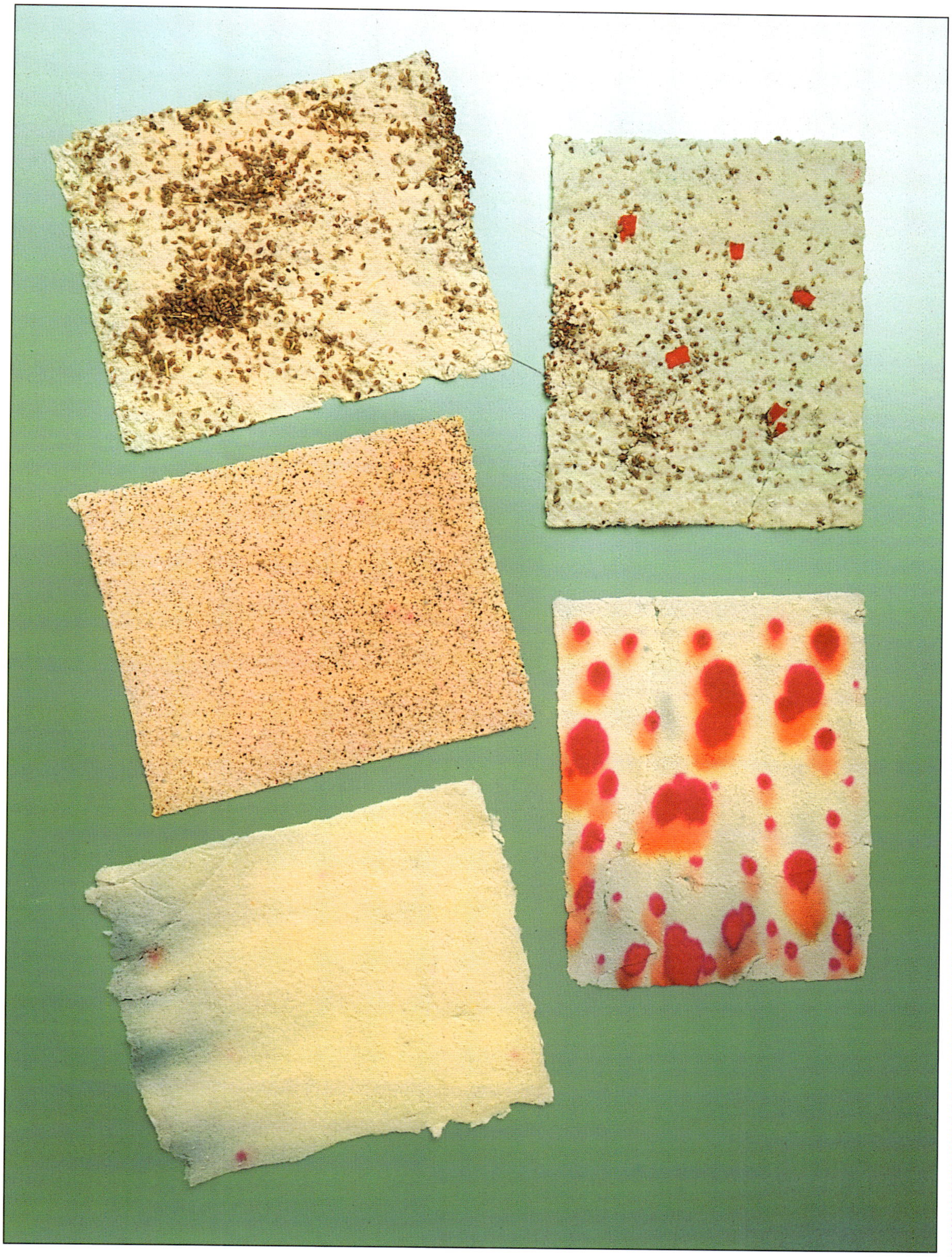

DECORATIVE SPONGING

Sponging has been used as a form of decoration for many years, especially on pottery. The process gives a pleasing mottled effect to plain surfaces, and can be very bold and dramatic; or, if you prefer, a more subtle background pattern can also be obtained.

YOU WILL NEED
Selection of poster or gouache paints
Piece of natural sponge
Paper
Newspaper

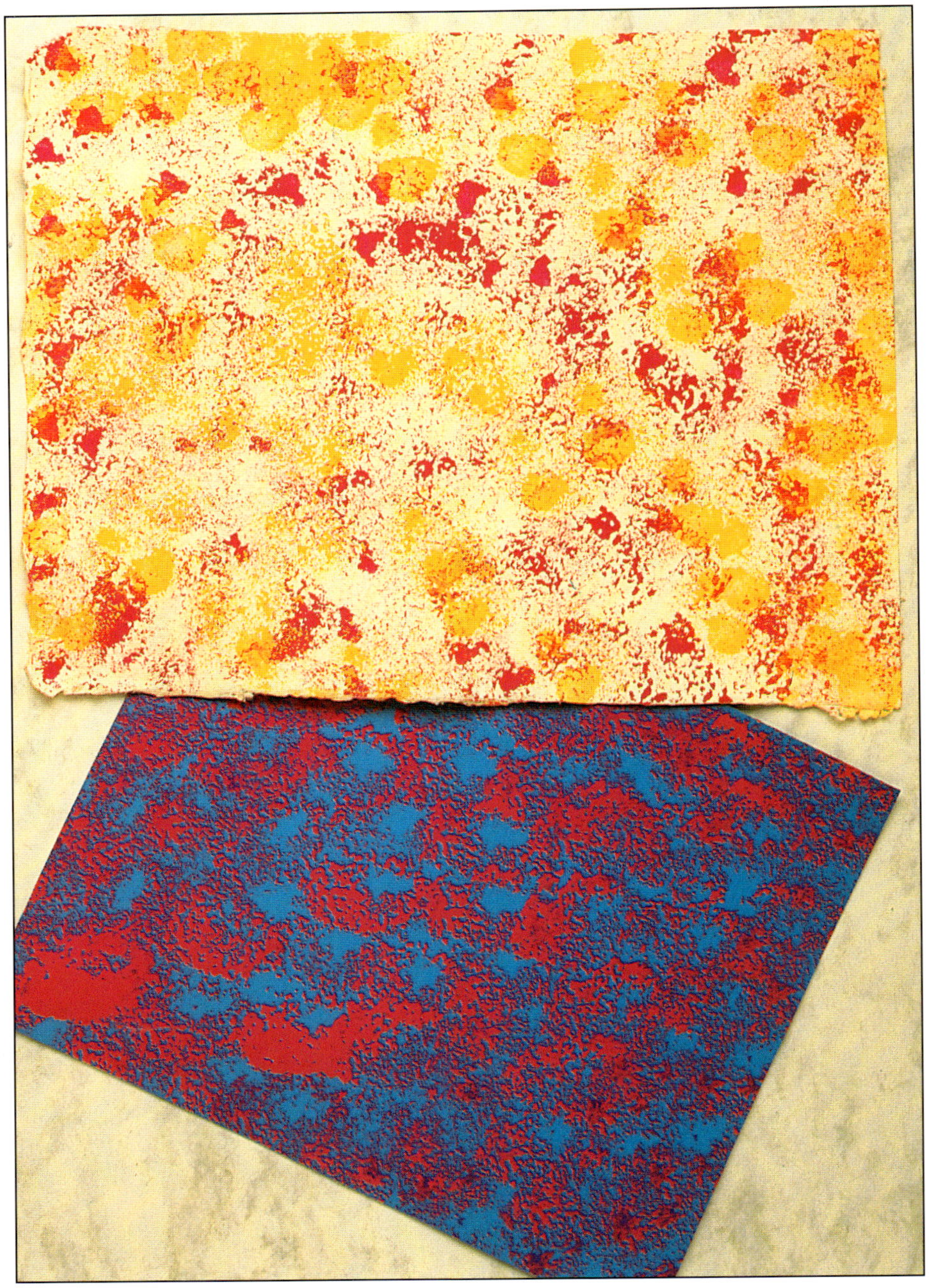

1 Mix a little paint in a saucer or on a small palette. The paint should be fairly sticky. Dip the sponge into the paint and dab it lightly over the surface of the paper, making a random pattern. If you want to be certain of the thickness of the pattern, test the density of the paint first by dabbing the sponge on newspaper.

2 To create patterns with two or more colours, wash the sponge thoroughly and squeeze it almost dry. When the first layer of sponging has dried, add more colours one by one, making sure each has time to dry before the next coat.

RIBBON ROSETTES

Make gifts look extra special with ribbon rosettes that match your wrapping paper. There are many ways of making ribbons into rosettes, pom-poms or just simple bows. Choose from all the types of plain and fancy ribbons available, or make your own by cutting strips from the wrapping paper.

YOU WILL NEED

Ribbon
Double-sided tape

1 Cut eight lengths of ribbon, four 30 cm (12 in) long and the other four measuring 24 cm (9 in). Make each one into a loop by using double-sided tape.

2 Assemble the rosette by crossing two of the longer loops and taping them in the middle. Then make another cross and join to the first cross, making the bottom layer.

3 Repeat with the shorter loops and join these to the base.

4 Finish off by putting a small loop into the centre and fixing it onto your wrapped gift.

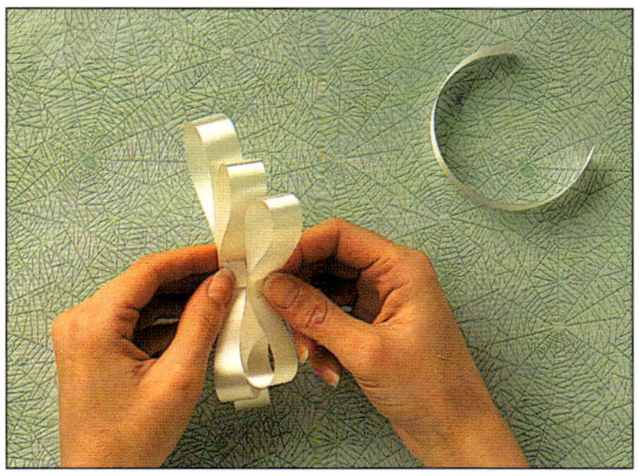

5 To make a different ribbon trim, grade the loops to start with a 30 cm (12 in) loop and make each layer smaller by 5 cm (2 in). Holding the loops in the middle, glue them one on top of the other, starting with the largest at the bottom and getting smaller to form a fan shape.

TO MY VALENTINE

This centre opening style of card can be used for any type of message. It could be to wish a Happy Christmas or just an abstract design to say Hello! Some variations are shown below.

YOU WILL NEED

Thin card in two colours
Tissue paper
Glue

1 Take a piece of card 34 × 14 cm (13½ × 5½ in). Instead of folding the card in the usual way, mark the centre of the card and fold each side to the centre point so that they meet. In another colour of card draw and cut out a heart shape. Cut the heart in half.

2 Cut out long strips of tissue paper and fold in half lengthways. Spread glue around the outer edge on the back of the heart shape and then make a frill with the tissue by gathering it up and sticking down. Finally glue both halves of the heart onto the two opening flaps of the card.

CUT-AND-THREAD PAPER

Make plain writing paper extra special with simple strips of crêpe paper threaded through in unusual patterns. Practise first on spare paper to get the right effect.

YOU WILL NEED

Sheet of writing paper
Craft knife
Crêpe paper

1 Take a sheet of writing paper and mark two sets of two vertical lines at the top, in the centre. The lines should be approximately 2 cm (¾ in) long and 2½ cm (1 in) apart. Cut through the lines using a craft knife.

2 Cut a piece of crêpe paper in a toning colour to your writing paper. Thread it under the 'bridges' taking care not to break them.

3 Once the crêpe paper is centred arrange the bow by fanning out the sides.

4 Repeat the bow design on the extended back flap of an envelope to complete the writing set.

5 Another effect can be achieved by marking and cutting out a series of vertical lines across the top of the page. Cut a piece of crêpe paper the same width as the slots, and a thinner strip in a stronger colour.

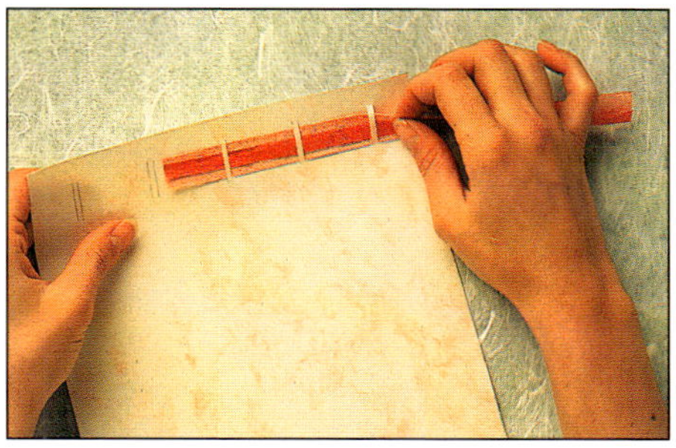

6 Fold the paper in half to thread the strips through easily, and then open up.

7 Instead of using vertical lines this version uses two staggered lines of horizontal slits. Once again thread the strip of crêpe paper through and see the diagonal pattern it makes.

BLOCK PRINTING

Quite sophisticated printing blocks can be cut from potatoes, and some lovely effects are possible. To make a more permanent block, use pieces of eraser. These can be used with paint or an ink pad.

YOU WILL NEED

Potatoes
Craft knife
Erasers
Poster or gouache paints
Ink pad
Paper
Nail brush
Stiff cardboard

1 To make a potato block, first cut the potato in half, making sure that the cut surface is straight and flat so that the design will print evenly onto the paper. The design can be cut directly into the potato, or else it can be drawn first with a pencil and then carefully pared away using a craft knife. Use the same process to make blocks from erasers.

2 Mix the paint with a little water and dab it onto the surface of the block with a paint brush. Firmly press the block onto a piece of paper and lift it up again, taking care to use a direct upwards movement to avoid smudging the printed image.

3 Rubber blocks can be used with ink pads as well as with paint.

4 Block printing can be combined with speckling in contrasting colours to create a very lively effect. Here, purple paper with a black block design is speckled using a nail brush dipped in yellow paint. Hold the brush over the paper and draw a piece of stiff cardboard over the bristles, making sure the cardboard is pulled towards the body (to avoid splashing yourself with paint!).

5 Cut a set of symbols into some erasers and use them on letter-heads and envelopes for a personalized look to your stationery.

DECORATIVE WALLET

Make this tidy wallet out of a favourite colour paper or piece of wrapping paper. You could even design the pattern yourself. Use the wallet to store banknotes, photographs or special letters.

YOU WILL NEED

Stiff paper or wrapping paper
Craft knife
Glue

1 Scale up the template to the size required and transfer the pattern onto the paper. Cut around the edges using a craft knife. Fold the sides inwards and glue one long edge to the other.

2 Glue the bottom flap to seal the end of the wallet, and it is ready for use.

21ST BIRTHDAY POP-UP

This unusual card is perfect for celebrating a special birthday. Once you have mastered the simple pop-up technique you could use different numbers for a variety of birthday years.

YOU WILL NEED

Craft knife
Stiff white and coloured paper
Paints
Glue

2 Next, fold a piece of stiff paper into two to form a card shape. Glue one tab to one half of the backing card, so that the bottom of the crease down the middle of '21' exactly touches the crease on the card.

1 Scale up the '21' shape to the size required and transfer to a piece of white paper. Cut it out using a craft knife and paint the numbers. When the paint is dry, fold the '21' in half and glue the underside of each tab.

3 To finish off, apply glue to the second tab and fold the empty half of the backing card over the top of the second tab. When unfolded, the card will stick to this second tab, pulling up the '21'.

COLLAGE TAGS

When you want to keep things simple and have perhaps used a plain paper to wrap your present, a collaged gift tag can be the perfect finishing touch. They can be as easy or as complicated as you want to make them.

YOU WILL NEED

Orange card
Green paper
Glue
Coloured thread

1 For the Grecian-style tag cut out a Grecian urn and decorative dots in green paper.

2 Glue them onto a folded piece of orange card.

3 Punch a hole and thread through a length of coloured thread.

WRAPPING A SPHERE

A sphere-shaped present is always a difficult shape to wrap up and it can be approached in two ways. The gift can either be placed in the centre of a piece of paper which can then be gathered up into a bunch above the present and tied with ribbon, or the paper can be pleated. Alternatively, pleat the paper as here.

YOU WILL NEED

Wrapping paper
Sticky tape
Double-sided tape

1 Place the present in the centre of a square piece of paper. Make the square into a circle by rounding off the corners.

2 Start by bringing one section of the paper up to the top. Now work around the circle by pleating the paper so that it hugs the shape of the sphere. Use tape to secure the pleats as you go round.

3 Continue to pleat neatly until you have gone all the way around. To finish off the top, make a pleated fan. Take a long strip of paper and fold in half with the right side outside. Pleat the paper along its length.

4 Then, pinch the pleats together at the bottom and fan out the sides. Attach it to the present by fixing with double-sided tape.

PLACES ON A THEME

Simple ideas are often the most striking, and so here are some suggestions for place cards made using a collage technique, creating a theme for your table setting.

YOU WILL NEED

Two pieces of contrasting coloured card or paper
Glue
Gold metallic pen
Metallic crêpe paper

1 Draw and cut out a snail shape from coloured paper. Glue it onto the front of a contrasting place card. Use any animal image: you could even give each person an individual animal!

2 For a Mexican theme for your table setting, cut out a cactus shape in green paper or card and stick it onto a yellow place card. Draw on small dots with a gold pen to indicate the prickles.

3 To introduce a touch of frivolity to your table, make up this jolly bow-tie card. Take a rectangle of metallic crêpe paper and fold the ends to the middle. Glue ends in place. Take a smaller strip of crêpe paper and wrap around the centre of the bow to pull into shape. Glue ends in place.

4 Finally glue the bow-tie to the top of the place card.

DECORATIVE DOILY

A circle of lightweight coloured card in a contrasting colour forms a base for this tissue paper doily and sets it off to best effect.

YOU WILL NEED

Lightweight card
Tissue paper
Glue

1 To get a good-sized doily, draw around a dinner plate and cut out two circles, one in card and the other in tissue paper.

2 Fold the tissue paper in half three times to form an eighth and cut a scalloped pattern around the curved edge.

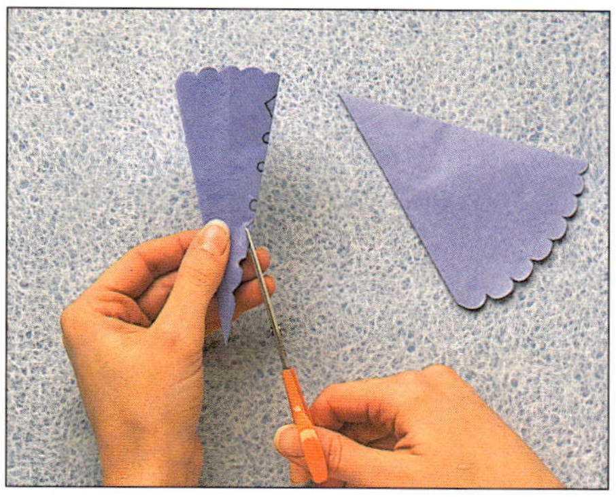

3 Fold it in half again and lightly draw a small geometric design along the edge and then cut these shapes out.

4 Unfold back to an eighth of the circle and fold the two edges of the segment to the centre. Draw and cut out your design as before on both edges. Unfold the doily and place on the card for a decorative effect.

CONE HATS

With a simple change of decoration this basic cone hat can make a clown's hat or an elegant medieval headdress fit for a lady.

YOU WILL NEED

Card
Crêpe paper
Glue
Sticky tape

1 For the basic cone you will need to cut out a 60 cm (23 in) diameter semi-circle in card. You can make this measurement larger or smaller depending on the finished size you require. Roll the semi-circle into a cone and fasten with tape or glue.

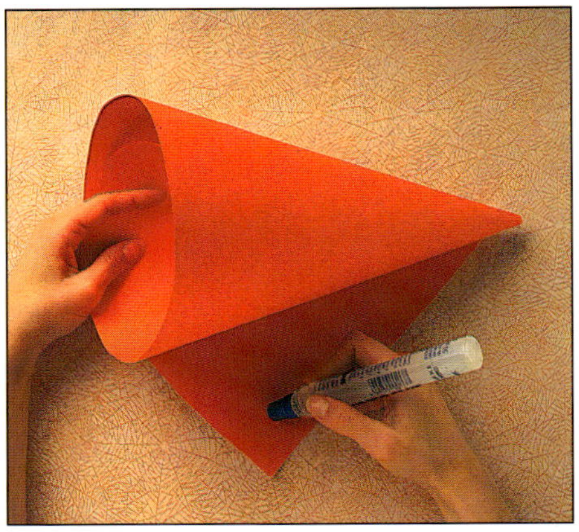

2 To make the medieval cone cut streamers of crêpe paper in three different colours and push them through the end of the hat. Secure with sticky tape on the inside.

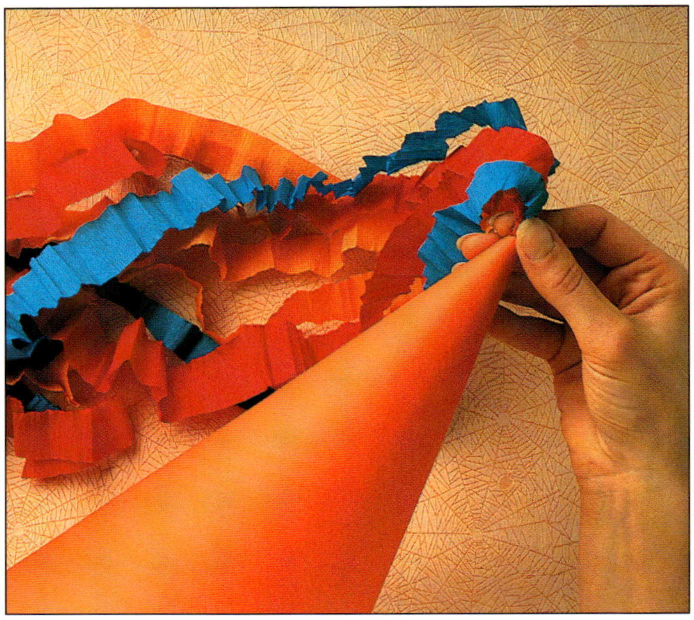

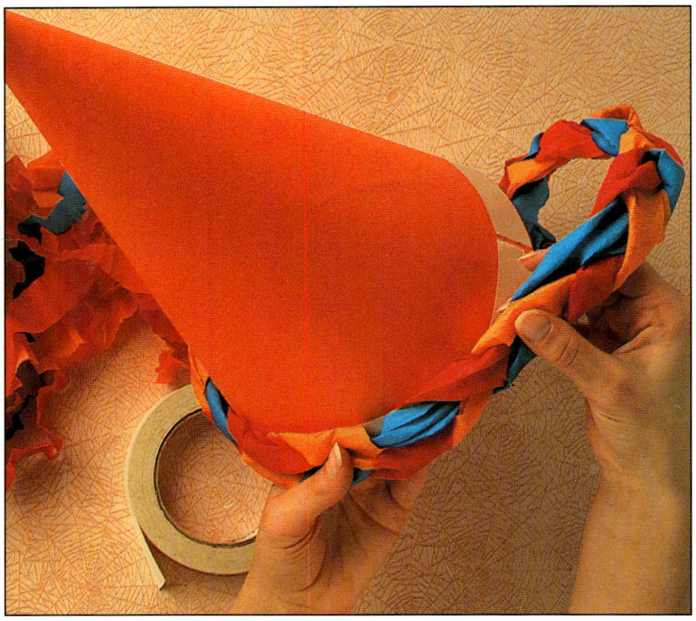

3 Now plait wider strips of the three colours of crêpe paper. Stick the plait onto the base of the cone.

4 To make the clown's hat make up pom-poms by cutting out three 20 cm (8 in) diameter circles of crêpe paper. Pinch each circle in the centre and twist. Now scrunch up the excess paper and mould it into a ball shape.

5 Push the first pom-pom through the top of the cone, then carefully make two slots one above the other down the front of the cone. Push the centre of the pom-poms through the slots and tape them on the inside to secure.

CHRISTMAS GIFT TAGS

If you want to get away from the traditionally shaped gift tag, here is an idea for making them with a stand-out effect.

YOU WILL NEED

Red and green card
Glue
Red paper

1 Take a long strip of red card and fold it so that one end is slightly longer. Draw and cut out a Christmas tree shape on a separate piece of green card.

2 Stick the tree onto the front flap and now cut away the part above the top branches so that it has a shaped top.

3 Then, glue on circles of red paper to decorate the tree.

4 Experiment by making up abstract designs in card, sticking these onto the front and then cutting around the shapes you have created.

SECRET MESSAGES

Give a sense of mystery to your gifts by adding a tag tied with a ribbon bow to conceal your message. A perfect idea for sending notes to loved ones.

YOU WILL NEED

Coloured card
Contrasting coloured paper
Gold metallic pen
Glue
Ribbon

1 Take a rectangle of card and fold in half. Open out the card and make a small narrow slit for the ribbon on the centre of both leading edges, back and front.

2 On a separate piece of black paper draw a design with a gold pen and stick this onto the card.

3 Write your message inside and then thread a length of gold ribbon through the slits and tie a bow to keep the wording a secret.

COMBING AND FEATHERING

Paint can be mixed with cellulose wallpaper paste to make a coloured 'gel' which can be used to create a variety of effects.

YOU WILL NEED

Poster or gouache paints
Large bowl
Cellulose wallpaper paste mixed according to manufacturer's instructions
Paper
Small piece of cardboard
Craft knife
Serrated pottery tools or forks

1 Feathering
Add a quantity of paint to the bowl of paste and mix it thoroughly until the desired colour is obtained. Test the depth of colour on a scrap of paper before you use it. Next, take two pieces of paper of the same size (trim if necessary) and, with a paint brush, coat them with a layer of coloured paste.

2 Put one piece of paper on top of the other so that the pasted sides touch. Then gently pull the sheets apart, starting at one corner. This process results in a delicate feathered pattern.

3 Combing
To make your own combing implement take a scrap of cardboard and cut 'teeth' into one end using a craft knife. Alternatively, ready-made implements such as pottery tools and forks can be used to achieve the combing effects. First, coat a piece of coloured paper with a layer of the paste. Then draw the combing tool through the paste, leaving behind a trail. This method produces many intricate effects when a variety of tools with different size 'teeth' are used on the same sheet of paper.

LIDDED BOX

This box can be used to keep things safe – or to conceal a surprise. Make several in a variety of colours to form a set or give one to each of your friends.

YOU WILL NEED
Thin coloured card
Craft knife
Glue

1 The box and its lid are made in the same way. Scale up the template to the size required and transfer the pattern to thin coloured card. Carefully cut out the pieces using a craft knife. Fold in the side tabs to form the upright sides.

2 Next, assemble the box by applying glue to the central tabs and folding them over the sides, fixing down firmly. Repeat this process to make the lid, and slide it over the base to complete the box.

CANDY CONES

Pretty and simple ideas for arranging sweets at a wedding or party. For another alternative wrap a red ribbon upwards around a cone made from elegant wrapping paper and use matching red tissue paper inside.

YOU WILL NEED

Square of wrapping paper
Glue
Rosette
Tissue paper
Sugared almonds

1 All you need is a 20 cm (8 in) square of coloured paper in patterned or plain design. Roll the paper into a cone, starting with a corner and shaping it into a rounded form.

2 Glue the cone together along the edge and stick a rosette on the overlapping point. Flatten the cone at the closed end.

3 Scrunch up some matching tissue paper and push this into the open end. Fill with sugared almonds or candies.

You can vary the design of the cones, depending on the occasion, using different paper and ribbons.

YOU WILL NEED

Black and gold paper
Glue
Ribbon or bow
Tissue paper
Chocolate coins

1 For a variation, cut one square in black paper and another in gold paper. Zigzag the edges along two adjacent sides of the black square, first drawing a line about 1½ cm (¾ in) from the edge as a guideline.

2 Then glue the black paper onto the gold and roll up into a cone form, gluing along the overlapping edges.

3 Slightly flatten the end of the cone and stick on a bow or pieces of ribbon.

4 Take some tissue paper and scrunch it up and insert it into the cone. Fill with chocolate coins.

ACROSS THE BORDER

By making the back half of this card slightly wider than the front it enables you to decorate the created border in many ways.

YOU WILL NEED

Assorted coloured paper or card
Silver metallic pen
Glue
Felt-tip pens
Tissue paper

1 To make the basic card fold a rectangle in two so that the top side is slightly shorter than the back.

2 Now shape the front fold by cutting a zigzag border.

3 Stick a contrasting coloured card behind to make the serrated edge stand out.

4 Alternatively, cut out a wavy edge on the front side and then decorate it with a silver line following the curved line. To finish the decoration draw a row of whirls.

5 This version is slightly more complicated. Take a piece of bright card and fold into the basic shape, then glue a panel of contrasting wrapping paper onto the front. When it is fixed, trim at the sides and then draw an arch and bauble design onto the leading edge. Cut out the arch and bauble shape.

6 On the inside of the card glue down a panel of contrasting tissue paper.

7 Cut further small circles in the tissue paper and glue them along the border.

SPOT-ON NAPKINS

This is a quick and bright way to decorate your paper napkins for children's parties or a special theme dinner. The basic idea is to split the layers of two different coloured napkins, then join them together and cut out shapes in one colour in order to reveal the other.

YOU WILL NEED

Two packets of contrasting coloured paper napkins
Glue

1 Take two paper napkins of different colours. Here a light and a dark colour are used. They should be the same size and preferably the same make so that they fit together exactly. Most napkins are three-ply (three layers). Start by splitting them so that you are working with two layers of each colour. The reason for this is so that the finished napkin is not too thick.

2 Fold the lighter coloured napkin diagonally and cut into two.

3 Carefully glue one half onto the darker napkin. Cut out light-coloured spots from the other half and glue them onto the dark triangle.

4 Now cut out spots from another dark napkin and glue these to the lighter triangle.

GIFT BAG

This gift bag is simple to make and adds a touch of elegance to any present. It can be used instead of separate wrapping paper and is sturdy enough to hold a variety of gifts.

YOU WILL NEED

Decorated paper
Craft knife
Glue
Hole punch
Ribbon

1 Scale up the template to the size required and transfer the pattern onto the decorated paper. Cut out carefully using a craft knife. Score lightly along the back of the creases so that they will fold more easily. Fold down and glue the flaps along the *top* edge of the bag.

2 Next, glue the long, side tab to form the bag shape.

3 Then glue the base of the bag, folding in the short end tabs first.

4 Form the pleats down the sides of the bag by pressing the long edges together gently so that the paper is pushed inwards.

5 Using the hole punch, make two holes on each of the top sides near the upper edge. Cut two short lengths of ribbon and thread each end through the holes to make two looped handles. Knot the ends at the back of the holes to secure.

STENCIL STYLE

Use ready-made or cut your own stencils to make this stylish writing paper. Dab on stencil paints or colour with soft crayons for speedy results.

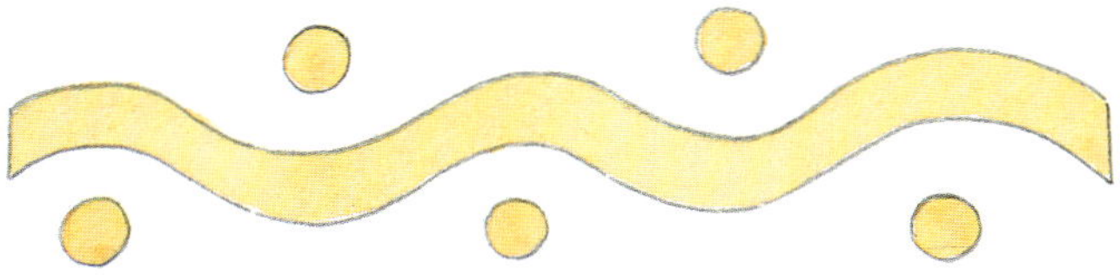

YOU WILL NEED

Stencilling card
Craft knife
Paint
Stencil brush
Writing paper
Crayon

1 Using the template transfer the motif onto stencilling card in the size you require and cut out using a craft knife.

2 Prepare the paint on a saucer and collect the colour onto a stencil brush. Then, holding the stencilling card firmly with one hand, use the other to dab the brush onto the writing paper using a circular movement.

3 Instead of using paint, a coloured crayon could be used. Once again hold the stencilling card firmly in one hand and lightly fill in the pattern, remembering to work the crayon strokes in the same direction each time.

PLACES PLEASE!

Here is a selection of attractive name cards for the table, using a technique of slotting decorative paper shapes through the card to create an interesting three-dimensional effect. Experiment with your own ideas!

YOU WILL NEED

Black, orange and white card
Craft knife
Red, orange and green paper
Sticky tape
Wrapping paper
Glue
Crêpe paper
Gold metallic pen

1 First, fold a piece of black card, 13 × 10 cm (5 × 4 in) in half lengthways. Open out again and place flat. On the bottom half of the card, cut two short lines just above each other in the top left hand corner area, using a craft knife. Then, cut out flame shapes in red and orange paper.

2 Push the flame shapes through the slots, from the back to the front of the card, and arrange so that they extend at varying angles and lengths.

3 Turn the card over, and secure the ends on the back with sticky tape.

4 For this fishy collage card, make an orange card and glue on a green fish. Cut a slot at the bottom of the card. Cut wavy strips of green paper for weeds, and push them up through the slot and arrange. Secure on the back as before.

5 As a decorative alternative, you could cover the card with patterned wrapping paper. Fold the card in half, then cut a long slot in the top edge of the front side. Cut two lengths of crêpe paper twice as long as the slot and fold up to make a frill, a little longer than the slot. Push the frills through the slot. Secure at the back with tape as before. To complete, stick a small piece of white card in the centre, and decorate with a gold pen.

NOTELET HOLDER

Take an ordinary writing pad and envelopes and dress them up in a special notelet holder. All kinds of versions are possible, made from decorative papers and cards.

YOU WILL NEED

Writing paper and envelopes
Card
Glue
Brown paper or wrapping paper
Gold metallic pen
String
2 paper fasteners

1 To make the notelet holder use one of the envelopes to determine the size, and cut a piece of card, measuring the length of the envelope and adding 8 cm (3 in), by three times the height of the envelope plus 8 cm (3 in).

2 Cut out the card with or without the pointed flap according to the finished style that you require.

3 Apply glue to the unmarked side of the cut out card, and then cover in brown paper, trimming the edges where necessary. In this example the paper covering is decorated by hand, but you could use a favourite wrapping paper or a piece of wallpaper.

4 Taking a gold pen draw a design onto the brown paper.

5 On the inside, score along the marked lines and cut the tab lines.

6 To make the notelets take six sheets of paper from the writing pad and glue a piece of brown paper or wrapping paper onto each sheet of writing paper. Trim to size.

7 Decorate the brown paper with the gold pen as before. Fold the paper in half and pop the six notelets and envelopes into the notelet holder.

8 Now fold and glue the notelet holder together. To make the closure push the fasteners through the paper at the point of envelope flap and in the front of the box to one side of the flap. Secure the case with a loop of string round the fasteners.

CONCENTRIC TWIST

Hang this impressive paper sculpture in a window; if it is made from metallic-coated card it will catch the light as it moves gently in the air currents.

YOU WILL NEED
Thin coloured card
Craft knife

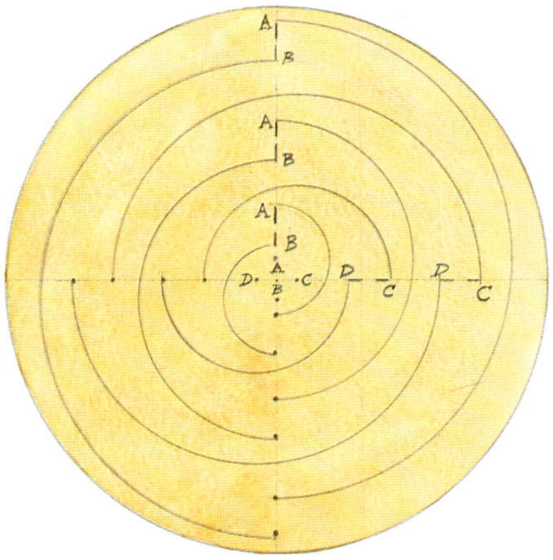

1 Scale up the template to the required size and transfer to coloured card. Cut the slits using a craft knife. Gently twist the central circle away from its frame.

2 Starting at the rim, form the first twist again by gently turning the central section at an angle of 90 degrees to the outer ring.

3 Continue to form the twists by turning each ring at the same angle, moving progressively towards the centre, until the twist-out is complete.

3-D CHRISTMAS TREE

Make a paper Christmas tree stand out by adding extra layers. Smother it with self-adhesive stars for a quick and easy decorative touch.

YOU WILL NEED

Coloured card in three colours
Glue
Self-adhesive stars
Ribbon

1 Cut out three Christmas tree shapes, in three different colours, so that they are gradually smaller in size.

2 Now cut twelve small squares of card and glue six of them together one on top of the other to make a block. Glue the other six in the same way. Glue one card block onto the top of the largest tree and the second one onto the middle-sized tree.

3 Glue the tip of the middle-sized tree onto the largest tree and the smallest tree onto the top of the middle-sized tree.

4 Now decorate all three trees with sticky stars. Attach a ribbon at the back so that it can be hung up to be displayed.

ABSTRACT POP-UP

This stunning pop-up sculpture is always impressive. Once you have mastered the basic technique you can start to experiment with your own designs.

YOU WILL NEED

Sheet of stiff paper
Metal rule
Craft knife
Sharp blade

1 Scale up the template to the size required and transfer onto the paper. Place a metal rule or other strong, straight edge along each strip and cut through each line with a craft knife.

2 Next, score along all the short creases with a scissor blade or similar implement, taking care not to cut right through the paper.

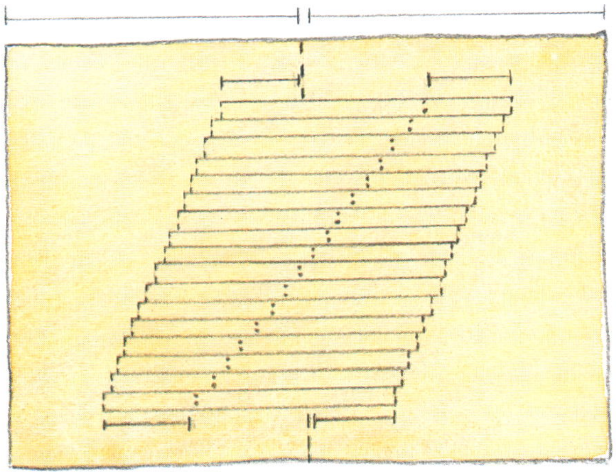

3 Take the piece of paper in both hands and very carefully begin to bend the pop-up in half. The strips of paper should begin to bend outwards but remain parallel to each other.

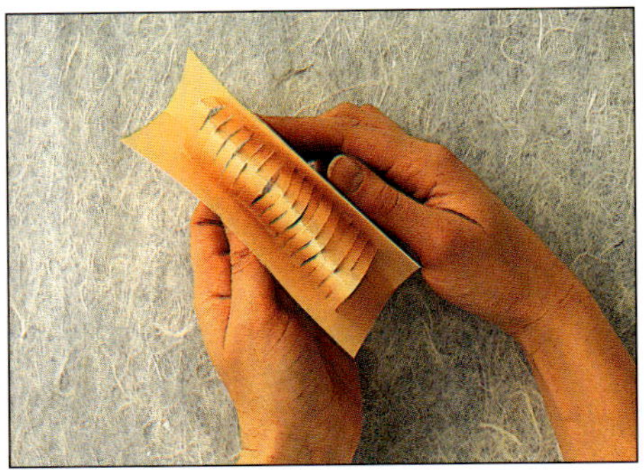

4 Close the two sides of the sheet of paper, ensuring that all the strands are lying side by side, folded evenly.

5 Lay the paper flat and, using gentle pressure, push down on all the creases to strengthen them. Open out the card and watch the design appear.

PRACTICAL ENVELOPE

Home-made envelopes can be cheaper and a lot more fun than shop-bought ones. Make a set from a variety of different papers, both plain and patterned. In order to write the address on a patterned paper simply add a little white label.

YOU WILL NEED

Stiff paper
Glue

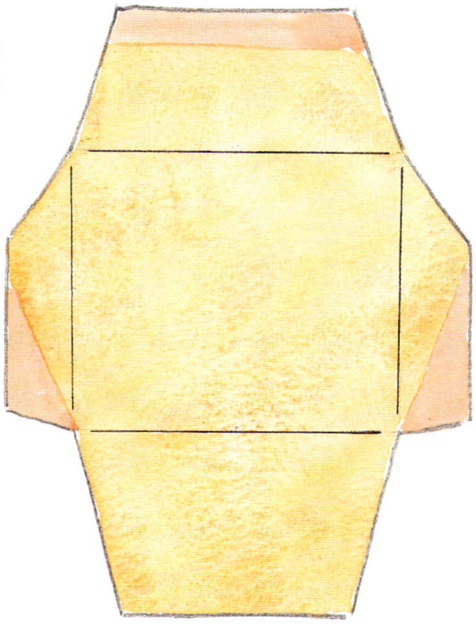

1 Scale up the template to the size required and transfer to the stiff paper. Using a scissor blade, gently score along the back of the creases that are to be folded. Next, fold in the side flaps.

2 Glue the bottom flap to the side flaps to form the envelope. Pop in your letter or card, seal with a dab of glue and send it off!

RING THE CHANGES

Using small pieces of coloured card you can create several different eyecatching napkin rings. Add contrasting coloured motifs, or simply cut and slot them into interesting shapes.

YOU WILL NEED

Coloured card
Contrasting coloured paper
Glue

1 Take a plain band of card measuring 15 × 5 cm (6 × 2 in). For the classical column design cut out the 'capital' and 'flutes' from contrasting colour paper and stick them onto the plain strip.

2 When the strip has been decorated, dab some glue onto one end and bring the other end around to join. Hold the ends in place until the glue has dried.

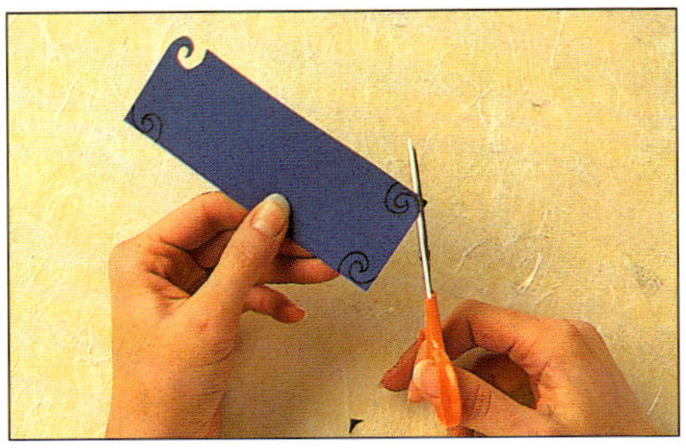

3 For the blue napkin ring, shape the ends by drawing and cutting out a design, so that when the ends are brought together the band looks more interesting.

4 To finish off add a contrasting colour circle with a blue dot in the centre.

5 For the asymmetrical rings, take a strip the same size as before and cut a 4 cm (1¼ in) slot, 1 cm (⅜ in) in from the end and parallel to it. Repeat the same on the other end but making sure that the slot is cut from the opposite edge.

6 Now cut the ends and interlink the slots so that they hold together. Decorate the ends by fringing or cutting triangles in them. By varying the size of the darts you can experiment with different effects.

BOW-TIE GIFTWRAP

Here is an interesting way to present your gifts by making your own three-dimensional bow-tie wrapping paper.

YOU WILL NEED

Crêpe paper in two or three contrasting colours
Double-sided tape or glue

1 First wrap your gift in a plain crêpe paper. To make the bows, cut out 5 cm (2 in) wide strips of contrasting crêpe paper and then cut them into 6 cm (2½ in) lengths.

2 Gather each piece in the middle and then twist to make the bow shape.

3 Now attach the bows to the wrapped gift either with double-sided tape or some glue.

4 To make your present really stand out, make up the bows in two different colours twisted together.

CUT-OUT STATIONERY

A fleur-de-lys motif is used for this writing paper cut-out, but you could choose a simple heart shape or your initial as decoration.

YOU WILL NEED

Plain writing paper
Craft knife
Contrasting coloured paper
Glue

1 Scale the motif from the template up or down to the required size or design your own and transfer it onto the centre of the top of the writing paper.

2 Carefully cut out the background area with a craft knife. Using a pair of scissors cut out a small rectangle of a different coloured card just larger than the motif.

3 Turn the writing paper over, glue around the opening and then stick down the contrasting coloured card. Turn the paper back again and see how the motif stands out.

TEARING HURRY

Using pieces of torn paper to create an abstract design, these cards are unusual and unique! Experiment with colours and cards for the best effect.

YOU WILL NEED

Envelope
Card
Ruler
Craft knife
Paper scraps
Glue

1 Using the size of an envelope as a guide, cut out a piece of complementary card three times as wide. Divide and mark the card into three equal parts. In the central panel cut out an opening with a ruler and a craft knife to create the frame.

2 Tear up pieces of paper into similarly-sized, irregular shapes and start to arrange them on the left hand panel.

3 Once you are happy with the arrangement of the collage pieces they can be glued into position. Complete the card by gluing around the frame in the centre panel and sticking it down over the artwork. Fold the blank sheet round to form the card shape and add your message.

DESK TIDY

Simple boxes can be used for many purposes; this one is ideal for keeping all those essential bits and pieces in one place on a desk.

YOU WILL NEED

Thin card
Craft knife
Glue

1 Scale up the pattern to the size required. Transfer onto a piece of thin card and cut it out using a craft knife. First of all fold in the side tabs.

2 Next, 'lock' the box by applying glue to the central tab and folding it over the side tabs, sticking it down firmly. Fill the box with pencils, pens and ink or other useful items.

ANTIQUE MARBLING

There are several methods of marbling paper to achieve the beautiful effects seen on old bookbinding and traditional Italian stationery. The process involves suspending pigment on top of water, arranging the colour into patterns, and transferring these to paper.

YOU WILL NEED

Metal roasting pan or deep tray
Paper
Oil paints in various colours
White spirit
Paint brush or metal skewer

1 Half fill a clean metal roasting pan or a deep tray with cold water. Cut a piece of paper to fit the size of the tray. Thin a little oil paint with white spirit, and dot the diluted paint onto the surface of the water with a brush.

2 The paint will disperse, creating patterns on the surface of the water. Hold the paper by the top right- and bottom left-hand corners and lower it across the surface of the water in a rolling movement.

3 Carefully lift the paper from the tray. The paint will adhere to the paper, giving a marbled effect. Lay the sheets out to dry at room temperature.

4 To create multi-coloured patterns add two or more colours of oil paint to the surface of the water. Use the end of a paint brush or a metal skewer to move the colours around before laying the paper down on the water. Before marbling subsequent pieces of paper, skim the surface of the water with scrap paper to pick up excess paint and keep the water clean.

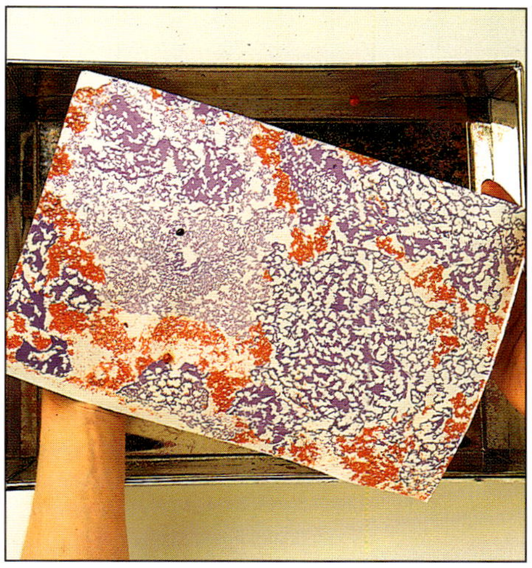

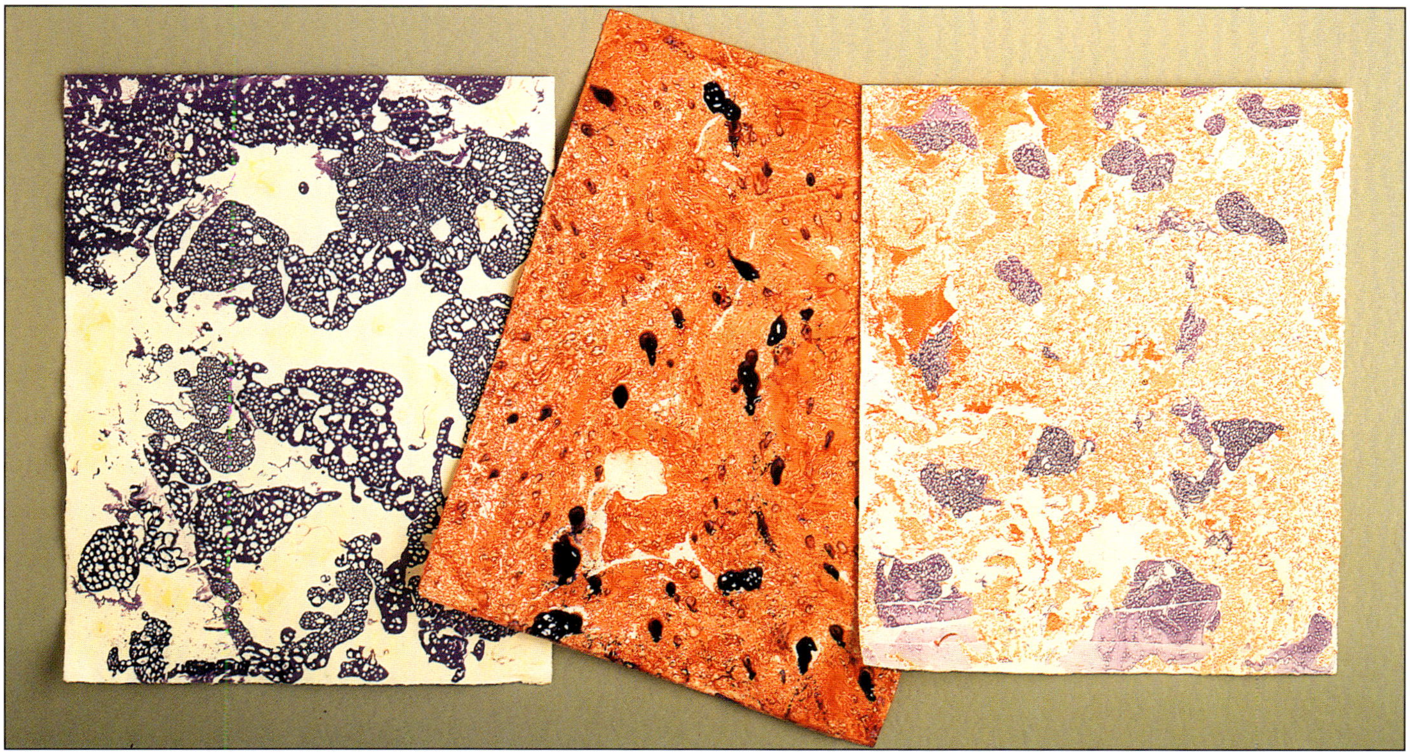

ONE-PIECE GIFT BOXES

This box is constructed from a single piece of card and can be closed tightly, making it an ideal container, either vertical or horizontal, for sweets or small biscuits.

YOU WILL NEED

Thin card
Craft knife
Glue

1 Scale up the template to the size required, and transfer it to the card. Cut it out using a craft knife. Score along the back folds of the tabs. Fold up the sides of the box and glue the end tab to make a tube shape.

2 Interlock the tabs at the base of the box and the base should lock securely without glue.

VALENTINE'S HEART

This pop-up surprise will add a touch of fun to Valentine's Day. The same technique can be used to make cards for other occasions, such as a tree for Christmas time, or a house for a friend's moving day.

YOU WILL NEED

Stiff paper in two different colours
Glue

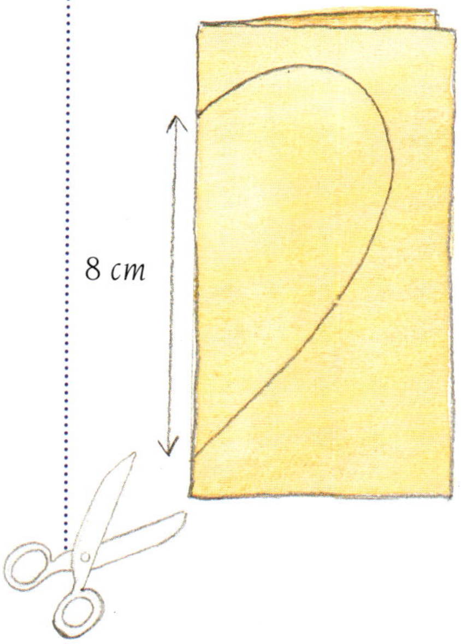

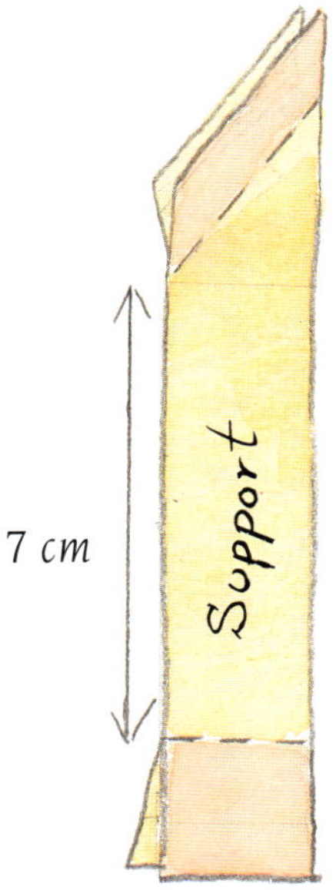

1 Scale up the support from the template to the required size and cut out of a piece of stiff paper. Then fold a matching piece of paper into two halves to form a card. Fold the support to the correct shape, creasing the tabs upwards.

2 Next, glue the support to the backing card near the top, ensuring that the crease on the support exactly touches the crease on the card. Note that the support is symmetrically placed over the crease.

3 Cut out a heart shape in red paper and glue it to the tabs at the top of the support. Decorate the inside border of the card to match. When the card is opened the heart will spring out and surprise the recipient!

EGYPTIAN EVENING

Ancient Egypt is the inspiration for this exotic place setting of place mat, napkin holder and name card embellished in bronze and gold.

YOU WILL NEED

Thin card
Bronze, black and blue paper
Glue
Gold metallic pen
Black felt-tip pen (optional)
Sticky tape

1 Place mat
In order to make up this place mat, cut out a piece of card in the shape of a Pharoah's head which should measure 30 cm (12 in) across the bottom and have a height of 27 cm (11 in). Cover the card in bronze coloured paper and, in the centre area, very lightly mark out the shape of the face in pencil. Cut the beard out of black paper, glue in place, and then make a criss-cross design on it with a gold pen. Scale up to the size required the features of the face from the template and cut out of black paper and glue into position or use a black felt-tip pen to draw them in.

2 Cut strips of blue paper 2 cm (¾ in) wide for the headdress decoration and start to glue them in parallel lines onto the bronze card. The strips at the top of the head are slightly curved. Add blue dots for the earrings.

3 Napkin holder
To make the Egyptian napkin holder, first cut out an 18 cm (7 in) square of card. Cover one side in bronze paper and the other side in black paper. Fold up one side not quite half-way, with the bronze side inside, and add blue strips, fanning them out as shown. Trim the strips level with the edge of card. Cut out an Egyptian eye motif in bronze paper and fix it onto the front.

4 Name place card
Cut out two triangles in card. Cover one side in black paper. Join them at the top by cutting off the top corner and taping them together at the back. Cut out a bronze motif, glue on the front then use a gold pen to write on the names required.

BROWN PAPER STATIONERY

Sometimes you need very little to make a good impression. For this project recycled brown paper is used to decorate the sheets of writing paper.

YOU WILL NEED

Brown paper
Plain writing paper
Glue
Gold metallic pen
Black felt-tip pen

1 For the first idea, tear a thin strip of the brown paper and glue it down, either on the right-hand side of the page or across the top as illustrated.

2 Then take a gold pen and draw a design along the strip. Remember that you can invent your own designs.

3 As an alternative suggestion, stick down pieces of brown paper to make two corner strips. Take the gold pen, draw in a design and then give it a three-dimensional effect by outlining it in a black felt-tip pen.

4 Another variation on the same theme is to tear a wider strip of brown paper and then tear it into four squares. Glue these down at the top of the paper and then decorate with black spots using a felt-tip pen.

FLOWER POWER

A simple idea for a get well or Mother's Day card. As an alternative, choose yellow backing paper for a birthday design.

YOU WILL NEED

Thin card in three colours
Craft knife
Glue

1 Take a rectangle of card and fold it in half. Draw the 'daisy' pattern onto one half of the card and with the card opened out flat cut out the shapes using a craft knife.

2 Cut a piece of pink card to the same size as the folded card. On the inside of the main card spread glue around the cut-out areas and place over the pink card.

3 Cut out orange circles from the remaining card and glue in place to make the centres of the daisies.

FRUIT 'N' VEG

Here is a fruity number that makes a collection of fun gift tags. These are just a few ideas from the wide variety of interesting shapes that can be found in fruit and vegetables, such as peas and bananas.

YOU WILL NEED

Orange, green and yellow card
Sticky tape
Coloured felt-tip pens

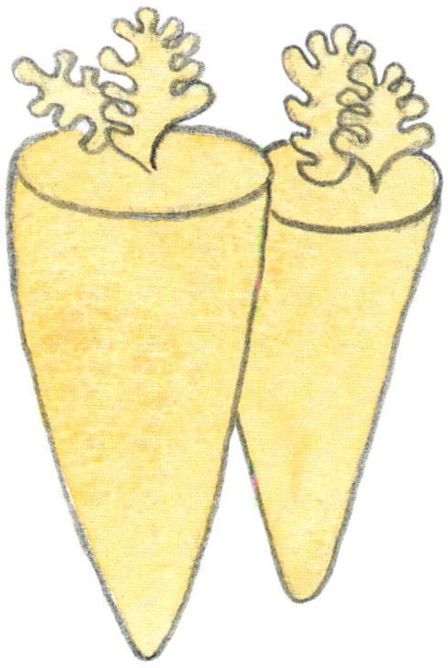

1 For a carrot gift tag scale up the template and transfer to the orange card. Cut out the pair of carrots, making sure that the top is not cut in order to leave the fold intact. Now cut out some greenery.

2 Open out the card and cut two slots with a craft knife at the top of the carrots.

3 Next, push the greenery through the slots and secure on the back with some tape.

4 The last stage is to draw the shading marks onto the carrot with a brown felt-tip pen.

BEAUTIFUL BINDING

If you have an old book or album and want to brighten them up you can learn how to cover your own pages. For this project you will need to determine the size of your book. If you are making a photograph album, for instance, the size will be determined by the album pages.

YOU WILL NEED

Book or photograph album
Thick card
Adhesive cloth tape
Patterned and plain wrapping paper
Glue
Hole punch
Ribbon

1 First cut two pieces of thick card that are about 1 cm (½ in) wider and longer than the pages to be covered. If you are covering a loose-leaf album, measure the side strip of the album sheet which has the holes punched in it, and mark the same amount onto the top of one of the cards, which will eventually be the top cover. Cut a small strip off one side of this.

2 Using the other back card as a measure, place the trimmed top card onto it and put the narrow strip above so that there is a gap between them where the strip has been removed. Tape the pieces together using adhesive cloth tape. Turn the block over and put another piece of the cloth tape onto the other side. This will make the hinge for the top cover.

3 Now glue on a decorative paper to cover the outsides. A toning or contrasting plain colour is used to cover the inside.

4 Next lay an album or page sheet on to the bottom cover and draw where the holes are onto it. Punch them through using a hole punch. Repeat the process with the front cover.

5 Now place the pages onto the back cover so that the holes are aligned and put the front cover on top. To finish off, thread a good quality ribbon through the holes.

MARBLED TAGS

Inevitably, after wrapping presents with marbled or decorated paper, there are small scraps left over that are too large to justify throwing away. Matching gift tags will make good use of these scraps as well as brightening up your present even further. You could even make them into a collection of ten gift tags and present them as a gift for a friend.

YOU WILL NEED

Marbled wrapping paper
Contrasting coloured card
Glue
Ribbon

1 First of all cut out some interesting shapes from the left-over marbled paper.

2 Then choose some contrasting coloured card which will bring out the beautiful colours in the marbelling. Glue the marbled motif onto the card and trim the card to suit the shape of the motif.

3 Make a hole in the tag to thread some ribbon through.

STAND-UP PLACE NAMES

Make your place cards really stand out with these novelty motifs that project above the cards. Choose simple, recognizable shapes cut out from contrasting coloured card.

YOU WILL NEED

Green, orange, red and white card
Glue
Gold metallic pen
Craft knife

1 Take a square of green card and fold in half. Cut out an octopus shape from orange card but instead of gluing it directly onto the green card, position it so that the top half is above the fold line. Cut out the facial features from the green card and glue in place.

2 For a festive name place, cut out two holly leaves in green. Fix them onto the top of a red place card so that the holly is sticking upwards. Cut out and glue on red dots to make the berries.

3 To make this rocket name card, fold then unfold the name card and lay flat. Draw on the spaceship shape onto the lower half with gold pen so that the top of the rocket extends over the halfway line. With a craft knife, cut around the top part of the rocket only. Then fold the card in half again and the rocket will stand up.

LOCKING BAG

This bag has a flap which 'locks', keeping the contents safe inside. Choose a favourite paper or decorate plain paper with your own design.

YOU WILL NEED
Decorated paper
Craft knife
Glue

1 Scale up the template to the size required and transfer it to the decorated paper. Cut out the shape using a craft knife. Score along the back edges of the creases to allow them to fold more easily. Fold down and glue all flaps along the *top* edge except for the lid flap.

2 Next, glue the end tab to form the bag shape.

3 Glue the base of the bag, folding in the short end tabs first.

4 Form the pleats down the short sides of the bag by gently pressing the long edges together so that the paper inbetween is pushed inwards. Close the top by folding the excess tab down into the *front* half of each pleat.

SCULPTURED TOPS

For this style of card it is best to have a tall image so that the majority of the folded card remains intact and is able to stand up. A palm tree card is described here, but you could use similar techniques to create the architectural variations shown.

YOU WILL NEED

Assorted coloured card
Orange and brown paper
Glue

1 Take a square of coloured card and fold in half. Draw out the shape of the palm tree leaves on the front and cut out the uppermost ones through both layers.

2 Then cut out coconuts from orange and brown paper and stick them onto the card at the base of the leaves.

3 Draw a tree trunk shape on light green card and cut out. Cut a zigzag edge along one side and glue this onto the card.

ENVELOPE LETTERS

There is no need for an envelope if you make this clever stationery that folds up like a notelet. Seal it with a sequin and pop it in the post.

YOU WILL NEED

Sheet of writing paper
Glue
Sequin
Double-sided tape

1 Fold a sheet of writing paper into three parts so that the top third is slightly smaller than the others.

2 On the top fold draw a line from the centre to each corner to make an envelope flap and then cut off the corner triangles.

3 To decorate the top, glue a sequin at the point. A piece of gold, metallic or shiny card would work as well.

4 Just under the flap attach a small piece of double-sided sticky tape and then draw in address lines on the reverse.

5 There are lots of different ways to decorate the envelope letter. You can glue on strips of contrasting coloured paper so that when the paper is folded up it looks like a present.

6
15
8
25
18
11
20
9
4

Paper Projects

TIGER, TIGER

Dress up as a big cat with this colourful tiger mask that will set the scene for a jungle theme party.

YOU WILL NEED

Orange card
Black felt-tip pen
Black ribbon
Craft knife
Sticky tape
Sewing needle
Elastic

1 Use the template, scaled up to size required, and cut out the tiger mask in some bright orange card.

2 Now draw on the tiger stripes with a black felt-tip pen.

3 For the whiskers cut thin strips of black ribbon about 12 × ½ cm (5 × ¼ in). Using a craft knife make four small slots on either side of the nose.

4 Push the whisker strips through the slots and use tape on the back to secure them.

5 Now sew on some elastic to either side of the mask and adjust to fit.

EASTER EGG BASKET

Make Easter egg-stra special by giving this pretty gift-wrapped basket of eggs. Choose daffodil yellow card and tissue, or bright pink as here.

YOU WILL NEED
Old bowl-shaped container
Coloured card
Glue
Metallic tissue paper
Pink tissue paper
Pink ribbon
Chocolate eggs

1 Cut a strip of card large enough to go around the bowl and just a bit deeper. Then cut a wavy line along the top edge.

2 Glue the strip onto the bowl.

3 Now take a square of metallic tissue paper and place it in the bottom of the bowl.

4 Scrunch up a large sheet of bright pink tissue paper and arrange it in the bottom of the bowl. Place the chocolate eggs inside on the pink tissue paper. Bring the metallic tissue paper around and tie together with some pink ribbon.

PAPER PROJECTS

CHOCOLATE BOX

This box is quick and easy to assemble. It needs only a spot of glue and a few tucks. Fill it with chocolates or homemade truffles for the perfect gift.

YOU WILL NEED

Thin coloured card
Craft knife
Glue

1 First, scale up the pattern from the template to the size required and transfer to the piece of card. Cut out using a craft knife, scoring along the back of the creases. Glue the end tab to form the basic box shape.

2 Next, interlock the tabs at the base of the box. If the pattern has been carefully cut out, the base will lock strongly without glue. Fill the box with sweets and fold down the lid.

RING AND BANGLE

A very simple way to make attractive jewellery is by twisting paper. Sheets of newspaper are twisted into a tight 'rope' and fitted around the wrist or throat to form bangles and rings, which can be covered with papier-mâché and decorated.

YOU WILL NEED

Newspaper
Masking tape
Diluted PVA glue
Fine sandpaper
White paint
Selection of poster paints
Glass 'gems', sequins, shells etc.
Non-toxic clear gloss varnish

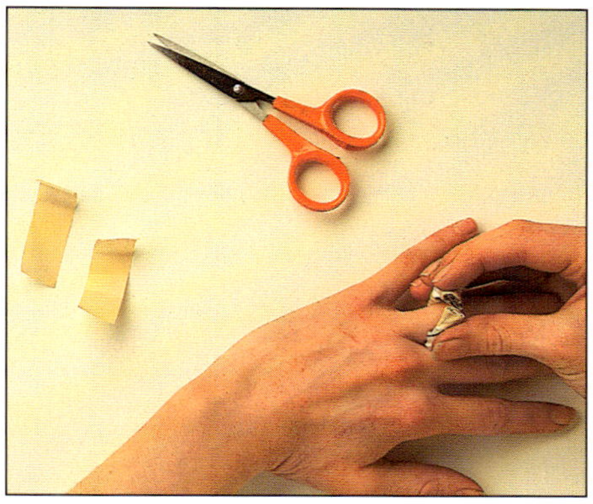

1 Ring
Take quarter of a sheet of newspaper and roll and twist it into a thin rope. Secure the rope along its length with strips of masking tape. Hold the rope around your finger, cut it to size, and tape the ends firmly together.

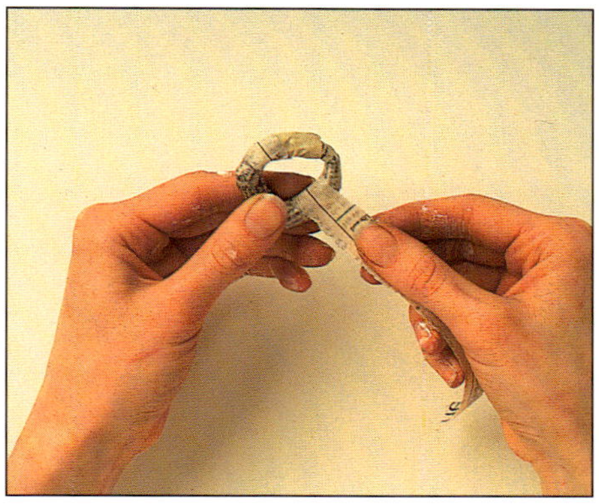

2 Tear small thin strips of newspaper, about 1 × 5 cm (½ × 2 in), coat them with diluted PVA glue, and stick them around the ring. Three layers of papier-mâché strips will be sufficient.

3 To add decorative knobbles to the ring, perhaps to imitate jewels, squash short pieces of newspaper between your fingers to form pellets, and stick in place.

4 Allow the ring to dry for 24 hours in a warm place. Lightly sand down the ring, and prime it with two coats of white paint.

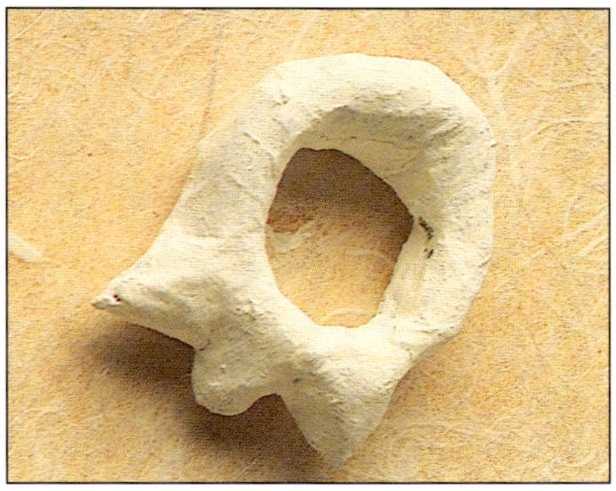

5 Bangle
To make the bangle, simply roll up a double sheet of newspaper to make a thicker rope, cut it to fit your wrist and then follow the same process you used to make the ring. Decorate the ring and bangle with poster paints. You may like to paint them in one colour, and then augment them with sequins, 'gems' or shells. Leave them to dry overnight, and then seal with two coats of non-toxic clear gloss varnish.

PLAQUE

Your family may have a coat of arms or a heraldic device that could be displayed on a wall plaque – if it hasn't, why not invent one? Add a Latin motto or phrase for authenticity – the wittier the better!

YOU WILL NEED

Thick cardboard
Strong clear glue
Masking tape
Diluted PVA glue
2 picture hangers
Newspaper
Fine sandpaper
White paint
Selection of poster paints
Non-toxic clear gloss varnish
Chain or cord to hang plaque

1 Cut three identical pieces of cardboard to the required dimensions, and stick them together with strong clear glue, securing the edges with masking tape. Paint the plaque with a coat of diluted PVA glue and allow it to dry. Stick two picture hangers to the reverse of the plaque with strong clear glue, and secure the stem of each hanger with a piece of masking tape.

2 Next, let the glue behind the hangers dry for at least an hour, and then cover the plaque with five layers of papier-mâché, using strips of newspaper approximately 2½ cm (1 in) wide, soaked in PVA glue.

3 Lightly sand down the surface of the plaque, and then apply two layers of white paint. Leave time for the paint to dry thoroughly.

4 Finally, draw in your design with pencil, and decorate the plaque with poster paints. Seal the finished plaque with two coats of non-toxic clear gloss varnish. Attach a chain or cord to the hangers on the reverse side to suspend it from the wall.

FRAMED PIECE

If you have a spare frame or a gap on a wall that you have been wondering how to fill, here is a way to make a charming abstract seashore scene. You can vary the images to make a series of pieces for different sized frames.

YOU WILL NEED

Stencilling card
Craft knife
Assortment of coloured papers
Glue

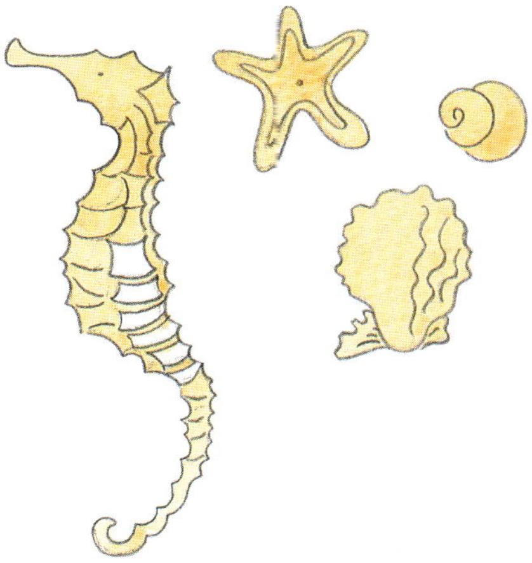

1 Scale up the design on the template to the size that you require for your frame. Draw it out onto a piece of stencilling card and carefully cut out the lines using a craft knife so that the shapes show through. Take care not to cut through any 'bridges' in the card.

2 Next, place the cut-out stencil onto the piece of coloured paper which will form the main background. Then cut out squares or rectangles of different coloured papers until you have enough to fill the spaces in the stencil design.

3 Arrange the coloured papers by placing them between the stencilling card and the background paper, and see how they give form to the shapes.

4 When you have decided on the colours for the final picture, glue all the pieces into position. Finally, trim the pieces of coloured paper that extend beyond the stencil and secure the picture into a frame.

PIRATES AHOY!

This hat is simple to make, but looks good and would make a very realistic pirate outfit. For added authenticity cut out an eye patch and tie with elastic.

YOU WILL NEED

Gold card
Stiff black paper
White paint
Double-sided tape
Black elastic

1 Cut out a strip of gold card measuring 6 × 60 cm ($2\frac{1}{4} \times 23\frac{1}{2}$ in) and join the ends together to make the basic headband.

2 Next cut out two pirate hat shapes in stiff black paper. On the front piece mark out a skull and cross bones (the pirate's hallmark) and paint it in white.

3 Apply two pieces of double-sided tape to the back and front of the headband and stick on the black paper hat shapes.

4 Now stick a small square of double-sided tape at either end of the hat so that the back and front sides join together.

5 For the eye patch, cut out a small triangle in the same black paper just large enough to fit over your eye. Attach elastic to either side so that it can be worn around your head to make the eye patch.

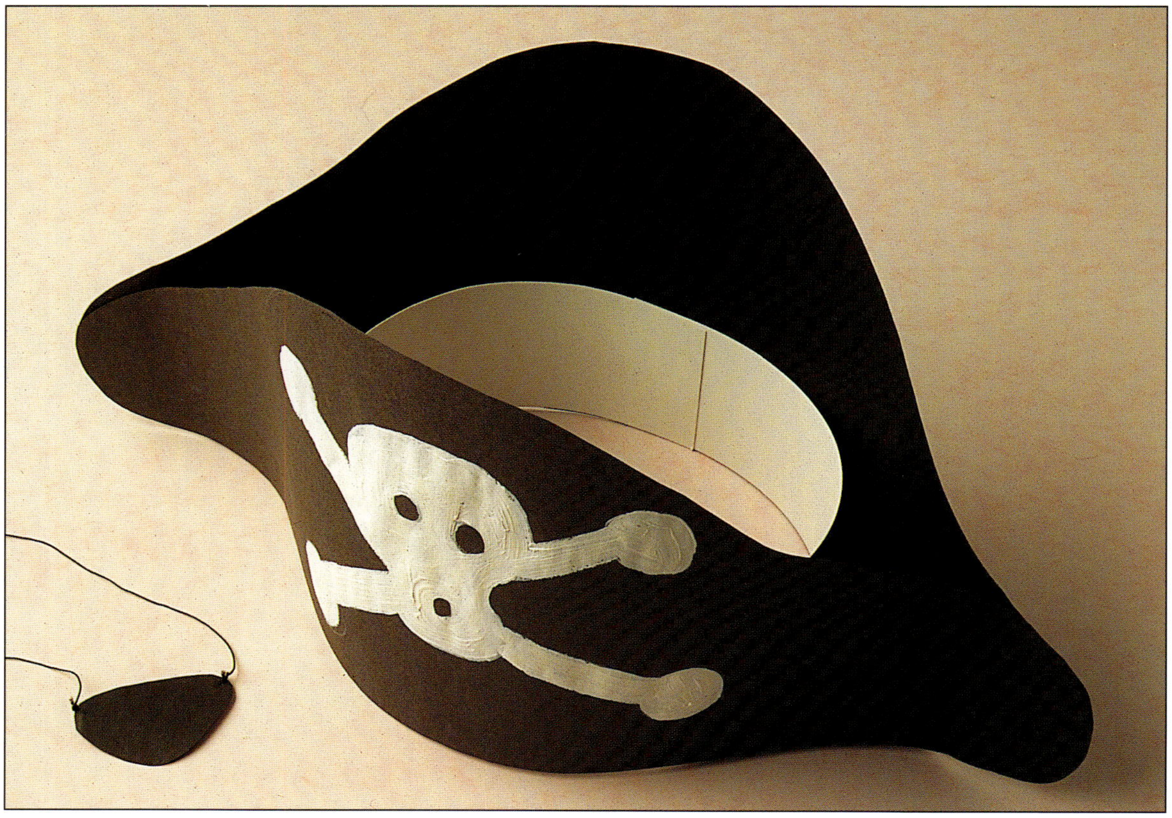

SANTA'S STOCKING

Children will love these Santa tree decorations to hang on the tree. Make a larger one to hang up by the fireplace on Christmas Eve.

YOU WILL NEED

Red card
Pale pink and dark pink paper
Glue
Black felt-tip pen
Cotton wool (surgical cotton)
Ribbon

1 Scale up the Santa from the template to the size required and transfer to the red card. Cut out carefully.

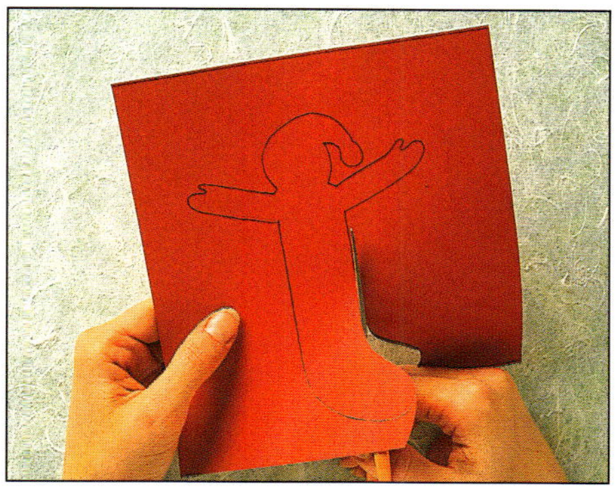

2 Next cut out the face shape in a pink paper and cut out two rosy cheeks in a darker coloured pink paper. Stick these onto the face area on the red card. Alternatively, colour in cheeks with felt-tip pen.

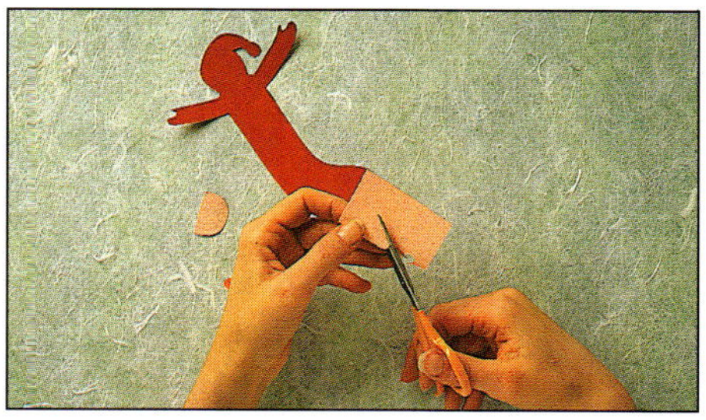

3 Draw in the smiling eyes and mouth with a black felt-tip pen.

4 Now glue the cotton wool (surgical cotton) onto the hat, the cuffs, the top of the Christmas stocking, and finally Santa's beard. Make a loop with some coloured ribbon and attach it to the back of the stocking so that it can hang on the Christmas tree.

PAPIER-MÂCHÉ PUPPET

Papier-mâché has long been associated with puppet-making, being a cheap, lightweight alternative to wood or clay. The simple construction of this puppet makes it easy to handle, and sumptuous costumes can be made out of exotic fabric scraps.

YOU WILL NEED

Newspaper
Masking tape
Diluted PVA glue
Fine sandpaper
White paint
Selection of poster paints
Black ink (optional)
Non-toxic clear gloss varnish
Piece of doweling rod about 40 cm (16 in) long
Thin string
Strong clear glue
Scraps of fabric, torn or cut into strips

1 Beginning with the puppet's head, crumple a double newspaper page into a ball, then sculpt it with masking tape into the desired shape. Do not forget to give your puppet a neck, as the top of the doweling crossbar will be glued inside.

2 Tear newspaper into strips and soak in diluted PVA glue. Cover the puppet's head with four layers of papier-mâché.

3 Form the puppet's features by squashing glue-soaked strips of newspaper into small pellets of pulp and sticking them in place. Cover over the pulp with two layers of short thin newspaper strips.

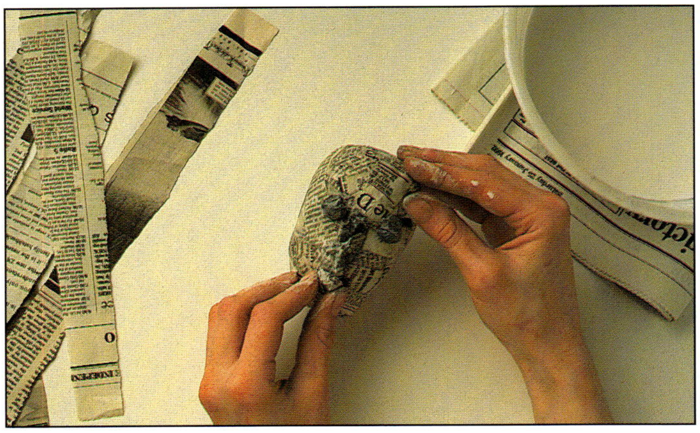

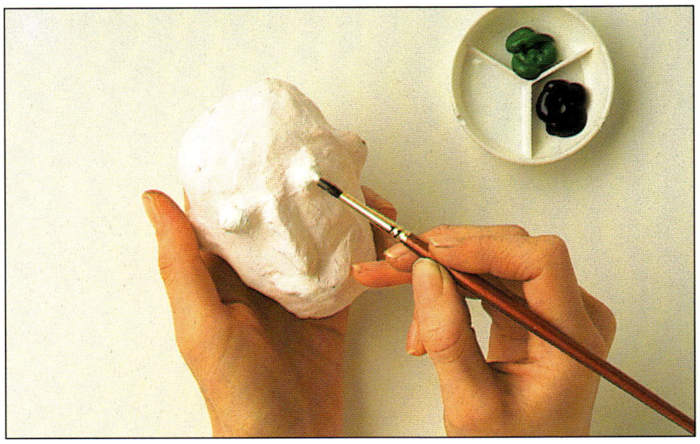

4 Allow the head to dry overnight in a warm place. Lightly smooth it with fine sandpaper and then prime it with two coats of white paint. When it is quite dry, draw in the puppet's features, and decorate the head with poster paints, adding detail with black ink if desired. Let the head dry overnight and seal it with two coats of clear gloss varnish.

5 Cut the doweling rod into two pieces 10 cm (4 in) and 30 cm (12 in) long. Place the shorter piece of rod across the longer piece, and tie them together in a cross. Make a hole in the puppet's neck and glue in the rod. Leave in a warm place to dry overnight.

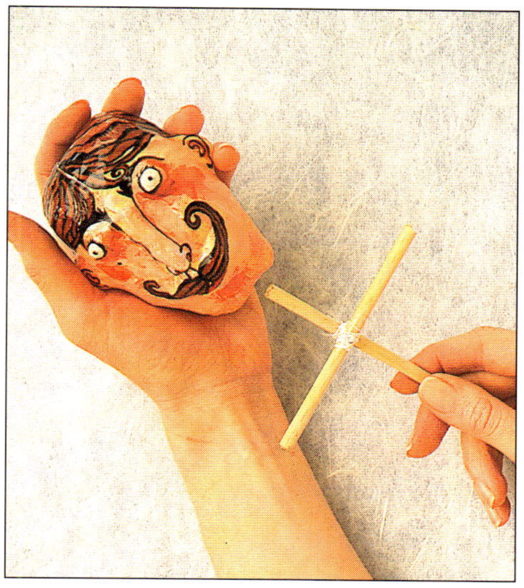

6 Finally, tear or cut strips of fabric about 2½ cm (1 in) wide and long enough to cover the doweling rod. Tie the strips along the length of crossbar that forms the puppet's arms. You might like to tie some fabric around the puppet's neck as well, to disguise the point where it joins the rod.

MASK

This handsome king mask could be used for plays or pantomimes, or for fancy-dress parties. It is made from heavy-weight paper and is strong but still flexible. By using the same basic face shape, and changing the crown to hair or a hat, you could make all sorts of masks, both male and female. Remember to cut the chin round rather than pointed if you do not want the mask to have a beard!

YOU WILL NEED
Thick paper in various colours
Gold paper
Glue
Thin elastic
Darning needle

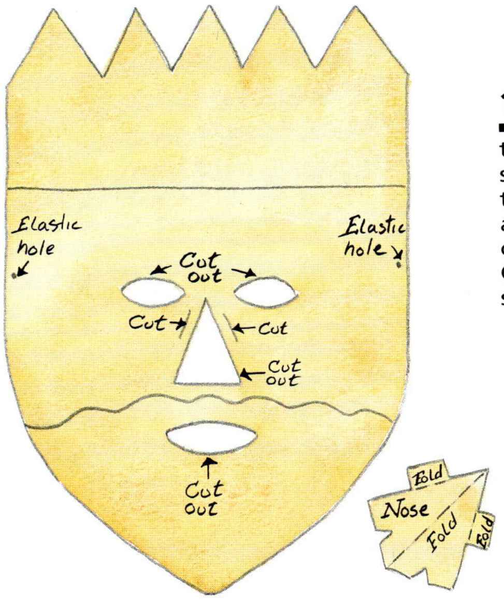

1 Scale up the basic mask shapes from the template to the size required, and transfer them to appropriately coloured papers. Carefully cut out the shapes.

2 Next, take the face shape and stick the nose, beard and gold crown onto it using a thin coating of glue.

3 Decorate using smaller pieces of coloured paper. Embellish the crown with jewels, and define the beard with strips of lighter coloured paper. Before wearing, carefully push a length of thin elastic through the mask using a darning needle. Knot the ends inside the mask.

SPOTTY DOG

This spotty dog is made from tightly rolled and twisted newspaper. It is a very good method for the construction of other animals, giving a firm armature or support for papier-mâché. It might be fun to make a giraffe or an elephant to go into a papier-mâché ark!

YOU WILL NEED

Newspaper
Masking tape
Diluted PVA glue
Fine sandpaper
White paint
Assortment of poster paints
Non-toxic clear gloss varnish

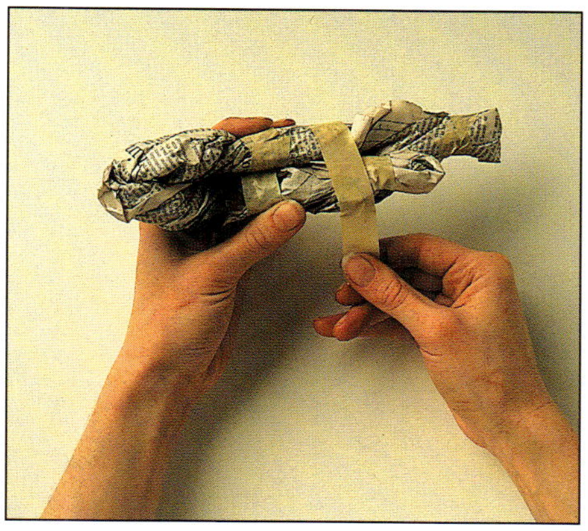

1 Take two double spread sheets of newspaper and twist them tightly to form a 'rope'. Tape the ends of the rope, and then bend it to form a fat rectangle about 15 cm (6 in) long, with one end extending about 5 cm (2 in). This end will form the dog's head. Firmly tape the rectangle to hold it in place.

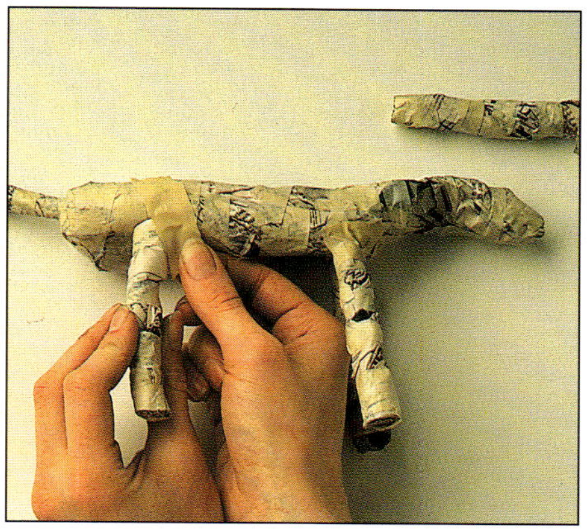

2 Make the dog's limbs in the same way as the body and head. Using a single sheet of newspaper, form a thinner 'rope', and tape it along its length. Cut it into four pieces about 7–10 cm (3–4 in) long, and fix each one in place on the dog's body using masking tape. Add the dog's ears and tail with small, thin rolls of paper.

3 Soak newspaper strips in diluted PVA glue and cover the dog with three layers of papier-mâché strips. Leave it to dry overnight in a warm place.

4 Sand down the papier-mâché dog shape, and prime it with two coats of white paint. Decorate the dog with poster paints, and then seal with two coats of clear gloss varnish.

STAINED GLASS PENDANT

Hang this 'stained glass' pendant in your window and enjoy the bright colours as the light shines through. You could choose your own design from a plate or a piece of jewellery or you could base it on the Celtic ship used here.

YOU WILL NEED

Black cartridge paper
Craft knife
Coloured tissue paper
Glue
Ribbon

1 Trace and draw out your designs twice in black cartridge paper and then cut out the shapes with a sharp craft knife. Be careful to cut inside the lines so that the shape remains intact.

2 Select which colour tissue paper is to go where and trace off and cut to shape. Start to glue your tissue paper on to the back of one of the black frames, using a separate piece to cover each area. You can use as many or as few colours as you wish. When you feel more confident you can start to shade your picture by putting one layer of paper over another, giving a darker tone.

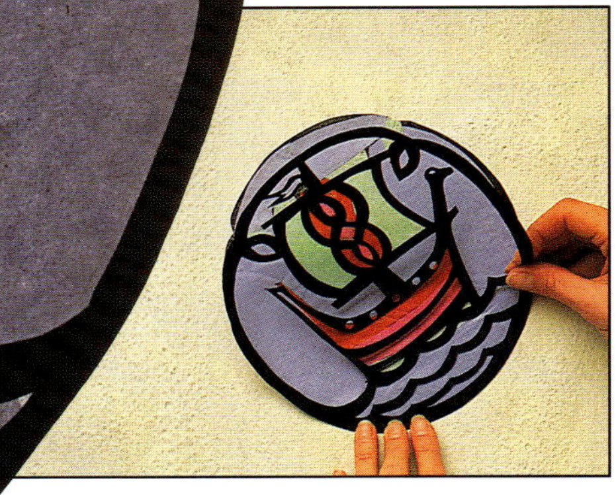

3 When all the shapes have been filled, glue and fix the other black frame on to the back to neaten. Attach a ribbon to the top and display in your window.

ABSTRACT STAINED GLASS

This is a very effective but easy way to make an abstract piece of 'stained glass' work, which is great fun to do and because the pieces are torn it is always slightly unpredictable.

YOU WILL NEED
Two sheets of black paper
Coloured tissue paper
Glue

1 Cut out two identical frames from the sheets of black paper. Take the coloured tissue papers and tear them into strips.

2 Cut out two pieces of tissue paper just larger than the frame opening, one in a light colour and one in a darker colour. Glue the lighter one onto the back of one of the frames. Arrange the torn strips so that they overlap the edges of the lighter tissue paper, and glue them into place.

3 Finally, stick down the darker piece of tissue paper, sandwiching the strips in place. Glue down the other black frame on top.

VASE

This vase is not waterproof, but it can be used to hold artificial or dried flowers, and is a very decorative 'objet d'art' in its own right. It is made using a simple basic method that can be easily adapted to make other shapes or sizes of vase.

YOU WILL NEED

Heavy corrugated cardboard
Strong clear glue
Masking tape
Newspaper
Diluted PVA glue
Fine sandpaper
White paint
Assorted poster paints
Non-toxic clear gloss varnish

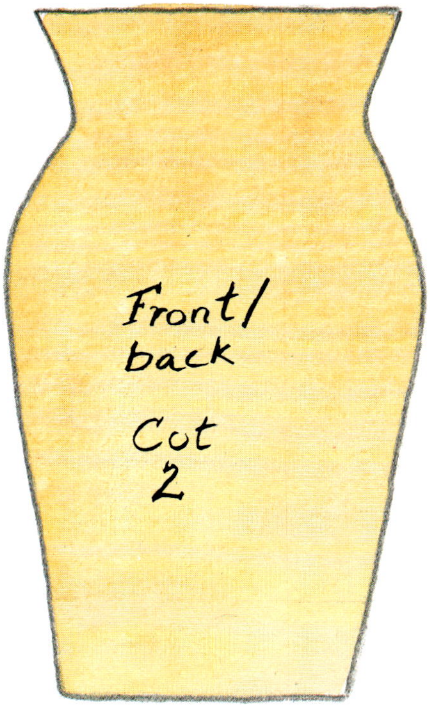

1 Scale up the shapes from the template to the size required and transfer onto heavy corrugated cardboard and cut out. The vase wall should be placed on the cardboard so that the corrugations run vertically down the wall's width. This will make it easier to bend the wall into shape. Glue and tape the wall into place right around the inside edge of one of the vase pieces. Cover the pieces with a coat of diluted PVA glue to help prevent warping, and let them dry for three to four hours in a warm place.

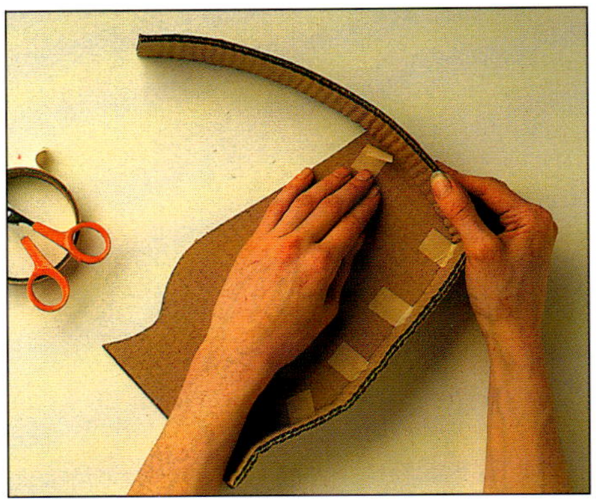

2 Next, tear narrow strips of newspaper and soak in diluted PVA glue. Cover the pieces of vase with four layers of papier-mâché strips. Leave to dry flat in a warm place overnight, and then smooth them lightly with fine sandpaper. Cover the inside of the vase and wall, and the remaining vase piece with two coats of white paint.

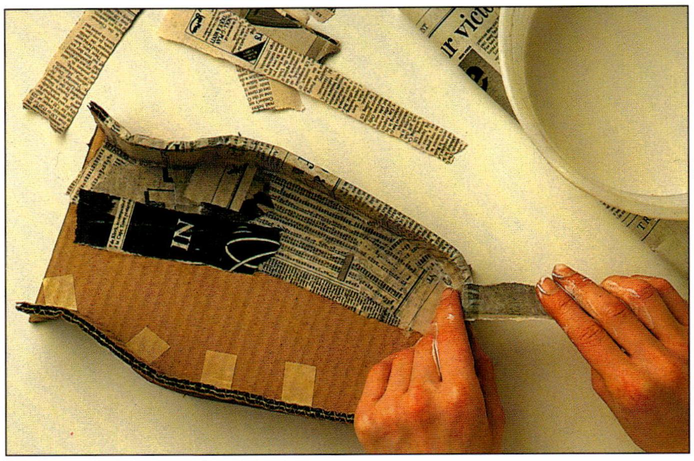

3 Join the vase together, with the painted surfaces to the inside. Glue the pieces together with strong clear glue and tape over the join with masking tape.

4 Leave the vase to dry for at least an hour. When dry seal its joined edge with three layers of papier-mâché strips, taking care to ensure a smooth surface by pushing out any small air bubbles or excess glue.

6 To decorate, lightly draw on the design with a pencil and then fill in using poster paints. When the paint is completely dry, apply a coat of clear gloss varnish.

5 Let the vase dry overnight, sand it lightly, and prime with two coats of white paint.

PERFORMING PIERROT

Children will love to watch the clever movements of this traditional Pierrot puppet. Why not make a couple and put on a show?

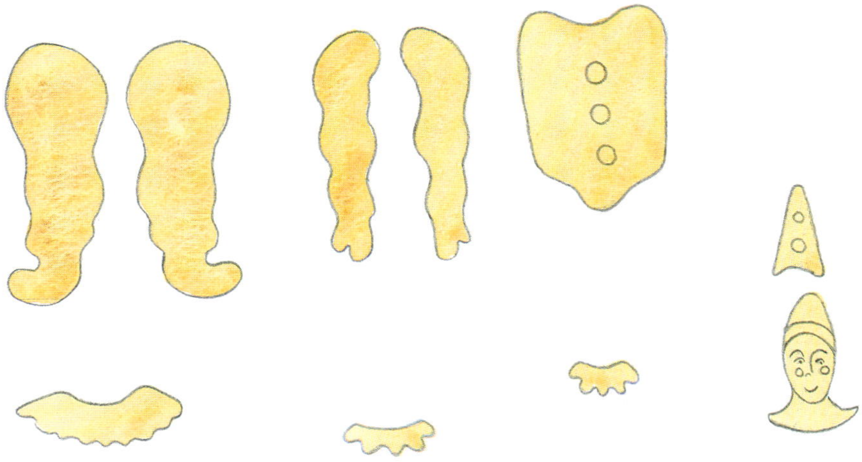

YOU WILL NEED

Blue, white and red paper
Black felt-tip pen
Glue
4 paper fasteners
Metal skewer or scissor blade
Curtain ring
Thin string

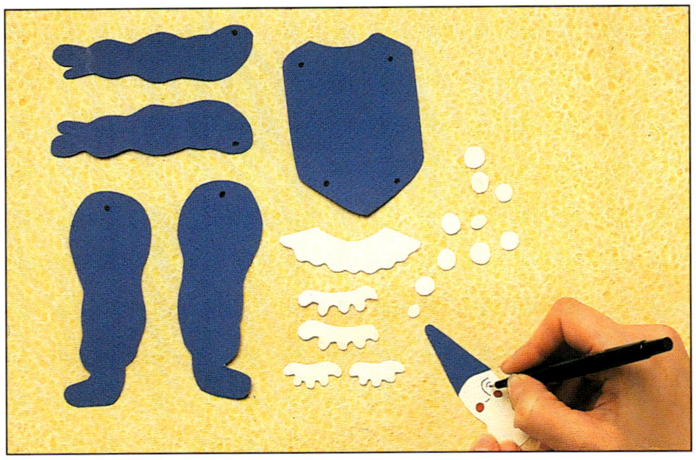

1 Scale up the pieces from the template to the size required and transfer to the coloured paper. Cut out the shapes for the clown: one body, two legs, two arms and a hat in blue, collar, cuffs and pom-poms in white. Mark on reference dots with a black pen. First make up the face by gluing on his hat and rosy cheeks. Draw the face details in with a black felt-tip pen.

2 Glue the pom-poms onto the hat, front and Pierrot's boots, and stick on the collar and cuffs.

3 Match up the dots on the body and limbs and join them all together by pushing the paper fasteners through both layers. Open out the fasteners on the back.

4 On the reverse side, pull the limbs downwards and pierce a hole at the top of each arm using a skewer or scissor blade. Thread a length of thin string through each hole and knot at both ends, on the reverse side. Repeat this with the legs to form two 'cross bars'.

5 Thread a long piece of string through a curtain ring. Attach one end to the centre of the arm string and the other end to the centre of the leg string. Trim where necessary. The strings should not be slack when the limbs are 'at rest'. When the strings are firmly fixed, pull the ring and watch Pierrot perform.

PICTURE CALENDAR

A simple idea that even children can make to give as presents. Calendar booklets are available from stationery shops.

YOU WILL NEED

Chosen picture
Card
Coloured paper
Glue
Calendar booklet
Matching ribbon
Sticky tape

1 Cut out a favourite picture from an old greetings card or a magazine.

2 Now cut out a larger piece of card and then choose a coloured paper which will match the colours in your picture. Glue the paper onto the card to cover.

3 Position and glue the picture onto the card, making sure that it is centred, but leaving more space at the bottom in order to accommodate the calendar booklet. Glue the calendar in place. Make a loop at the top with some matching coloured ribbon, and fix it at the back with sticky tape. For an added detail, make a little bow from the same ribbon and glue it just above the booklet.

A GREAT CATCH

This handsome fish is displayed proudly on a papier-mâché stand, rather like a trophy. It would be fun to make a papier-mâché case displaying a similar 'catch' to hang on the wall!

YOU WILL NEED

Heavy corrugated card
Strong clear glue
Masking tape
Diluted PVA glue
Newspaper
Fine sandpaper
White paint
Assortment of poster paints
Black ink (optional)
Non-toxic clear gloss varnish

1 Scale up the fish shape and stand from the template to the required size, and transfer onto the corrugated card. Remember to cut out two pieces for the stand. Stick the two halves of the stand together with strong clear glue, hold the joins with masking tape and leave to dry.

2 Soak newspaper strips in diluted PVA glue and apply three layers of papier-mâché to the fish and stand. Leave them to dry overnight in a warm place.

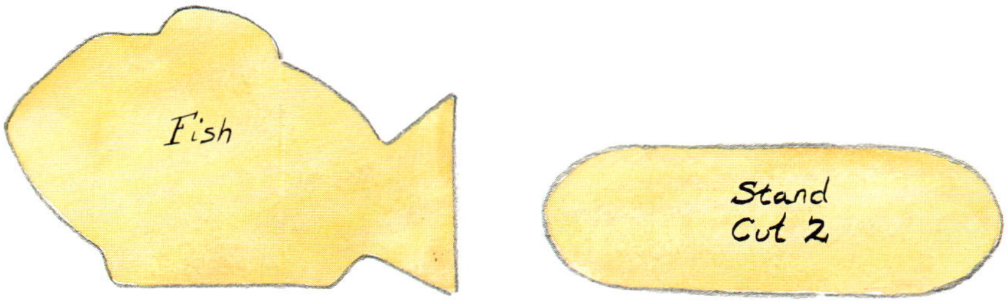

3 Lightly sand down the fish and stand. Prime with white paint.

4 Draw in the fish's face, fins and other features, and then decorate it with poster paints. Use black ink to draw in the detail, if required. Let the fish dry overnight and then seal it with two coats of clear gloss varnish.

SOPHISTICATED CRACKER

This cracker is easy to make and will add a designer look to your dinner table. Choose sophisticated black and white or match colours to your table setting.

YOU WILL NEED

Crêpe paper
Cardboard tube, 10 cm (4 in) long
Glue
Acetate paper
Silver metallic pen
Ribbon

1 Cut a piece of crêpe paper 30 × 20 cm (12 × 8 in). Wrap the crêpe paper around the cardboard tube and glue in place.

2 For the next stage an acetate paper with small white dots printed on it is used. Cut a strip 7 cm (2¾ in) wide and long enough to cover the tube. Wrap the strip around the centre and glue at the back.

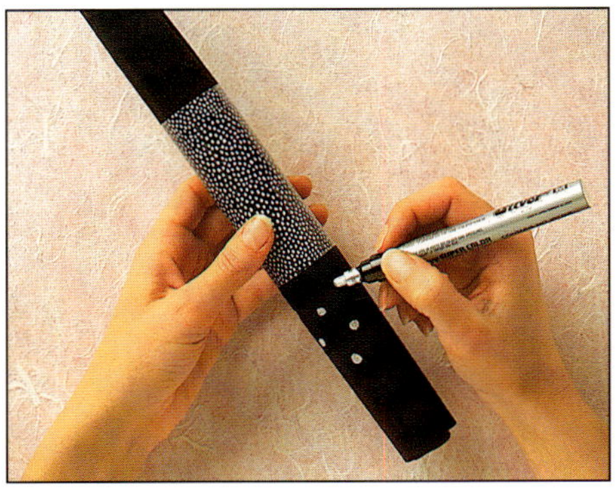

3 On either end of the cracker paint silver dots with a metallic pen.

4 Now ease an extra piece of tube into one end, and tie a piece of silver ribbon between the rolls to make the cracker shape. The tube will give form to the end. Remove the extra tube and repeat with the other end of the cracker.

5 Frill the ends of the cracker by stretching the paper between the finger tips.

WHIRLING CIRCLES

Festoon your room with garlands of whirling circles. Double-sided crêpe paper is used here so that one side is a slightly darker colour.

YOU WILL NEED

Drinking glass
Double-sided crêpe paper
Wide ribbon
Craft knife

1 First of all draw round a drinking glass and cut out circles of crêpe paper in all different colours. Now cut a spiral towards the centre leaving a small 'bobble' in the middle.

2 When you have cut out enough circles in all the different colours, take some wide ribbon and, using a craft knife, make small cuts parallel to the sides, at intervals along the tape.

3 Now push the 'bobble' centre of the whirls through the cut in the ribbon so that they are held in position. Make sure that you alternate the colours along the ribbon.

CHINESE HAT

Celebrate Chinese New Year with a stylish Oriental hat. There is no fixed design to follow, so you can have fun adding your own characters.

YOU WILL NEED

Beige and white card
Black ink or paint
Double-sided tape

1 Cut a 48 cm (19 in) diameter circle out of beige card. Using black ink or paint, make up Chinese characters and decorate the beige card with them.

2 Now cut a line from the edge of the circle to the centre and overlap one edge over the other to give form to the hat. Stick in position with double-sided tape.

3 Take a strip of narrow card, long enough to go around your head, and tape the ends together to make a headband.

4 Fix the headband to the underneath of the Chinese hat with pieces of tape as illustrated.

POT-POURRI PUNNET

Bring the sweet smell of your favourite flowers into the room all year round with a basket of pot-pourri. Stir it occasionally to bring out the scent.

YOU WILL NEED

Small basket
Tissue paper
Needle
Silver thread
Pot-pourri

1 Take a small gift basket and line it with coloured tissue paper. A bright pink has been chosen here to bring out the colours of the pot-pourri.

2 Now take another piece of the same tissue paper and roll it up into a sausage shape and twist.

3 Take a needle and some silver thread. Oversew the twisted tissue paper around the top edge of the basket.

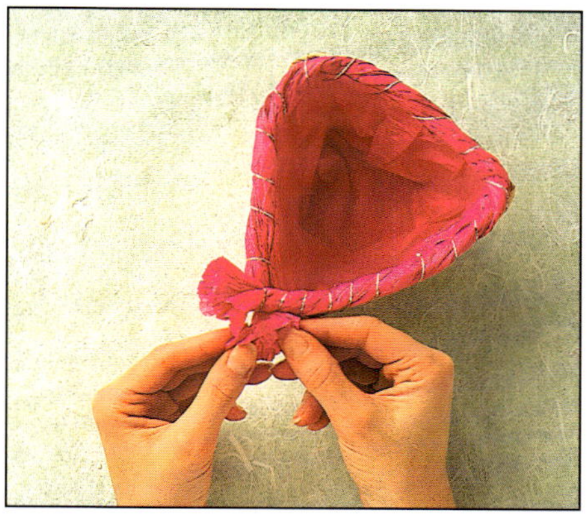

4 Fix the two ends of the sausage so that they overlap and secure them with a couple of stitches or a dab of glue. Now place the pot-pourri into the basket to give your room a lovely aroma as well as look attractive.

POPULAR POPPIES

The stark simplicity of bright red poppies with their black centres makes them an ideal flower to craft in paper.

YOU WILL NEED

Garden wire
Cotton wool (surgical cotton)
Green, black and red crêpe paper
Glue
Sticky tape

1 To make the stem cut a length of garden wire. Bend the top to make a loop and trap a small amount of cotton wool in the loop. Cover this in a cut-out circle of green crêpe paper. Secure by wrapping tape around.

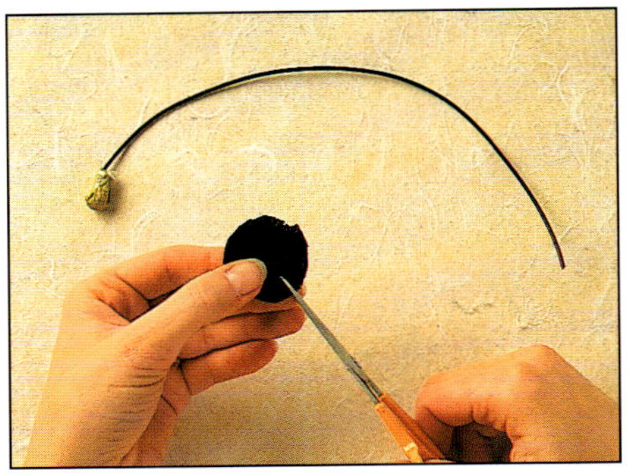

2 Next cut three small circles of black crêpe paper. Fringe the outer edges and then poke the other end of the wire through the centre and slide up to the green bud.

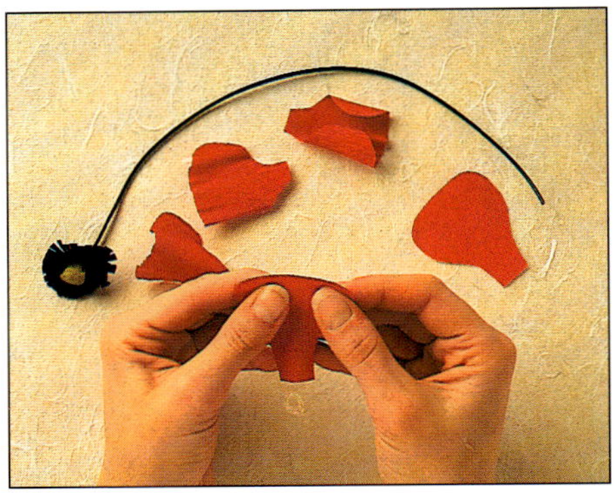

3 Cut out five petal shapes in red crêpe paper and stretch the outer edge with your finger tips so that they frill.

4 Glue the petals one by one around the base of the centre.

5 Finally, cover the stem in green crêpe paper by winding a long strip around diagonally and securing it at the base with sticky tape.

LEAFY FOLIAGE

This foliage can be used to add to other flower arrangements you can make out of paper.

YOU WILL NEED

Garden wire
Double-sided tape
Green crêpe paper

1 Take a length of green garden wire and wrap small pieces of double-sided tape at intervals along the wire.

2 Cut out double leaf shapes in thick green crêpe paper.

3 Twist each leaf shape in the centre and fix them onto the wire by twisting them around the taped parts.

4 Tape a long strip of the same green paper to the bottom of the wire and wind it up the stem, making sure to cover the tape as you go. Bend and mould the finished greenery to suit your flower arrangement.

CHRISTMAS TREE BOWS

Dress up your tree with shimmering bows for a glamorous film-star style Christmas. Match bows to baubles for a co-ordinated look.

YOU WILL NEED

Metallic corrugated paper
Stapler
Metallic tissue paper
Double-sided tape
Ribbon

1 From the metallic corrugated paper cut out an oblong measuring 18 × 12 cm (7 × 4½ in). Gather in the centre to make the bow shape and staple in position.

2 Now take a length of metallic tissue paper and wrap it around the centre of the bow to cover the staples. However do not wrap the whole length around but leave some excess to fall at the front. Fix at the back with double-sided tape.

3 Now cut two rectangles for the tails in the metallic paper measuring 20 × 8 cm (8 × 3 in). Cut darts at one end of each tail.

4 Make one pleat at the top of the tails. Staple each pleat and then staple the tails together.

5 Now attach the tails to the back of the bow with double-sided tape. Make a loop with a piece of ribbon and stick it to the back of the finished bow for hanging.

SOAP-BOX

Guest soaps come in all shapes and colours. Decorate a box in pretty shades to match your soaps for an attractive present.

YOU WILL NEED
Empty circular box
Assorted coloured card
Glue
Tissue paper
Soaps

1 Cover the outside of the box by gluing a strip of coloured card around the side.

2 This particular gift uses shell-shaped soaps, so draw shell shapes onto coloured cards that complement the colours of the soaps.

3 Cut out the shell shapes and stick them onto the outside of the box.

4 Scrunch up a large piece of tissue paper and arrange it inside the box. Place the soaps on top of the tissue paper.

BOWLED OVER

This bowl is made by a traditional method where layers of papier-mâché are laid into a greased mould and removed when dry. For this project, an ordinary china bowl has been used, but all sorts of items can make interesting moulds – just remember to grease them first, otherwise they will be permanently lined with paper!

YOU WILL NEED

Bowl suitable for using as a mould
Petroleum jelly
Newspaper
Diluted PVA glue
Heavy corrugated card
Strong clear glue
Masking tape
Fine sandpaper
White paint
Assortment of poster paints
Non-toxic clear gloss varnish

1 Coat the inside of the bowl with five layers of PVA-soaked newspaper strips, allowing for an overlap of 2½ cm (1 in). Leave to dry in a warm place for 48 hours.

2 Gently prise the paper bowl from its mould with a blunt knife, and leave it upside down to dry for a few hours.

3 Trim the ragged edge to about ½ cm (¼ in).

4 Cut a zigzag bowl rim from the thick cardboard and lay it on the top of the papier-mâché bowl rim. Stick the rim on the bowl with strong clear glue, and hold it in place with masking tape. Allow the glue to dry for an hour or so and then paper over the rim, covering the joins carefully.

5 Paper the underside of the rim in the same way. Leave the bowl to dry for 24 hours. Lightly sand down the surface of the bowl, and then prime it with two coats of white paint.

6 Draw in any decoration with pencil first, and then decorate the bowl with poster paints. Let the bowl dry thoroughly, and then seal it with two coats of clear gloss varnish.

TAKE A LETTER

As well as paper and card, this letter rack also requires a block of wood to give it a firm base. Cover it in patterned paper to match your desk accessories.

YOU WILL NEED

Block of wood 19½ × 4½ × 2 cm (7½ × 1¾ × ¾ in)
Patterned paper
Glue or waterbased wood adhesive
Mounting card

1 Entirely cover the block of wood in the patterned paper and glue in place. Trim it where necessary.

2 Cut three pieces of mounting card, one piece measuring 25 × 13 cm (10 × 5 in) and the other two measuring 20 × 9 cm (8 × 3½ in). With each bit of card, measure and cut out a piece of paper slightly larger than the card itself. Glue the paper onto the card, and mitre the corners carefully by snipping off the corners diagonally and folding the turnings on to the back, making sure that they are well stuck down. Repeat with each piece of card.

3 Now stick a piece of paper slightly smaller than the card onto the back.

4 Using a strong glue or waterbased wood adhesive stick the smaller, front card to the narrow edge of the covered piece of wood, making sure it is centred. Glue the back card in the same way.

5 To complete the letter rack, position and glue it onto the covered base.

ADVENT CALENDAR

Make the countdown to Christmas even more exciting with this beautiful tree advent calendar. The windows are decorated with pictures cut out from old Christmas cards.

YOU WILL NEED

Red, green and orange card
Thin cardboard
Craft knife
Old greetings cards
Glue
Silver metallic pen

1 Cut out two tree shapes, one in red card and the other in green. Use a 2 cm (¾ in) square template of thin cardboard to mark out 25 windows at random on the green tree. Now cut along three sides of each window with a craft knife.

2 Place the green tree onto the red tree so that it is slightly higher and gives the green tree a red line on the bottom edges. Carefully open each window and mark their position on the red tree in pencil. Remove the green tree. Cut out 25 small pictures from old Christmas cards and glue them onto the pencilled squares on the red Christmas tree.

3 Now glue the green tree onto the red one making sure that all the windows line up.

4 Decorate the tree with cut-out circles of red and orange card to suggest the Christmas tree baubles.

5 Using a silver pen draw a bow above each bauble and then number the windows 1 to 25.

WASTE PAPER BOX

Waste paper boxes can make elegant gifts that can be put to use straight away. They can be covered in paper that matches the decor of the room they are intended for, or else in paper of your favourite design.

YOU WILL NEED

Thick card
Dark contrasting or toning paper
Impact adhesive
Decorative paper

1 For this waste paper box, cut out one square in thick card measuring 20 cm (9 in). Now measure and cut out from the same type of card the four sides so that they are 20 cm (9 in) wide, with a height of 25 cm (11 in). Cover one side of all these pieces with a dark toning paper.

2 Next glue the sides onto the base and to each other using an impact adhesive.

3 Now cut out a square of decorative paper measuring 24 cm (10 in). Firmly glue it onto the base and cut the corners diagonally. Glue the turnings around and up onto the sides of the container to give the box extra strength.

4 To cover, cut a piece of the decorative paper large enough to go around the whole of the box. Stick it on and trim where necessary at the base to create a neat finish.

5 At the top, turn the excess paper over and glue down onto the inside of the box, after mitring the corners. This will produce a very professional look.

ELEGANT LAMPSHADE

Add a designed look to your room by using a left-over piece of wallpaper, or a paper of a complementary colour, to make this lampshade.

YOU WILL NEED

Lampshade frame
Coloured paper or wallpaper
Craft knife
Coin
Glue

1 First of all take a lampshade frame and place it onto your chosen paper. Draw around the shape while slowly moving the frame round to obtain the correct measurement. Now cut out the shape slightly outside the drawn line using scissors or a craft knife to give a piece of paper larger than the frame. Using a coin, draw a scalloped edge along the bottom edge.

2 Then cut along it until the edging is complete.

3 Now apply a layer of glue to the frame and carefully attach the paper to it, smoothing it out to avoid bumps or creases.

4 Finally, cut small darts around the top and glue them down, working around until the frame is completely covered and the shade ready to be fitted to a lamp.

DESIGNER PENCIL POT

This pencil pot is a lovely idea to cheer up your own desk, or it can make a beautiful personalized gift for a friend. The matching pencils add an artistic touch.

YOU WILL NEED

Empty cardboard tube or salt container
Patterned paper
Glue
Pencils

1 First of all you will need to cover the inside of the container. Measure the height and circumference of the pot and cut out two pieces of paper, slightly larger. You could use wallpaper, wrapping paper or marbled paper.

2 Take one of the pieces, glue it and carefully slot it into the inside of the pot, pressing it around the inside walls.

3 Cut darts on the excess paper at the top and glue them down to the outside one by one.

4 Take the other piece of paper and stick it to the outside so that the edge is flush with the top of the pot.

5 Once again cut darts into the excess length at the bottom and glue them onto the base.

6 Now draw around the base of the pot onto the patterned paper and cut out a circle slightly smaller. Glue this and drop it inside the bottom.

7 Cut out another circle and glue it to the outside base.

8 To make the matching pencils, cut out a strip of the same patterned paper the length of the pencils and approximately twice the width. Glue it and place the pencil at one edge and roll. Trim the paper where necessary.

DESK BLOTTER

To make the blotter special it is a good idea to select a wrapping paper to suit the type of desk area. You could choose a hand-made marbled paper for a very traditional look, or an abstract paper or two co-ordinating plain papers for a more modern effect.

YOU WILL NEED
Thick card
Patterned paper
Glue
Thin card
Coloured paper
Blotting paper

1 Cut a piece of thick card 46 × 30 cm (18 × 12 in). This will be the finished size of the blotter. Cut your chosen paper 3 cm (1 in) larger all around than the card.

2 Next fold and glue the edges onto the back of the card, mitring the corners by trimming them diagonally.

3 For the corner pieces cut four triangles in thin card measuring 10 × 10 × 14 cm (4 × 4 × 5½ in) and cover them in coloured paper cut to the same size first. Glue and turn down the bottom edge and the top point. Repeat this for all four corner pieces.

4 Position the corner pieces onto the corners of the blotter. Turn the board over and fold the edges around, gluing them securely.

5 Cut another piece of coloured paper the same size as the blotter and glue it on to the back. Trim where necessary.

6 Insert a piece of blotting paper under the corners.

SWEET THOUGHT

Chocolates are always a treat, especially when they are gift-wrapped. Simply cover an empty container with vibrant tissue paper and fill with sweets.

YOU WILL NEED

Empty bowl-shaped food container
Tissue paper
Glue or tape
Metallic card
Pencil or paint brush

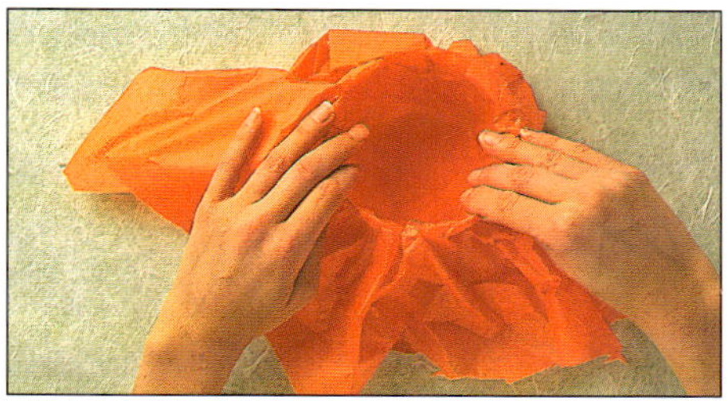

1 Cover the bowl with tissue paper by placing the centre of the paper inside, pushing it down and then moulding it out and around the sides.

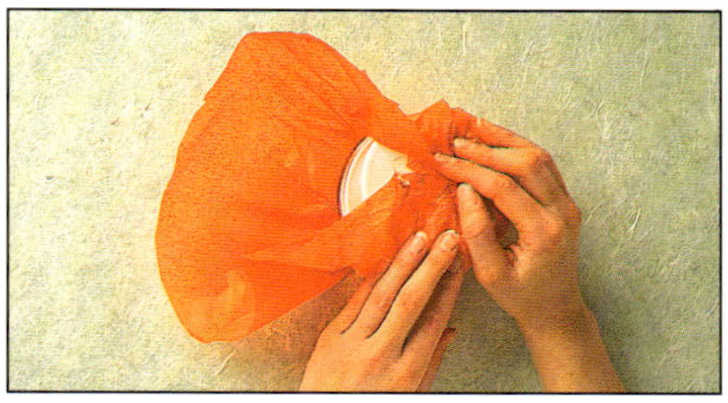

2 Glue or tape the tissue paper to the underside, trimming where necessary.

3 Now cut two strips measuring 3 × 50 cm (1¼ × 20 in) of coloured metallic card. Tightly roll each end of the card strips around a pencil or paint brush so that it curls.

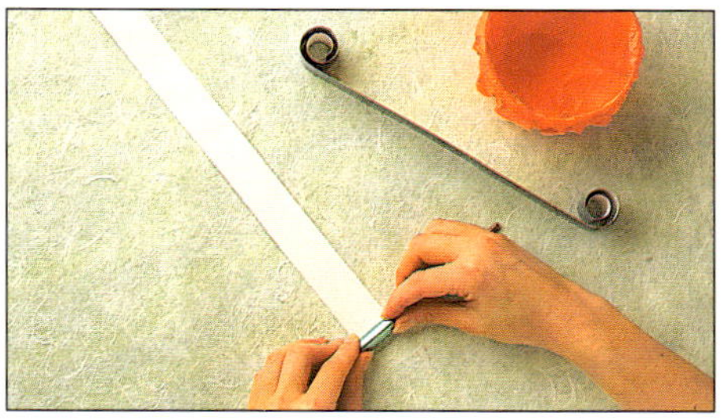

4 Now glue the centre of the cards and place them into the bowl at right angles. Place another piece of tissue paper that has been scrunched up into the bottom of the container, and arrange the chocolates on the top.

NECKLACE AND EARRINGS

This beautiful necklace with matching earrings is created from only a small piece of decorative paper. A printed feather marbled pattern is used here.

YOU WILL NEED

Patterned paper
Pair of earring fittings
Leather cord
Glue

1 For the earrings, cut out two tab shapes from the decorative paper, using the template as a guide to the shape. Now fold the tab in half to the point and continue to pleat out from the centre.

2 Pierce the top and push an earring fitting through to create a fan shape. Make a second earring in the same way.

3 For the necklace you will need to make five 'fans' in the same way and then pierce them at the top.

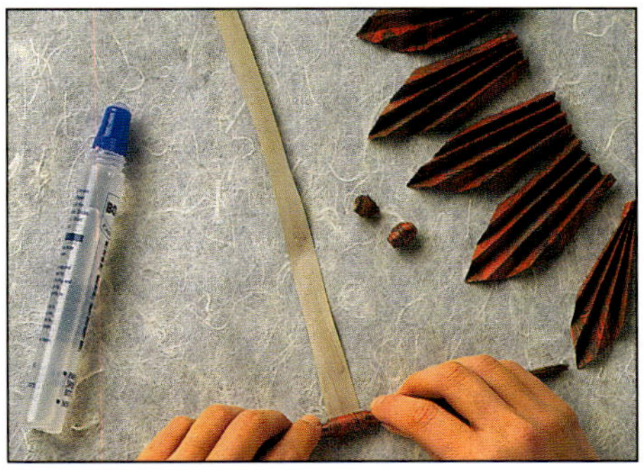

4 To make the beads which sit inbetween the fans, cut 30 cm (12 in) strips of paper into elongated triangles measuring 4 cm (1½ in) at the base and tapering to 1 cm (½ in) at the tip. Starting at the wide end, roll up the strips around a pencil and glue the end. Now thread a piece of leather cord through the tops of the fans, alternating them with the beads.

FESTIVE CRACKERS

Here is an economical way to make your own festive crackers as well as to give your guests a personal surprise present by adding a small gift.

YOU WILL NEED

Crêpe paper in two colours
Thin writing paper
Cracker snaps
Thin card
Two cardboard tubes
Glue
Strong thread
Double-sided tape

1 First of all cut a length of crêpe paper measuring 35 × 20 cm (14 × 8 in). Lay it flat and place a piece of thin writing paper centrally on top. Place a cracker snap on top and then place a piece of card measuring 15 × 8 cm (6 × 3 in), across the centre.

2 Place two cardboard tubes onto the papers so that their ends meet in line with the right hand side of the piece of card. Roll the crêpe paper around and glue at the edges.

3 Pull the right hand tube out slightly and use some strong thread to tie inbetween the tubes and gather the paper as illustrated. Now pop your gift in at the other end. Pull the other cardboard tube so that you can feel a gap between the tube and the inner card, and tie the end as before with some strong thread.

4 Remove the cardboard tubes and, using a strip of contrasting coloured card, stick over the threads to neaten. Now cut another strip of the same card and a strip of contrasting coloured crêpe paper twice this length. Put double-sided tape on the back of the card and gather up the crêpe paper onto it.

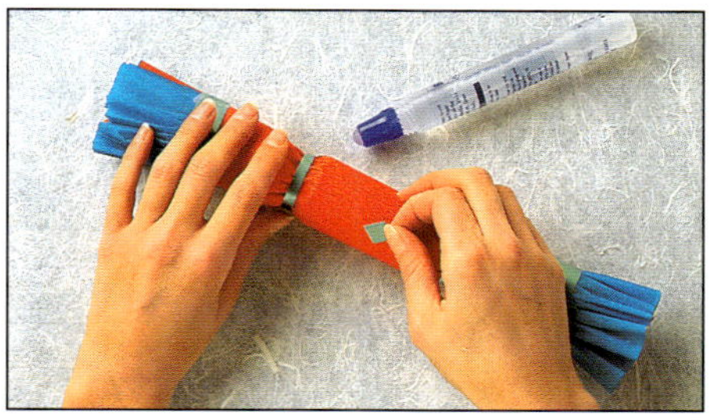

5 To finish off decorate the cracker with a diamond of card.

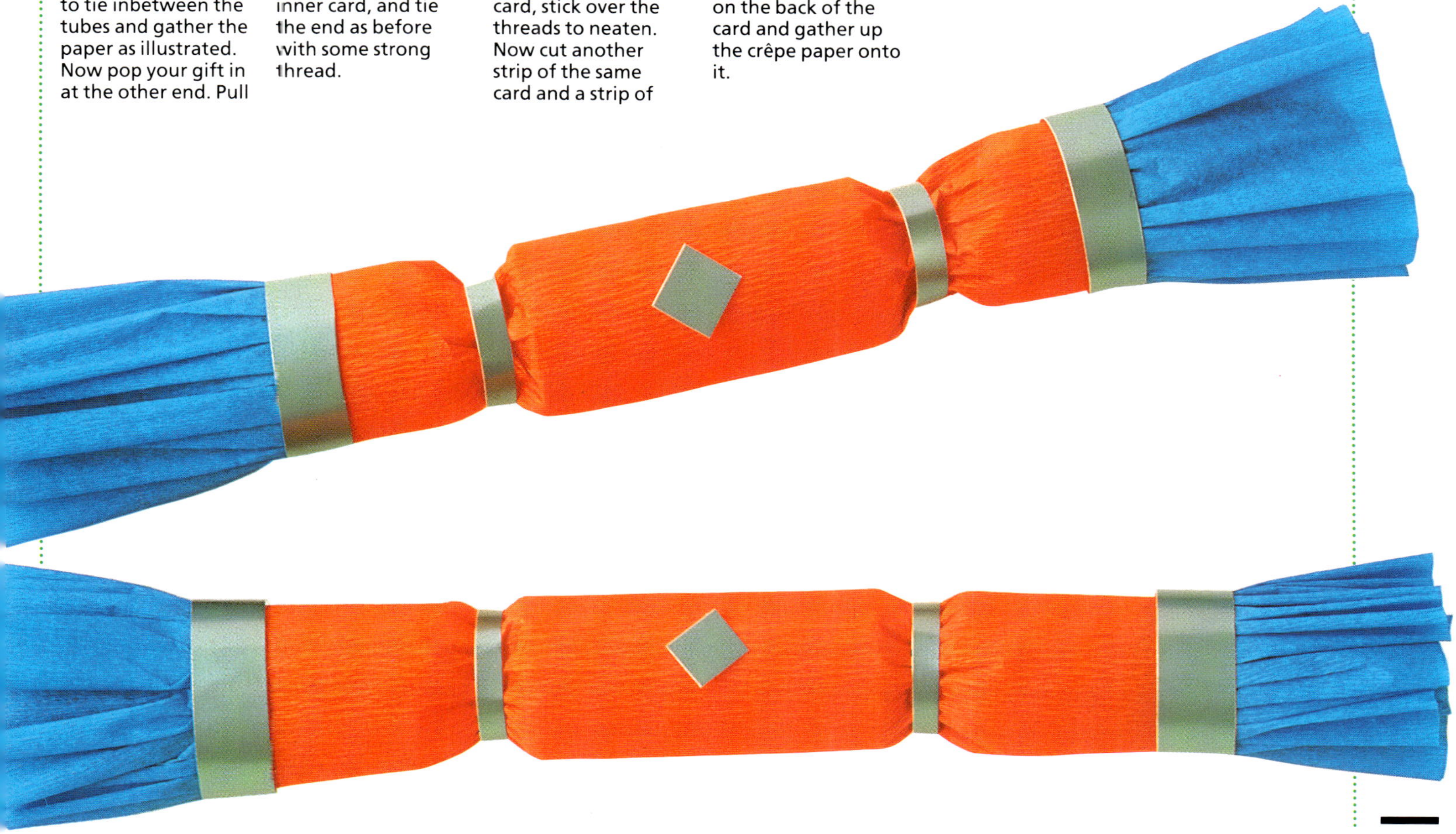

SUNNY MOBILE

Mobiles come in many forms, from very simple brightly coloured abstract shapes, to highly sophisticated motor-driven extravaganzas. This one is made in a traditional way and features a soothing arrangement of the sun with clouds, which will move gently if hung in a breeze.

YOU WILL NEED

Thin card
Thin wire jewellery hangers, one for each piece of mobile
Strong clear glue
Masking tape
Newspaper
Diluted PVA glue
Fine sandpaper
White paint
Assortment of poster paints
Black ink (optional)
Non-toxic clear gloss varnish
Fishing line or similar nylon cord
Thin florists' or model-makers' wire

1 Scale up the mobile shapes from the template to the size required and transfer them to the thin card. Make a total of four cloud shapes. Cut out each shape. Stick a wire hanger to the back of each mobile piece with strong clear glue, and secure the hangers with a piece of masking tape.

2 Let the glue dry for an hour, and then cover each card shape with three layers of papier-mâché, using short, narrow strips of newspaper soaked in diluted PVA glue. Allow the shapes to dry overnight in a warm place.

3 Lightly sand down each piece of mobile, and then prime them with two even coats of white paint.

4 Draw in any design with pencil first, and then decorate the mobile shapes with poster paint. Accentuate details with black ink if desired. When the decoration has thoroughly dried, seal all the pieces with two coats of clear gloss varnish.

To assemble the mobile, cut two pieces of thin florists' or model-makers' wire to a length of about 15 cm (6 in). Suspend one piece of wire from the centre of the other. Attach the shapes to the wires using short lengths of nylon cord tied through the fasteners. Attach a length of cord to the middle of the top wire and hang the mobile in place.

WINDMILL

This traditional toy is easy to make as well as being fun to watch turn in the wind. For a children's party you could make one for each guest in a variety of colours.

YOU WILL NEED

Square of stiff paper
Map pin
Empty ballpoint pen casing
Piece of cork
Plastic drinking straw or short bamboo cane

1 First, scale up the pattern from the template to the size required and transfer it to the square of paper. Cut along the lines from each corner nearly to the centre. Bend each alternate corner to the centre, securing each one with a map pin. It is easier to create the pin hole when the sheet is flat.

2 Next, push the pin through the centre of the windmill to the back.

3 Cut a small piece off the end of a ballpoint pen ink casing to act as a bearing, and put it onto the point of the pin behind the paper. Push the pin through a drinking straw, and then into a small piece of cork for safety.

Alternatively, push the pin into a garden cane, making sure the point is well inside the wood so that no sharp end is protruding.

DANCING FINGER PUPPETS

Finger puppets are traditional toys that have been made to amuse children (and adults!) for many years. Here are a flying Scotsman and a member of the corps de ballet for you to make.

YOU WILL NEED

Thick white paper
Felt-tip pens or coloured pencils
Glue
Thin card
Craft knife

1 Scale up the puppet designs from the template to the size required and transfer them to the paper.

2 Colour in the Scotsman and the ballerina with felt-tip pens or coloured pencils.

3 Then stick the puppets onto the thin card, and cut carefully around each one with a craft knife. Cut out the finger holes with a craft knife, and your puppets are ready to dance the night away!

NECK TIES AND BOW-TIES

A tie always creates a good impression, and these paper ties add a touch of fun without the formality. All you need is a sheet of wrapping paper or crêpe paper.

YOU WILL NEED

Neck tie
Wrapping paper
Glue
String or elastic
Crêpe paper
Double-sided tape

1 To make this party tie cut out a piece of suitable wrapping paper using the front part of a real neck tie as a guide. Make sure that the paper is slightly larger all round to allow for turnings.

2 Glue and fold back the turnings to get a good finish.

3 To make the 'knot', cut out a fairly large rectangle of paper. Cut a piece of string or elastic long enough to go around your neck, and place it across the rectangle. Glue and fold the rectangle in half. Now glue the 'knot' to the top of the tie and knot the elastic at the ends.

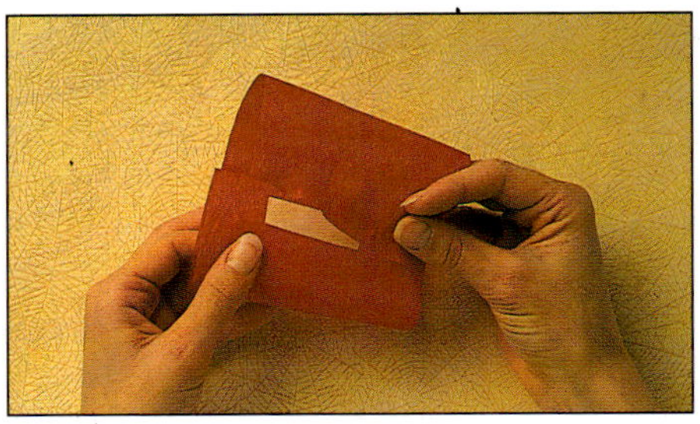

4 To make a bow-tie, use some crêpe paper, measuring 25 × 10 cm (10 × 4 in). Join the ends together to form a ring with double-sided tape.

5 Gather in the centre and cut a thin strip of crêpe paper and wind it around the middle. Apply glue to the end, but before sticking it down, insert a neck-length of elastic.

6 Glue on coloured spots to make an impression at the party!

PAPER PEAR

You could make any sort of fruit or vegetable from papier-mâché using this method. It is possible to make quite convincing shapes by 'sculpting' the crumpled newspaper with masking tape. You might even be inspired to attempt something really exotic, like a star fruit!

YOU WILL NEED

Newspaper
Masking tape
Diluted PVA glue
Fine sandpaper
White paint
Assortment of poster paints
Non-toxic clear gloss varnish

1 Loosely crumple a sheet of newspaper into a large egg shape. Twist and tape the paper. You may have to add smaller wedges of crumpled paper to achieve the shape you want.

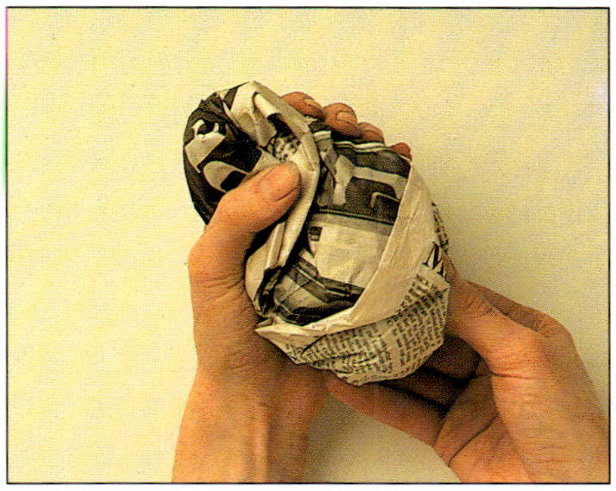

2 To make the stalk, roll a small piece of newspaper into a thin tube, bend the top over, and tape it firmly. Make a hole in the top of your pear, and push the stalk in, fixing it with masking tape.

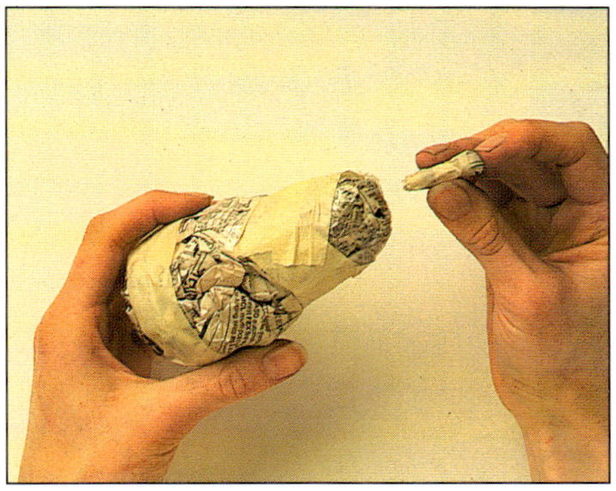

3 Soak strips of newspaper in diluted PVA glue. Cover the pear with three layers of paper strips. Smooth its surface with your hands.

4 Let the pear dry overnight in a warm place, such as an airing cupboard. Lightly sand the surface of the fruit, and prime it with two coats of white paint.

5 Colour your pear with poster paints. When it has dried, seal the surface with two coats of clear varnish. You might like to use satin finish rather than gloss varnish to give a more naturalistic look.

DECORATIVE CUP

This papier-mâché cup is formed in an exotic style from heavy cardboard. This method of making a frame which can be built up with layers of papier-mâché allows great versatility of style: almost any design on paper can be reproduced in card with a little planning.

YOU WILL NEED

Heavy cardboard
Diluted PVA glue
Masking tape
Newspaper
Fine sandpaper
White paint
Selection of poster paints
Non-toxic clear gloss varnish

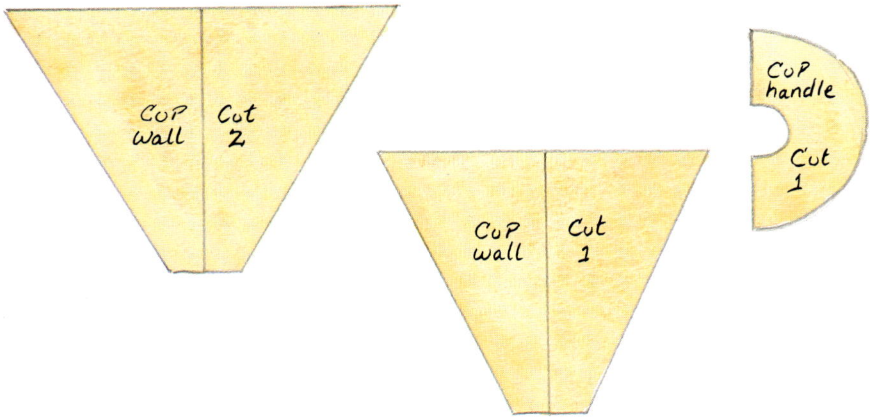

1 Scale up the cup pieces from the template to the size required and transfer them onto heavy cardboard. Assemble the cup by first sticking the three triangles of card together using PVA glue. Strengthen with strips of masking tape, and then assemble the base.

2 Stick the handle to one side of the cup and secure with masking tape. To stick the bowl and base together, make a hole in the centre of the base using a sharp pencil. Apply glue to the 'point' of the bowl and rest this on the base. Finally, fix in place with masking tape for extra strength.

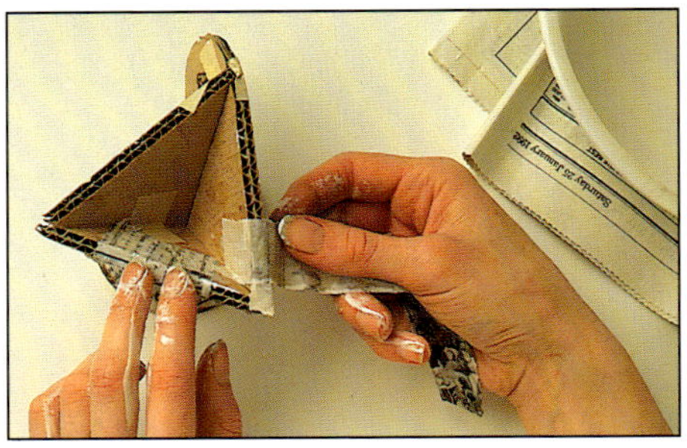

3 Next, paint the cup with one coat of diluted PVA glue to prevent it from warping, and then cover it with four layers of papier-mâché. Use short thin pieces of newspaper soaked in diluted PVA glue. Make sure the pieces of newspaper are thin enough to go around the handle.

4 Leave the cup to dry overnight in a warm place. Then lightly sand down the dried cup, and prime it with two coats of white paint.

5 Decorate the cup with poster paint. When the paint has dried thoroughly, apply a coat of clear gloss varnish.

MASKED BALL

Keep the guests at the party guessing with this stylish evening mask. Choose crêpe paper to match your ballgown and trim with matching ribbon.

YOU WILL NEED
Gold foil card
Gold doily
Glue
Foil crêpe paper
Sticky tape
Doweling rod
Ribbon

1 Scale up the template to the size required and cut out a mask shape in gold foil card.

2 Now cut the scalloped edge from a gold doily and glue it to the top of the mask.

3 Gather a strip of foil crêpe paper and stick it to the back of the mask along the top edge. You might need to secure this further with some tape.

4 Now cut out some other motifs from the doily and stick them onto the mask front to decorate.

5 Take a piece of doweling rod, wrap a length of ribbon around it and glue the ends. Curl further pieces of ribbon and stick them to the top of the doweling. Tape the doweling rod onto one side of the mask and set off for the ball.

INDIAN CHIEF

Transform a strip of card into an exciting headband fit for an Indian chief. Why not make one each for the whole tribe?

YOU WILL NEED

Coloured card
Assorted coloured card
Glue
Sticky tape

1 First of all cut out a length of stiff coloured card measuring 60 × 6 cm (24 × 2½ in). Now decorate it by cutting out zigzag lines from brightly-coloured card and sticking them onto the band.

2 Draw and cut out feather shapes from the brightly coloured card and make lots of small scissor cuts along the sides of the feathers to make them more realistic.

3 Apply glue to the inside of the band and stick the feathers in place. To secure them really well use a strip of tape on top.

4 Fold the two ends together, adjust the size and tape to fit.

SUNFLOWER

Brighten up a room with some crêpe paper sunflowers that will bring a ray of sunshine all year round.

YOU WILL NEED

Brown card
Brown and green crêpe paper
Glue
Bright yellow paper
Doweling rod
Green paper
Sticky tape

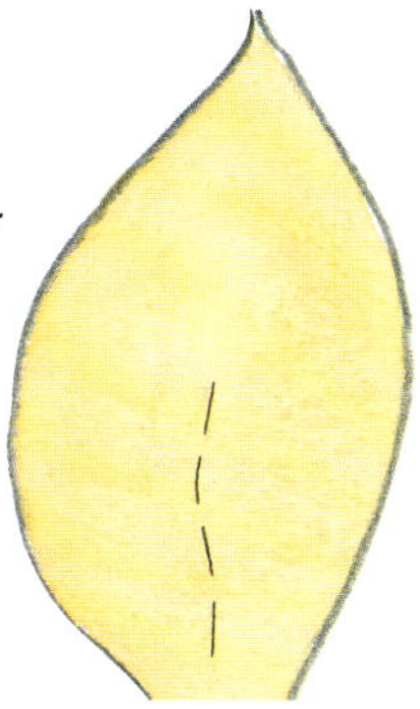

1 Cut out two 10 cm (4 in) diameter circles from brown card. Next cut 4 cm (1½ in) squares of brown crêpe paper and attach them to one side of one of the brown circles by screwing up each one and gluing it on.

2 Using the petal template, scaled up to the size required, cut out petals in bright yellow paper.

3 Pleat and glue them into position onto the back of the covered brown circle so that they follow the edge.

4 To make the stem take a piece of doweling rod approximately 50 cm (20 in) long. Cut leaf shapes in green paper and twist the ends to make a small stem.

5 Attach the leaf stems to the doweling rod at intervals, securing with tape.

6 Cover the stick completely by winding a long strip of green crêpe paper around it.

7 Tape the flower head to the front of the stick, then turn over and glue the remaining brown circle to the back to neaten.

FLYING IN THE WIND

This regal kite will look very grand flying in a blue sky with its gold bows trailing behind. If it is made with fairly stiff paper, it should withstand quite strong gusts of wind. It is possible to make the kite in a variety of sizes: just follow the basic rule that the cross bar is two-thirds the length of the long doweling rod.

YOU WILL NEED

Two lengths of wooden doweling rod, one measuring 40 cm (16 in) and one 60 cm (24 in)
Lengths of strong thin string
Craft knife
Large sheet of stiff coloured paper
Strong glue
Curtain ring
Ball of kite string
Contrasting scraps of coloured paper for decoration and tail ribbons
Length of coloured ribbon for kite tail

1 First, take the two pieces of doweling rod. Using a pen, mark the shorter piece halfway along its length. Mark the longer piece a third of the way down its length. Join the pieces of doweling rod together so that the marks touch; the shorter piece should lie horizontally across the longer, forming a cross. Tie the sticks tightly together with thin string.

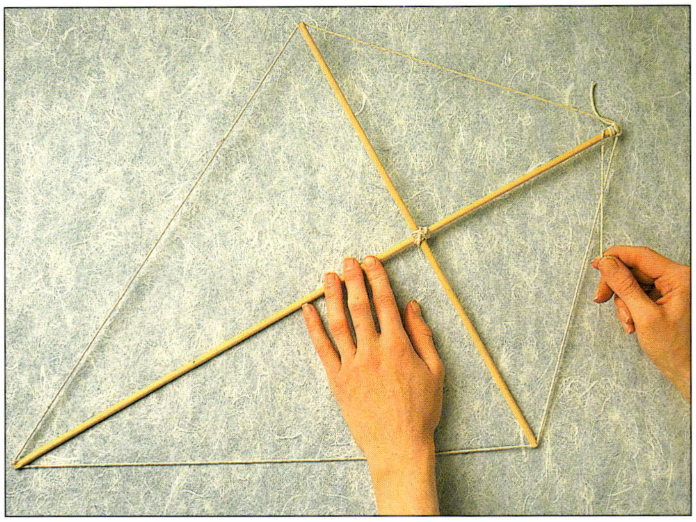

2 Using a craft knife, make a notch at the end of each piece of doweling rod. Then tie the end of a length of string around the notch in the top of the kite frame, and wind the string around the outside, securing it around each notch in turn. Tie the ends of the string together when you reach the top of the frame again.

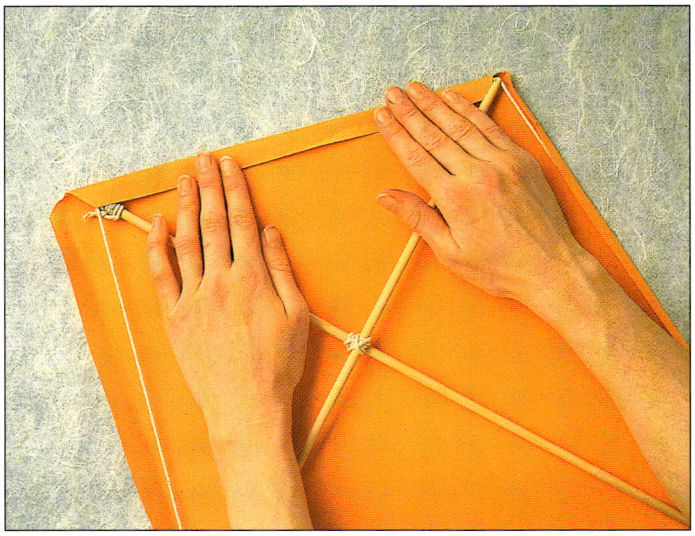

3 Next, place the kite frame on the large piece of coloured paper and cut around it, leaving 1 cm (½ in) of paper spare outside the edges of the string. Cut the corners of the paper back to the ends of each piece of doweling rod, and then smear glue along the edges of the paper, folding them over to enclose the string.

Tie a length of string to each end of the short rod, and a piece to either end of the long one. Pull the strings together so that they overlap, and secure them where they touch with a curtain ring. Tie the ball of kite string to the curtain ring.

4 Decide on the colour of the tail decoration and stick it to the front of the kite with strong glue. Secure the tail ribbon at the bottom of the kite frame, and stick paper bows in place along its length with a dab of glue or small pieces of tape. Alternatively, tie the kite tail around each bow to keep them firmly in place.

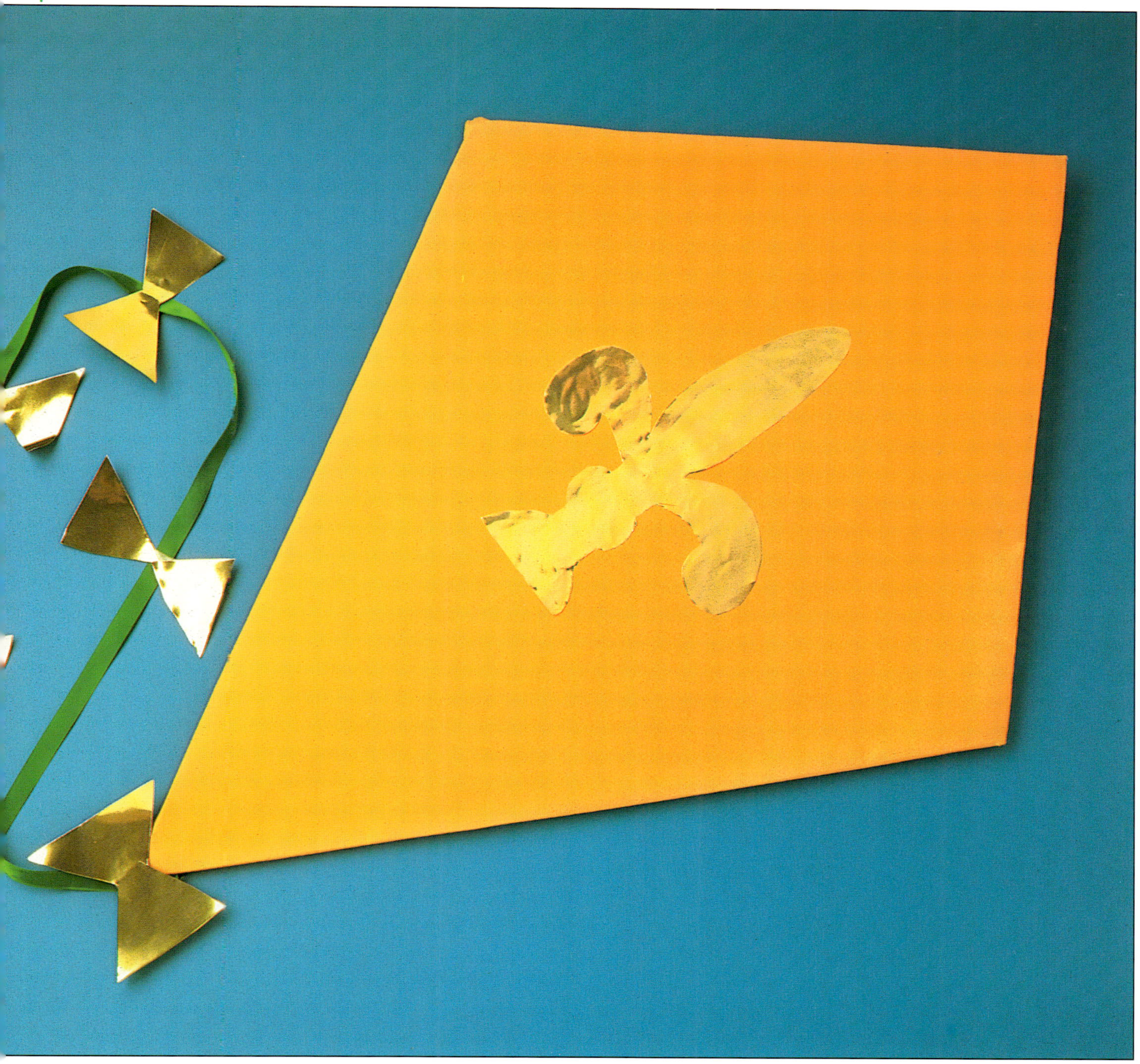

CANDLE DECORATIONS

This is a very quick and decorative way to display candles, but remember that lit candles should never be left unattended under any circumstances.

YOU WILL NEED
Oasis or florist's sponge
Tissue paper
Candle
Thin paint brush

1 To make the candle holder, first cut a block of oasis or florist's sponge to the size that you require.

2 Now cut out small squares of tissue paper. This tissue paper is black on one side and gold on the other so that it has a two-tone effect, intended to match the elegant black candles used.

3 Push the base of the candle into the oasis so that it can stand by itself.

4 Taking a square of tissue paper, place the end of a paint brush in the centre of the paper and poke it into the oasis so that it is held in place. Continue to do this until the block is covered.

STAR GARLAND

For this star garland you will need lots of different colours of tissue paper. Four colours have been used here, but it is up to you how many you choose.

YOU WILL NEED

Coloured tissue paper
Double-sided tape

1 First of all fold up the sheets of tissue paper in individual colours and draw a star shape on top. Now cut out the stars and repeat in all the colours.

2 Stick double-sided tape onto four points of one star and place another star of a different colour on top.

3 Put a further piece of double-sided tape into the centre of the second star and place the next coloured star on top of this. Continue to build up the garland, sticking the stars alternately at sides and centre, until you have a chain long enough for the length that you require.

SPACE ALIEN

A hair band simply covered in shiny paper makes an effective alien headdress. Team with T-shirt or leotard and tights for a double-quick space outfit.

YOU WILL NEED

Rigid hair band
Blue metallic crêpe paper
Glue
Sticky tape

1 Use an old hair band and wind a strip of blue metallic crêpe paper around it, taking care not to tear the paper. Secure the end with glue or sticky tape.

2 Next cut two lengths of the crêpe paper and roll them up lengthways, gluing them to make a tube.

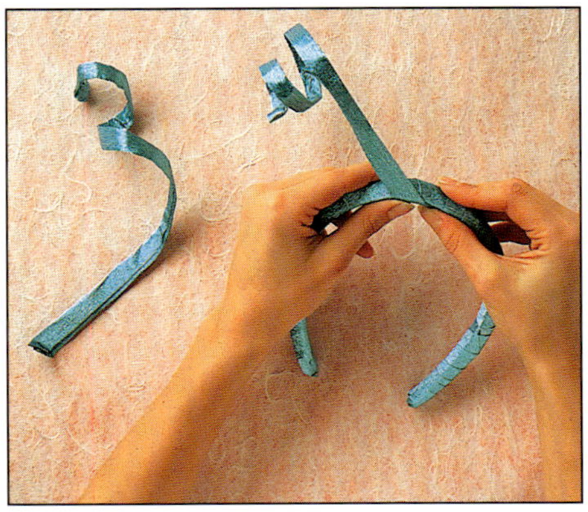

3 Now tightly wind the top part of the tube around a pencil or paint brush to make it curl. Repeat with the other length. Fix the Space Alien 'antennae' onto the hair band with clear tape and mould into a suitable shape.

CHRISTMAS TREE GIFT BOX

Here is a way to make a very attractive Christmas decoration to hang on the tree. Pop a sweet or small gift inside or leave it empty simply for decoration.

YOU WILL NEED

White card
Craft knife
Ruler
Glue
Wrapping paper
Ribbon

1 Using the template, scaled to the size required, draw and cut out the box shape in white card. You can make it smaller or larger by altering the size of the square as you like.

2 Score along all the lines using a craft knife and ruler, taking care not to cut through the card completely.

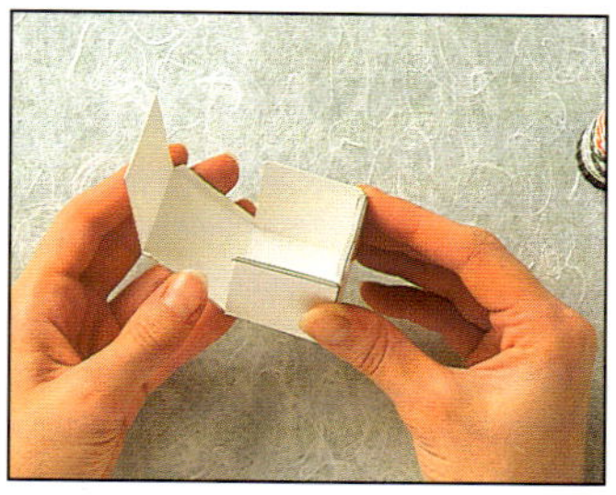

3 Shape the box by folding the sides up along the scored lines. Apply glue to the tabs and hold the box in position until it is fixed.

4 Now cover the box in an appropriate wrapping paper.

5 Finish off by tying a ribbon decoratively, and making a loop to hang the box on the tree.

SPARKLING FRAME

This frame is decorated with two different coloured foils, and will take standard-sized photographs. It opens at the side and could easily be made larger to accommodate bigger pictures.

YOU WILL NEED

Heavy corrugated cardboard
Thin corrugated cardboard
Strong clear glue
Diluted PVA glue
2 picture hangers
Masking tape
Newspaper
Fine sandpaper
White paint
Silver foil
Gold foil
Cord for hanging

1 Scale up the frame pieces from the template to the size required. Transfer the front to heavy cardboard and the spacer to thin cardboard. Cut a rectangle in thick cardboard to form the back of the frame. Stick the spacer to three sides of the reverse of this rectangle and secure with tape. One side is left open for inserting the picture. When the glue is dry, prime the pieces with diluted PVA glue to help prevent warping. Allow to dry for three or four hours. Glue and tape the hangers to the back.

2 Now cover both pieces of frame with three layers of papier-mâché, using strips of newspaper about 2½ cm (1 in) wide. Let the papier-mâché dry overnight, and then sand the layers lightly with fine sandpaper.

3 When they are dry, prime the frame pieces with two coats of white paint *before* they are joined. Although the paint will eventually be covered, you will be able to see much more easily where to stick the foil if the surface of the frame is white. Stick the back to the front of the frame with strong, clear glue, and hold the joins together with tape. Cover the joins with two layers of papier-mâché strips, and apply another coat of white paint.

4 When everything is dry, decorate the frame. Cut strips of silver foil to fit on the frame and glue them in place. Make sure that you cover the inside edges of the frame. Next, cut shapes from gold foil and stick them around the frame. Finally, attach some cord to the back of the frame, around the hangers.

MOSAIC STYLE

Mosaic tiling is a very ancient form of art and was used as a practical way to decorate floors. It is also an attractive way to make a picture using paper. It does need patience and the finished result makes a beautiful piece to frame and display.

YOU WILL NEED

White and brown card
Coloured papers
Glue
Craft knife

1 Scale up the design from the template to the size required and transfer it onto a piece of white card 30 × 20 cm (12 × 8 in).

2 Select the coloured papers you would like to use and cut them into strips first of all and then into squares. They do not have to be perfect as the variety of shapes and edges will add to the mosaic effect.

3 Organize the various squares of colours into separate piles and start to glue them onto the picture.

4 Continue to build up the squares in colour sections. In order to achieve a smooth line, it may be necessary to use a craft knife to trim the edges of the squares once they have been glued.

5 To make the border, cut two strips of the brown card 3 cm (1¼ in) wide and the length of the white board. Cut two yellow strips of paper in the same size and draw and cut the wave design onto them. Fix the yellow strips onto the brown and glue them onto the card. When all the areas have been covered, cut pieces to make the eyes and the mouths and glue them into place.

CIRCLE GARLAND

Festoon your room with these simple circular garlands made from vivid tissue paper. Alternate the colours individually or place together in blocks of colour.

YOU WILL NEED

Card
Coloured tissue paper
Glue

1 Cut two circles of card and lots of circles in different colours of tissue paper.

2 Take ten of the tissue paper circles and fold them in half, then half again into a quarter. Do not use any more than ten pieces as they will not fold properly. Now make a cut from the double-folded edge, following the line of the outside of the circle, two thirds down the wedge.

3 Undo the circle and fold again in half the other way. Fold again into a quarter so that you have a new fold line. Make a cut nearer the centre, following the outside line as illustrated. Undo the circle and lay it flat.

4 Glue the first circle onto one of the circular cards and then attach another tissue circle onto it by gluing it at the centre.

5 Glue the next circle to the top and bottom of the first. Continue to glue together alternately gluing them at the centre, and the top and bottom. Finally, glue the other circular card to the last tissue circle. Pull the cards away from each other to reveal the garland.

PARTY BOATER

Perfect for a fancy dress party, a theatrical production or a summer picnic, this boater is both elegant and easy to make.

YOU WILL NEED
Coloured card
Glue

1 Measure and draw a 24 cm (10 in) diameter circle on to a piece of coloured card and then draw a second circle with a 19 cm (7 in) diameter inside the first one. Cut out the larger circle.

2 Cut darts around the larger circle so that they end at the inner circle. Fold the darts down once they have all been cut. This allows the hat to fit perfectly.

3 Next measure and cut out a strip of card in the same colour measuring 8 × 60 cm (3 × 23½ in). Draw a straight line down the centre of the strip and carefully cut darts down one half. Glue the strip and then fix it to the circle by attaching the darts onto it in order to form the top of the boater.

4 Now push the side darts outwards; cut out a ring of coloured card that has an outside diameter of 30 cm (13 in) and an inside diameter of 19 cm (8 in).

5 Place the card ring over the top and onto the out-turned darts and glue into position.

6 Decorate by putting a band of suitable wrapping paper around it, to create a colourful band. You could make several hats and give each one a different band.

BRIGHT BEADS

Papier-mâché can be used to make beads in a huge variety of sizes, shapes and colours, and because of its lightweight nature you can make the most enormous necklaces, bracelets and earrings without being weighed down!

YOU WILL NEED

Newspaper
Diluted PVA glue
Darning needle
White paint
Assortment of poster paints
Non-toxic clear gloss varnish
Thin nylon cord or elastic to string beads

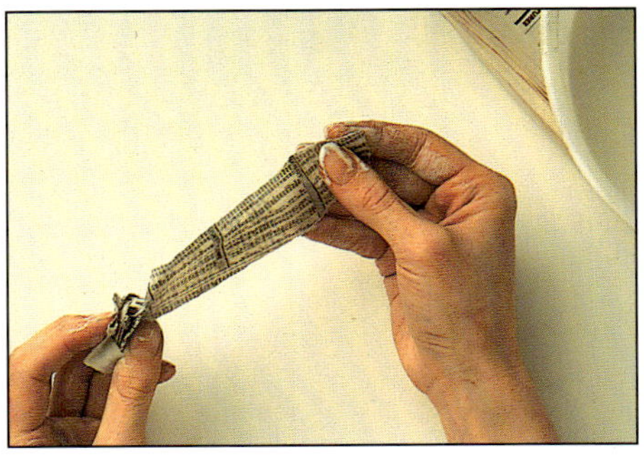

1 Tear the newspaper into long strips about 2½ cm (1 in) wide, and soak them in the diluted PVA glue for a few seconds. Shake off the excess glue, and roll up the paper between your fingers so that it forms round pellets of pulp.

2 Squash each ball of pulp so that it is tightly compacted, and most of the glue is squeezed out. Lay the beads in a warm place to dry for a couple of hours.

3 When they have dried for an hour or two, make a hole through the centre of each bead with a darning needle. Let the beads dry overnight.

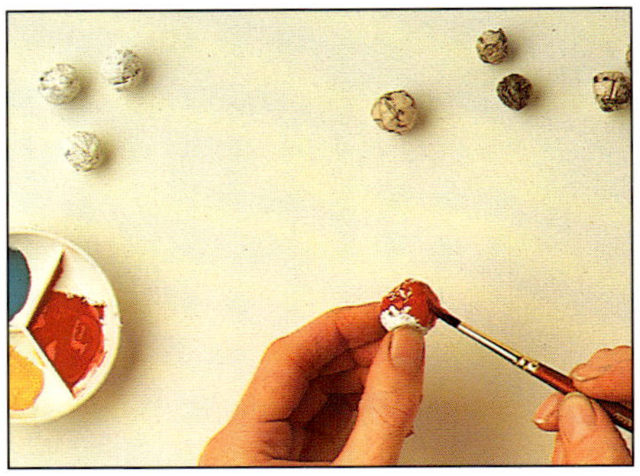

4 When the beads are completely dry, prime each one with two coats of white paint. Let the paint dry, and then decorate the beads with poster paints.

5 Varnish each bead with two coats of clear gloss varnish, and when dry, string them onto thin nylon cord or elastic using a darning needle.

CUT-OUT ANIMALS

The chicken, frog, and elephant are held together with paper fasteners and have moveable limbs. They are very simple in construction, and many other animals could be attempted using the same process.

YOU WILL NEED

Heavy paper or thin card
Felt-tip pens or coloured pencils
Craft knife
Paper fasteners
Glue

1 Scale up your chosen animal from the template to the required size, and transfer the pieces to paper or card. Cut two bodies for each animal. Remember that one will have to be cut *in reverse* so that the bodies can be stuck together. Next, cut two of each leg, wing, ear and so on. To transfer the pattern in reverse, simply turn it over.

2 Next, colour each piece of animal with felt-tip pen or coloured pencils, and cut them all out, keeping the parts separate.

3 To fix the animal together, make a small incision with a craft knife at the limb positions in each body, and at the top of each body part. Push a paper fastener through the front of each body part, through the body, and open it out on the other side to secure the animal.

4 To join the two halves together, spread a little glue along the top edge of one half of the animal's body, and stick it to the other.

MONOCHROME DECOUPAGE

Decoupage is the traditional art of decorating surfaces with paper cut-outs of Victorian-style images. This project has a contemporary feel, however, by using monochrome cut-outs and a modern box covered in brown paper.

YOU WILL NEED

Black and white pictures
Card or wooden box
Glue
Varnish (if needed)

1 Start by choosing your images. The ones used here are from a wrapping paper. Cut them out carefully following their outlines.

2 Arrange the images on a box and then glue them into position. A card gift box is used here but you could apply the paper cut-outs to a wooden box such as an old cigar box. However, you would need to coat the decorated box with a layer of varnish.

BANGLES AND BEADS

If you want some new accessories and to wear something that nobody else will have, this jewellery that is made from paper could be just what you are looking for.

YOU WILL NEED

Patterned paper
Contrasting coloured card
Pencil or paint brush
Glue
Bead thread
Sticky tape

1 To start, cut 30 cm (12 in) strips of marbled or decorated paper and taper them so that they measure 4 cm (1½ in) at the base and 1 cm (½ in) at the tip. Then cut a small length of contrasting coloured card, wrap it around a pencil or paint brush and fix it with glue.

2 Now apply some more glue to the length of the triangular strip and, beginning with the wider end, start to wrap around the card, so that the strip is kept central. Make several more of these beads, and thread them onto a length of bead thread to form a necklace.

3 To make a matching bangle, cut a long strip of white card and curl it round into a ring, large enough to slip over your hand. Fix by taping it.

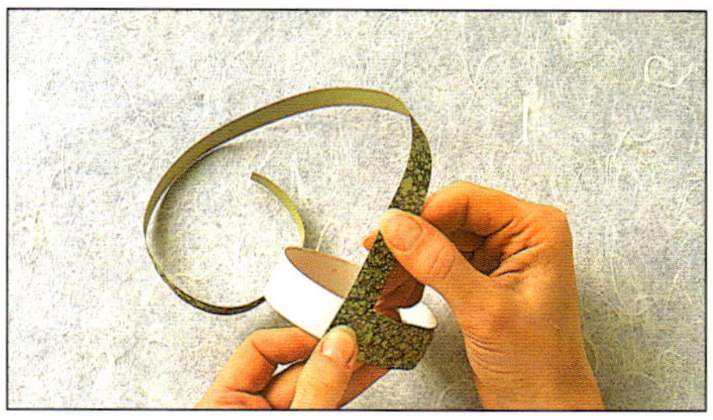

4 Now cut long strips of your chosen decorated paper and after gluing them at one end, start to wind them one by one around the bangle shape.

CUT-OUT DOLLS

This charming couple are modern versions of the cut-out dolls that have been popular for several centuries. They have 'casual' and 'smart' outfits, so are ready for any occasion!

YOU WILL NEED

Thick white paper
Felt-tip pens or coloured pencils
Glue
Thin card
Craft knife

1 Start by scaling up the designs from the template to the size required. Next transfer them to white paper.

2 Colour in the dolls and their clothes with felt-tip pens or coloured pencils according to your own fashion scheme.

3 Stick the dolls onto the thin card. Cut carefully around the dolls and their clothes with scissors. Using a craft knife, lightly score the fold line of the stand at the bottom of each doll, making sure you do not cut right through. Fold along the scored line to make a prop to help the dolls stand upright. To dress the dolls, simply fold each white tab over to the back of the body.

'BAROQUE' CHRISTMAS WREATH

The base for this beautiful wreath is an embroidery hoop. An oval one is used here but a round one would work just as well.

YOU WILL NEED

Gold crêpe paper
Glue
Oval embroidery hoop
Gold card
Paint brush or pencil
Black felt-tip pen

1 First cut a long strip of gold crêpe paper, glue it at one end of the hoop and start to wind it around the hoop until it is completely covered.

2 Now cut a strip of gold card approximately 1 × 30 cm (½ × 12 in) and wrap it tightly around a paint brush or pencil.

3 Attach one end of the curled gold strip half-way up the right-hand side of the hoop, wind round the hoop and fix the other end just beyond the bottom point.

4 Using the template, scaled to the size required, draw the angel playing the trumpet onto the back of some gold card and cut out. Draw on the features in a black felt-tip pen. Make a bow out of gold crêpe paper and stick it on to the top of the wreath.

5 Now fix the angel to the left hand side of the wreath.

FRAME UP

Make your own designer-look photograph frames from thick card and wrapping paper. Choose paper to pick out colours in the photographs or to co-ordinate with furnishings.

YOU WILL NEED

Thick card
Ruler
Craft knife
Wrapping or marbled paper
Glue

1 Cut two pieces of thick card to the required size and cut a window in one of them using a ruler and craft knife. As a guide allow 3 cm (1 in) for the frame but this can be varied depending on the photograph.

2 For the backing card, cut a piece of marbled paper to the same width but slightly longer, then glue and turn the excess length around the top edge.

3 Take the frame front, place it onto another piece of marbled paper and lightly mark and cut out a smaller window so that you have turnings of about 1½ cm (½ in). Glue the turnings on the window to the inside of the frame. Cut across the external corners of the paper and glue the top edge down.

4 Cut spacing strips out of thick card and stick them along the three sides of the back panel.

5 Apply glue to the strips and carefully fix the front frame on top. Glue and turn the edges at the side and base front so that they wrap around the three remaining sides of the back panel.

6 Now cut a piece of marbled paper exactly the same size as the frame and stick it onto the back to neaten.

7 To make the support strut cut out a piece of card approximately half the length of frame and cut a pointed end. Cover in paper leaving a long overlap of excess paper at the blunt end.

8 Use the excess paper to glue and attach the strut to the back of the frame.

9 Make a support strap from the same paper, and glue it to the back of the frame and the support.

TREE DECORATIONS

Good, unusual Christmas decorations are often hard to find. If you want an alternative to glittery baubles then you may like to design and make your own decorations in papier-mâché. These are very simple in design and structure, but you could easily make quite ornate, even three-dimensional, decorations to dress your tree.

YOU WILL NEED

Thin card
Craft knife
Small metal jewellery hangers, one for each decoration
Strong clear glue
Masking tape
Newspaper
Diluted PVA glue
Fine sandpaper
White paint
Assortment of poster paints
Black ink (optional)
Non-toxic clear gloss varnish
Cord to hang decorations

1 Trace the decoration shapes from the template, scaling up to the size required, and transfer them to the thin card. Cut out each shape.

Stick a hanger onto the back of each decoration with strong clear glue, and hold it in place with masking tape.

2 Allow the glue to dry for an hour, and then cover each decoration with three layers of small, thin newspaper strips soaked in diluted PVA glue. Let the decorations dry in a warm place overnight.

3 Then, sand the dry decorations lightly with fine sandpaper, and prime each one with two coats of white paint.

4 Draw in any design first with pencil, and then colour your decorations with poster paints. Define details with black ink if required.

Allow the decorations to dry thoroughly, and then seal them with two coats of clear gloss varnish. When they are dry, tie a loop of cord to the top of each decoration.

VICTORIAN BOOKLET

What could be more evocative of the Victorian age than a notebook that has been decorated by decoupage. This little book could be used as a diary, a notebook or a sketch pad.

YOU WILL NEED

Writing paper
Needle and embroidery thread
Victorian-style scraps or magazine pictures
Glue

1 First fold some sheets of writing paper in half to make the booklet, and press down in the centre to create the crease.

2 Now open out the book and, taking a needle and embroidery thread, make three large stitches to bind the booklet.

3 To give the booklet a nostalgic feel use Victorian-style scraps which can be cut out from magazines, or purchased. Arrange and stick them onto the cover of the notebook.

ROYAL CROWN

A regal crown fit for a king, queen, prince or princess! Make your decorations as simple or elaborate as you like, for a right royal celebration.

YOU WILL NEED

Foil card
Silver paper
Glue
Coloured foil paper
Double-sided tape
Foil crêpe paper

1 To make the crown, cut out a length of foil card about 55 cm (22 in) long and 15 cm (6 in) wide. On the back of the card draw out a shaped crown design and cut it out.

2 Now cut out small circles of silver paper and glue them onto the finials. Cut out diamond shapes in different coloured foil paper to make up the 'jewels' and glue them onto the crown.

3 Join the ends of the crown together with glue and stick a long piece of double-sided tape all the way around on the inside about half-way down.

4 Take a circle of matching foil crêpe paper, which is just larger than the crown, and carefully place it inside the top so that it is fixed to the tape. Make it billow out by pushing it up from underneath, to represent the velvet in a crown.

CHRISTMAS RING

This is a quick and easy way to make a new collection of Christmas decorations to hang on your tree without spending a fortune. They are made from wooden curtain rings, covered in vivid crêpe paper.

YOU WILL NEED

Crêpe paper
Wooden curtain rings
Glue
Thin ribbon

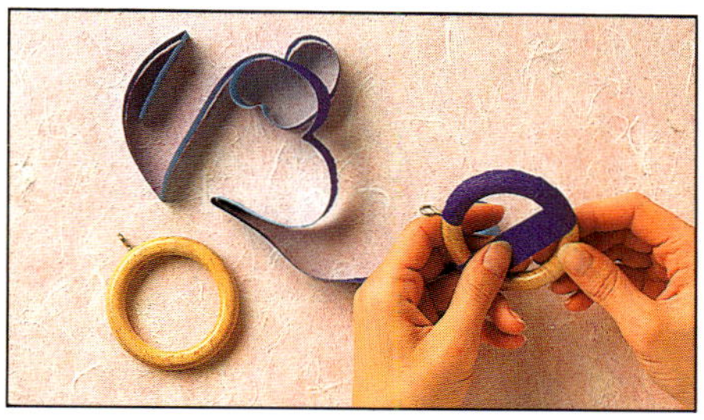

1 Cut 2 cm (¾ in) wide strips of coloured crêpe paper. Take a wooden curtain ring and wind the strips of crêpe paper around the ring to cover. Glue ends in place.

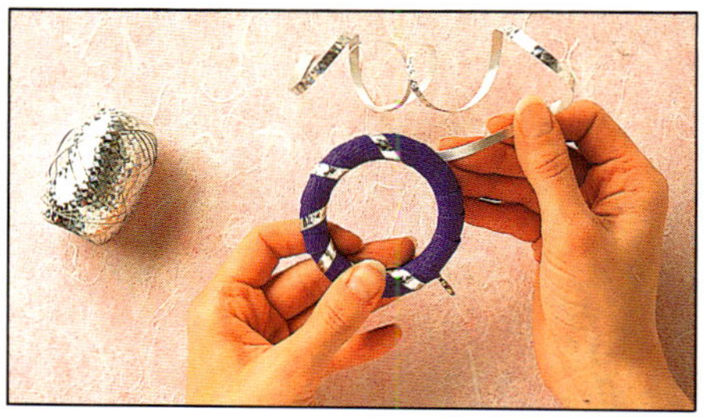

2 Now take a thin ribbon and secure it at the top of the ring. As before, wind it around the ring leaving gaps to reveal the paper. When you have worked the ribbon back to the top, secure it and then make a loop for hanging.

3 To finish off, make a bow out of the crêpe paper and stick it on at the top of the ring.

BUTTERFLY MOBILE

Mobiles can drift gently in the slightest breeze or draught, entertaining young and old alike. Here the pretty butterfly wings are particularly eye-catching as they sparkle in the light.

YOU WILL NEED

Brightly coloured card in different shades
Sequins or glitter (optional)
Glue
Cotton thread
Sewing needle
Sticky tape
Three mobile wires, or three thin lengths of thin wooden rod

1 Scale up the template to the required size and trace four butterflies onto different coloured cards and then cut them out. Then cut out a fifth butterfly, using a smaller scale so that it is approximately half the size of the other four.

2 Next start to decorate the butterflies by sticking on small pieces of card, making sure that the colours are strong and bright. You could use other materials such as sequins or glitter to add extra sparkle.

3 Thread a long length of cotton through the top of each of the large butterflies, knotting the end securely and fixing it with sticky tape. Attach the other end of each piece of thread to the mobile wires. Each piece of thread should be a different length to add variety to the positions of the butterflies.

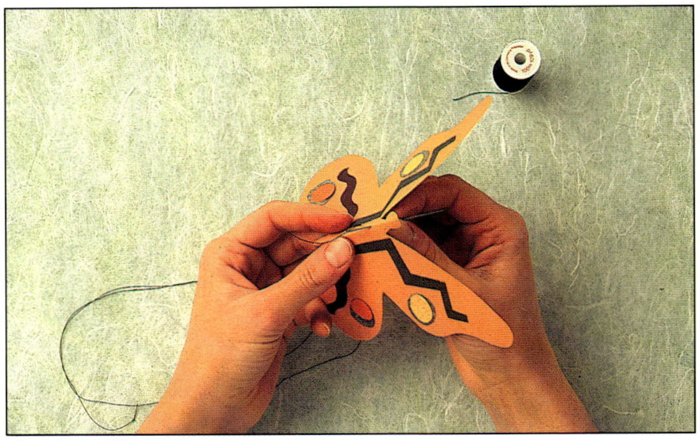

4 Last, but not least, decorate the smallest butterfly and stick it onto the top wire of the mobile, to make it look as if it is having a rest from flying around!

BAUBLE BOX

This box can be made in a variety of sizes, and could be filled with handmade sweets as a gift on a special occasion. It may be decorated in a variety of ways, perhaps with small pieces of brightly coloured pottery to emulate mosaic, or glass 'gems' from a theatrical costumiers.

YOU WILL NEED

Heavy and thin corrugated cardboard
Craft knife
Strong clear glue
Masking tape
Newspaper
Diluted PVA glue
Fine sandpaper
White paint
Assorted poster paints
Non-toxic clear gloss varnish

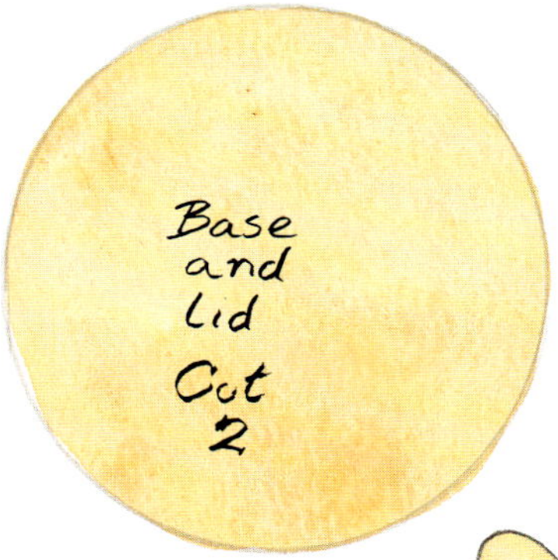

1 Scale up the box pieces from the template to the size required and, apart from the lid handle, transfer to heavy corrugated cardboard. Cut out using a craft knife. Place the box wall pattern so that the corrugations run vertically along its width. Cut the lid handle from thin corrugated card.

2 Next, assemble the body of the box and the lid. Bend the box wall at each corrguation so that it forms a circle. Glue and tape it in position on the box base. Then glue and tape the lip to the underside of the lid, and fix the handle in position.

3 Tear newspaper into thin strips and soak in diluted PVA glue. Cover the body of the box and the lid with four layers of papier-mâché. Make sure the strips of paper are thin enough to ensure a smooth surface, especially around the curved edges.

4 Leave the box to dry overnight in a warm place. When quite dry, lightly smooth the surface of the box with fine sandpaper, and prime it with two coats of white paint. Leave to dry thoroughly in a warm place.

5 Decorate the box and its lid, both inside and out, using poster paints. When the paint is completely dry, apply a coat of clear gloss varnish.

DOLL

This doll is formed from tightly taped and compacted newspaper twists. The resulting structure is very sturdy and quite large dolls or other toys could be constructed using this method.

YOU WILL NEED

Newspaper
Masking tape
Diluted PVA glue
Fine sandpaper
White paint
Selection of poster paints
Black ink (optional)
Non-toxic clear gloss varnish

1 First, twist a double sheet of newspaper together to form a 'rope' and tape the top, about 5 cm (2 in) down, to form the doll's head. Cut the remaining paper 'rope' to the desired length to form the body, and secure it with masking tape.

2 Cover the body and head with strips of masking tape to add extra strength. Next, make the arms and legs by the same process, twisting smaller pieces of paper and taping them along their length. Cut the resulting 'ropes' to the right length, and tape them firmly in place on the doll's body.

3 Tear some newspaper into thin strips and soak in diluted PVA glue. Then cover the doll with four layers of papier-mâché. To make the doll's hair, hands and feet, roll up small strips of glue-soaked paper between finger and thumb to form pellets of pulp and stick them in place on the head. Paper over the pulp hair with short, thin strips of paper.

4 Let the doll dry overnight in a warm place. When completely dry, lightly smooth the surface with fine sandpaper and prime it with two coats of white paint.

5 When the paint has dried thoroughly, draw in the features of the doll with pencil and fill in the design with poster paints. Define the decoration with black ink if more detail is needed. Seal the doll with two coats of non-toxic clear gloss varnish and allow to dry.

Origami

INTRODUCTION

It is not difficult to understand why origami is the most popular of all papercrafts: the art is very inexpensive, can be done anywhere at anytime and requires no equipment or facilities other than a sheet of paper and a firm surface to work on. Moreover, the transformation of an ordinary piece of paper into a pleasing origami design is a kind of alchemy, perhaps even more so in today's increasingly push-button, computer-controlled, battery-operated culture, than ever before.

The history of origami is rather obscure, but clearly cannot pre-date the invention of paper in China about two thousand years ago. The word 'origami' is not Chinese but Japanese, and is used worldwide out of respect for the ancestral home of the art. When China invaded Japan in AD 610, the secret of papermaking travelled with them and was immediately assimilated into Japanese culture, not just as origami, but more practically as screens, mats, bags, umbrellas, woven clothes and many other objects. As an indication of the importance of paper to the Japanese, the word 'origami' is formed from 'ori' (to fold) and 'kami' meaning paper and also God ('kami' becomes 'gami' when combined with 'ori'). Indeed, many of the early origami designs were created for symbolic or ceremonial purposes, not for recreation.

The growth of creative origami in the West began in the 1950s, though it was a minor Spanish tradition and practised by the occasional creative individual before that time. Curiously, since that same decade, the art has also undergone a major creative revival in Japan, so much so that there are now several hundred Japanese language books currently in print, most containing new creative work. A great amount of new work is also coming from the West, in all manner of styles ranging from the charmingly simple to the astonishingly complex and from the expressive to the geometric.

If you are new to origami the next few pages will introduce the basics. Readers who have folded before will find these pages a useful refresher. The designs which follow have been graded according to their level of difficulty and you are encouraged not to be too ambitious too soon.

ORIGAMI PAPER

Although origami is defined as 'the art of *paper* folding', most paper folders spend little time thinking about paper, preferring to get straight down to the business of folding, frequently with whatever paper happens to be to hand, however inappropriate it may be. A little consideration for paper, though, can significantly improve the look of what you make and increase your pleasure in folding it.

The easiest and cheapest source of good quality practice paper is photocopy (Xerox) paper. The photocopy and quick print shops now found in most shopping centres sell reams (packets of 500 sheets) of white or coloured photocopy paper, either A4 size or American Letter Size (both about the same size as a page in this book). The shop will trim a ream to square on a power guillotine for a nominal sum. Two or three reams can usually be purchased for a very reasonable price. Part-reams may also be purchased.

For two-tone models, origami paper bought in packets is ideal. However, it can be difficult to find and is relatively expensive. Also, the bright colours can make some designs look rather childish, so it should be used with care. Patterned gift-wrap paper is a good alternative if origami paper cannot be found. Other good practice papers include computer paper, typing paper, writing paper and even brown wrapping paper.

For displaying origami, perhaps at home or at a place of work, quality papers appropriate to the design should be used. A surprising range of interesting papers can be found in art, craft and graphic equipment supplies shops. It is also worth starting a collection of unusual papers such as old posters, discarded wrapping paper, wallpaper and telephone note blocks.

TIPS

In many ways, nothing could be more basic than folding a sheet of paper. Yet, despite this wonderful simplicity, there are a few guidelines to follow that will make the process of folding easier and very satisfying. Please follow them.

- Check that the paper you are folding is *exactly* square. The best method for making a square is described in the following pages. Nothing is more frustrating than trying to fold paper which is not quite square!
- Do not fold against a soft surface, such as a carpet, your lap or bedsheets. Fold against a hard surface such as a large hardback book or a table.
- Crease slowly, firmly and accurately. Form the early creases with particular care – if they are incorrectly placed, all the later, smaller creases will be difficult to place accurately and will look messy.
- Read the instructions and follow the symbols on each step. Many a mistake is made by ignoring written instructions or by not following all the written instructions on a step, particularly during complex manoeuvres.
- The instructions and symbols on one step will create a shape which looks like the next step but stripped of its symbols. So, you must always *look ahead* to the next step to see what shape you are trying to make. Never look at steps in isolation, but see them as being interconnected, like links in a chain.

ORIGAMI SOCIETIES

If you would like to know more about origami, here are addresses for two well-organized societies. Both accept overseas members and welcome beginners. Also, both publish regular magazines, hold conventions and regional meetings, sell a wide variety of books and paper, and publish booklets on specialist origami topics. The British Origami Society has a postal library service.

British Origami Society,
253 Park Lane,
Poynton,
Stockport,
Cheshire,
SK12 1RH,
England.

The Friends of the Origami Centre of America,
15 West 77th Street,
New York,
NY 10024,
USA.

The Japanese Paper Place,
966 Queen Street West,
Toronto M6J 1G8,
Canada.

The Australian Origami Society,
2/5 Broome Street,
Highgate,
Perth 6000,
Australia.

The New Zealand Origami Society,
79 Dunbar Road,
Christchurch 3,
New Zealand.

HOW TO MAKE A SQUARE

Most papers are bought as rectangular sheets that need to be trimmed square before being folded. Here, then, is a quick and simple way to accurately trim a large sheet to a smaller square, ensuring that the edges are kept straight and clean.

1 Fold over an edge of the sheet, lining up the edges at the sides to ensure square corners.

2 Carefully cut along the crease with a series of large, smooth slicing movements, made with a non-serrated kitchen knife (one with a 15 cm [6 in] blade is best). Set aside the unwanted portion of the sheet.

3 Fold over the short edge to make a triangle.

4 Bend the sheet backwards and make a crease underneath the bottom edge of the triangle.

5 Cut along the crease.

6 Unfold the triangle.

7 The square complete.

OTHER METHODS

Scissors

Duplicate the method shown in the photographs, but use scissors instead of a non-serrated knife. Be careful to control the cutting to ensure a straight edge.

Craft knife

Duplicate the method shown in the photographs, but unfold each crease and cut along them with a craft knife held against a metal rule. Before cutting, place thick card beneath the paper so that the knife does not damage your work surface.

Guillotine

Paper bought in bulk from photocopy print shops and cut on the premises on a power guillotine will be perfectly square, but paper cut by hand on a manually-operated guillotine has the annoying habit of never quite being square, whatever safeguards are taken. So, hand guillotining is not recommended if it is important that your paper is perfectly proportioned.

Tearing

Tearing is not recommended, but is acceptable if there is no other way to trim paper. Before tearing, crease the folded edge backwards and forwards several times, pressing firmly. This will weaken the crease and make tearing easier and neater.

SYMBOLS

No sequence of origami diagrams can be followed without an understanding of the symbols they use. The meaning of most symbols is obvious and it is not necessary to learn them all now, but it would be very helpful to at least learn the difference between the mountain and valley fold symbols. The other symbols can be learnt as they appear by referring back to this page.

The same symbols can be found in most origami books, whatever language they are written in, be it English, Spanish or even Japanese. This standardization means that the language of origami is truly universal, and that enthusiasts can fold from almost any book, East or West.

valley

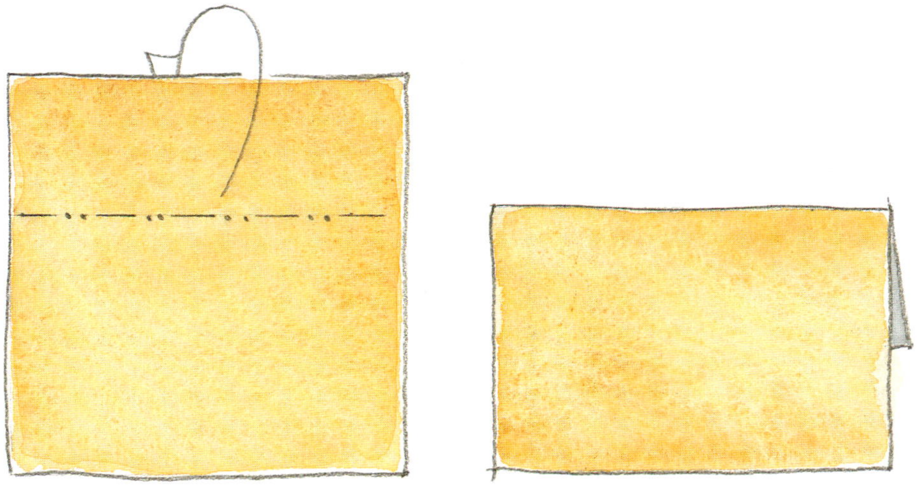

mountain

existing creases

turn over

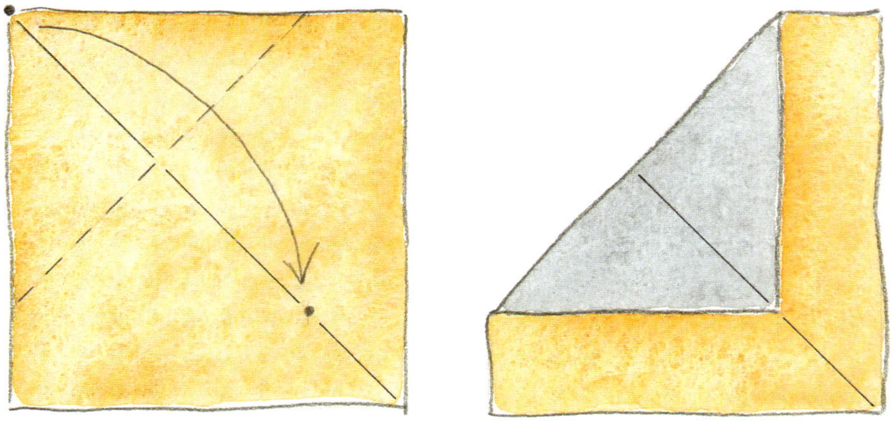

▮ fold dot to dot

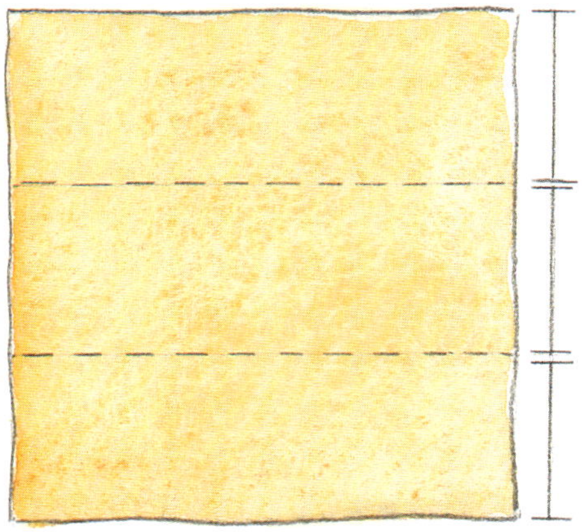

▮ these distances are equal

▮ unfold or pull out

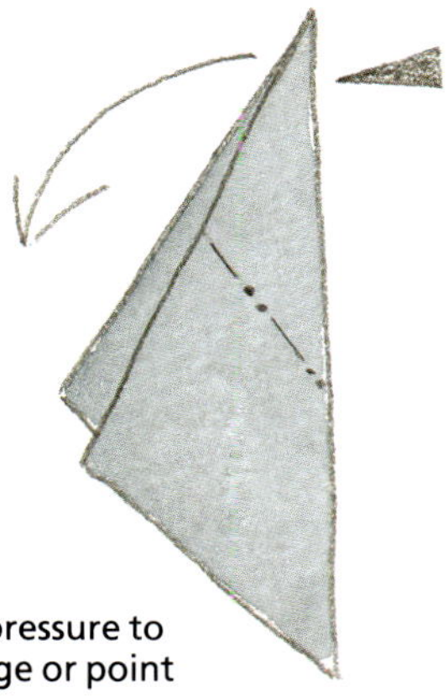

▮ apply pressure to this edge or point

▮ inflate

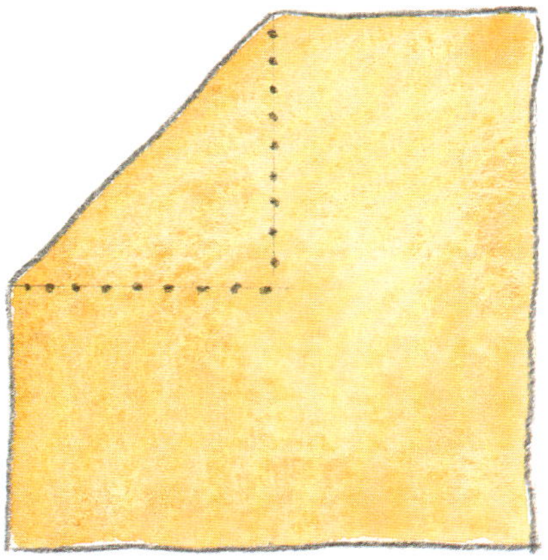

▮ x-ray view

▮ cut

ORIGAMI TECHNIQUES

Apart from the basic mountain and valley creases from which all origami designs are folded, there are four advanced techniques found in the designs that follow. These techniques are used in combination and are: the squash fold, the sink fold and the inside and outside reverse folds. However, not all designs use these advanced techniques, and only the Elephant uses them all together.

Squash and sink folds are the least common. To save space, a detailed explanation of each is given once in the book within a particular design. For an explanation of the squash fold see the Multiform House, Steps 4–6 for an explanation of the sink fold see the Star, Steps 8–12. When you come across a squash or sink fold in another design, refer to these designs for a step-by-step guide.

Inside and outside reverse folds are not more complex than squash or sink folds, but are more common and come in a greater variety. So, to simplify cross referencing, here are the basic forms of each. Refer to this page whenever you need to be reminded how to make them.

INSIDE REVERSE

Pull-through version

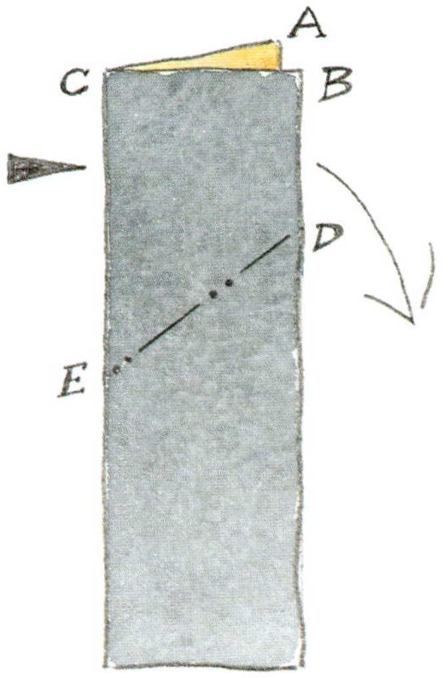

1 This is how the manoeuvre is illustrated in the book.

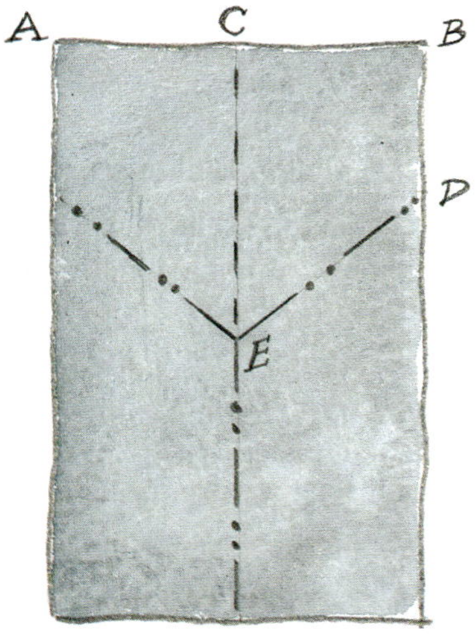

2 This is the crease pattern.

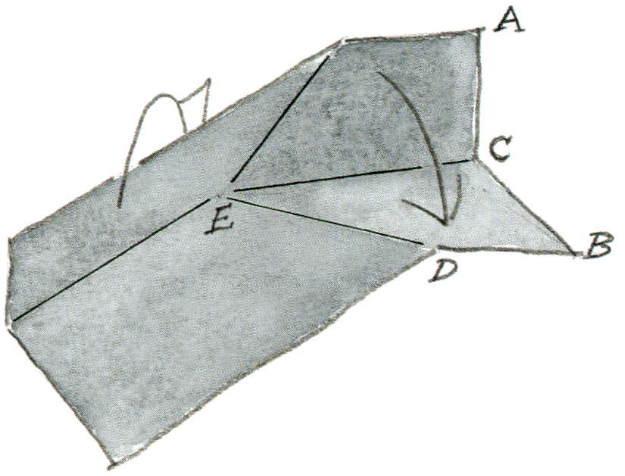

3 Collapse.

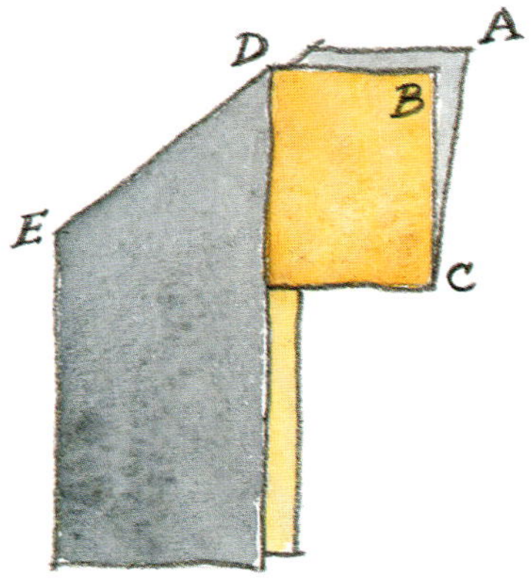

4 Complete.

Push-in version

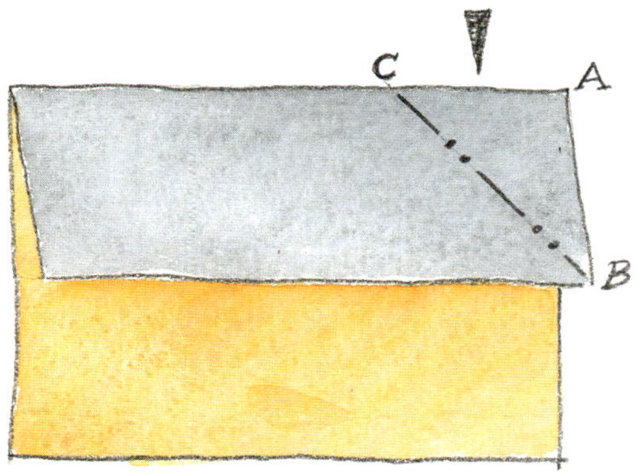

1 This is how the manoeuvre is illustrated in the book.

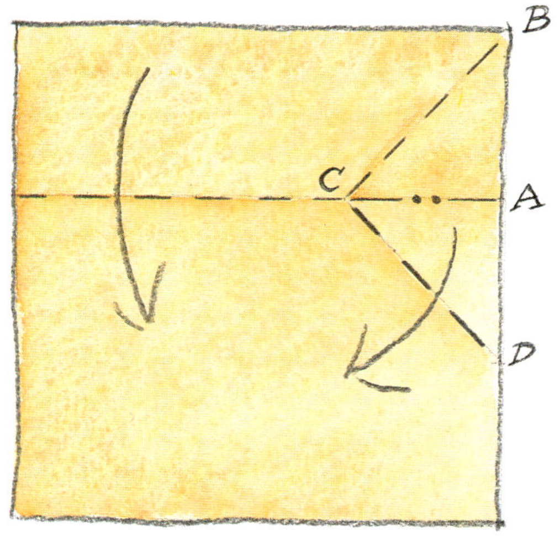

2 This is the crease pattern.

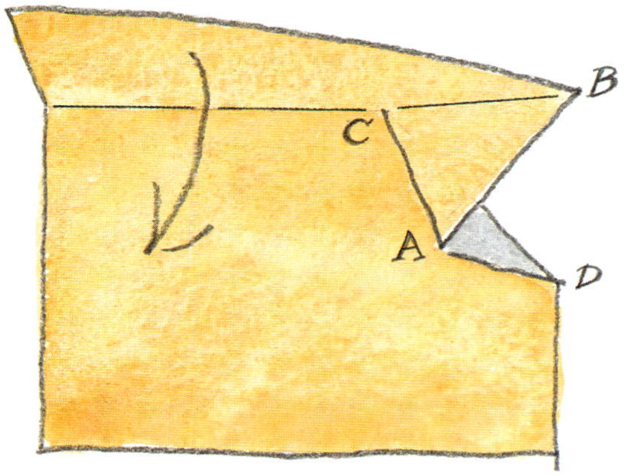

3 Collapse.

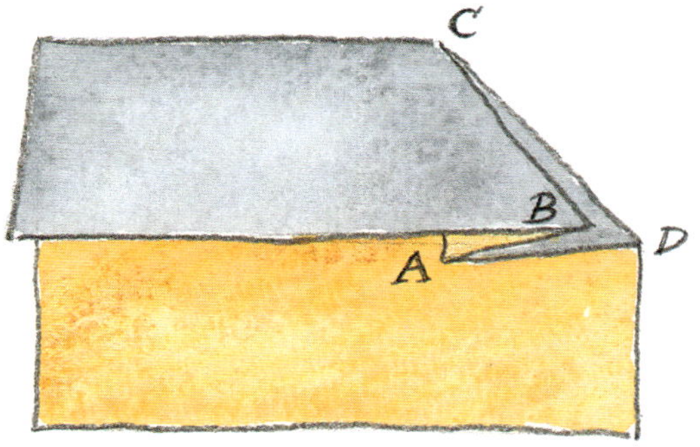

4 Complete.

OUTSIDE REVERSE

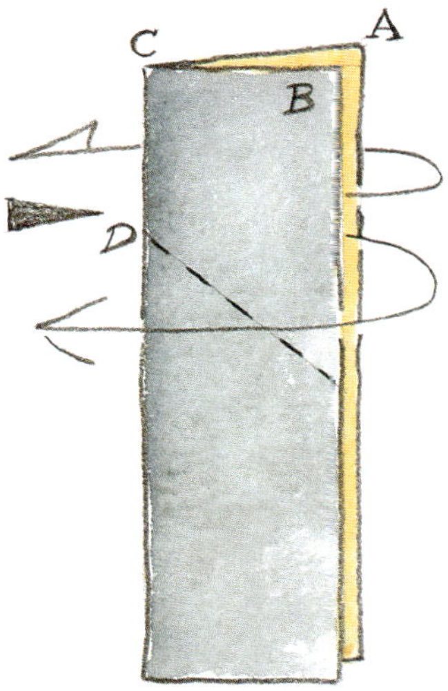

1 This is how the manoeuvre is illustrated in the book.

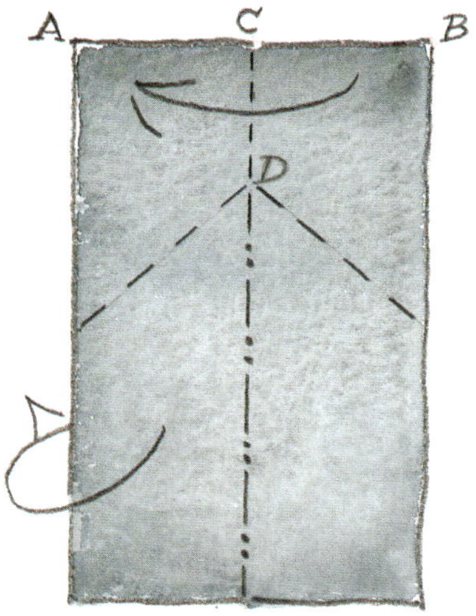

2 This is the crease pattern.

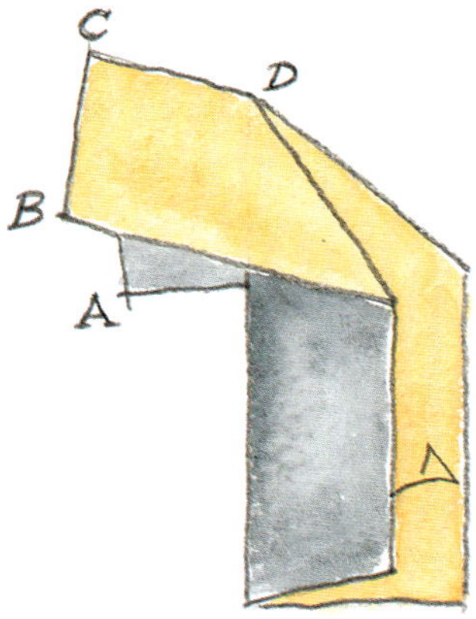

3 Collapse.

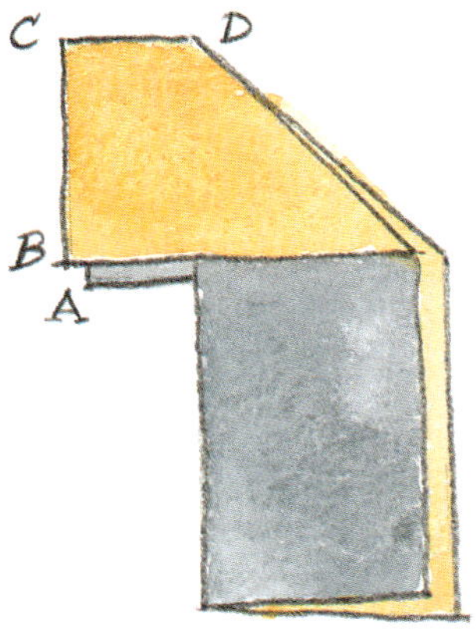

4 Complete.

SIMPLE PROJECTS

GLIDER

This design is one of a number of similar gliders of Chinese origin, all of which fly extremely well. The secret of good paper plane making is to fold with great accuracy and to practise a variety of launching actions – a carefully-made plane will not fly well if launched wrongly. Use an A4 or American Letter Size sheet of paper.

Traditional design.

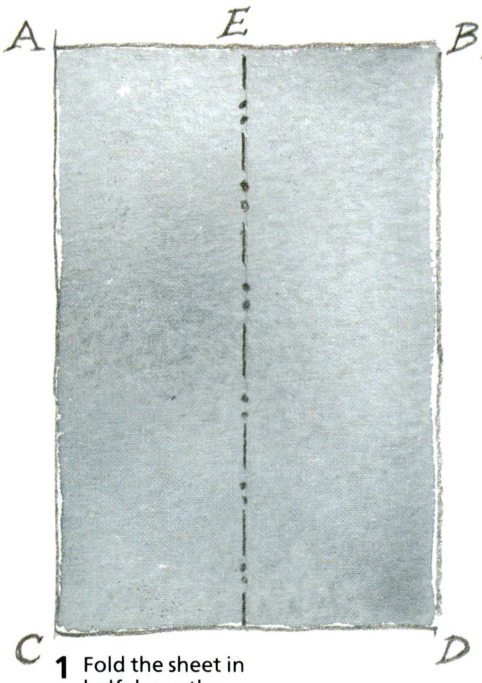

1 Fold the sheet in half down the middle, as a mountain fold (it is easier to make a valley fold, then to turn the sheet over). Unfold.

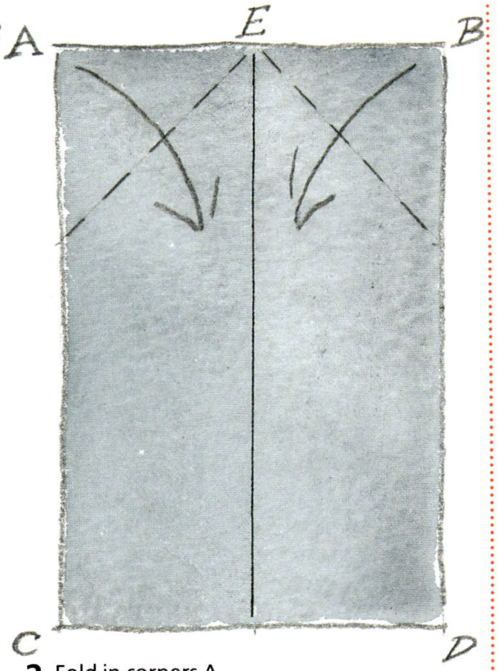

2 Fold in corners A & B to the centre crease.

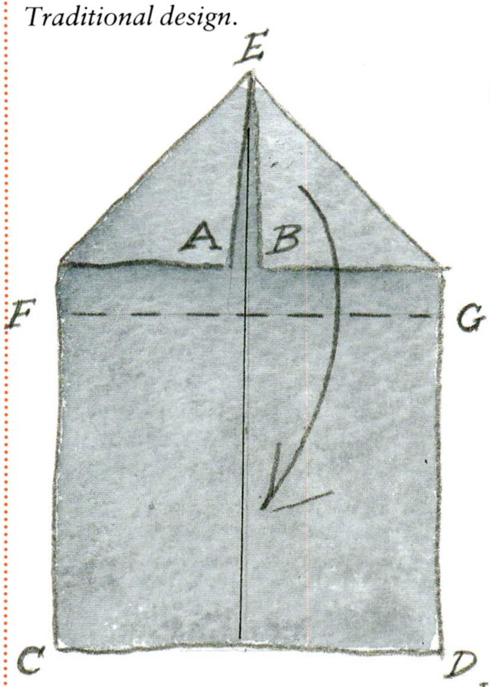

3 Fold down E along crease FG. Note that FG is a little below the level of AB.

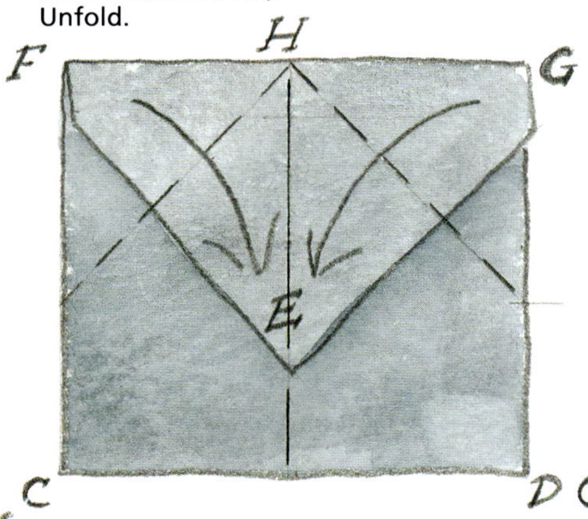

4 Fold in corners F & G, leaving E exposed.

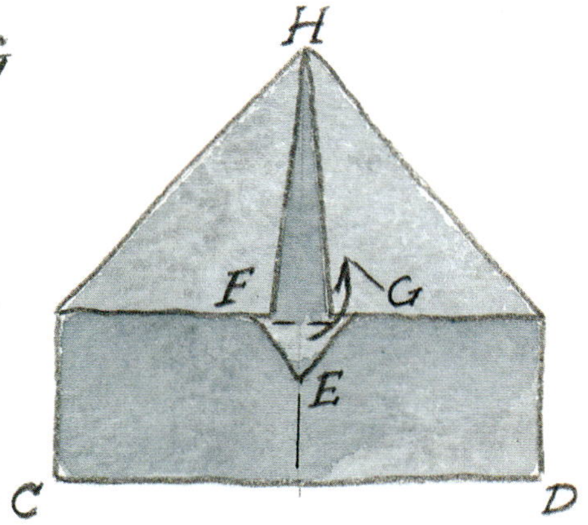

5 Fold up E over F & G.

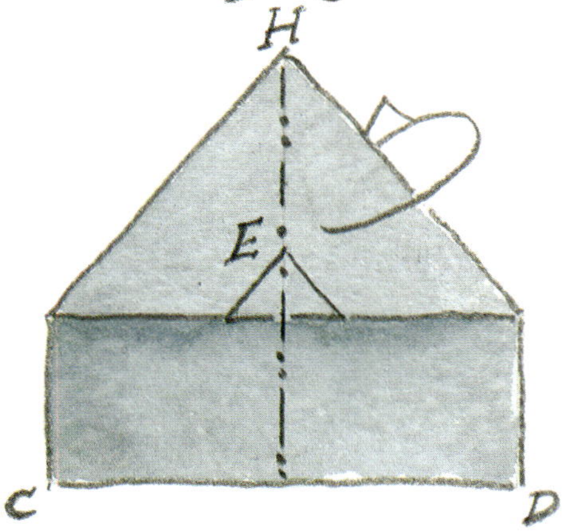

6 Mountain fold D to C.

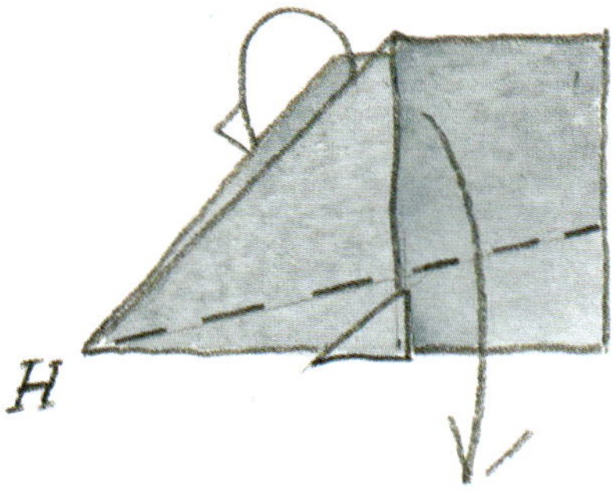

7 Before creasing, press flat the existing creases. Then, make the wing creases from the nose tip at H.

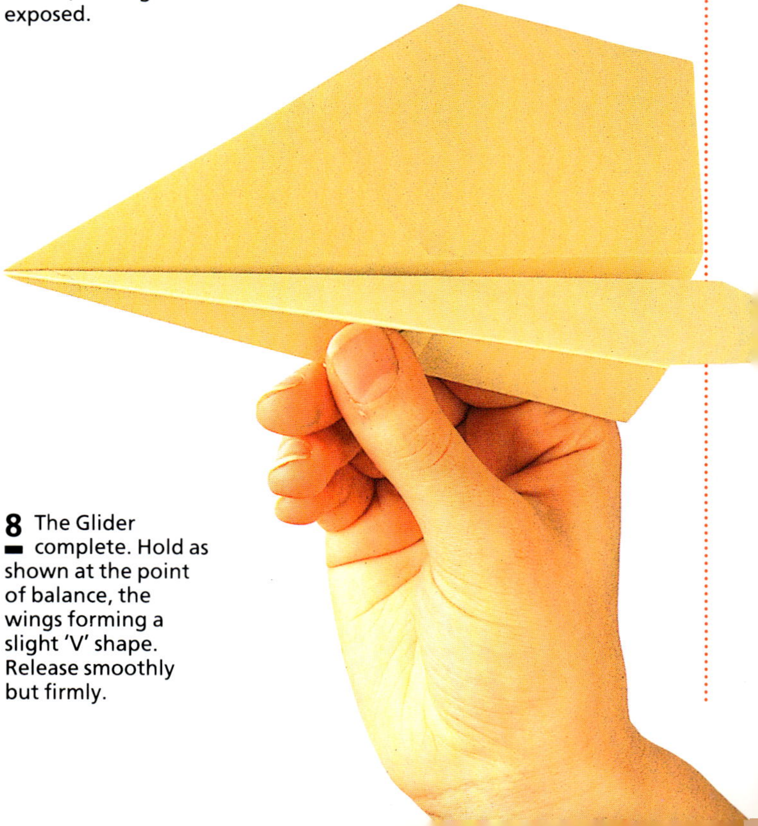

8 The Glider complete. Hold as shown at the point of balance, the wings forming a slight 'V' shape. Release smoothly but firmly.

CANDY BAG

If folded from greaseproof paper, this practical design will hold fries and other oily or sticky foods. For extra strength, fold two squares together. For sweets or candies, use any paper, not too thin. Use a 15–25 cm (6–10 in) square. If using origami paper, start coloured side up.

Designed by Paul Jackson.

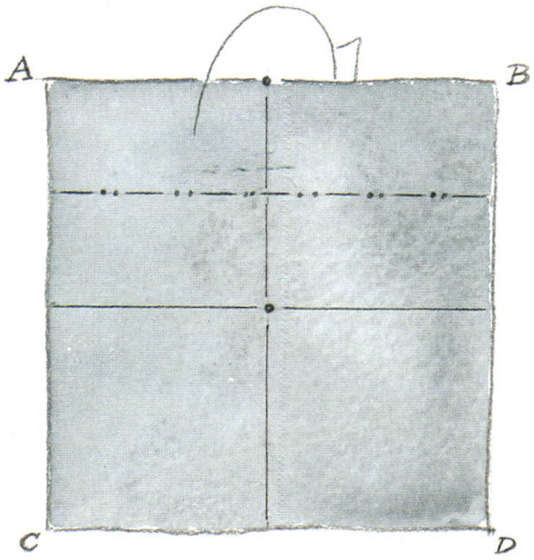

1 Fold and unfold the paper in half horizontally and vertically. Mountain fold edge AB to the centre crease.

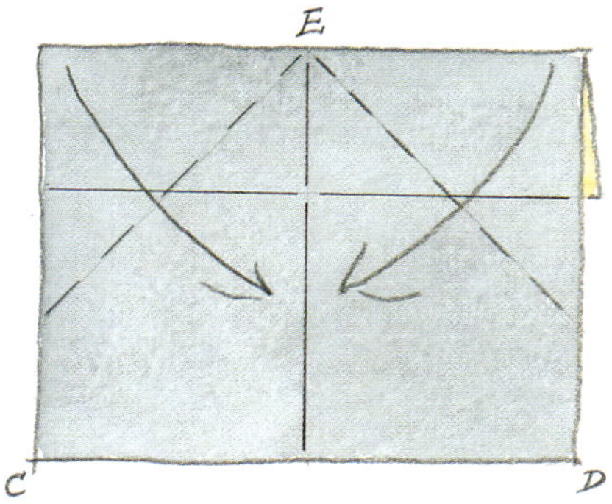

2 Fold in the top corners to the centre crease.

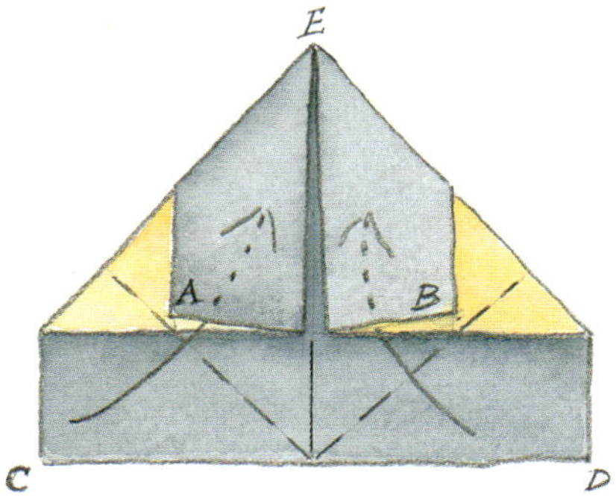

3 Similarly, fold in bottom corners C & D, but tucking them beneath A & B, to lock them flat.

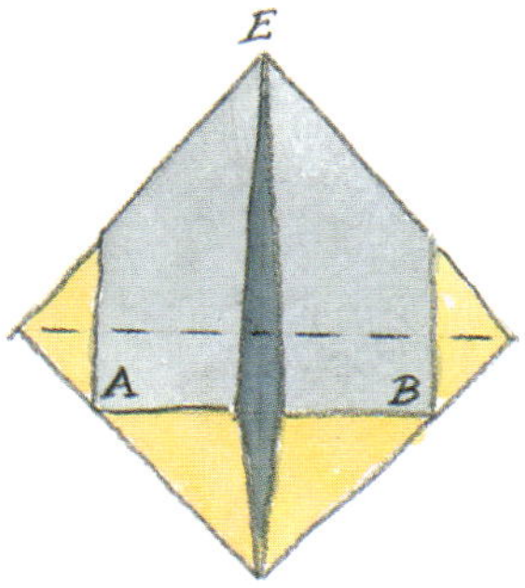

4 Valley fold in half across the middle, then . . .

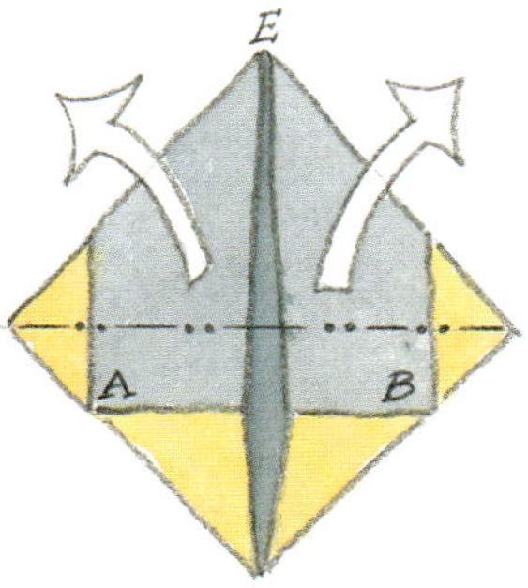

5 . . . mountain fold in half, to create a flexible crease. Open out the bag.

6 The Candy Bag complete.

BUTTERFLY

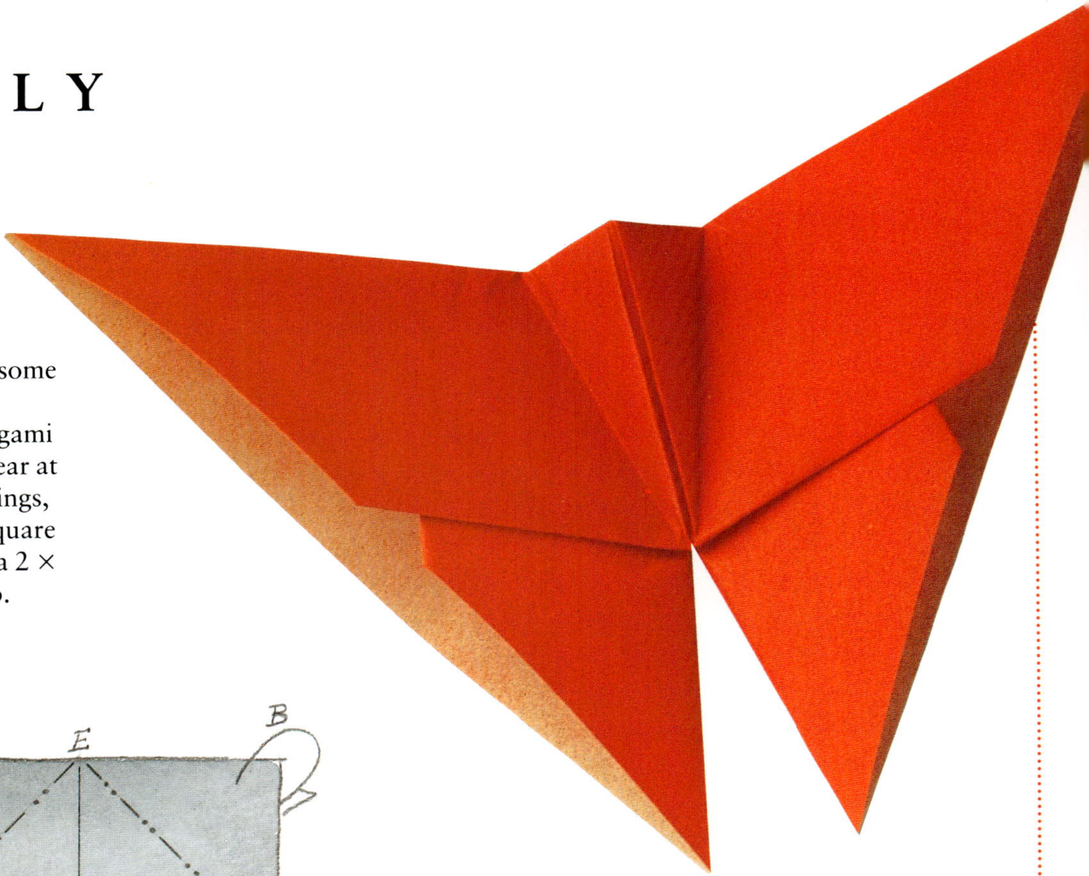

There are a great many origami butterflies in all manner of styles, some very complex. This is one of the simplest. It is important to use origami paper, so that white triangles appear at the edges between the coloured wings, to visually separate them. Cut a square of origami paper in half to create a 2 × 1 rectangle. Start coloured side up.

Designed by Paul Jackson.

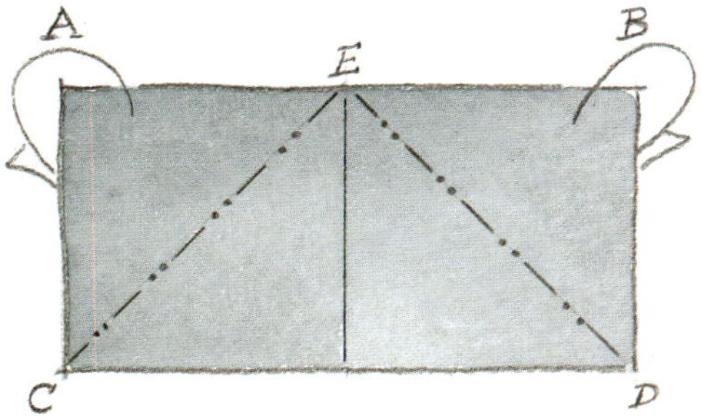

1 Fold corners A & B behind to the centre.

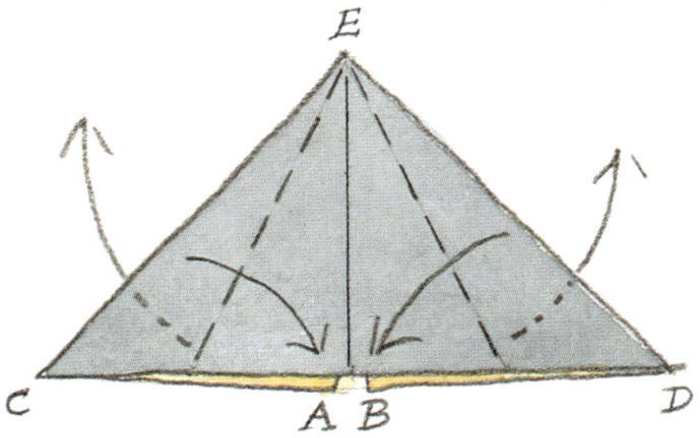

2 Fold EC & ED to the centre crease, allowing corners A & B to flip outwards . . .

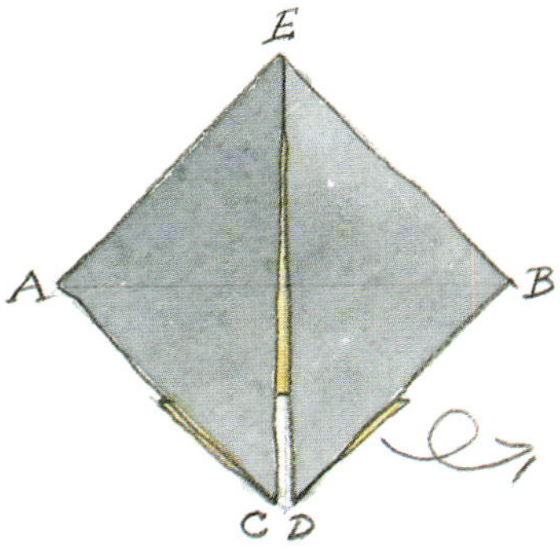

3 . . . like this. Compare the position of the lettered corners with their position in Step 2. Turn over.

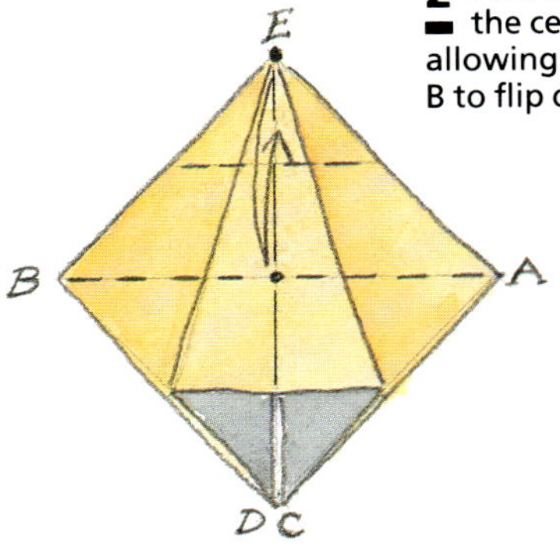

4 First, crease from B to A, across the middle. Then, fold E to the centre point.

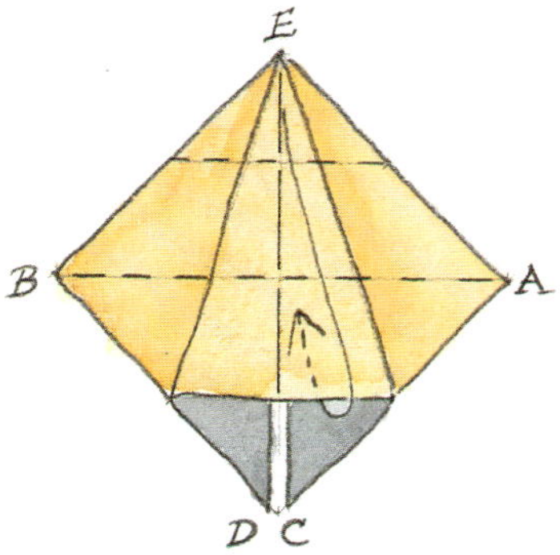

5 Re-form the Step 4 creases, but tucking E up under the horizontal edge.

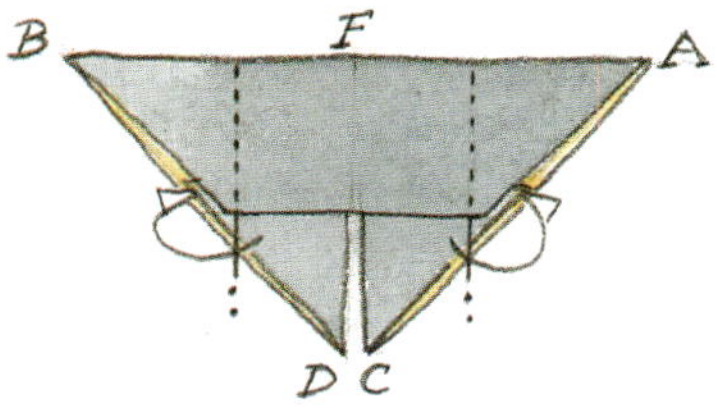

6 With vertical creases that run inside up to edge BA, mountain fold the loose corners behind as far as they will go.

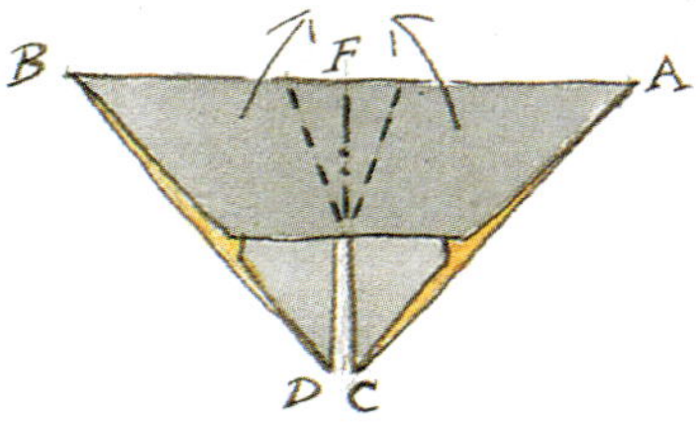

7 Make a mountain and two valley creases where shown, to create the body and to swivel D & C apart.

8 The Butterfly complete.

SAMPAN

This is a simplified version of a sampan with a canopy over each end of the boat. Both designs feature an extraordinary move, here shown in Steps 7–9, in which the entire shape is turned inside out. With a little extra folding, one end of the sampan can be blunted to create a rowing boat. Use a square of paper. If using origami paper, start coloured side up.

Traditional design.

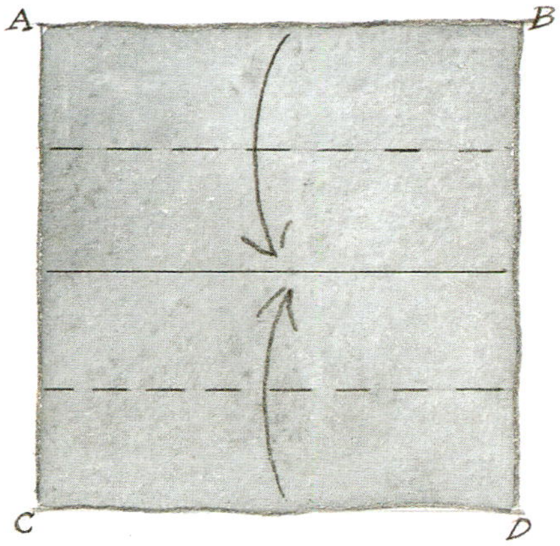

1 Crease and unfold across the centre. Fold the top and bottom edges to the crease.

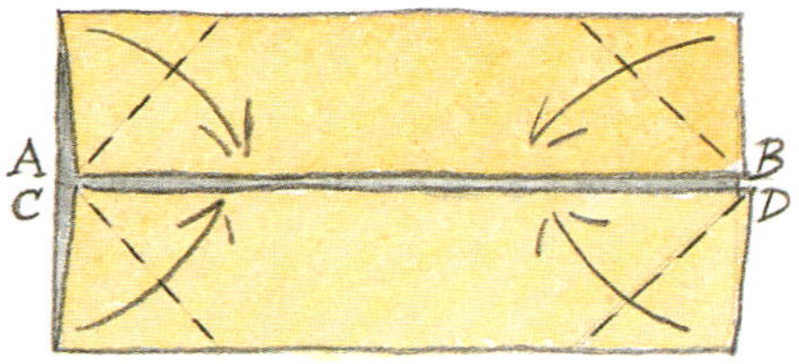

2 Fold in the corners.

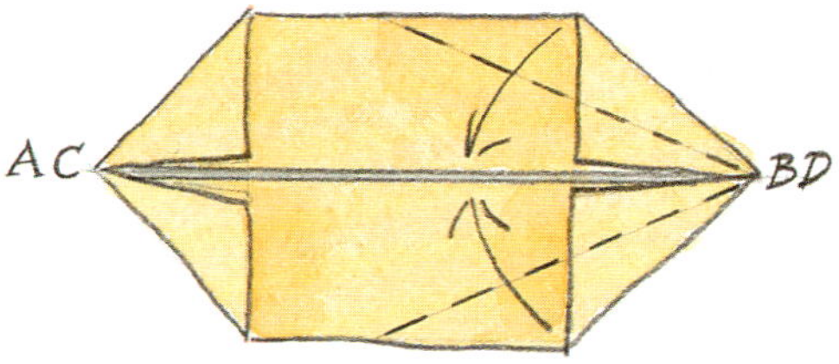

3 Narrow the corner at the right, as though making the familiar paper dart.

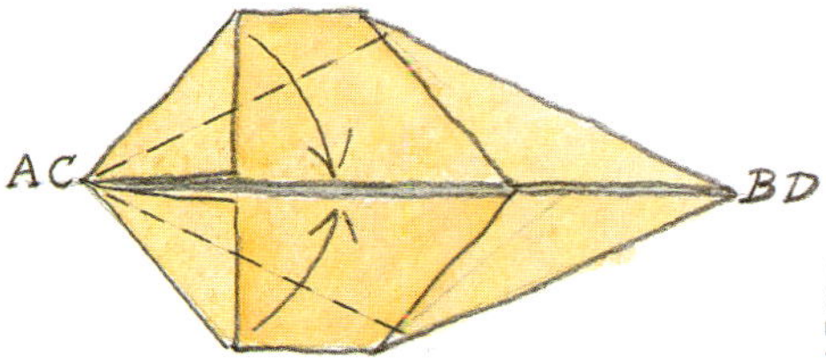

4 Repeat at the left, overlapping the Step 4 creases.

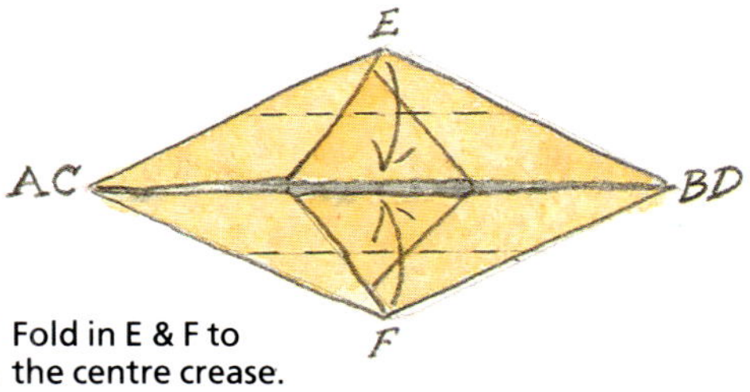

5 Fold in E & F to the centre crease. The paper is thick, so press firmly.

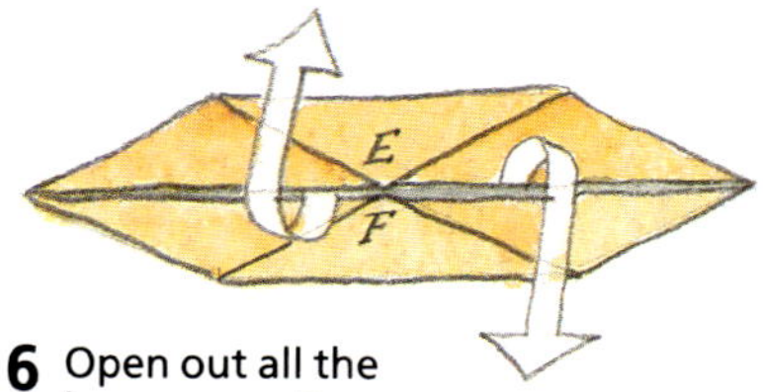

6 Open out all the layers revealing the coloured base . . .

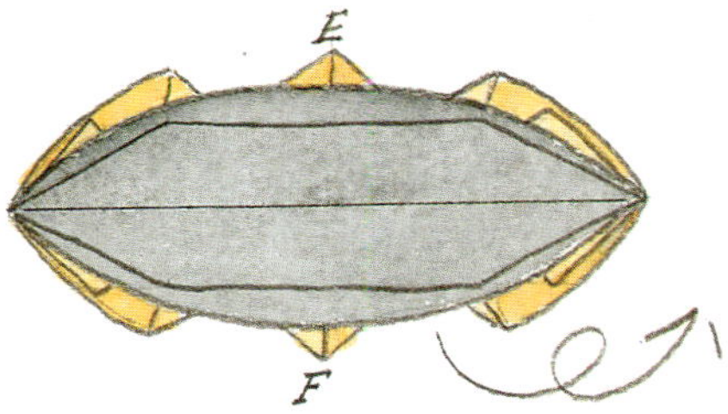

7 . . . like this, to form a loose boat shape. Turn over.

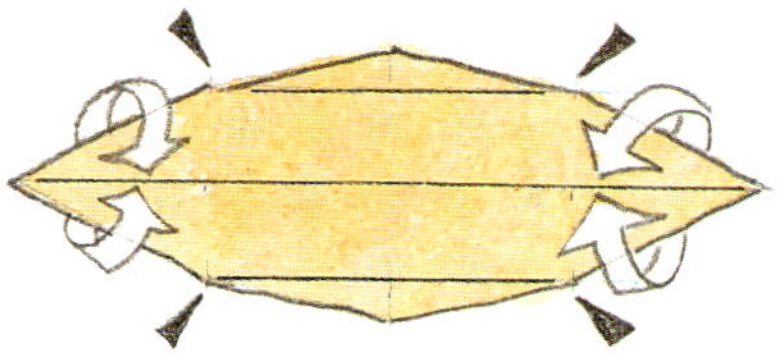

8 To lock the sampan, push down on the four arrowed corners, so that the whole of the structure inverts and turns inside out!

9 The Sampan complete.

NAPKIN FOLDS

Napkin folds always create a point of interest on a dining table. The Duck Step is a basic form from which other varieties of napkin fold can be made. The Cable Buffet server allows guests at a buffet or picnic to help themselves to food, a napkin and cutlery all at once, while the Bishop's elegant curves and free-standing structure create a strong impact on any table.

Designed by Paul Jackson.

DUCK STEP

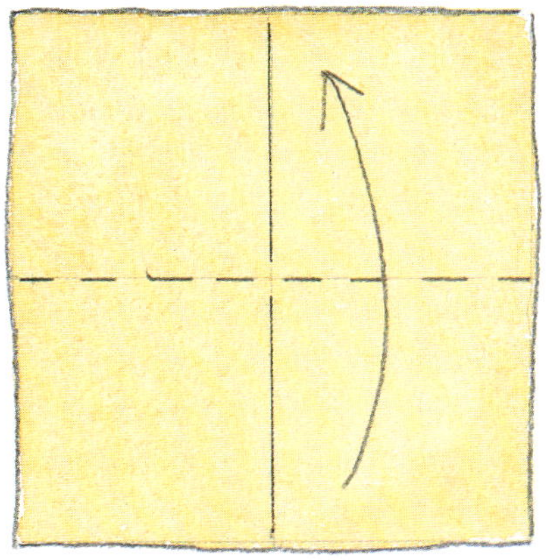

1 Completely unfold a napkin, then fold the bottom edge up to the top.

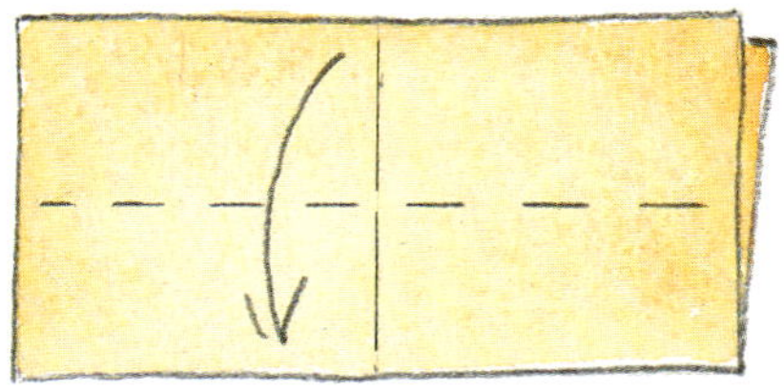

2 Fold the top edge down to the crease.

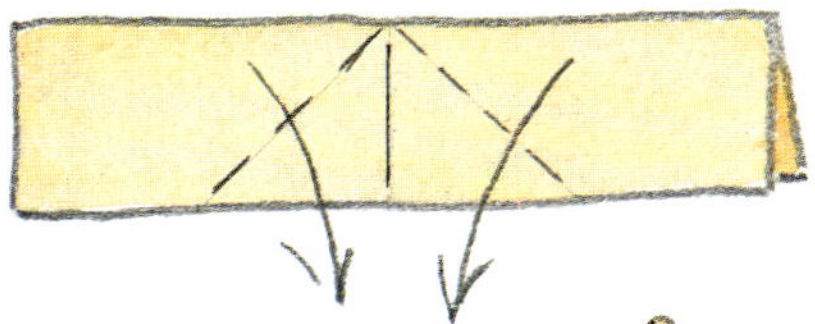

3 Fold each half of the top edge down the centre crease . . .

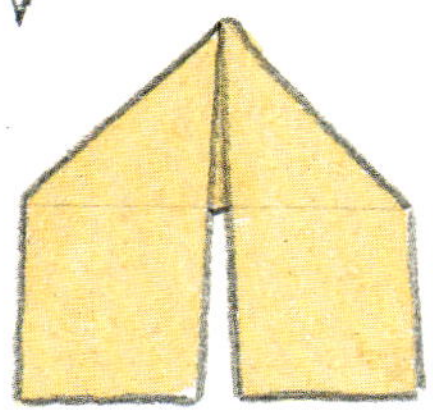

4 . . . like this. Turn the napkin over.

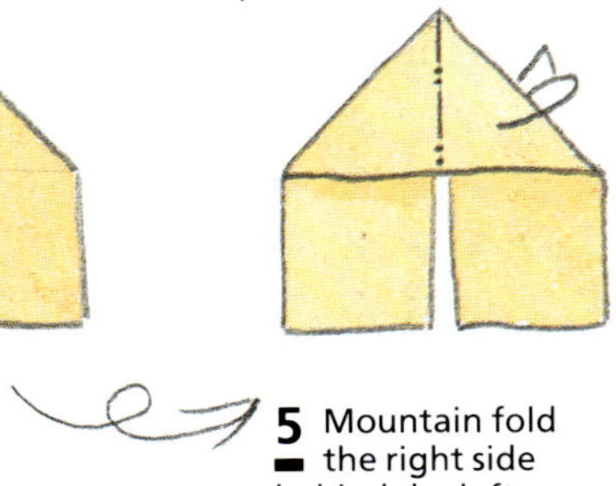

5 Mountain fold the right side behind the left.

6 Valley fold the front square up over the triangle. Repeat behind.

7 The Duck Step napkin complete.

CABLE BUFFET

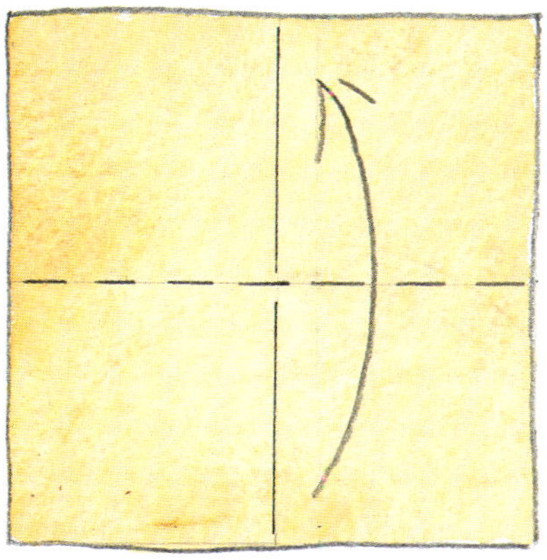

1 Completely unfold a napkin, then fold the bottom edge up to the top.

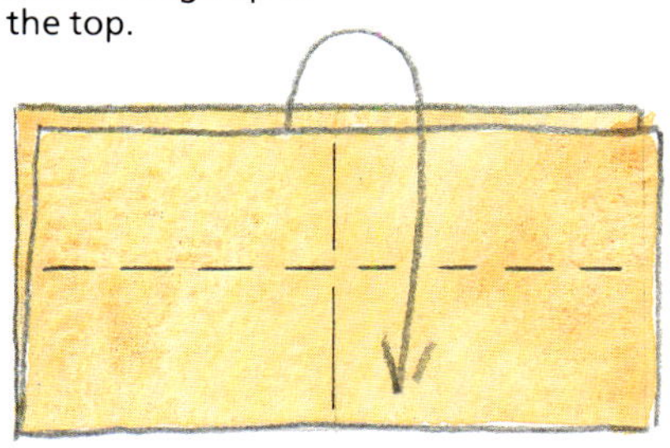

2 Fold the top layer down to the crease.

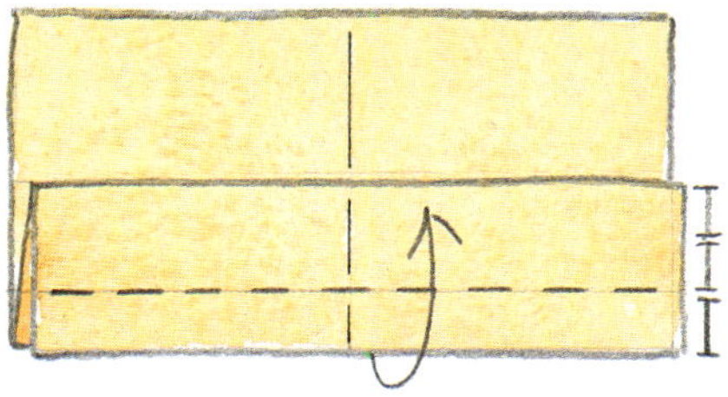

3 Fold the top layer back up a little way . . .

4 . . . like this. Turn the napkin over.

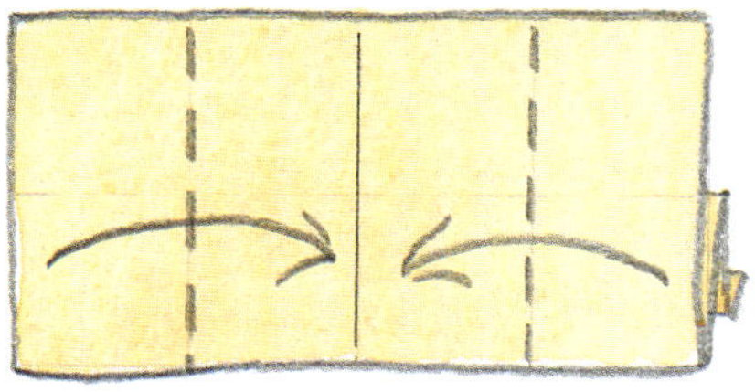

5 Fold the sides to the middle.

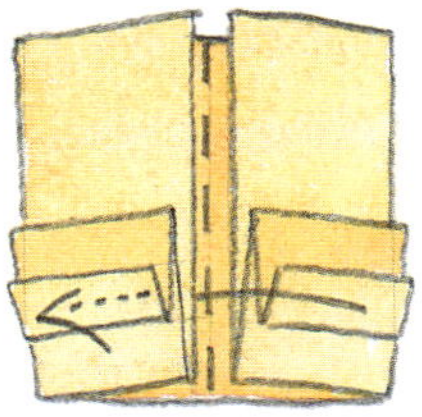

6 Tuck one half deep into the other, locking the napkin flat.

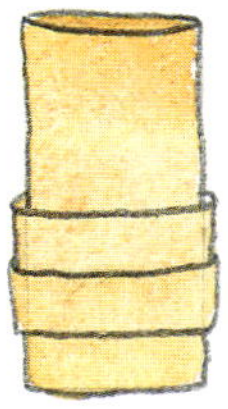

7 The Cable Buffet server complete. Insert cutlery into the pocket ready for the meal.

(Continued . . .)

(*Continued . . .*)

BISHOP

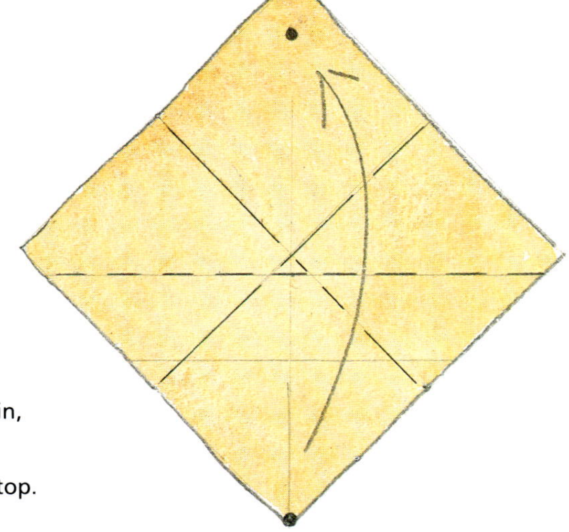

1 Completely unfold a napkin, then fold the bottom corner almost up to the top.

2 Fold up the bottom corners to the position shown in Step 3.

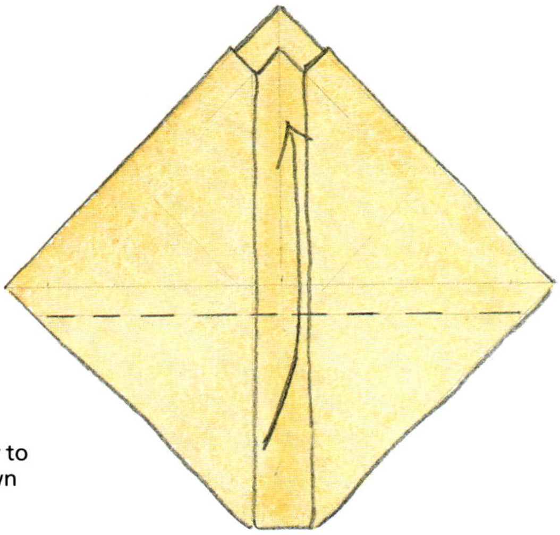

3 Fold up the bottom corner to the position shown in Step 4.

4 Fold down the front edge.

5 This is the basic shape. The proportions are important, so it may be necessary to adjust some of the folds. Turn the napkin over.

6 Bend the left and right halves forward. Interlock one half into the other to make a tube that will not spring open.

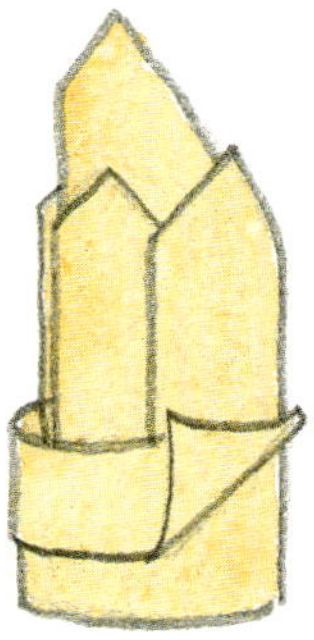

7 The Bishop napkin complete.

FISH

The creator of this fish is known for designs which are pre-creased and collapsed into shape. When pre-creasing, it is important to fold accurately (here, up to Step 5), otherwise the creases will not fall into place to achieve Step 6. For extra flatness, a speck of glue inside the mouth will close the layers. Use a square of origami paper, coloured side up, or a square with the same colour on both sides.

Designed by Jeff Beynon, UK.

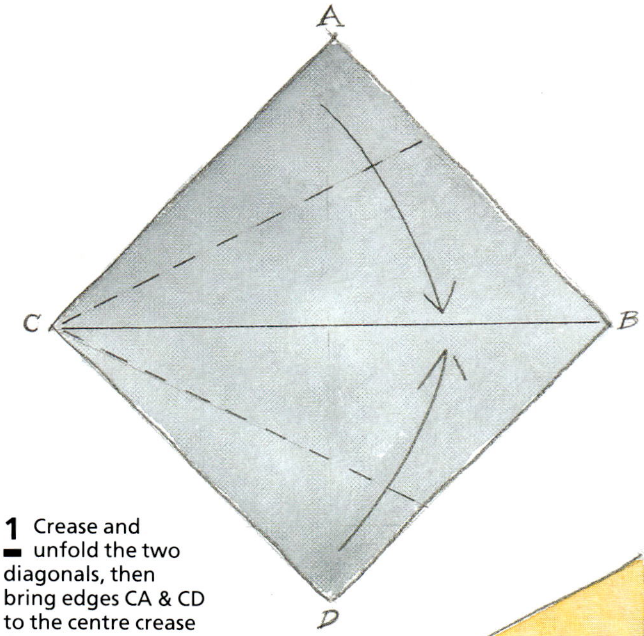

1 Crease and unfold the two diagonals, then bring edges CA & CD to the centre crease CB . . .

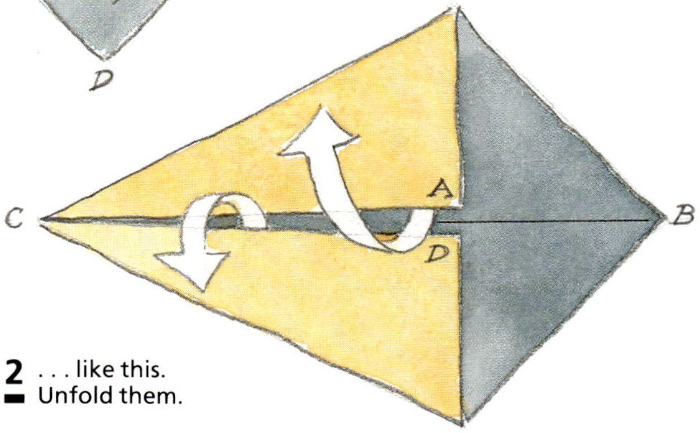

2 . . . like this. Unfold them.

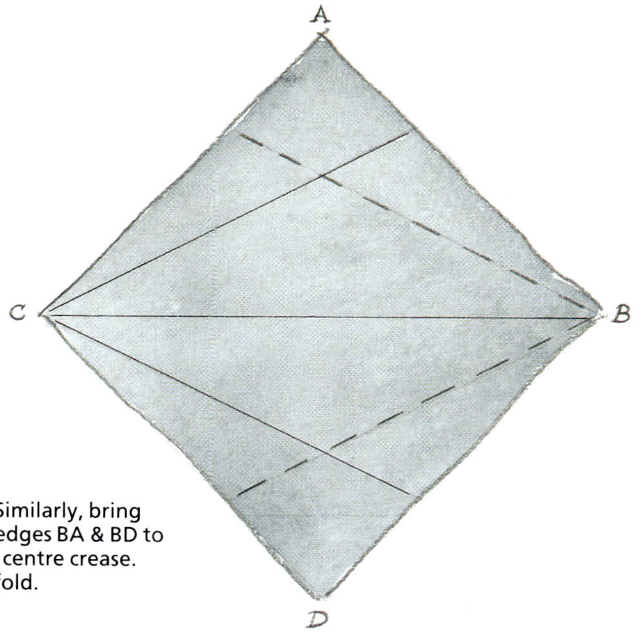

3 Similarly, bring edges BA & BD to the centre crease. Unfold.

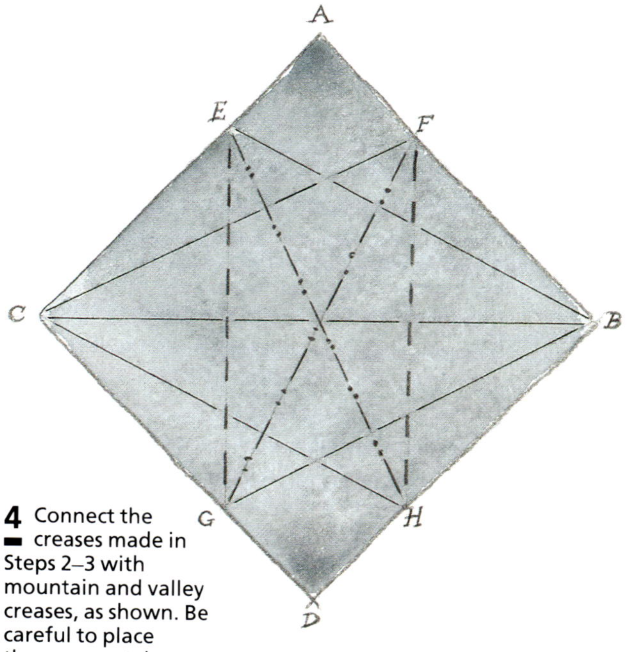

4 Connect the creases made in Steps 2–3 with mountain and valley creases, as shown. Be careful to place them accurately.

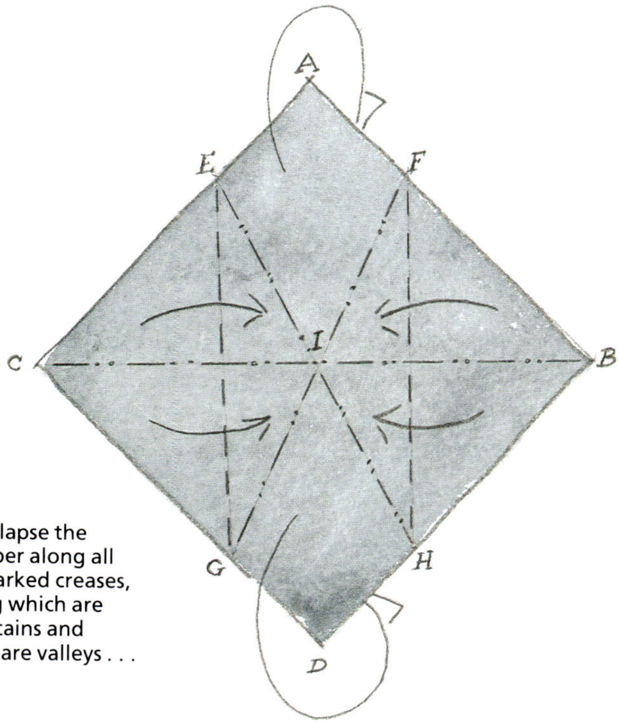

5 Collapse the paper along all the marked creases, noting which are mountains and which are valleys . . .

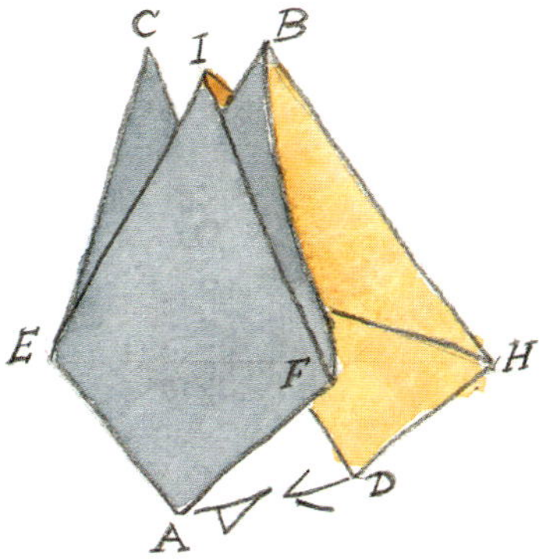

6 . . . like this. Bring A to D and F to H. Flatten the creases.

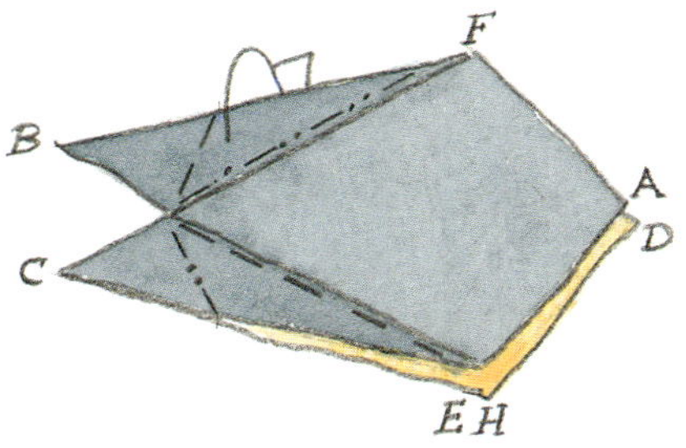

7 Lock by pleating one half of the tail fin into the body with a mountain fold and the other with a valley.

8 The Fish complete. Suspend it from a thread attached just behind the top corner at the point of balance.

SLEEPY DOG

The design is simple to make, but it is important to place C accurately in Steps 1 & 2. Once Step 3 has been achieved, the remaining folds fall naturally into place. Note the way in which the eyes are suggested. Use a square of origami paper, coloured side up.

Designed by Paul Jackson.

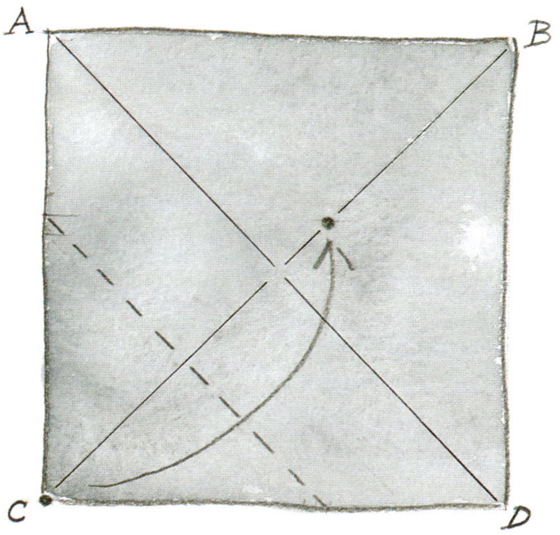

1 Crease and unfold the two diagonals, then fold in corner C to the point described in Step 2.

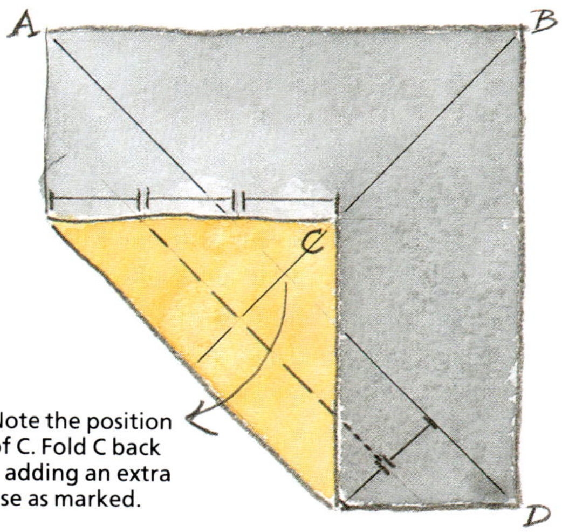

2 Note the position of C. Fold C back out, adding an extra crease as marked.

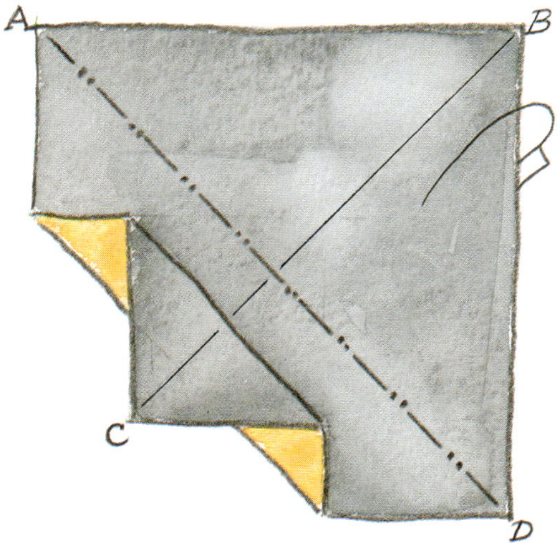

3 Mountain fold B behind, along the AD diagonal.

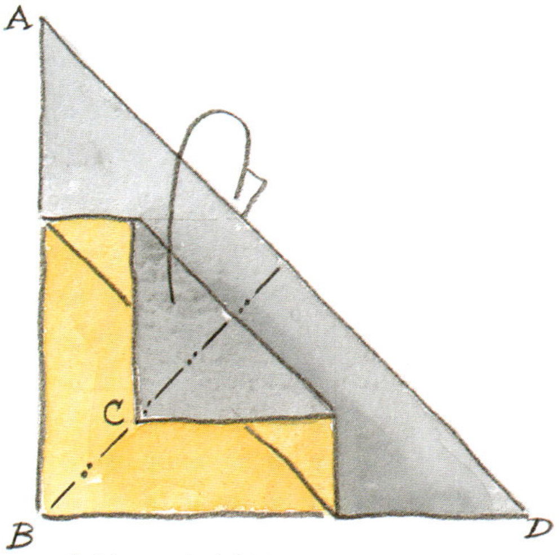

4 Mountain fold A behind to touch D.

5 Fold back points D & A to the outside.

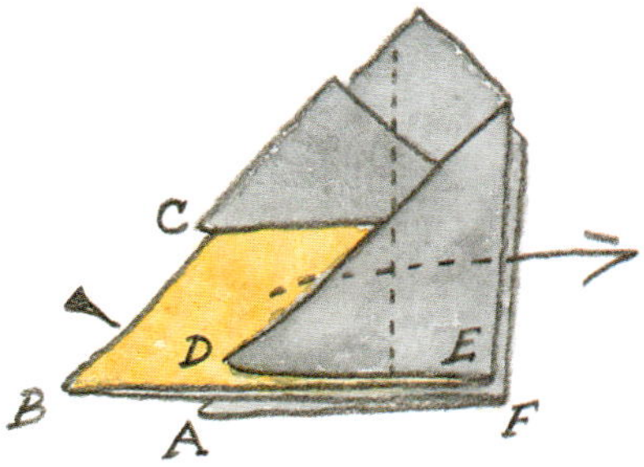

6 With a reverse fold, swing B through the middle. Note the position of the crease.

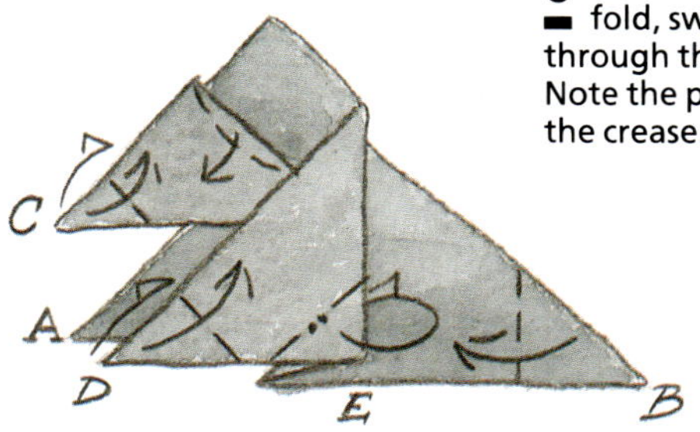

7 Mountain fold E behind. Repeat at F behind. Turn D, A & C inside out. Fold B forward. Curve the edge at the eye. Repeat for other eye.

8 The Sleepy Dog complete.

MODULAR DECORATION I

A modular design is one in which a number of identical units are folded, then locked together without glue to create a decoration or geometric form. Other modular designs are included and appear later. In recent years, it has become a very popular branch of origami, East and West. Method 1 begins with a rectangle, Method 2 with a small square.

Designed by Paul Jackson.

METHOD 1

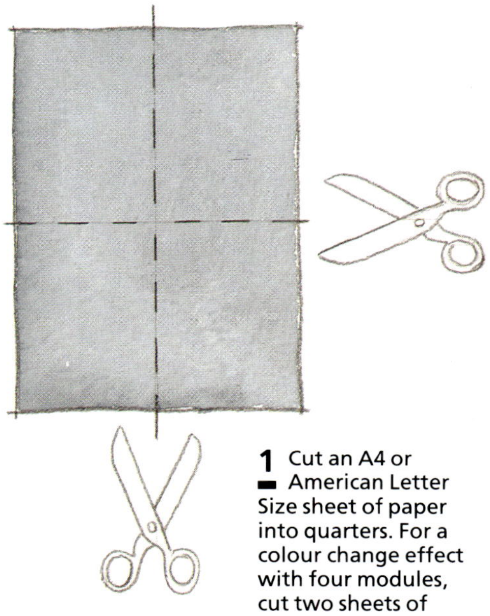

1 Cut an A4 or American Letter Size sheet of paper into quarters. For a colour change effect with four modules, cut two sheets of different colours.

2 Take one quarter sheet of paper and fold diagonal BC.

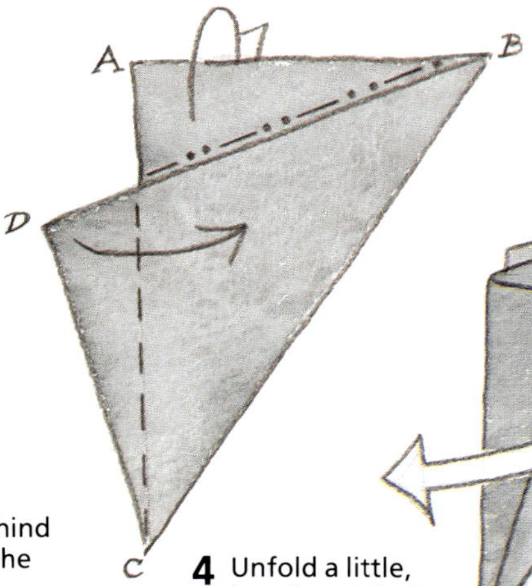

3 Fold A behind and D to the front.

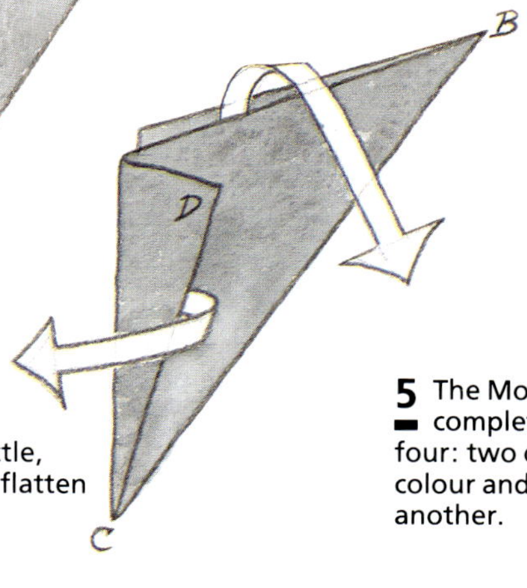

4 Unfold a little, but do not flatten the sheet.

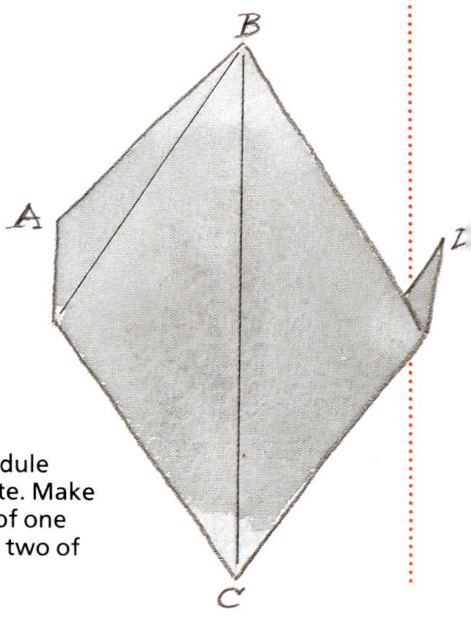

5 The Module complete. Make four: two of one colour and two of another.

METHOD 2

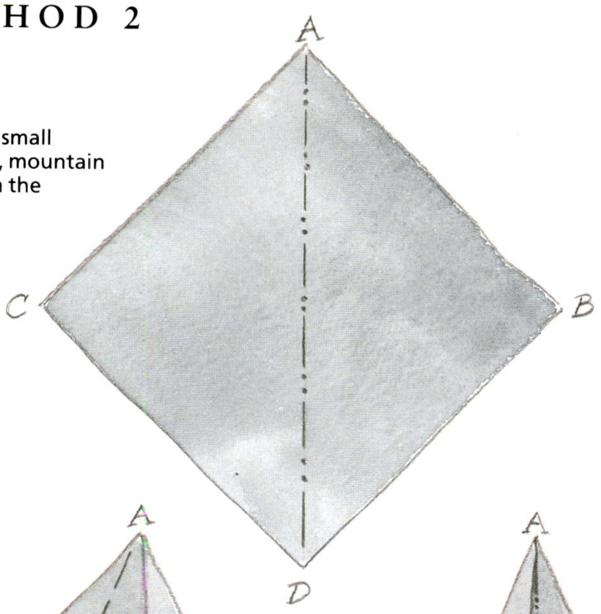

1 With a small square, mountain fold down the diagonal.

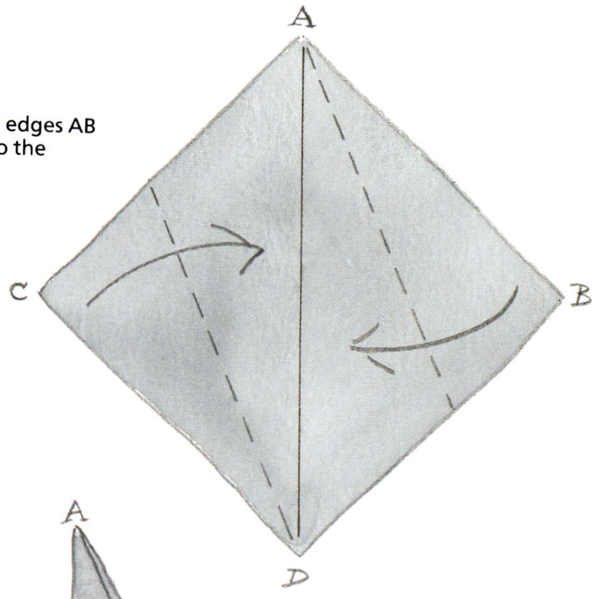

2 Fold in edges AB & CD to the crease.

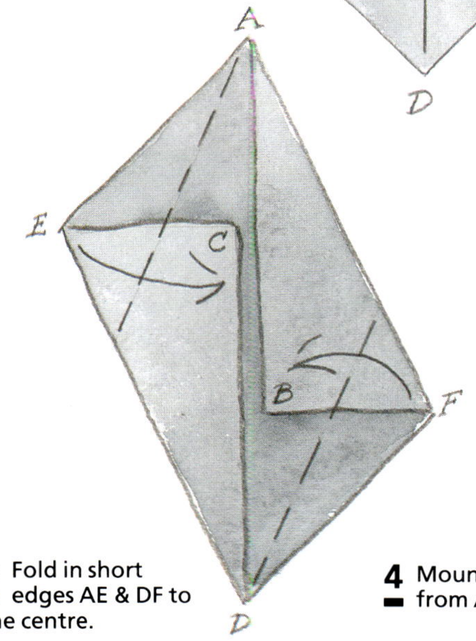

3 Fold in short edges AE & DF to the centre.

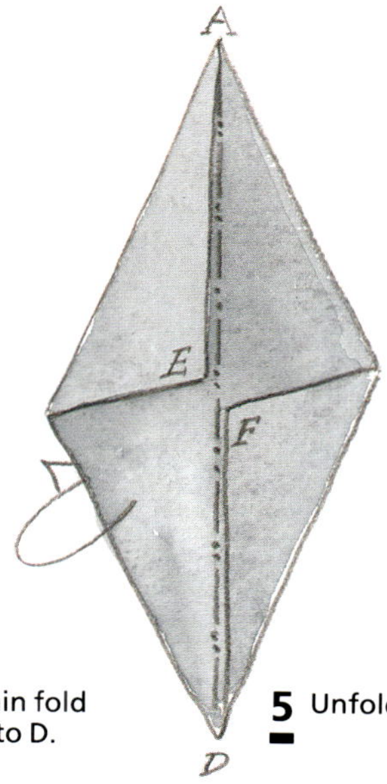

4 Mountain fold from A to D.

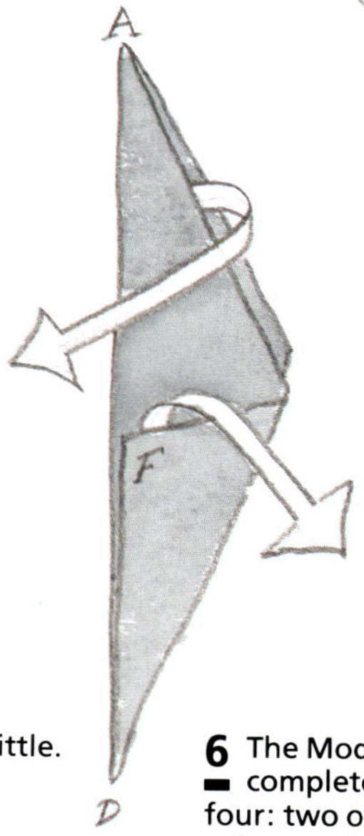

5 Unfold a little.

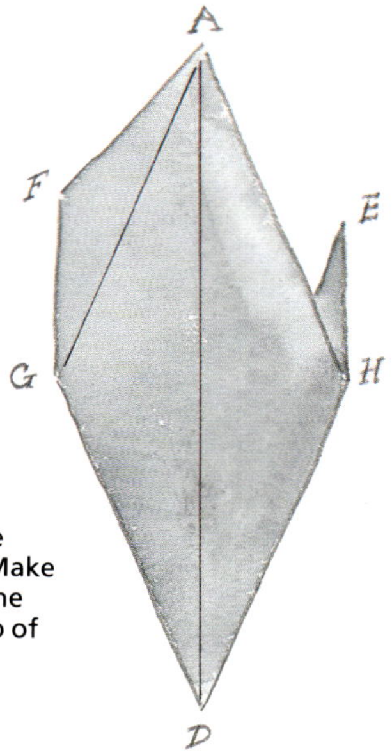

6 The Module complete. Make four: two of one colour and two of another.

ASSEMBLY

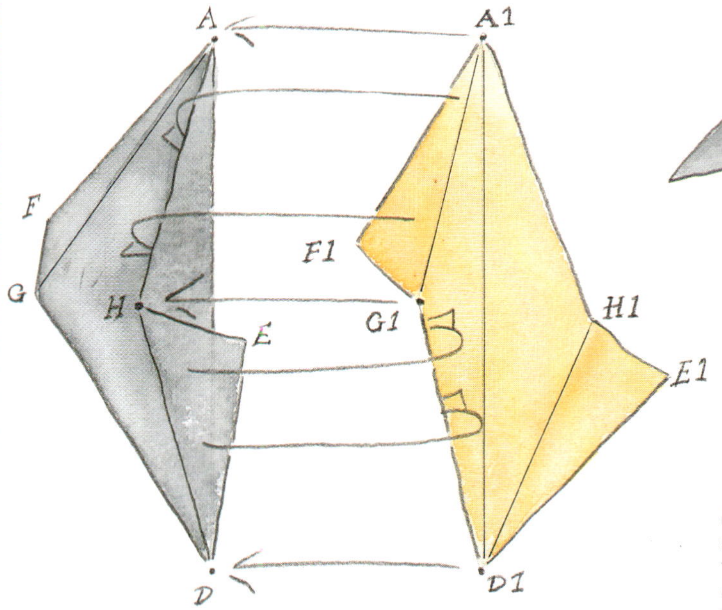

1 The method of assembly is the same for Methods 1 & 2. Edge A1,F1 on the right-hand module is tucked behind edge AH on the left-hand module. At the same time, edge DE on the left-hand module is tucked behind edge D1,G1 on the right-hand module. Note that A1 touches A, G1 touches H and D1 touches D.

2 This is the result. The lock is not strong, but when two other modules are locked in, so that the fourth locks into the first to close the circle, the complete structure will lock well.

3 The Modular Decoration complete.

COLOUR-CHANGE BIRD

This design is included because it is a particular favourite. The simple shape of the completed bird and the effectiveness of the colour contrasts are achieved by a fluent and concise sequence of folds. Perhaps it is too stylized for some readers, but less can sometimes be more. Use a square of origami paper, white side up.

Designed by Paul Jackson.

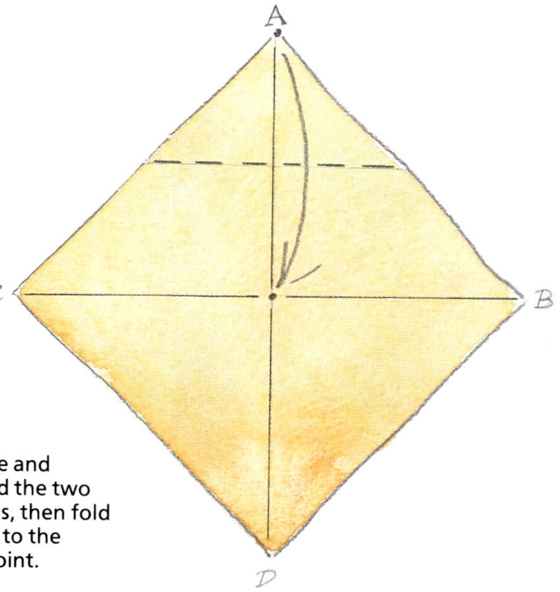

1 Crease and unfold the two diagonals, then fold corner A to the centre point.

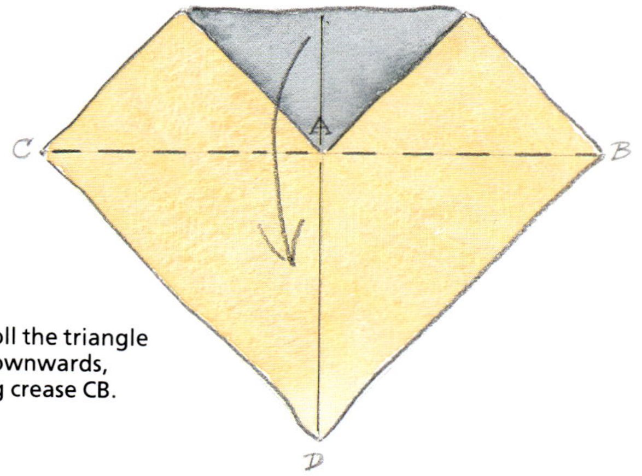

2 Roll the triangle downwards, along crease CB.

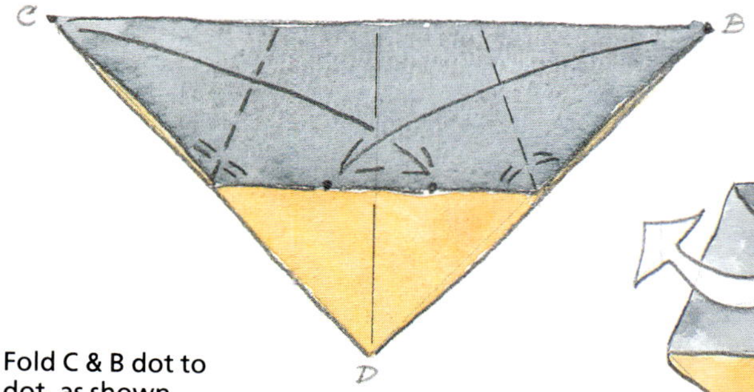

3 Fold C & B dot to dot, as shown.

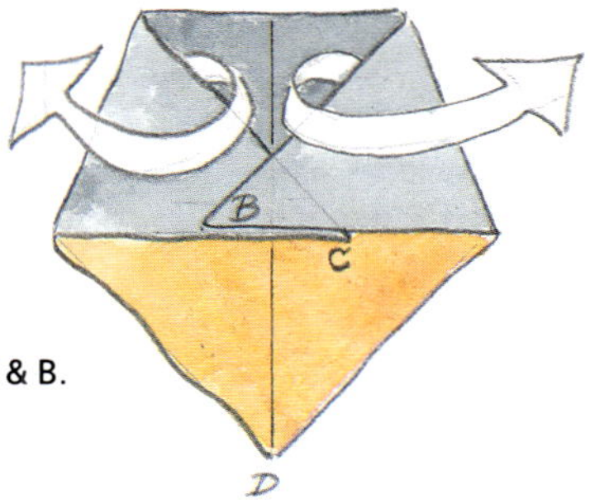

4 Unfold C & B.

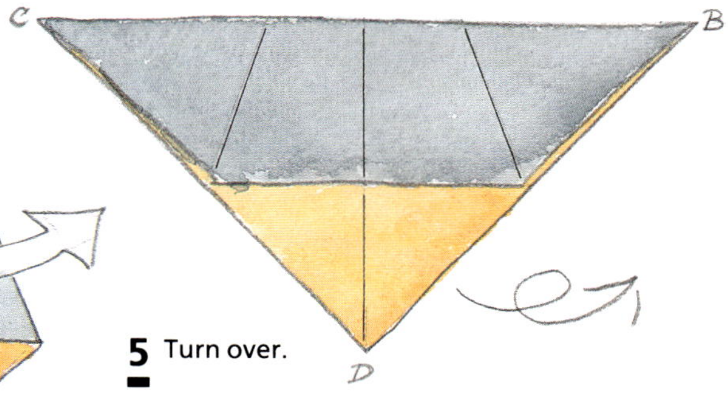

5 Turn over.

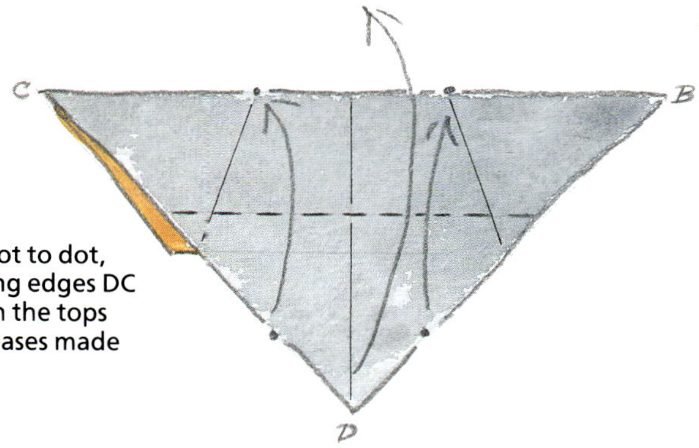

6 Fold dot to dot, aligning edges DC & DB with the tops of the creases made in Step 3.

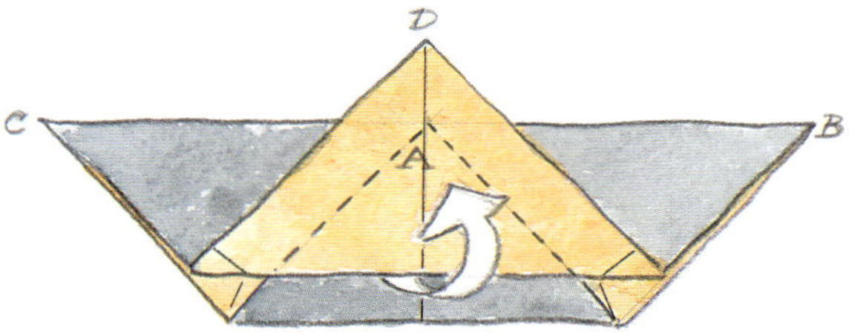

7 Pull out corner A.

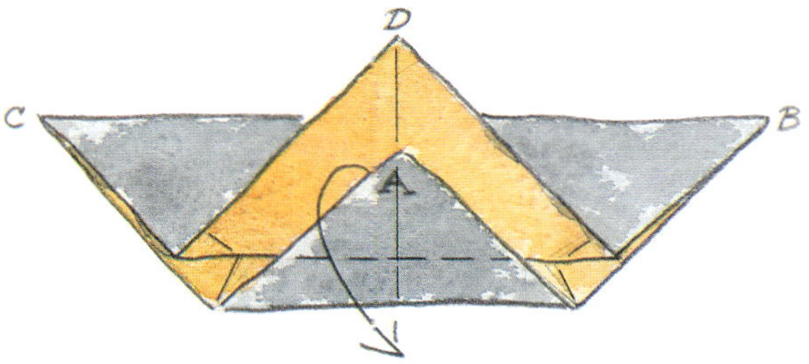

8 Fold down A, level with the folded edge.

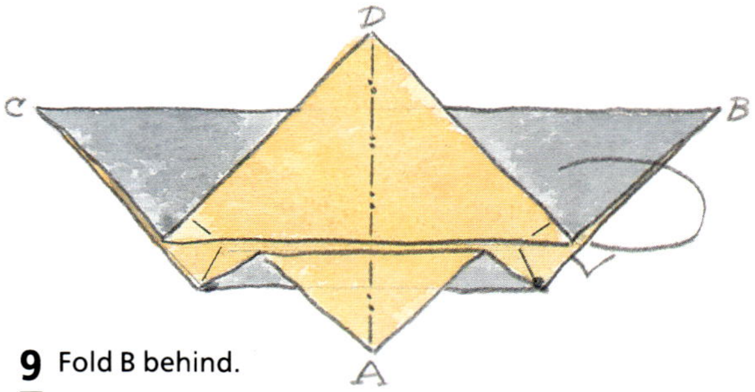

9 Fold B behind.

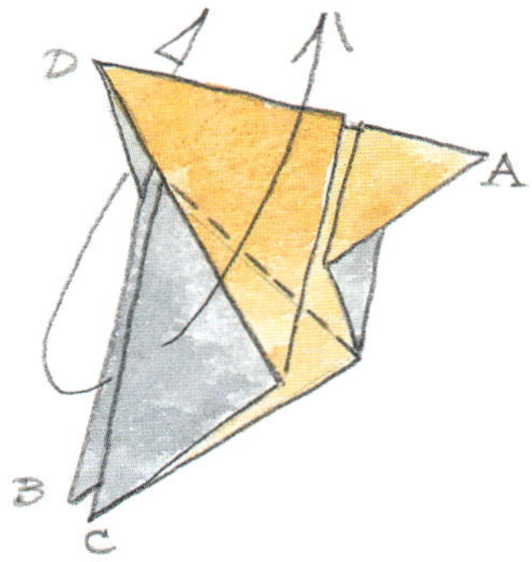

10 Fold up B & C along existing internal (hidden) creases made in Step 3.

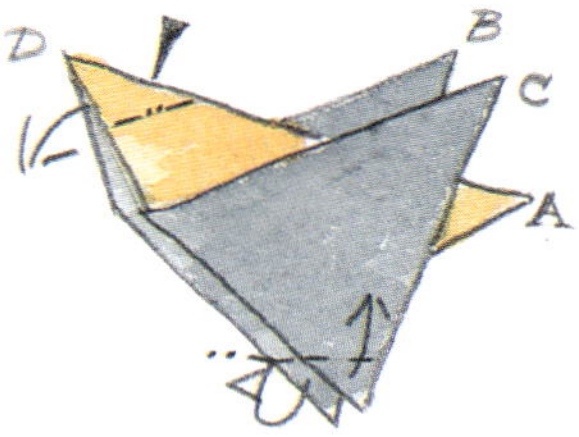

11 Reverse fold D to create the head. Fold out the feet to create a stable base for the bird.

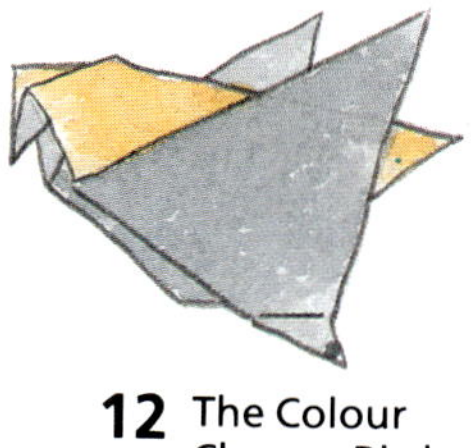

12 The Colour Change Bird complete.

MODULAR DECORATION II

The basic modules are very simple to make, but some thought must be given to assembling them correctly. Once locked, they will hold together very well. For re-use – perhaps from one Christmas to the next – the decoration may be flattened for easy storage. Use two 10–15 cm (4–6 in) squares of paper. If using origami paper, start with the white side up.

Designed by Paul Jackson.

METHOD

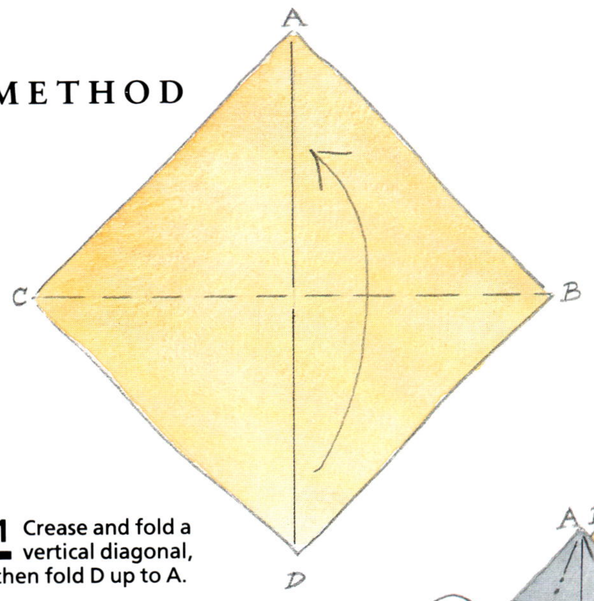

1 Crease and fold a vertical diagonal, then fold D up to A.

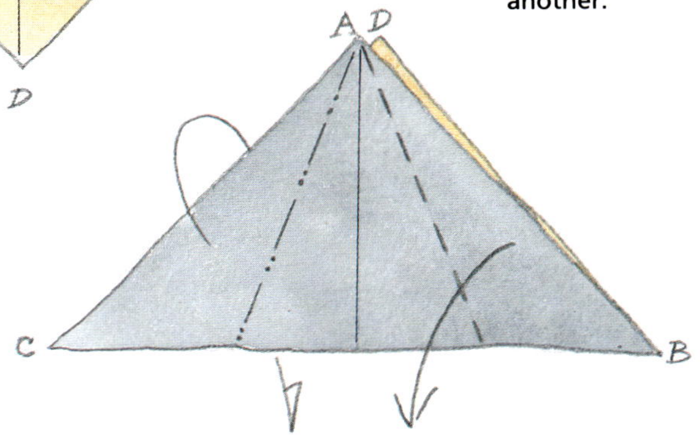

2 Fold edge AD,B forward to the vertical crease (valley fold) and edge AD,C behind to that crease (mountain fold).

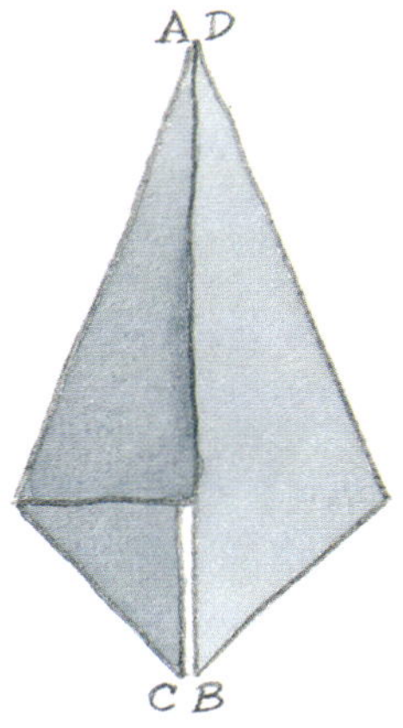

3 This is the completed module. Make another.

ASSEMBLY

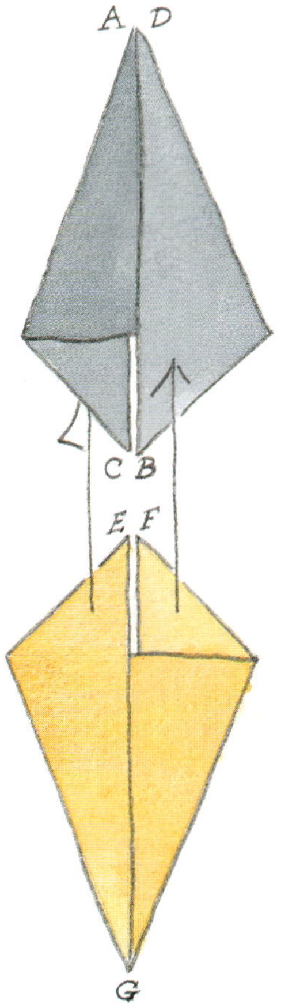

1 Take careful note of the lettered corners. Bring the two modules together, so that F is on top of B, and C is on top of E . . .

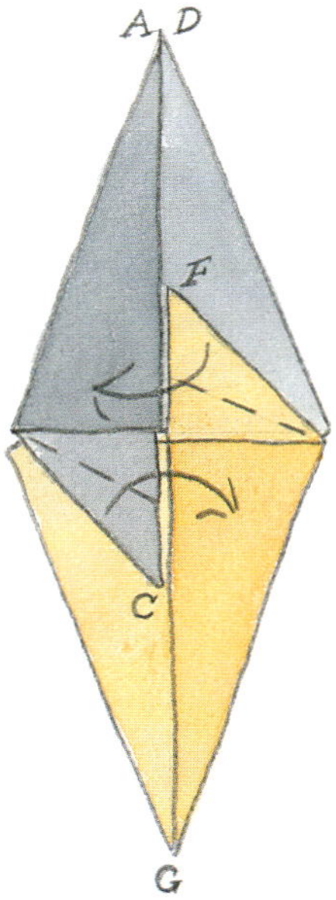

2 . . . like this. Fold F across to the horizontal. Repeat with C, then with E & B behind.

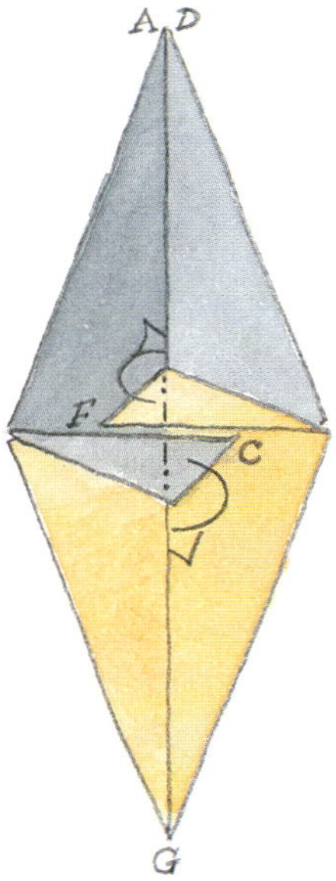

3 Lock the modules together by tucking F & C behind the vertical edges. Repeat behind with E & B.

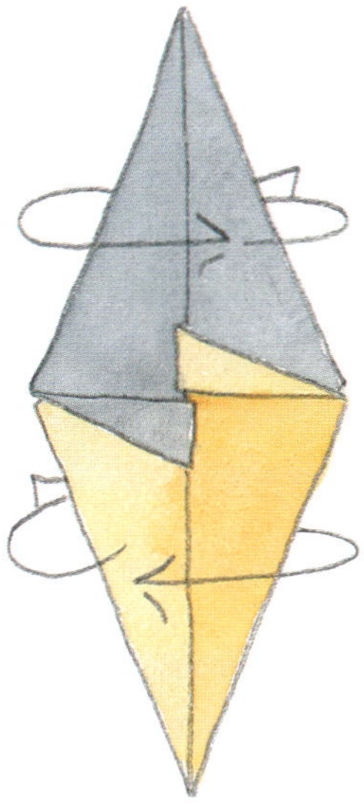

4 Separate the modules by twisting one away from the other, so that they lie perpendicular to each other.

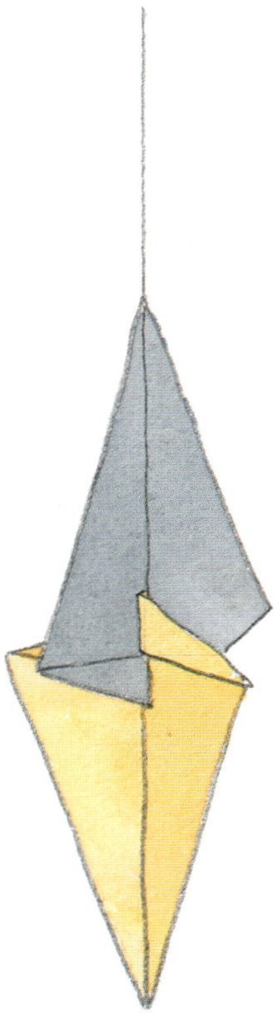

5 The Modular Decoration complete. Suspend from a thread.

MULTIFORM

Here is a remarkable sequence of designs which are all made from the same basic shape, the House. The designs shown here are not the full set: it is also possible to fold a dustpan, purse, fox puppet, crown . . . and very probably many others! Experiment by folding the paper this way and that to see what you can discover. Use a square of origami paper, white side up.

Traditional design.

HOUSE

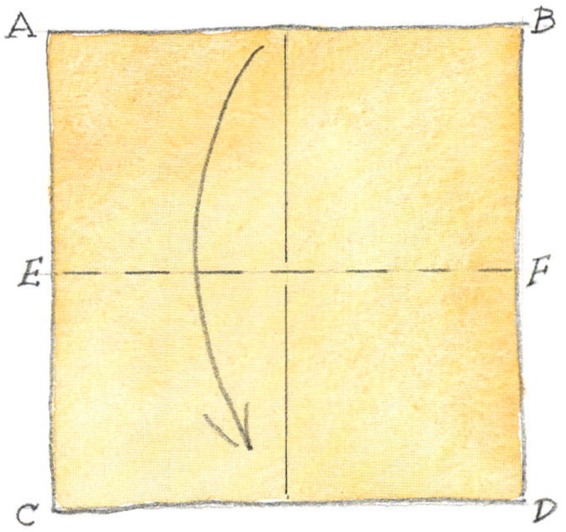

1 Crease and unfold down the middle of a square, then fold AB down to CD.

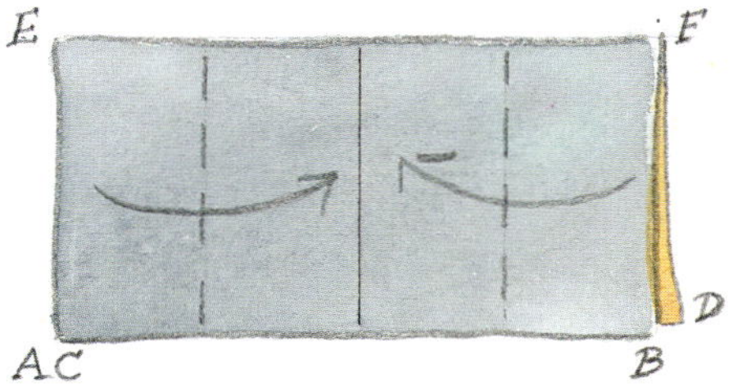

2 Fold the edges to the centre.

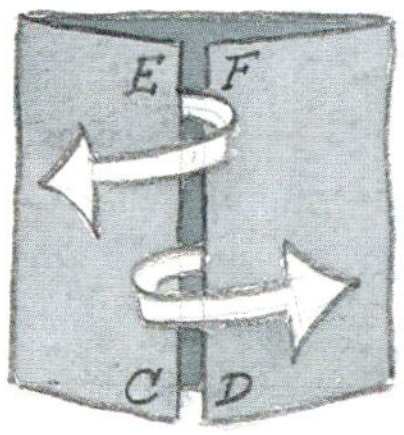

3 Unfold.

4 Lift up the edge BD,F. Separate B from D, applying pressure on the edges below F . . .

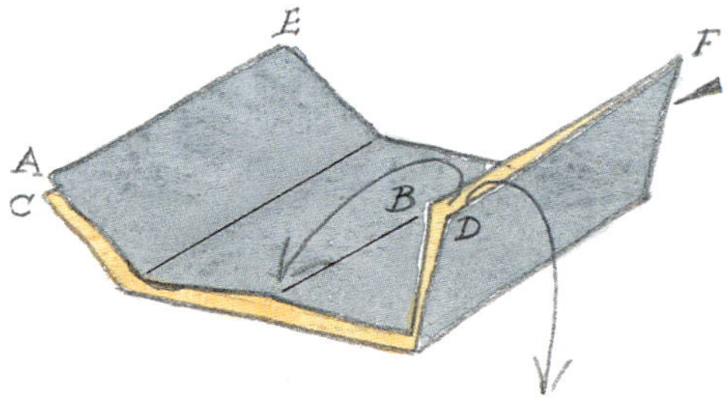

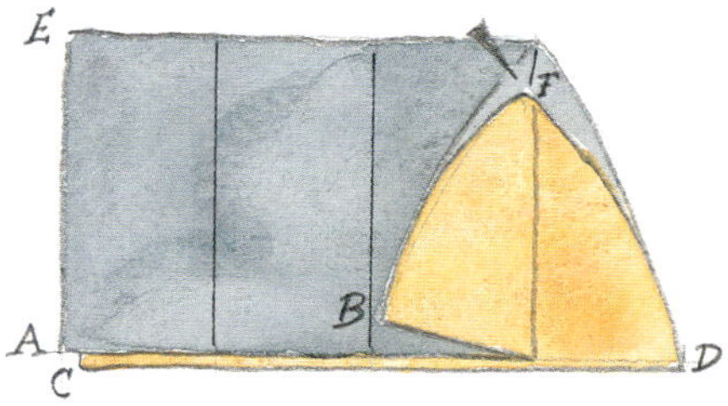

5 . . . like this. Pull B & D right apart and squash F flat.

6 Repeat Steps 4–5 on the left, separating A from C and squashing E flat. Let A touch B.

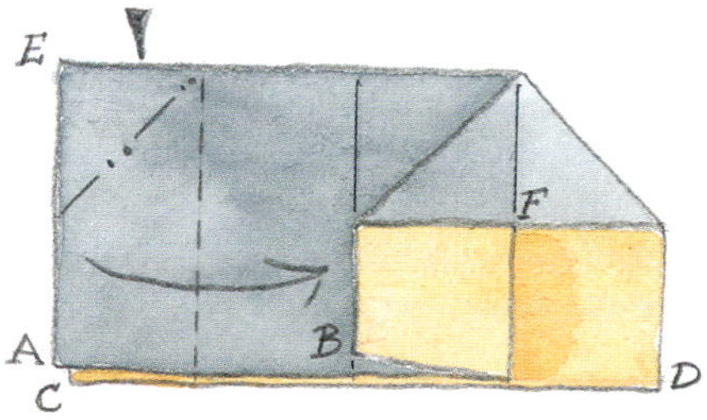

7 The House complete. Children like to draw windows and a door to finish the design.

3D HOUSE

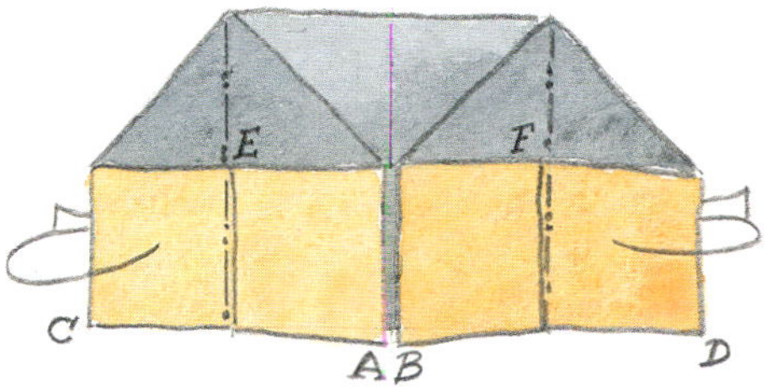

1 Begin with Step 6 of the House. Fold C & D behind.

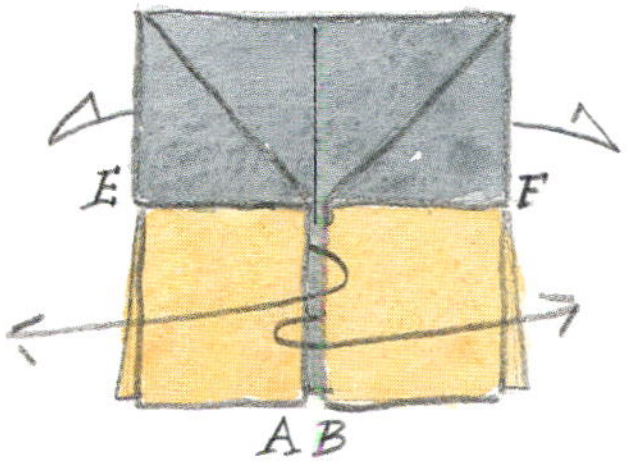

2 Unfold AC & BD.

3 The 3D House complete.

(Continued . . .)

SEAT

1 Begin with Step 6 of the House. Fold AB up to the top edge.

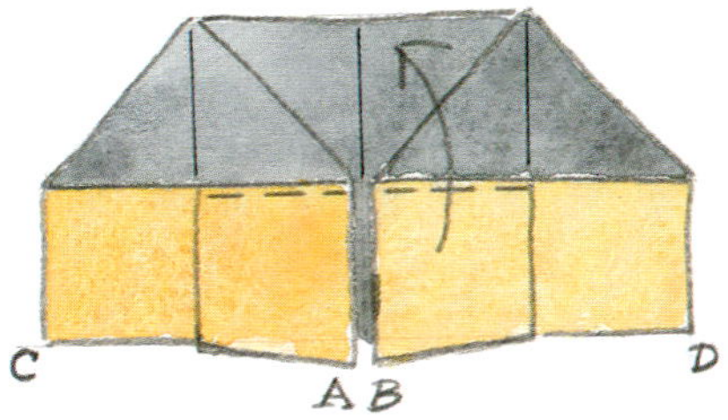

2 Fold in C & D.

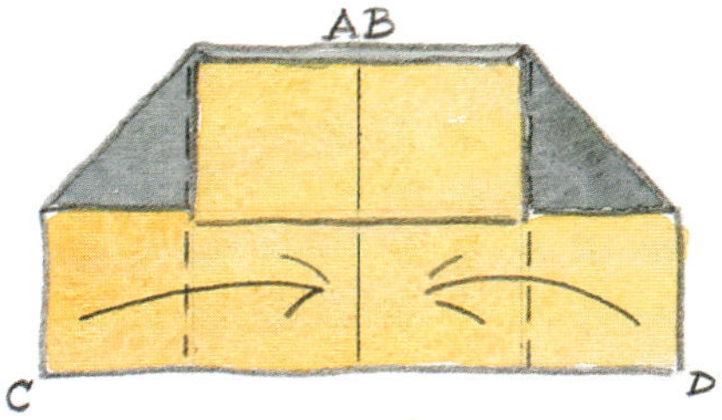

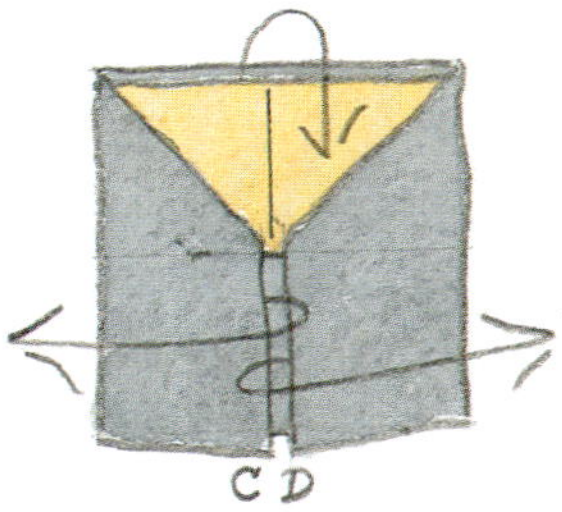

3 Swing open C & D and pull down AB.

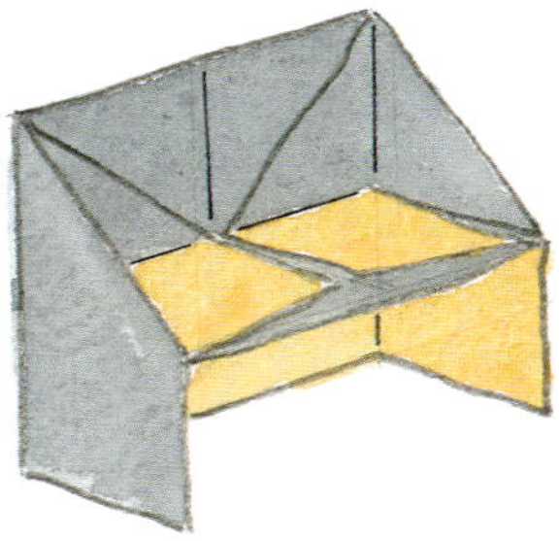

4 The Seat complete.

ORGAN

1 Begin with Step 2 of the Seat. Fold edge AB back down to the folded edge across the middle of the paper.

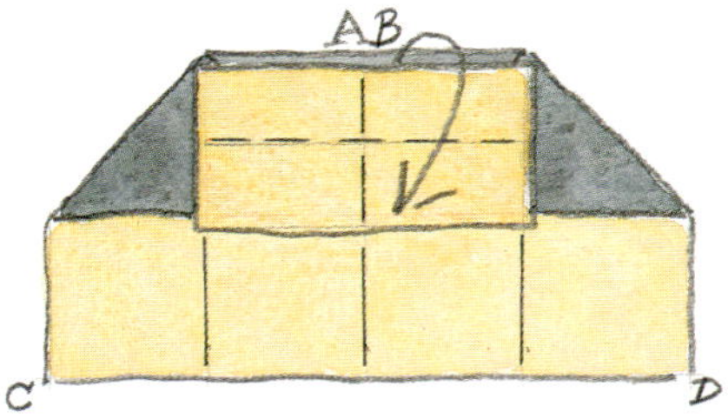

2 Fold in C & D.

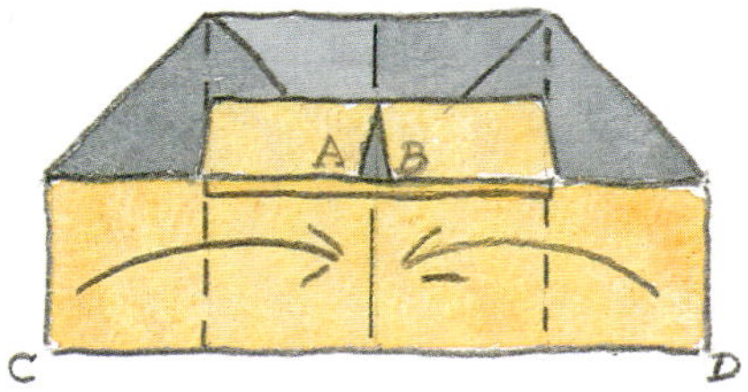

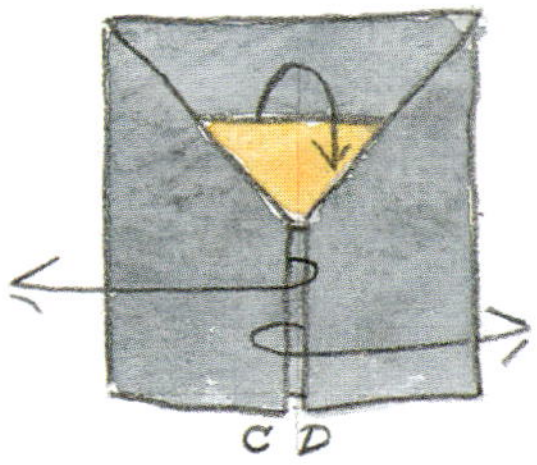

3 Swing open C & D and pull down the ledge.

4 The Organ complete.

G.I. CAP

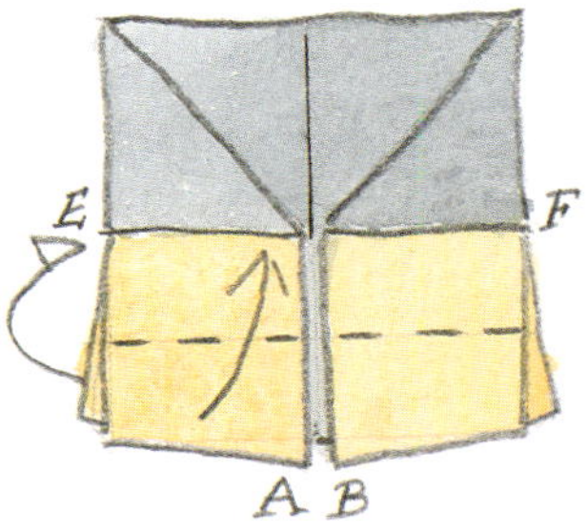

1 Begin with Step 2 of the 3D House. Fold AB up to EF. Repeat behind.

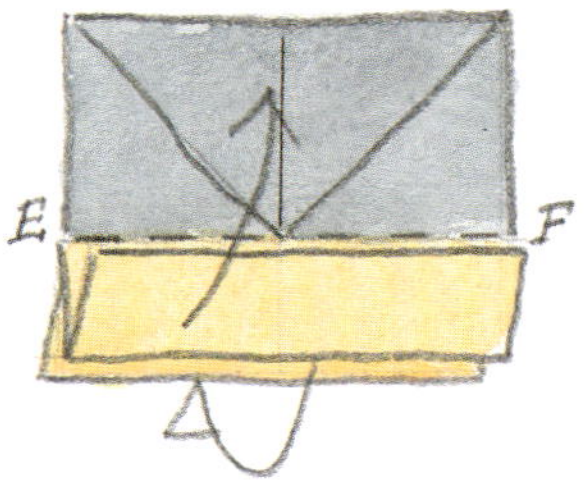

2 Fold up the bottom section along crease EF. Repeat behind.

3 Open out the cap.

4 The G.I. Cap complete. To make a full-sized cap, use a square trimmed from a large format newspaper.

STAR

The shape made in Step 7 is known in origami as the Preliminary Base, so called because other, more advanced bases can be developed from it, including the Bird and Frog bases and their stretched variants. Use a square of paper or perhaps paper-backed foil, coloured side up.

Designed by Florence Temko, USA.

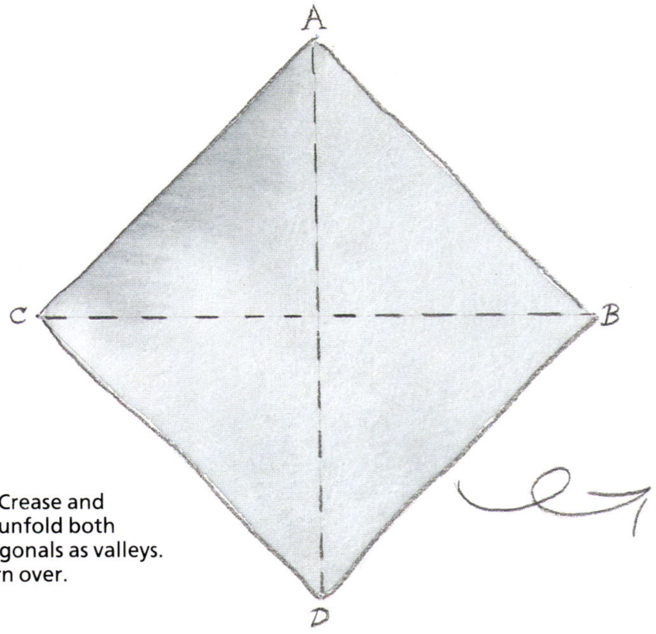

1 Crease and unfold both diagonals as valleys. Turn over.

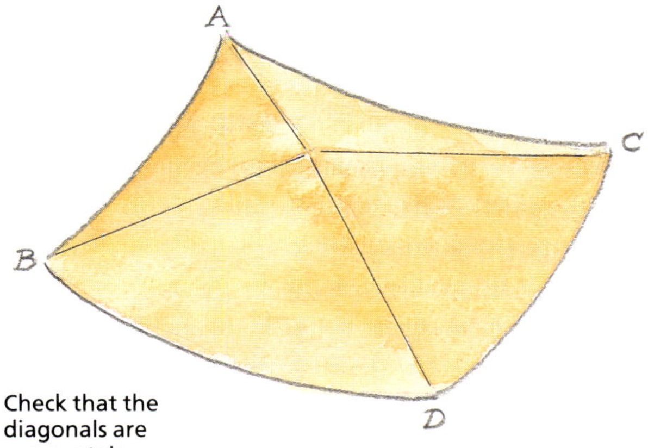

2 Check that the diagonals are now mountain creases.

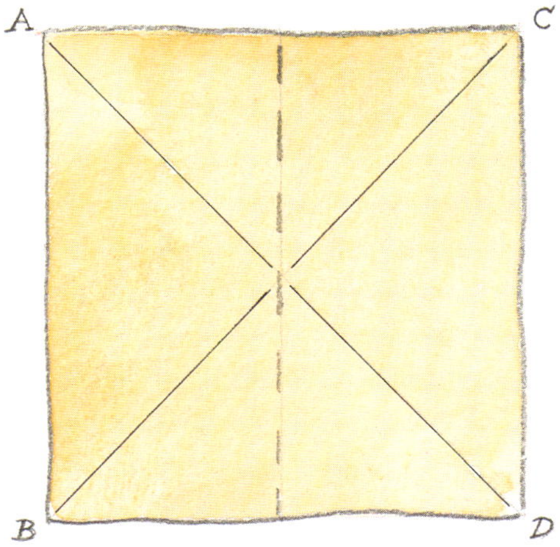

3 Fold and unfold in half down the middle, then . . .

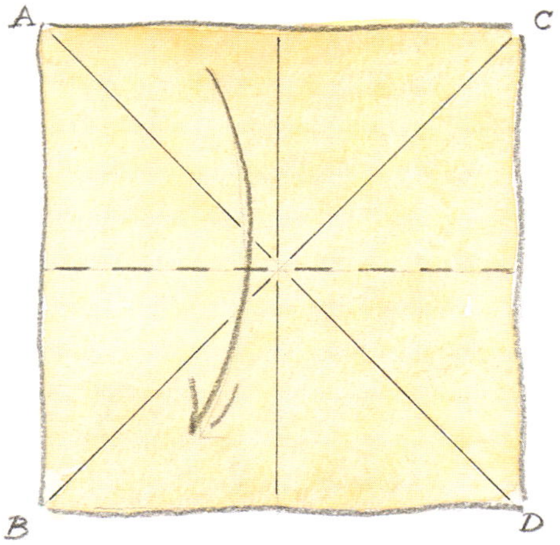

4 . . . fold in half across the middle.

5 Hold as shown. If the mountain and valley creases have been placed correctly, a 3D diamond shape will emerge when the hands are swung towards each other . . .

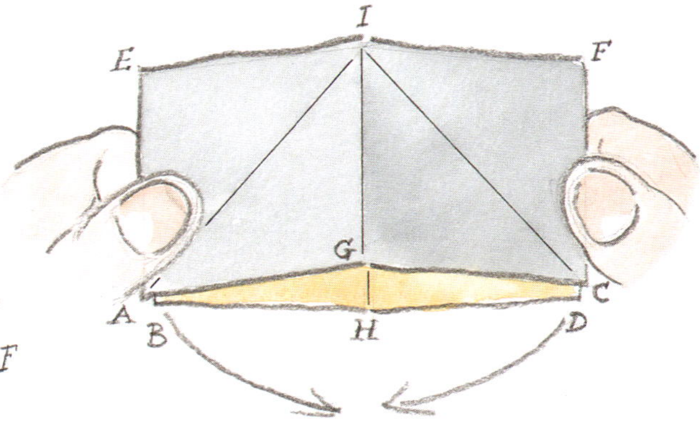

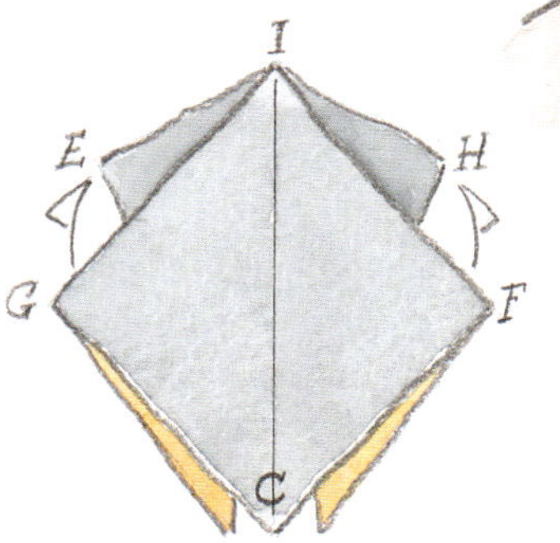

6 . . . like this. Flatten G against E and F against H.

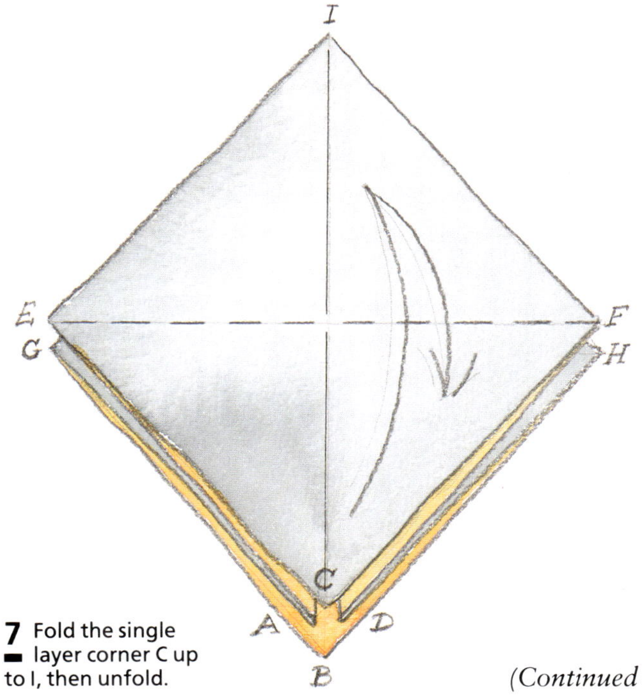

7 Fold the single layer corner C up to I, then unfold.

(Continued . . .)

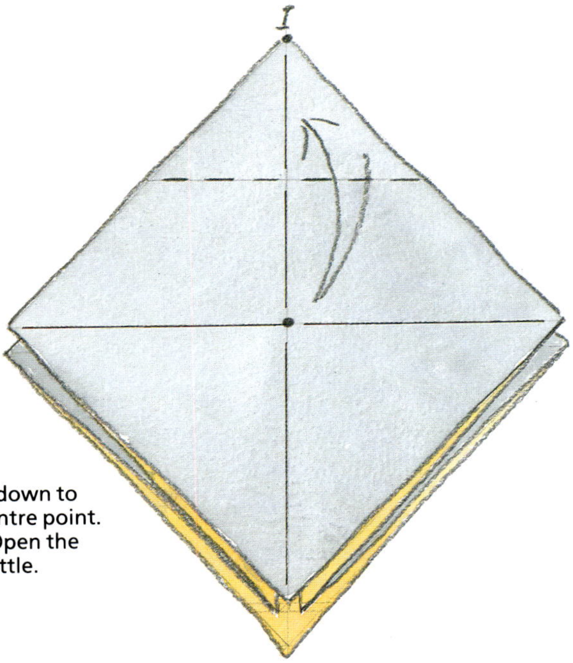

8 Fold I down to the centre point. Unfold. Open the paper a little.

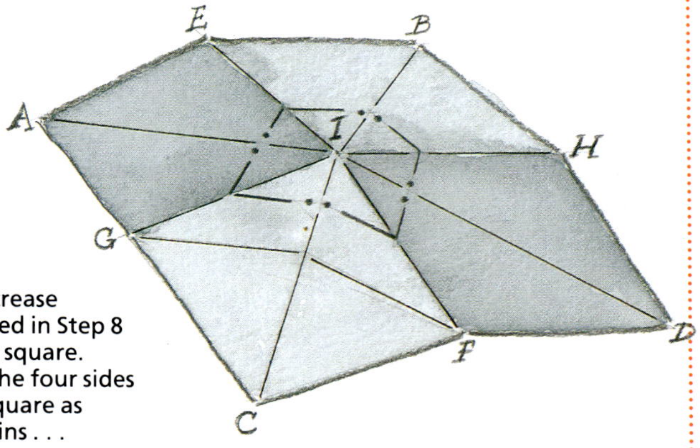

9 The crease formed in Step 8 makes a square. Crease the four sides of the square as mountains . . .

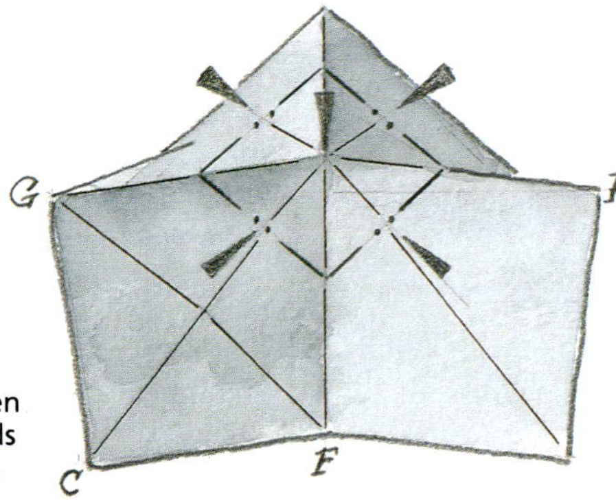

10 . . . like this. Flatten the centre square, then push it downwards into the paper . . .

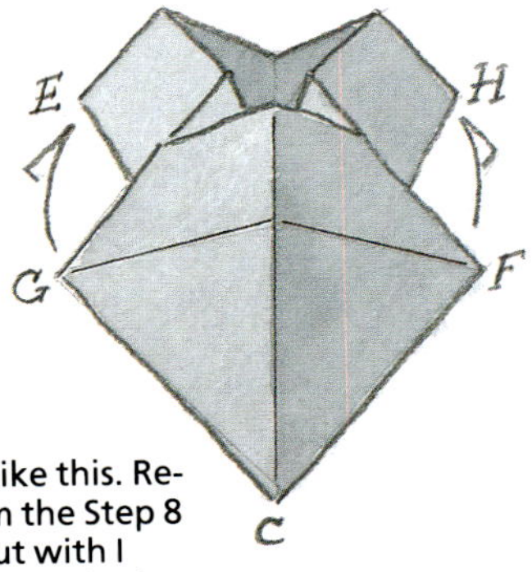

11 . . . like this. Re-form the Step 8 shape, but with I now sunk inside the paper.

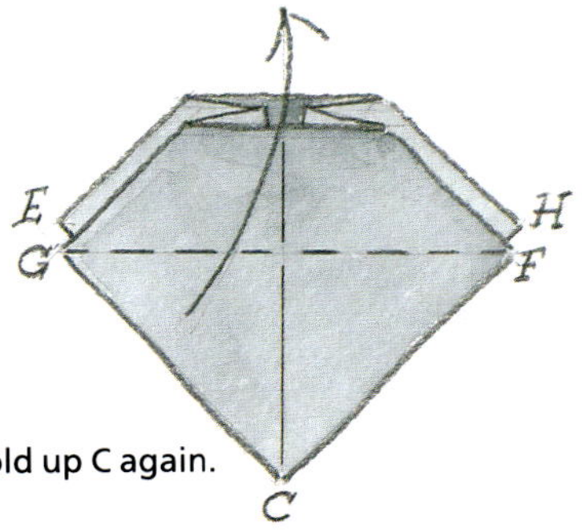

12 Fold up C again.

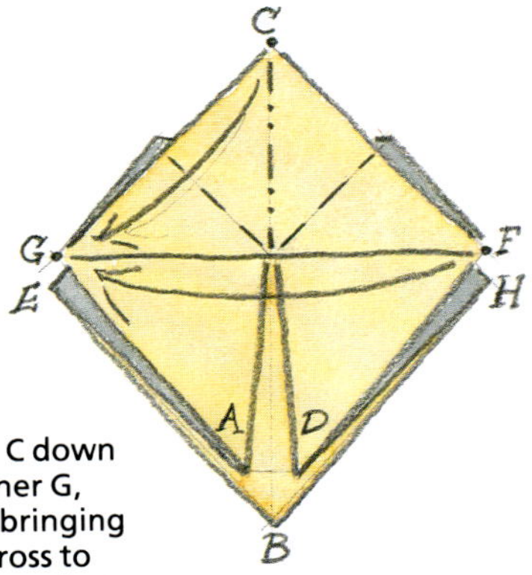

13 Swing C down to corner G, whilst also bringing corner F across to touch G. Note that the crease from G is a mountain, not a valley.

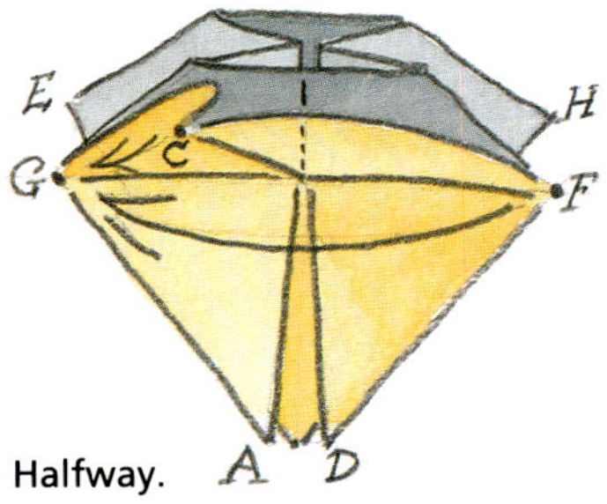

14 Halfway.

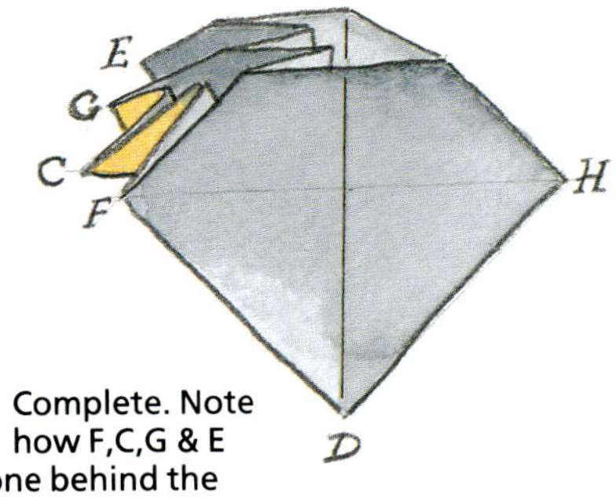

15 Complete. Note how F,C,G & E lie one behind the other.

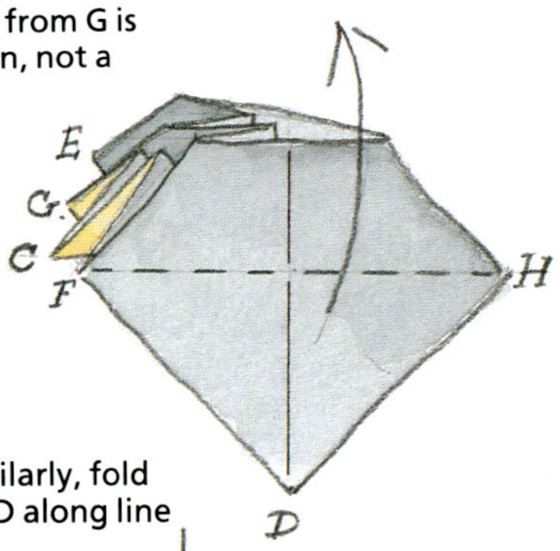

16 Similarly, fold up D along line FH . . .

17 . . . and swing towards corner F, bringing H across to touch corner F. Repeat this sequence with A then B, turning the paper over and around each time, to keep the same number of layers on each side of the paper. Fan out the points in a symmetrical pattern.

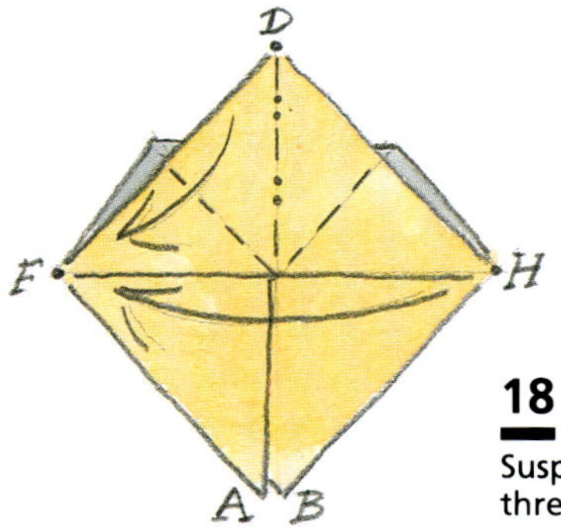

18 The Star complete. Suspend from a thread.

INTERMEDIATE PROJECTS

WATERBOMB

Many people – particularly mischievous children – have learnt how to make a waterbomb, but without practice, it is very easy to forget how to lock it. Without a good lock, it cannot contain the water it is designed to hold! More peaceably, it makes an excellent Christmas decoration if folded from a patterned paper. Use a square of paper. If using origami paper, start with the white side uppermost.

Traditional design.

1 Mountain fold horizontally and vertically across the paper. Unfold each time.

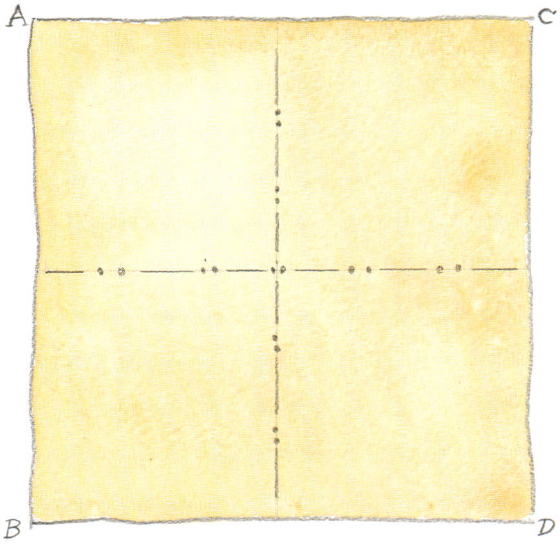

2 Form a vertical valley diagonal (the other creases are mountains). Unfold.

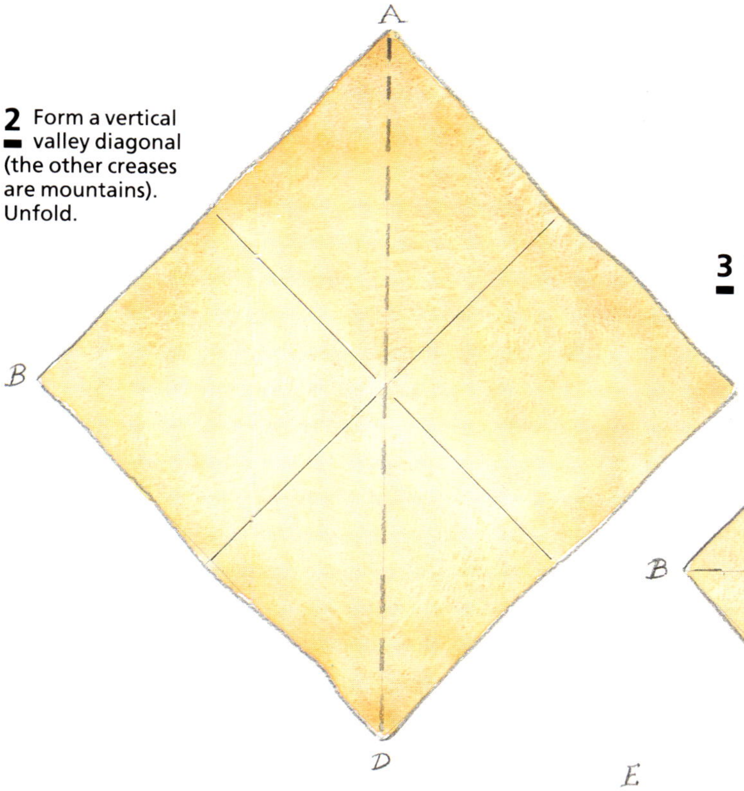

3 Fold A down to D.

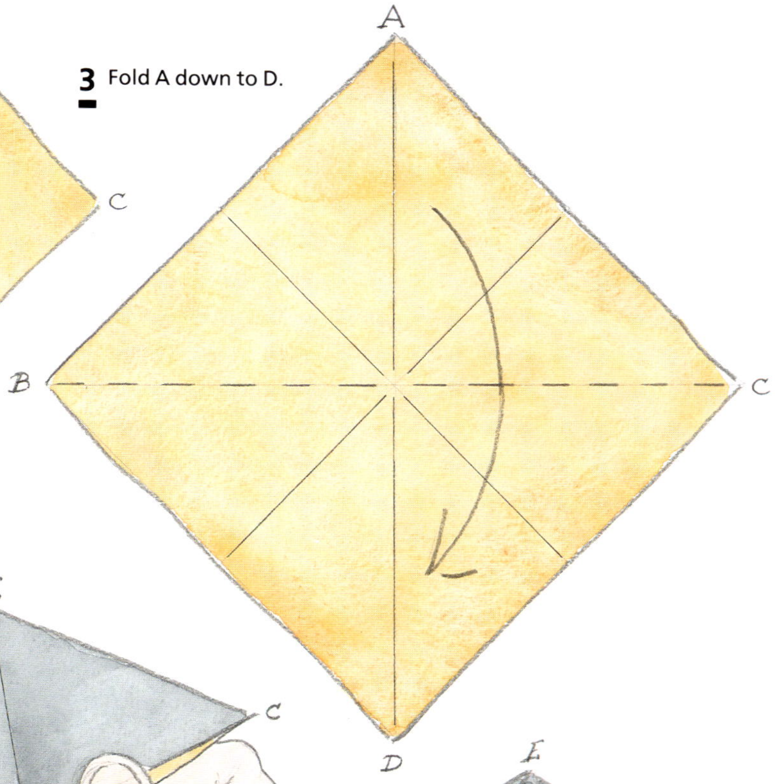

4 Hold as shown. If the mountains and valleys have been placed correctly, the paper will form a 3D pyramid when the hands are swung towards each other . . .

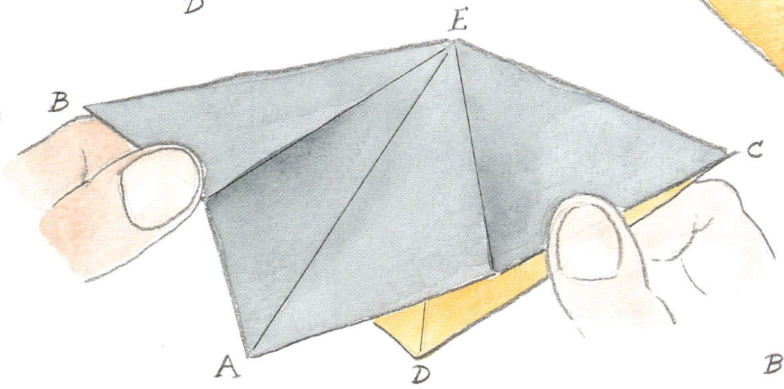

5 . . . like this. Flatten A against B, and D against C.

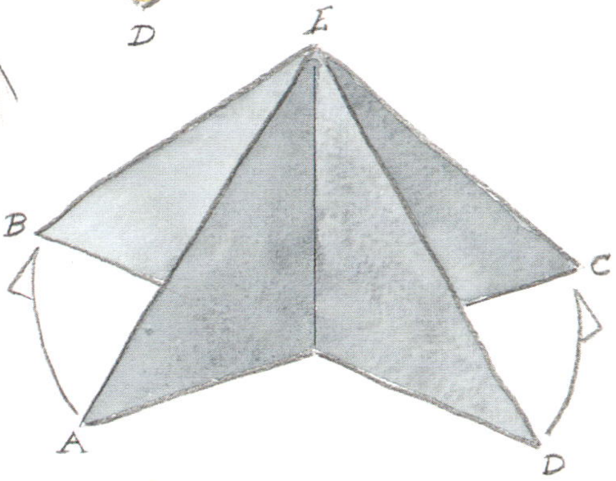

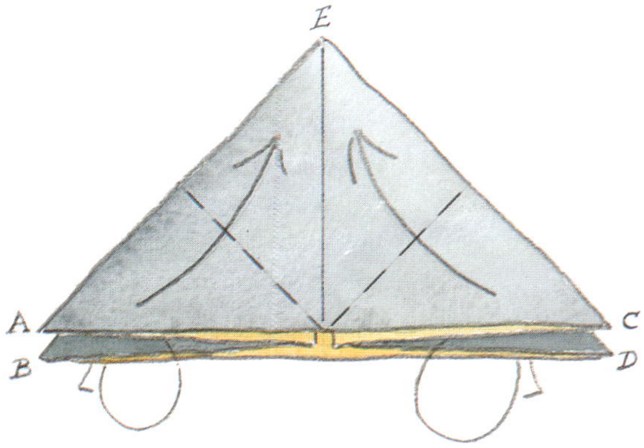

6 Fold A & C up to E. Repeat behind with B & D. (Note: to increase the size of the hole through which air is blown to inflate the Waterbomb, fold the corners *short* of E. A hole that is too small is difficult to blow through.)

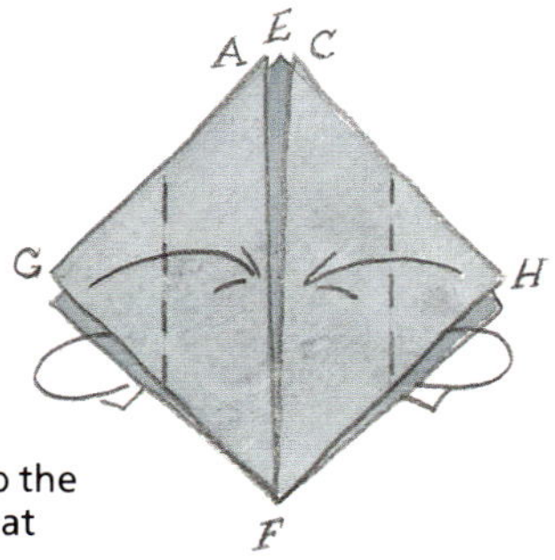

7 Fold G & H to the centre. Repeat behind.

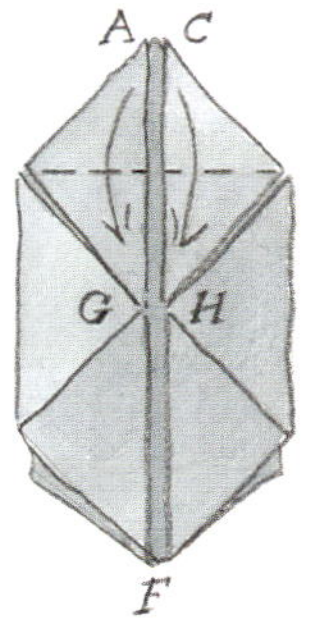

8 Fold A & C into the centre at G & H.

9 Valley fold the small triangle above A into the pocket made by separating the layers above G. Repeat with C on the right and twice more behind with B and D.

10 The Waterbomb is now locked, front and back. Blow into the bottom to make it 3D. If the hole is too small, enlarge it.

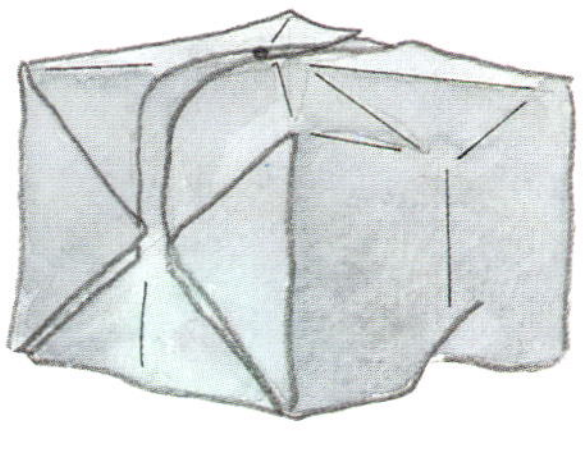

11 The Waterbomb complete.

TRADITIONAL BOX

This is perhaps *the* classic origami box. It is quick and simple to make, and locks strongly. A box made from a slightly larger square will form a lid. In Step 3, if the creases are not placed at the quarter points, but elsewhere, taller or squatter boxes can be made. Use a square of strong paper. If using origami paper, start white side up.

Traditional design.

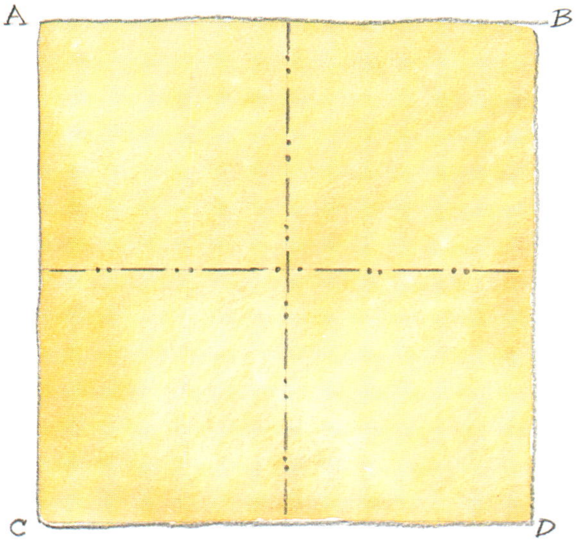

1 Mountain fold horizontally and vertically across the centre, unfolding each time.

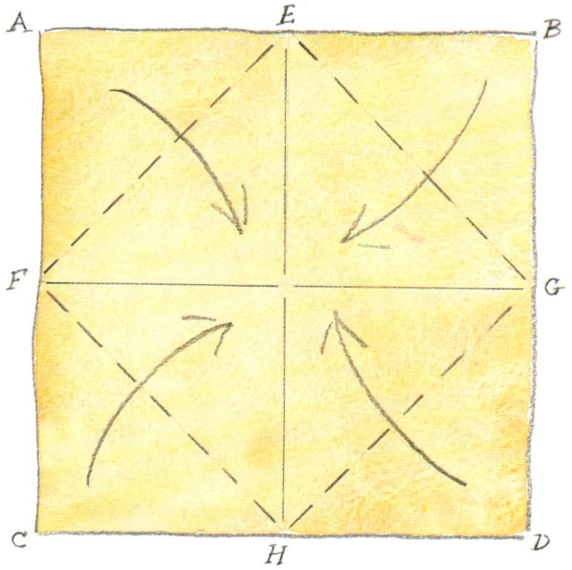

2 Fold the corners to the centre. (The existing creases are mountains.)

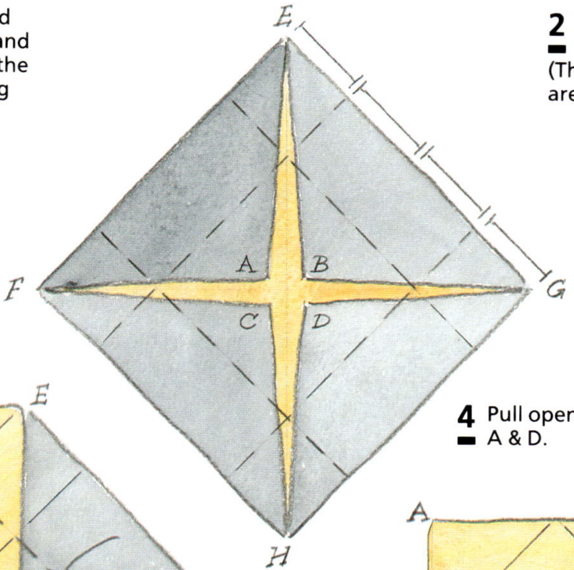

3 Fold each edge in turn to the centre point, unfolding each crease before making the next.

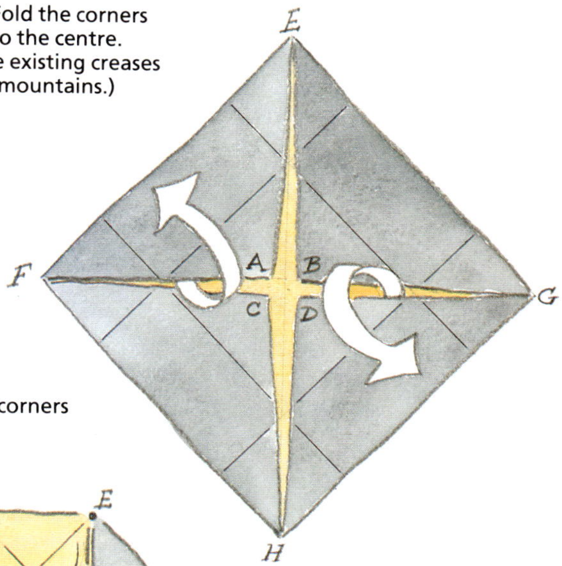

4 Pull open corners A & D.

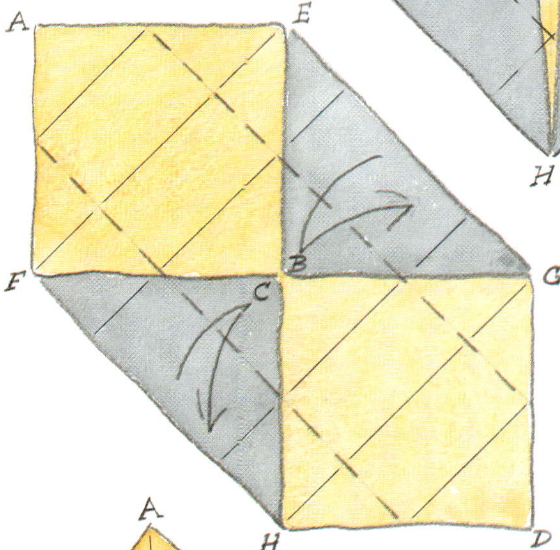

5 Re-crease valleys where shown.

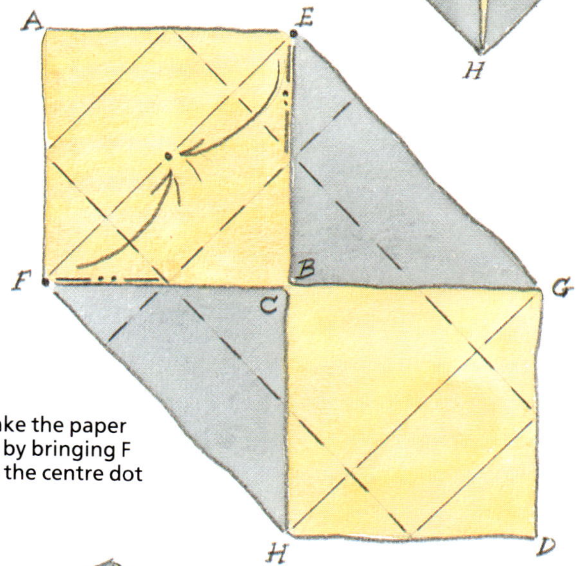

6 Make the paper 3D by bringing F & E to the centre dot . . .

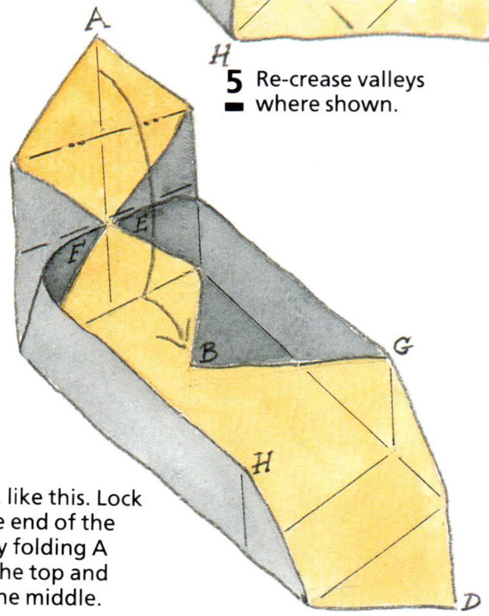

7 . . . like this. Lock the end of the box by folding A over the top and into the middle.

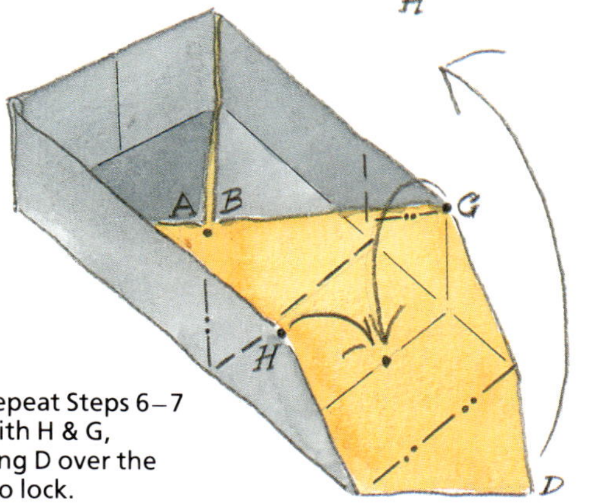

8 Repeat Steps 6–7 with H & G, folding D over the top to lock.

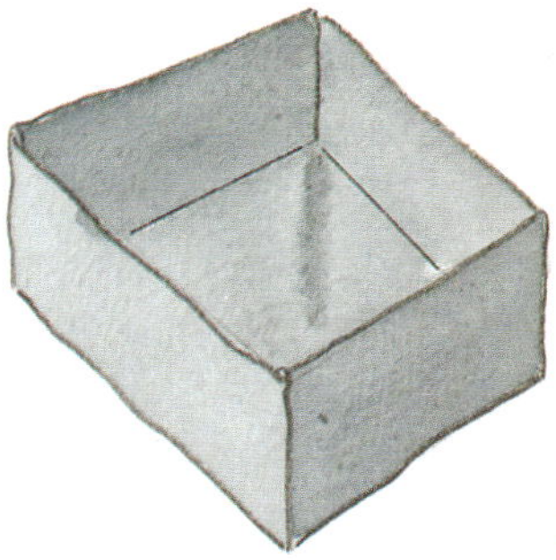

9 The Traditional Box complete.

NESTING BIRD

The design features a peculiar and little-used manoeuvre at Steps 4–5, when one spike is pulled out from inside another that envelops it. The move is very satisfying! What was a closed and rather unpromising shape in Step 4 becomes much more useful by Step 6, yet no new creases are made. Begin with a square of paper, same colour both sides.

Designed by Paul Jackson.

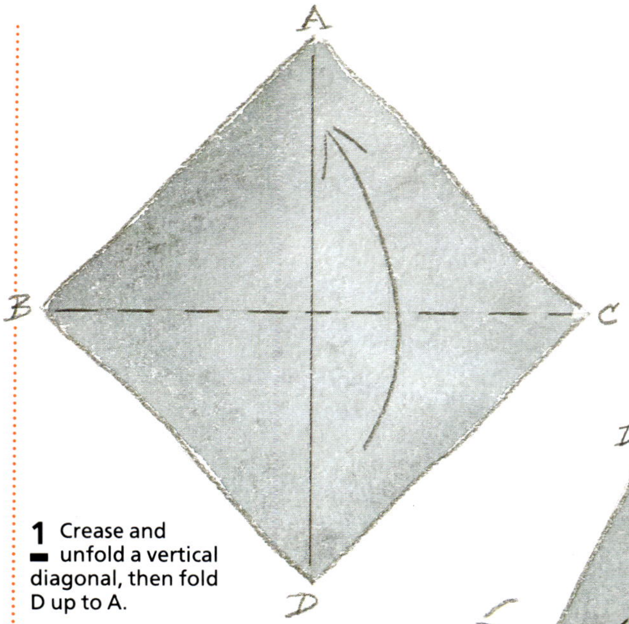

1 Crease and unfold a vertical diagonal, then fold D up to A.

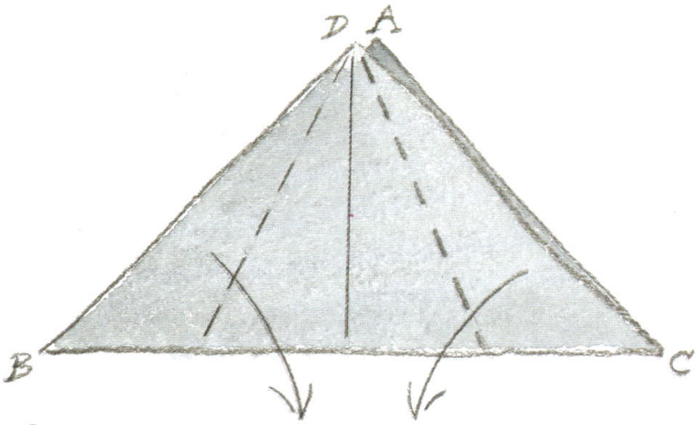

2 Fold edges AD,B and AD,C to the centre crease.

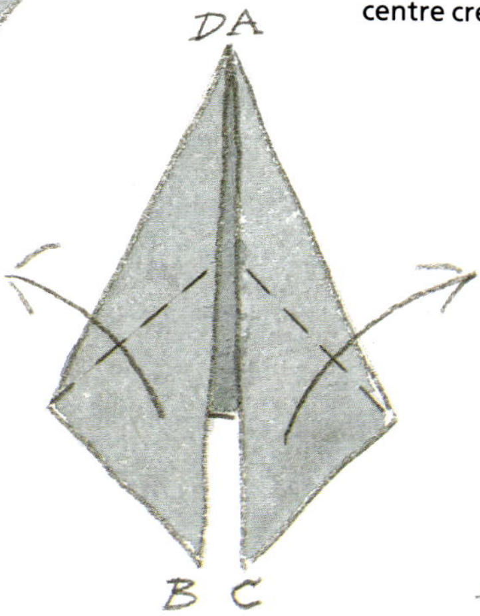

3 Fold out corners B & C.

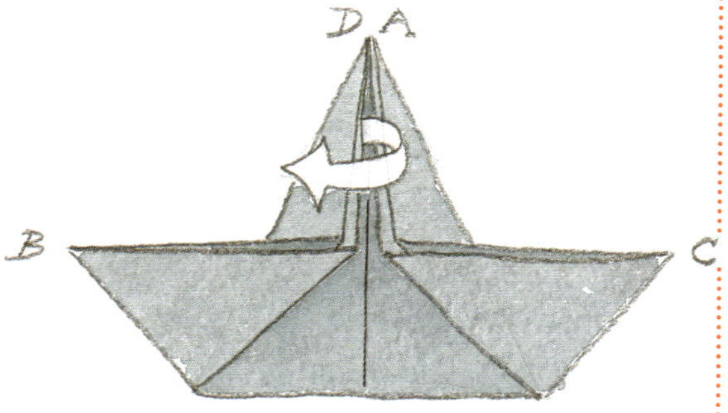

4 Note the shape of the paper. Pull out D from inside A . . .

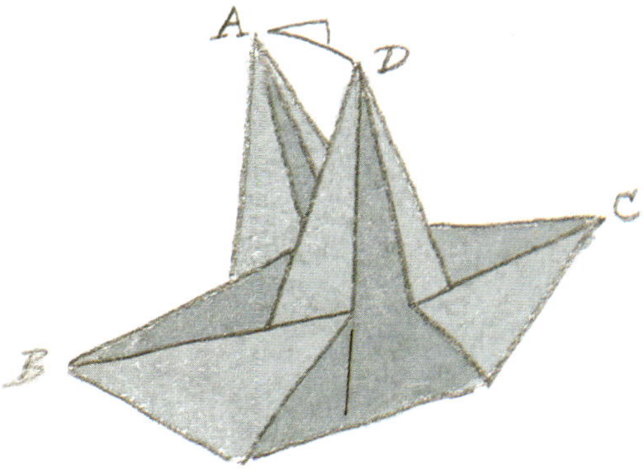

5 . . . like this. Flatten D on top of A.

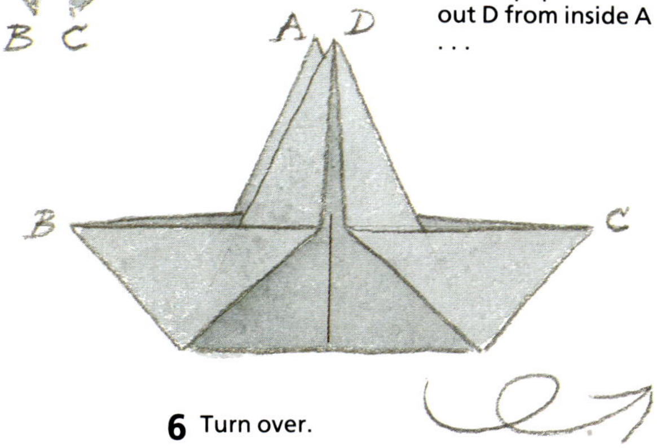

6 Turn over.

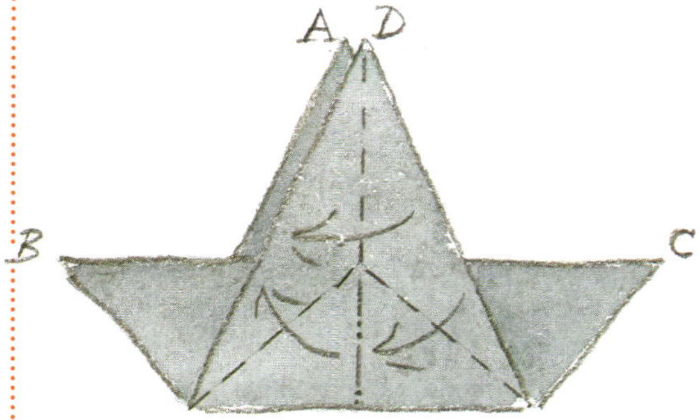

7 Collapse the paper as shown, separating A from D and bringing C to touch B.

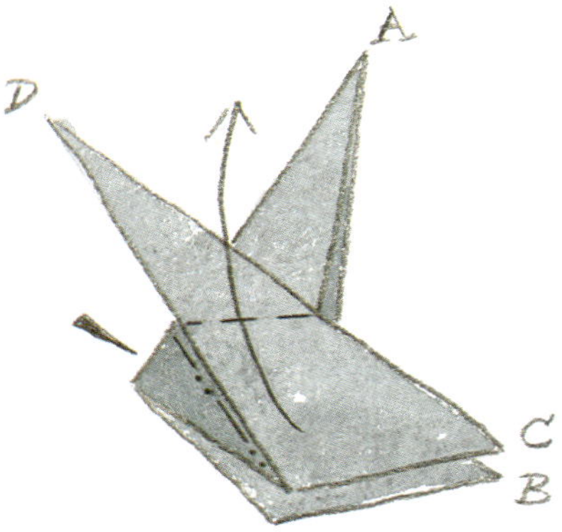

8 Lift up corner C, squashing the paper flat at the left.

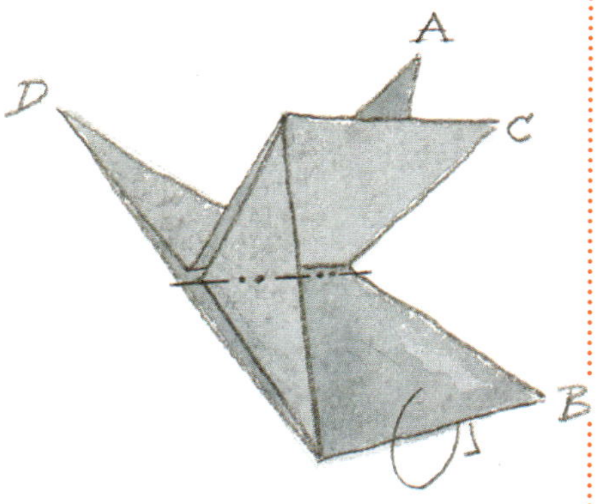

9 Fold B behind.

10 Reverse fold D. Fold out the bottom corners to stay away from the wings and so create a stable base for the bird to balance on.

11 The Nesting Bird complete.

BEAK

This is a variation on a well-known origami 'action' theme. The mechanism will be familiar to knowledgeable paper folders, but here the eyes are made differently. It is important to use origami paper, to achieve a contrast of colour for the eyes and the inside of the mouth. The colour should be on the outside in Step 1.

Designed by Paul Jackson.

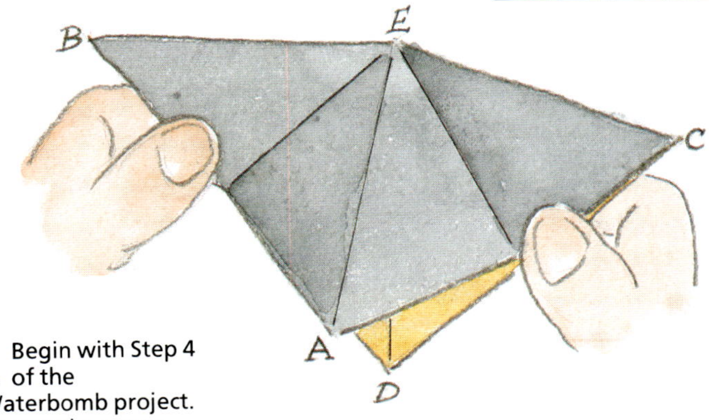

1 Begin with Step 4 of the Waterbomb project. Flatten the paper.

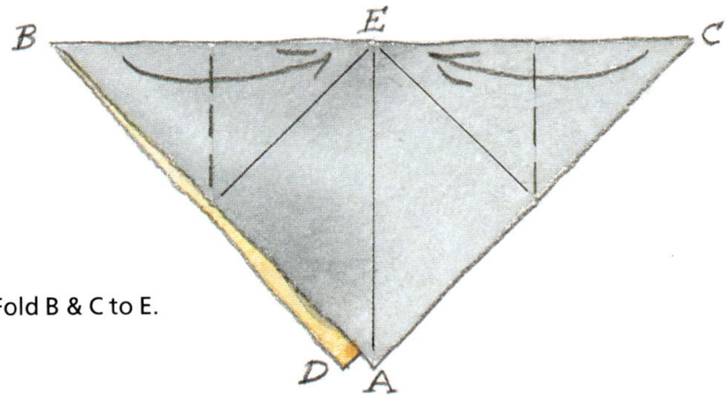

2 Fold B & C to E.

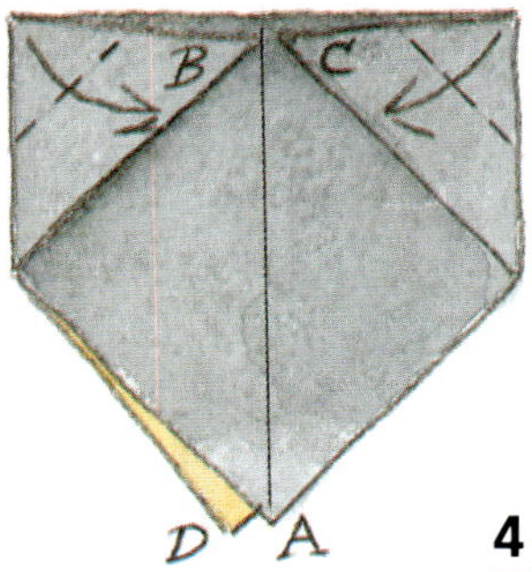

3 Fold in the corners.

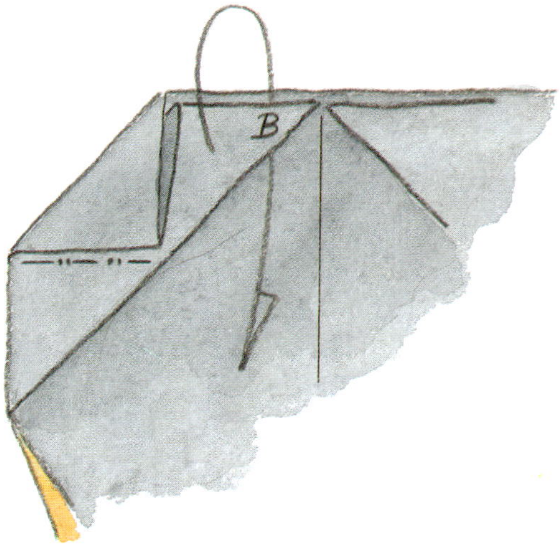

4 (The instructions now refer to B only, but repeat all Steps with C.) Swivel B behind and downwards . . .

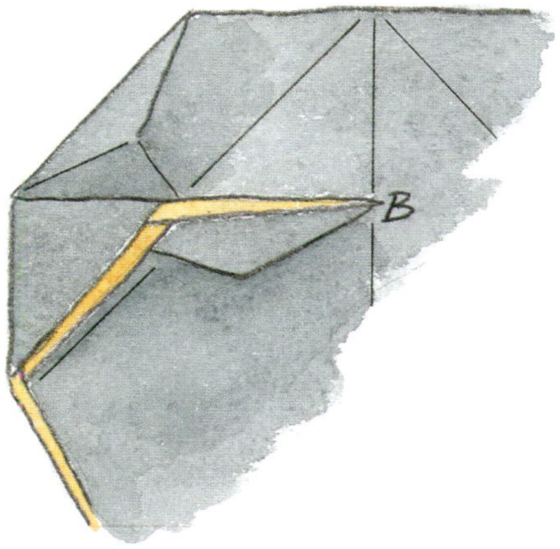

5 . . . like this . . .

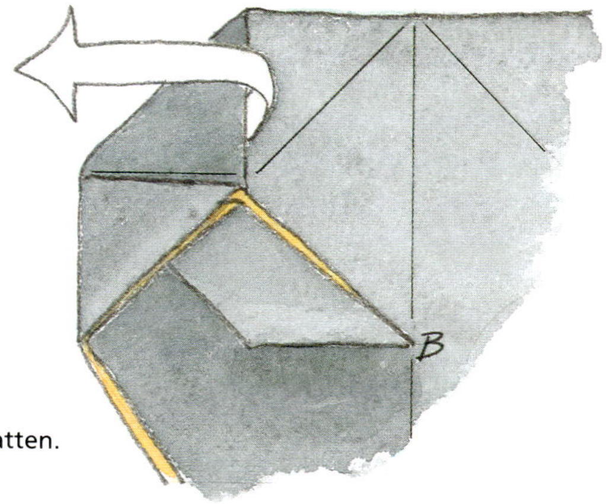

6 . . . and flatten. Unfold.

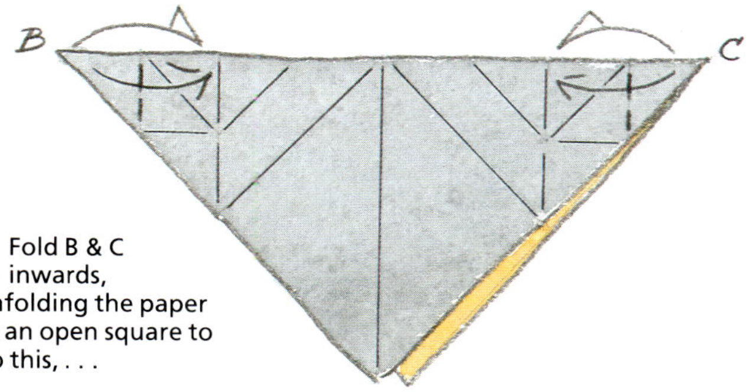

7 Fold B & C inwards, unfolding the paper to an open square to do this, . . .

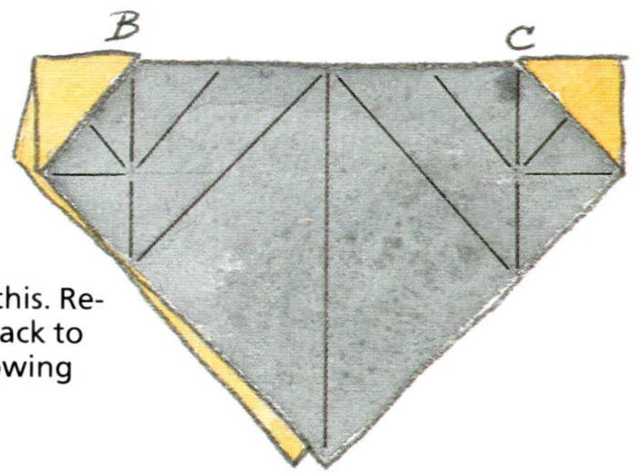

8 . . . like this. Re-crease back to Step 6 following Steps 2–6.

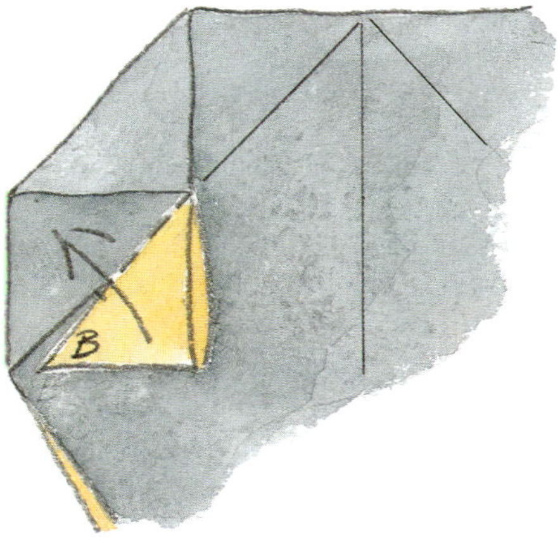

9 Note the new shape at B. Fold up triangle B.

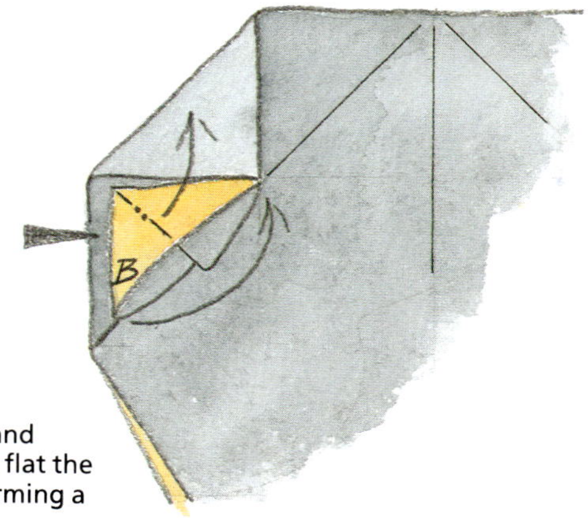

10 Open and squash flat the triangle, forming a square.

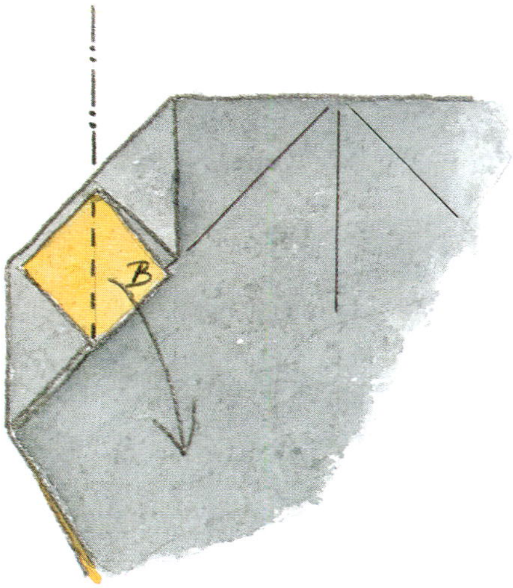

11 Swivel the square down and to the right along a hidden crease.

12 Pleat the eye.

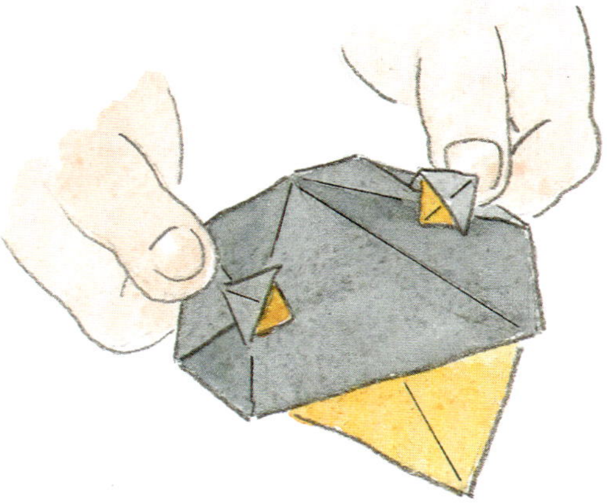

13 The Beak complete. Hold as shown and move your hands to and fro to make the mouth open and close!

LIGHTHEARTED

Original concepts are rare in origami. Most designs, however good, are created within relatively predictable themes, so it is pleasing to occasionally find a fresh approach. In this design, the final shape is unimpressive, but reveals a translucent heart when held against the light! Fold the paper carefully, particularly at Steps 2–3, or the heart will be poorly proportioned. Use a square of thin paper; thicker papers will not reveal the heart.

Designed by Wayne Brown, UK.

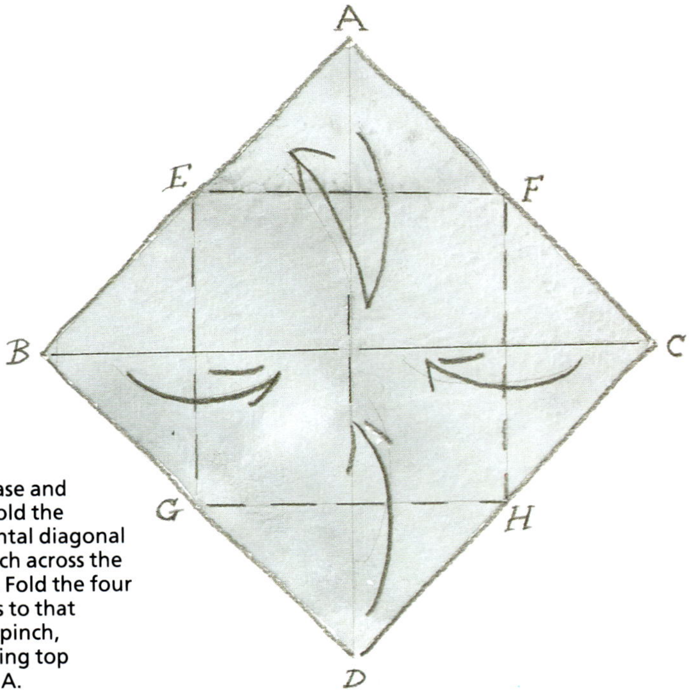

1 Crease and unfold the horizontal diagonal BC. Pinch across the centre. Fold the four corners to that centre pinch, unfolding top corner A.

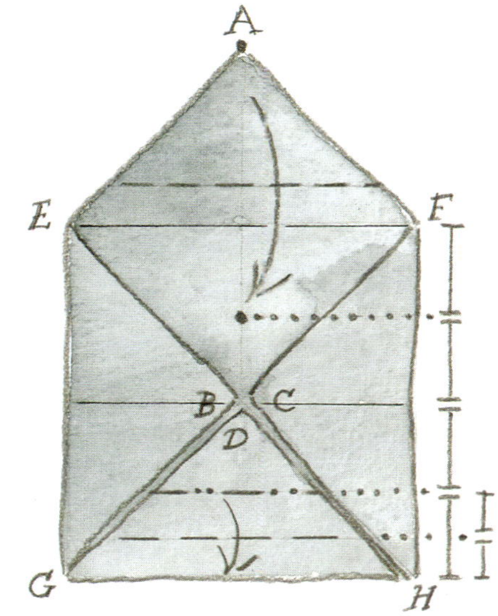

2 Fold down corner A as shown. Pleat triangle DGH as shown.

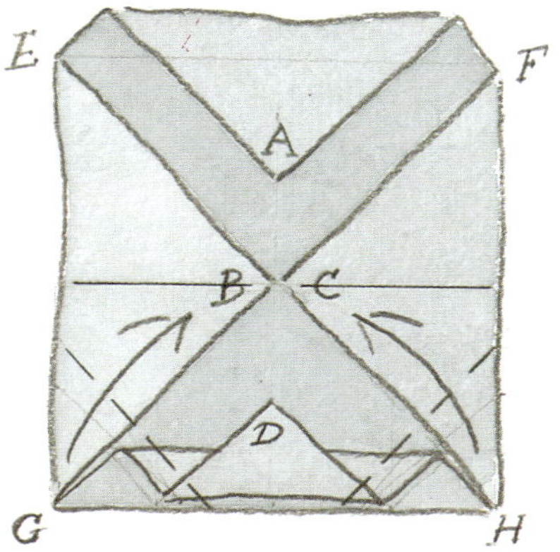

3 Fold in corners G & H. Note the very small intrusion of the crease into the D triangle. This is important, as it affects the proportion of the heart.

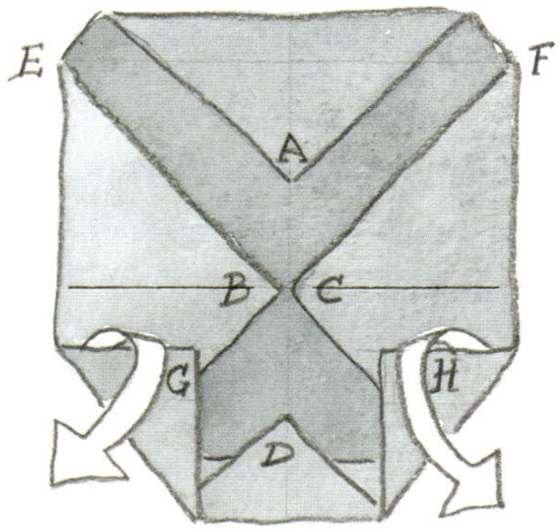

4 Unfold Step 3.

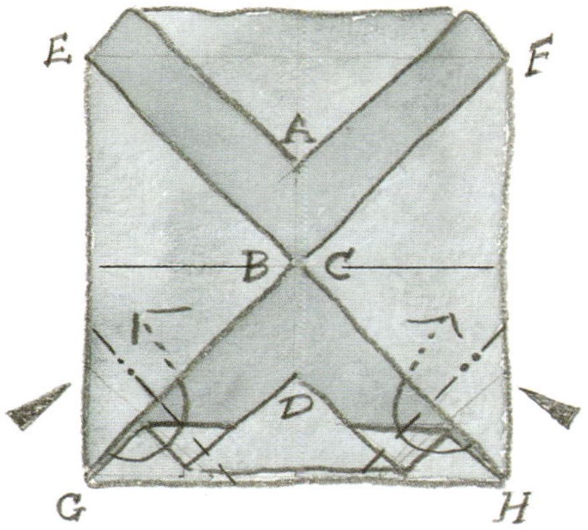

5 Re-crease Step 3, but reverse folding the top part of each crease to push G under B, and H under C.

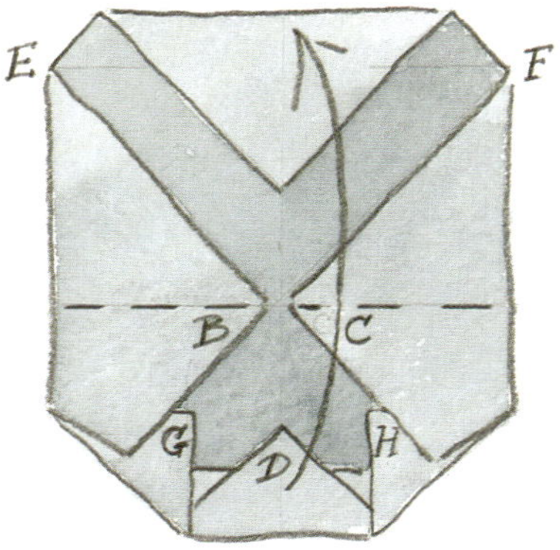

6 Fold in half.

7 Fold in E & F just a little way.

8 Fold over as shown, locking the edges into the pockets made in Step 5.

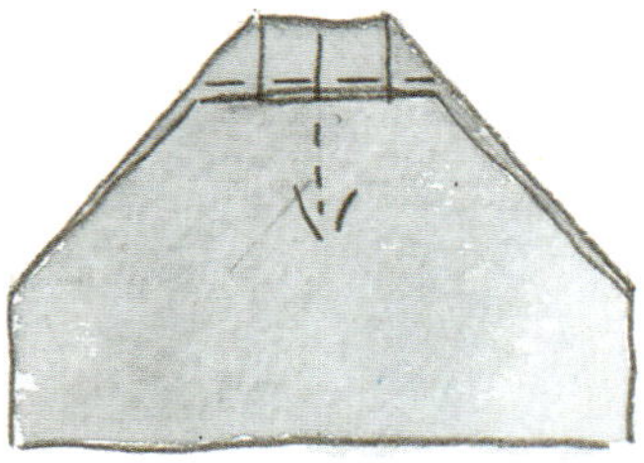

9 Fold the excess paper into the top pocket.

10 Note that the shape is locked flat.

11 To see the heart, hold the paper up to a window or other diffuse light source (but not the sun).

STAR BOX

This is one of the simpler decorative origami boxes. It is relatively easy to make a square, straight-sided box, such as the Traditional Box project, but the technical complexities increase as the final shape becomes less plain. Here though, the design is pleasingly bold. Use a square of origami paper, with the coloured side outwards.

Traditional design.

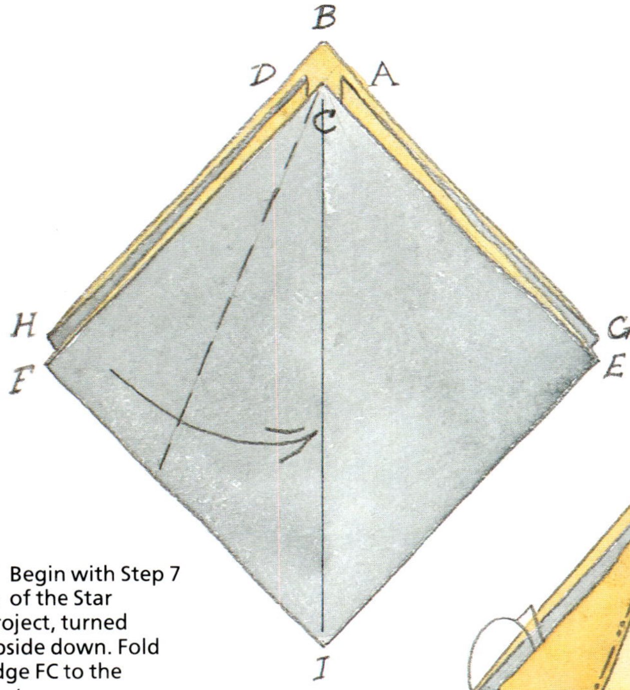

1 Begin with Step 7 of the Star project, turned upside down. Fold edge FC to the centre crease.

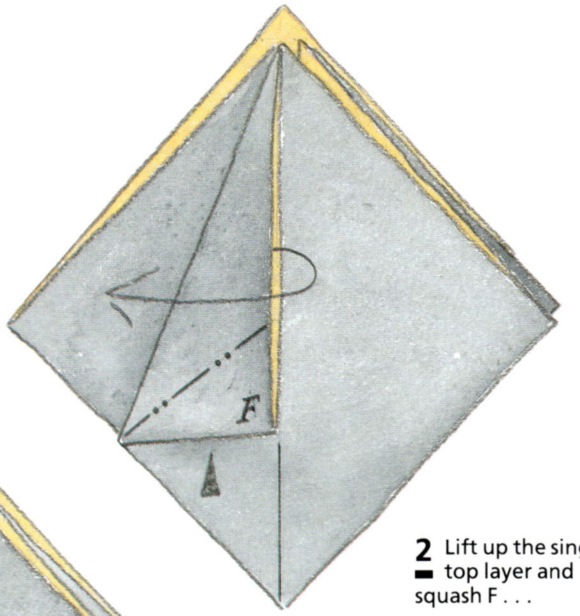

2 Lift up the single top layer and squash F . . .

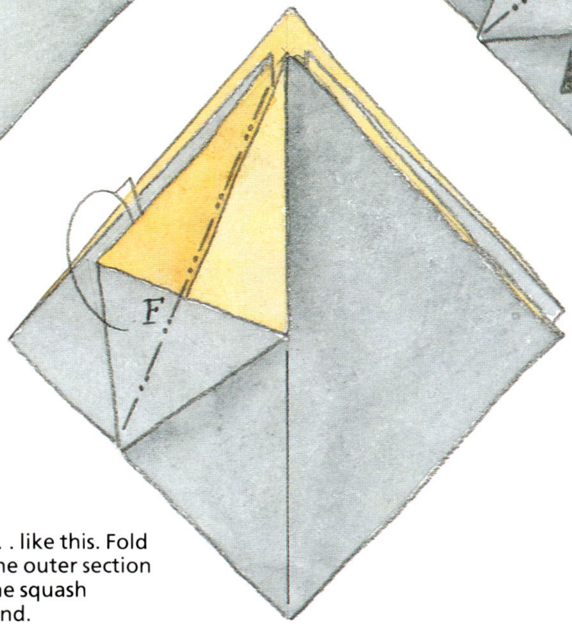

3 . . . like this. Fold the outer section of the squash behind.

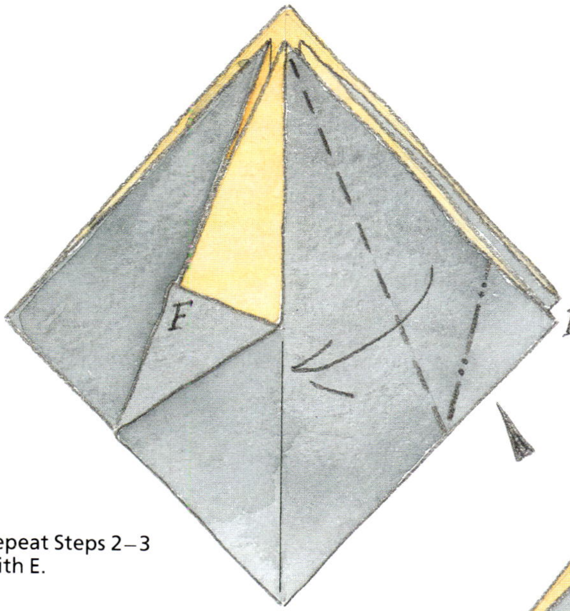

4 Repeat Steps 2–3 with E.

5 Turn over.

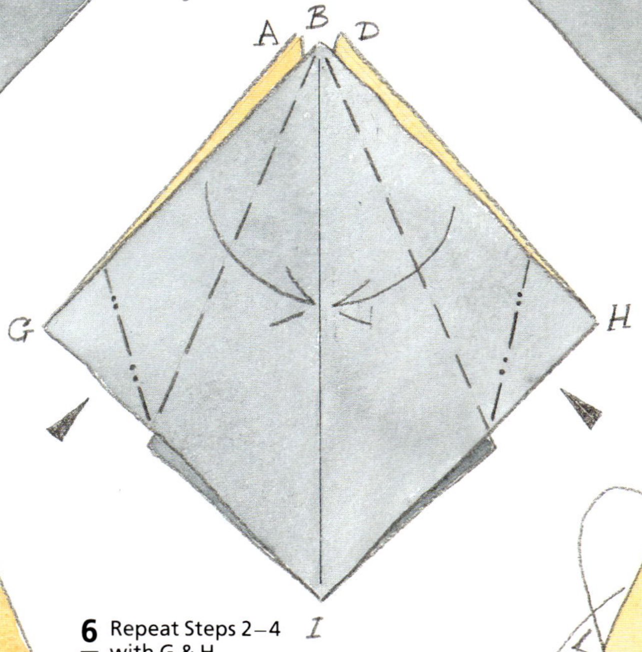

6 Repeat Steps 2–4 with G & H.

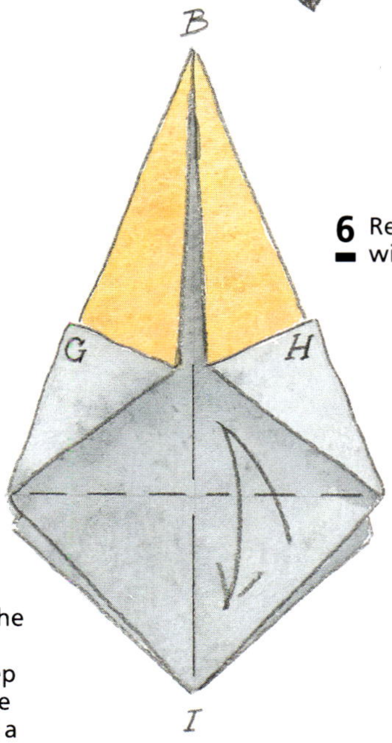

7 Crease and unfold across the full width of the paper. To help Step 9, the valley can be further creased as a mountain.

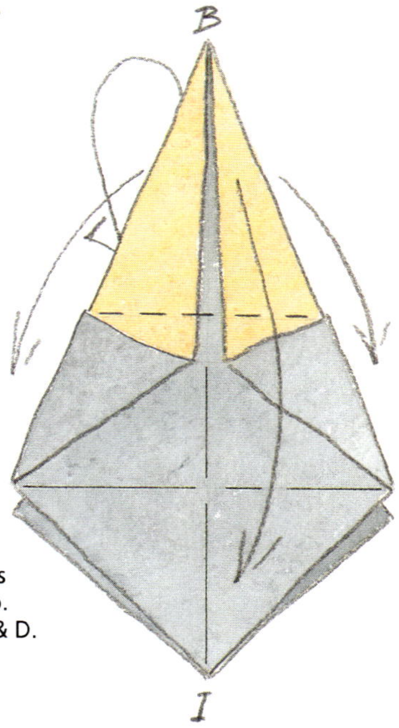

8 Fold down B as far as it will go. Repeat with A, C & D.

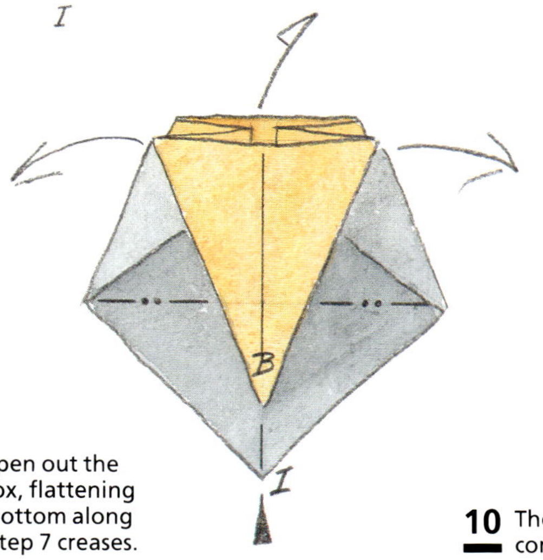

9 Open out the box, flattening the bottom along the Step 7 creases.

10 The Star Box complete.

JUMPING FROG

There are many origami jumping frogs, most – like this one – made by creating a frog shape, then pleating across the body to create the spring. This version is a particularly athletic jumper. Use a 20 cm (8 in) square of paper. A 2 × 1 rectangle of thick paper may also be used, starting at Step 2.

Traditional design.

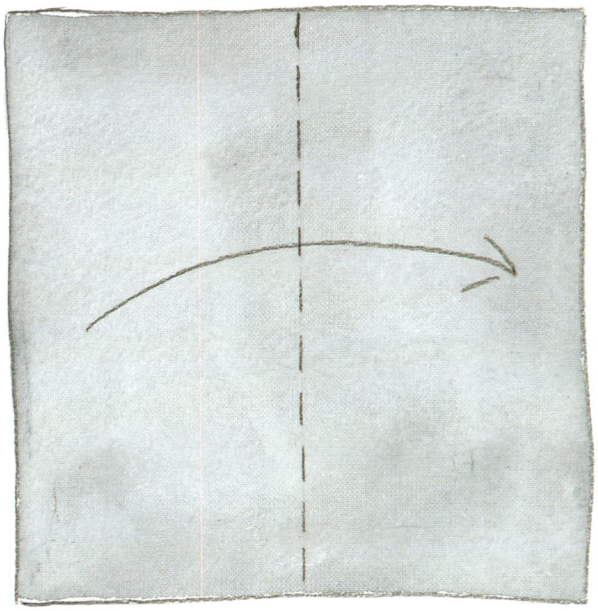

1 Fold a square in half down the middle.

2 The paper is now two layers thick, but will be referred to as though it was a single layer. Collapse AB to make the shape seen in Step 6 of the Waterbomb project.

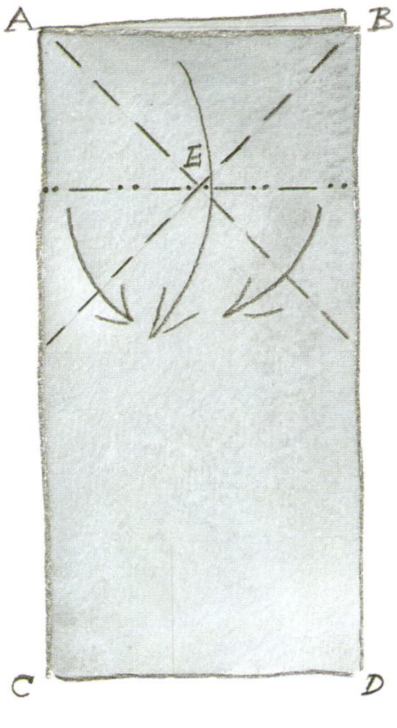

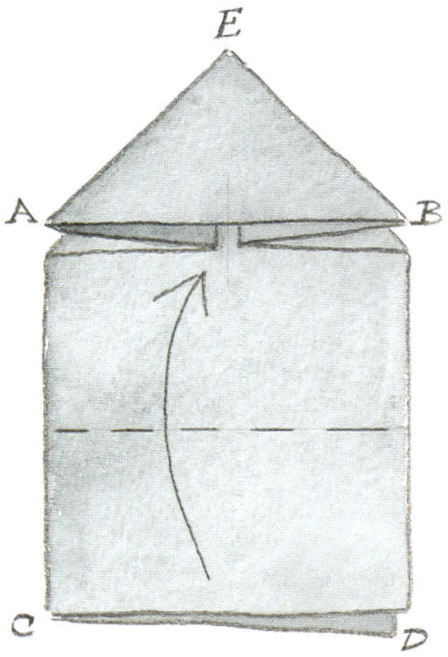

3 Fold up edge CD to AB.

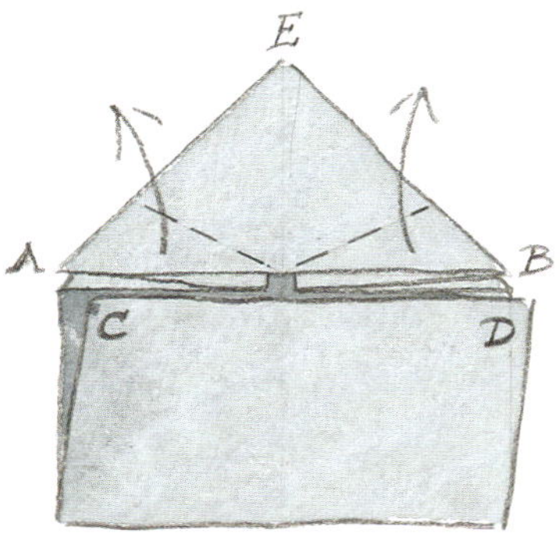

4 Swing out A & B. Note that they do not touch E, but protrude to the side.

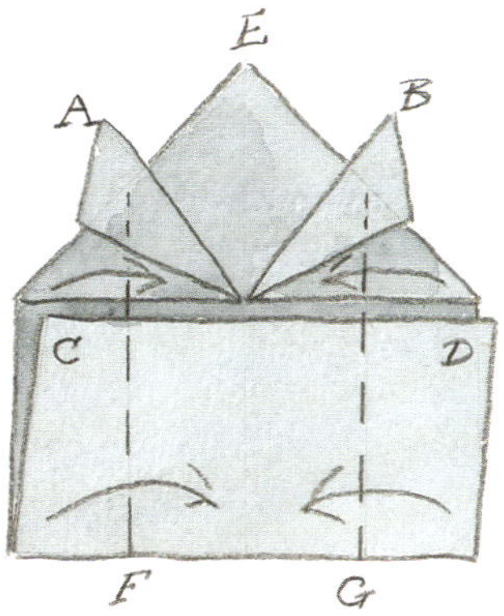

5 Fold in the sides.

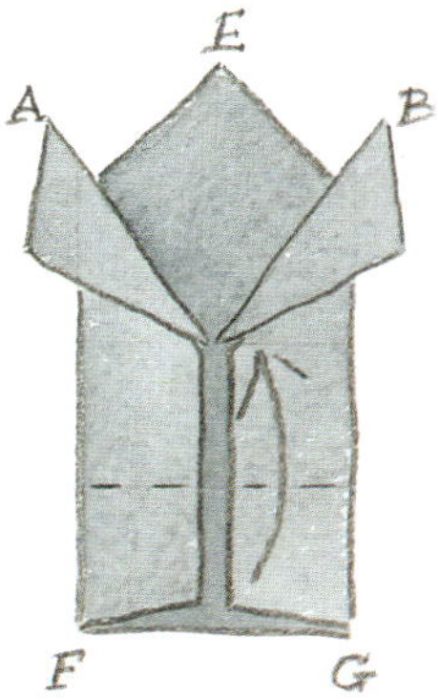

6 Fold edge FG to the centre point.

7 Fold down corners F & G . . .

8 . . . like this.

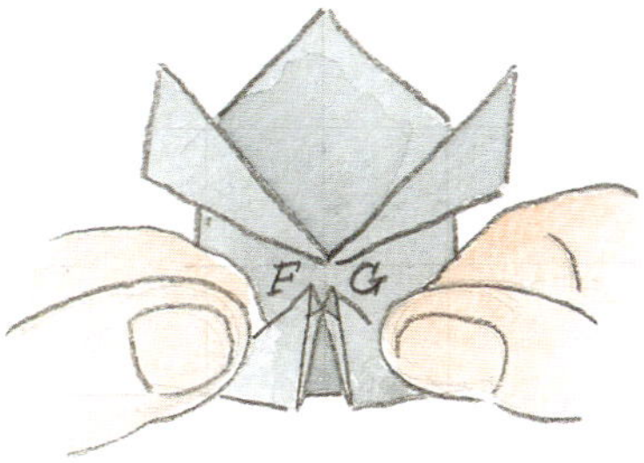

9 Hold tightly as shown. Slide F & G away from H . . .

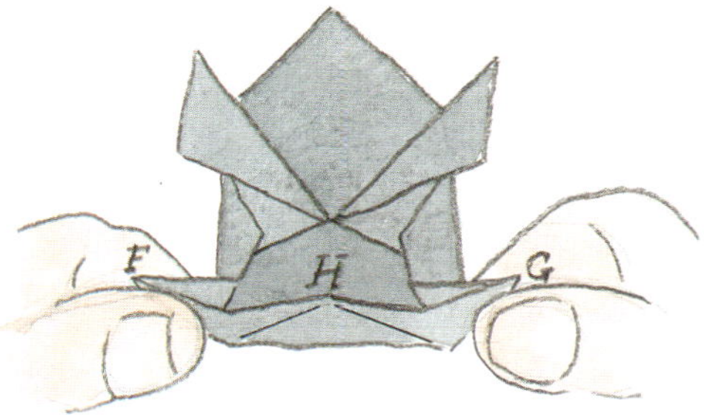

10 . . . like this, keeping firm hold of F & G. When F & G have been pulled out as far to the side as they will go, flatten the paper . . .

11 . . . like this. Fold down F & G.

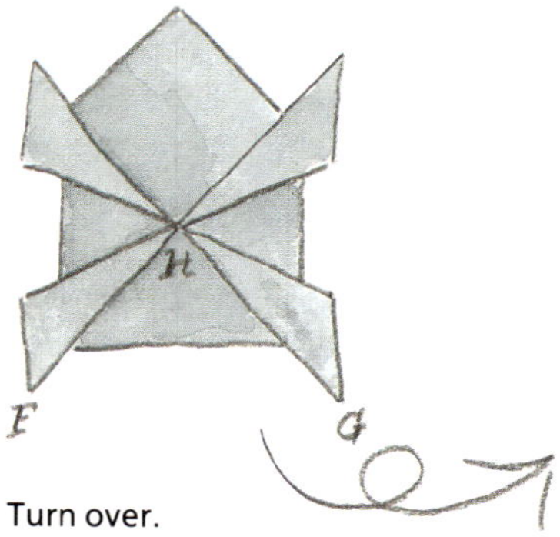

12 Turn over.

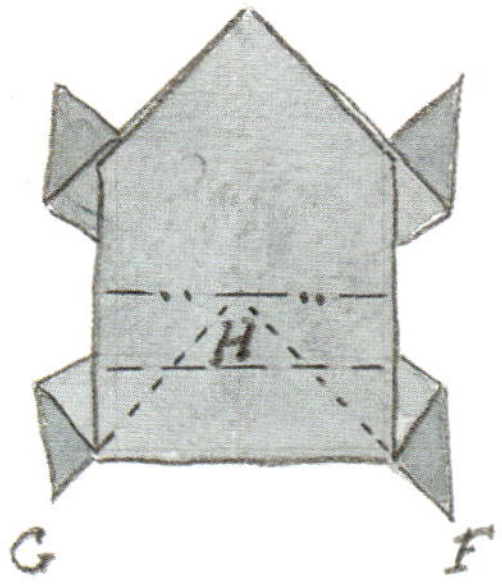

13 Make a pleat, with the mountain crease passing through H. The paper is very thick, so use considerable pressure.

14 The Jumping Frog complete.

15 To make it jump, put your finger on its back. Flatten the pleat and slide your finger off! With practice, it will jump quite a distance.

BIRD

This design is straightforward until Step 9, when the difficult 3D crimp transforms an ordinary flat bird into a 3D bird with a pleasingly rounded shape. Some origami creators argue that such '3D-ing' at the end of the folding sequence is a cheat, and that a *truly* 3D design is folded as such from the start. Use a 15–20 cm (6–8 in) square of paper, coloured the same on both sides.

Designed by Paul Jackson.

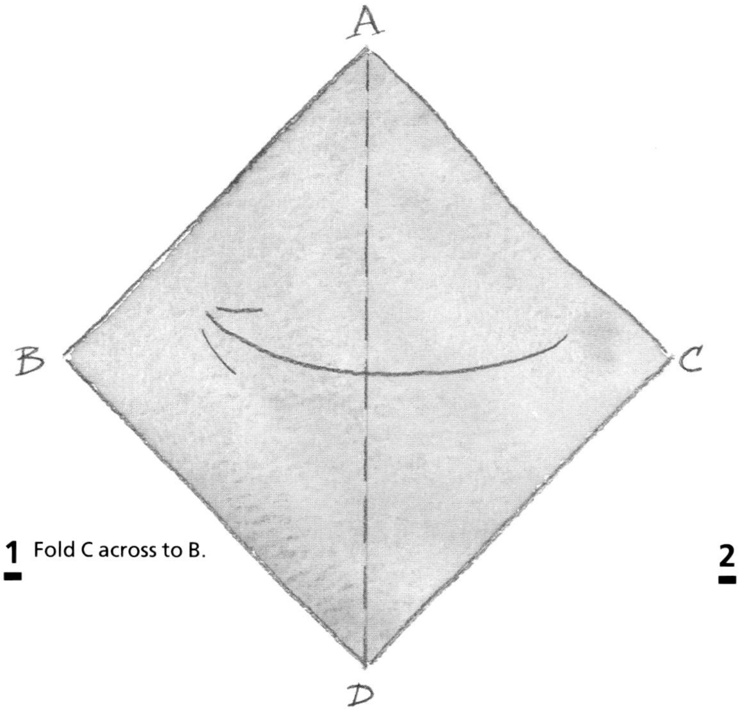

1 Fold C across to B.

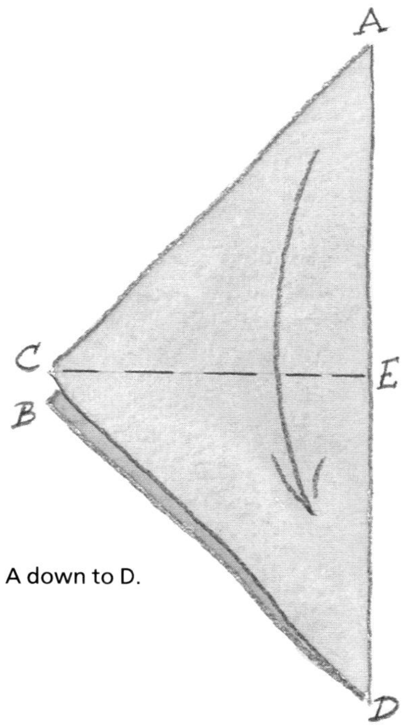

2 Fold A down to D.

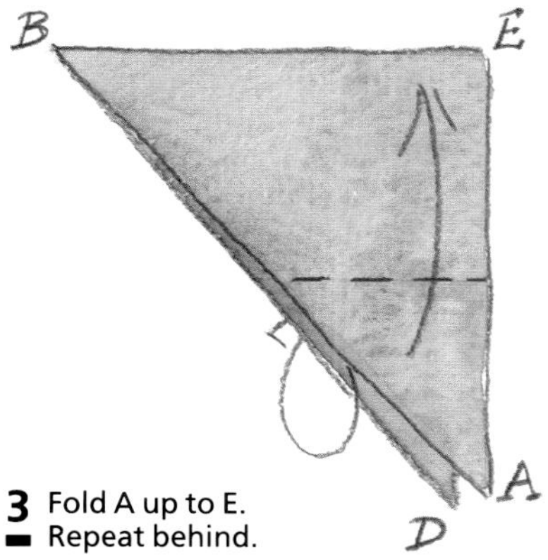

3 Fold A up to E. Repeat behind.

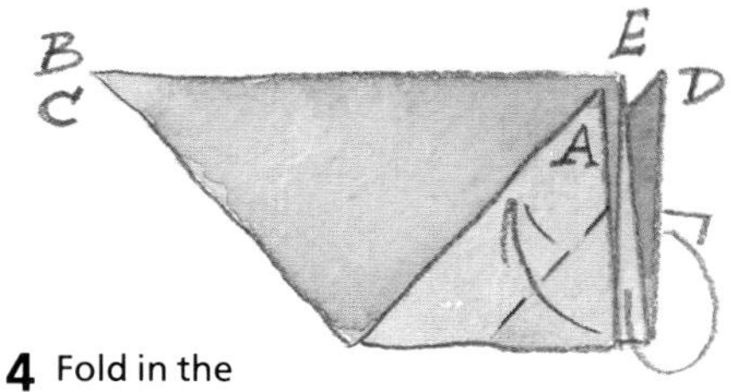

4 Fold in the corners.

5 Unfold crease BC,E.

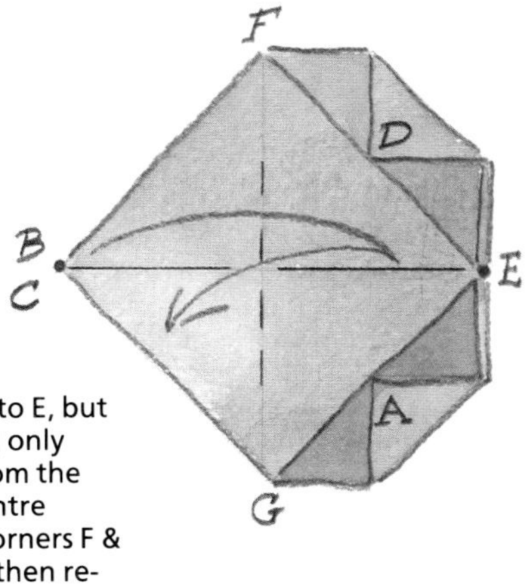

6 Fold BC to E, but creasing only halfway from the existing centre crease to corners F & G. Unfold, then re-fold back to Step 5.

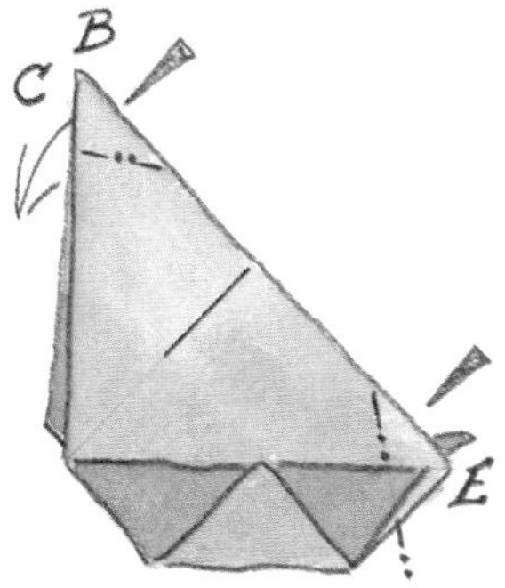

7 Reverse corners BC & E.

8 Reverse corner C only, creating the open beak.

9 Pull down the triangles front and back as a base for the bird to stand on. Crease a mountain fold front and back, so that when folded over the valley made in Step 6, the bird becomes rounded. Unfold the spine a little to assist with this crimp. Be patient! The bird has to be forced into shape, but will lock strongly when in position. Please persevere – this is definitely a move with a 'knack'! The fully-rounded shape of the body is achieved by pushing the paper outwards from the inside.

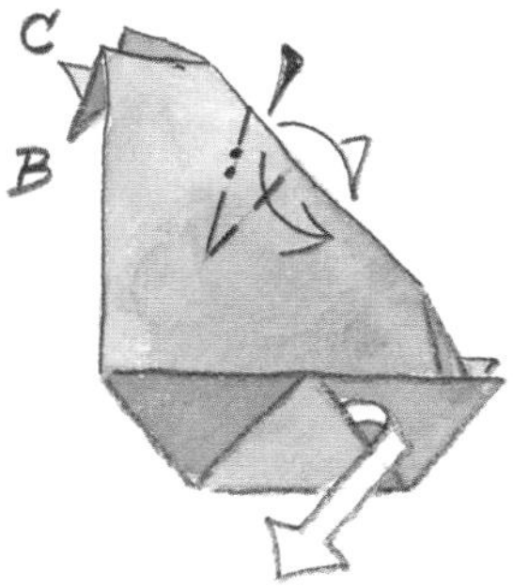

10 The Bird complete.

BUILDING

The design is included in the book to show how the rectangles and triangles that are created naturally by folding a square along halves and quarters, can be articulated to create a form such as this semi-abstract building, complete with colour-change roofs. Often, allowing the paper to do what it wants to do without contrivance is the best way to create. Use a square of origami paper, white side up.

Designed by Paul Jackson.

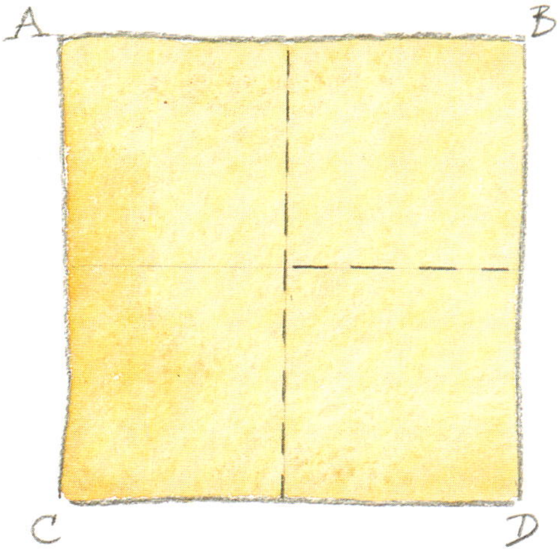

1 Crease as shown. Note the short crease at the right.

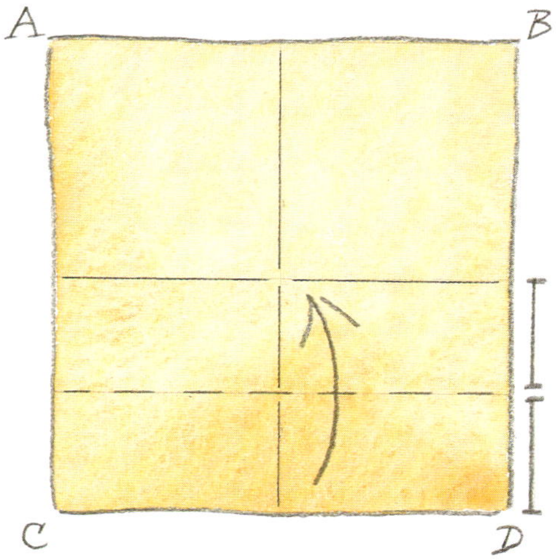

2 Fold edge CD up to the centre crease, then fold in half down the middle.

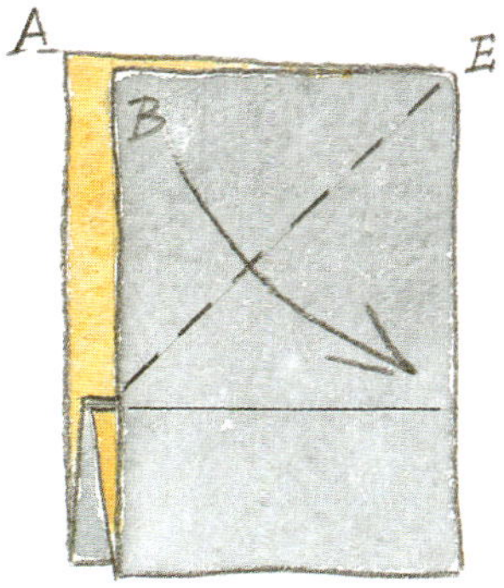

3 Fold down corner B.

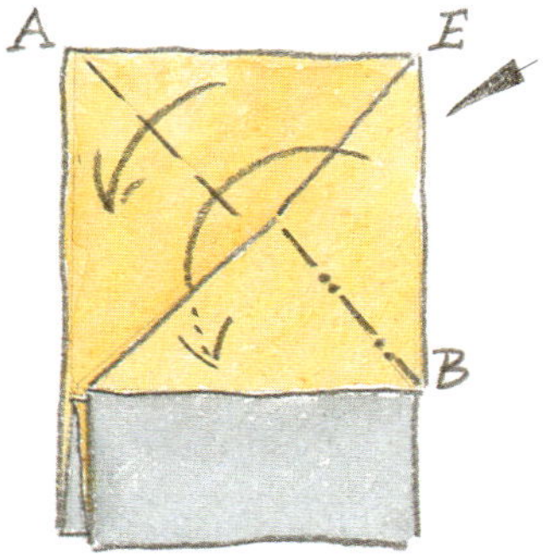

4 Reverse fold corner E behind B.

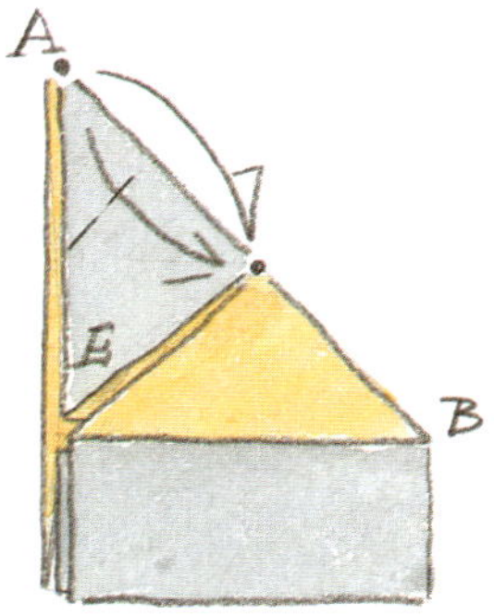

5 Fold corner A as shown, opening the paper to do this.

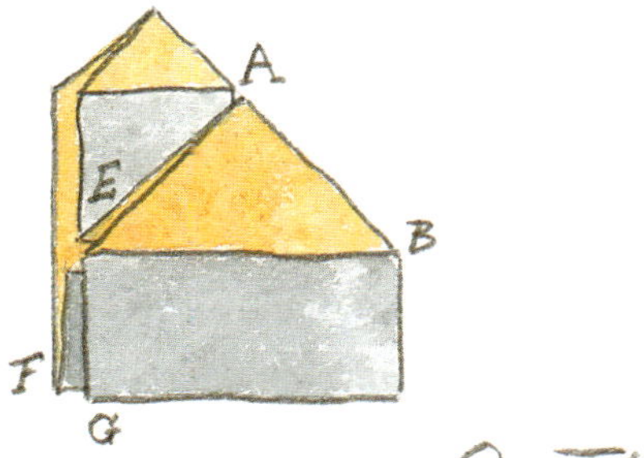

6 Turn over.

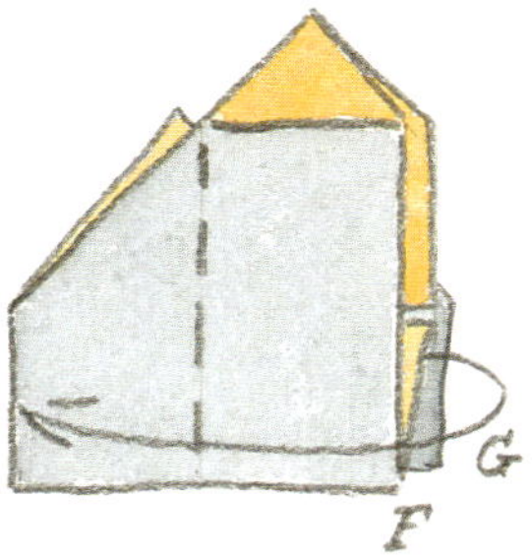

7 Swing F over to the left.

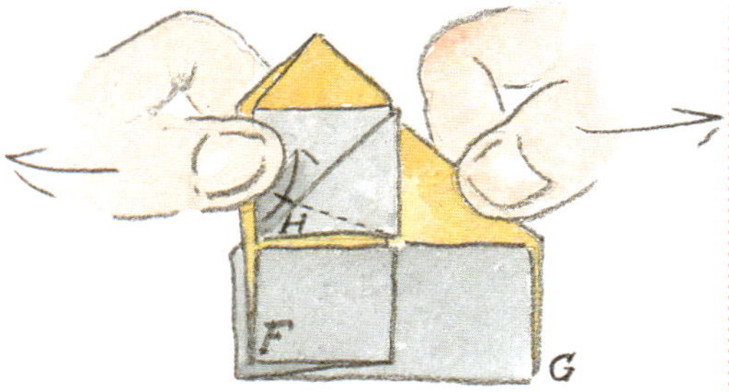

8 Hold as shown and move your hands apart. Corner H will lift. Crease and flatten H as shown . . .

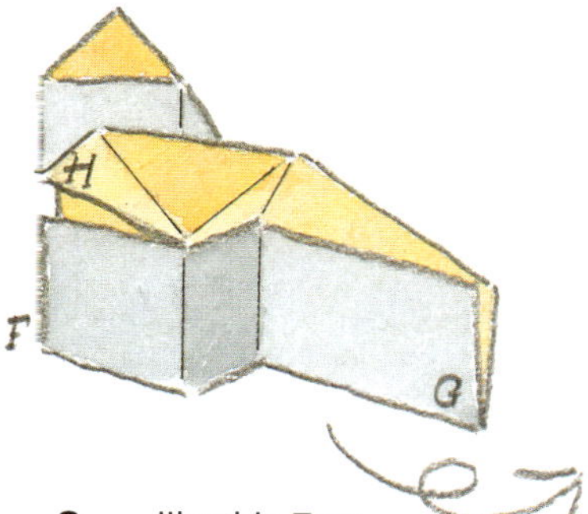

9 . . . like this. Turn over.

10 The Building complete.

PIG

The Pig, although a fairly complex project, is rewarding to construct, especially as the finished animal emerges in the final steps. Take time over the snout folds – they may appear complicated but do give a realistic result. Choose a 'pig'-coloured paper and use a 2 × 1 rectangle, the same colour on both sides. It is easy to create a whole 'family' of origami pigs: simply vary the size of the initial 2 × 1 rectangle.

Designed by Paul Jackson.

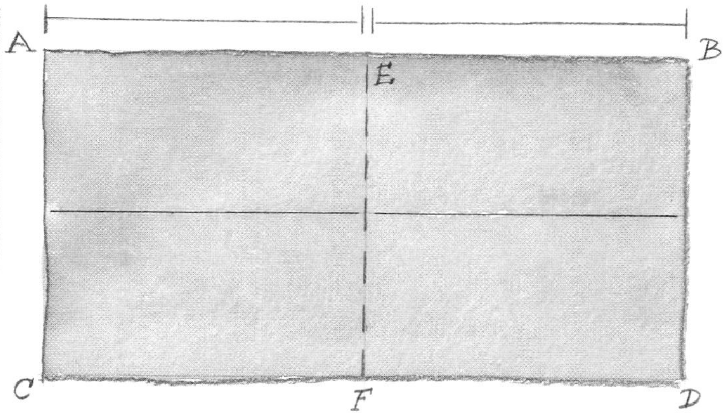

1 Crease and unfold the long horizontal centre crease, then crease and unfold down the shorter axis.

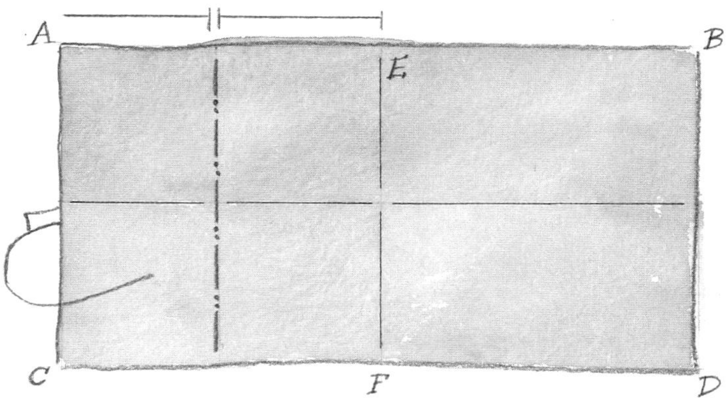

2 Fold edge AC behind.

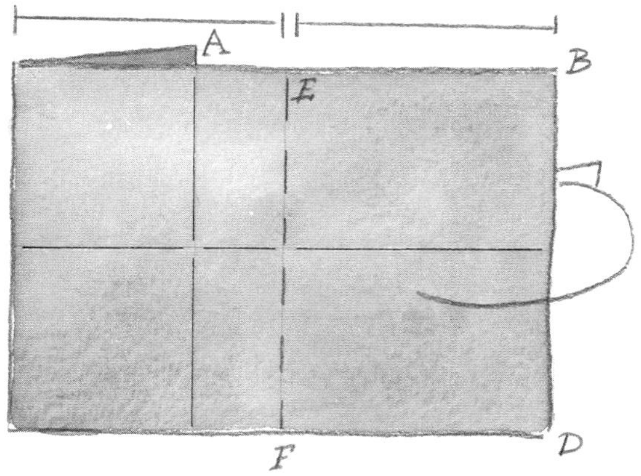

3 Fold edge BD behind to the crease made in Step 2.

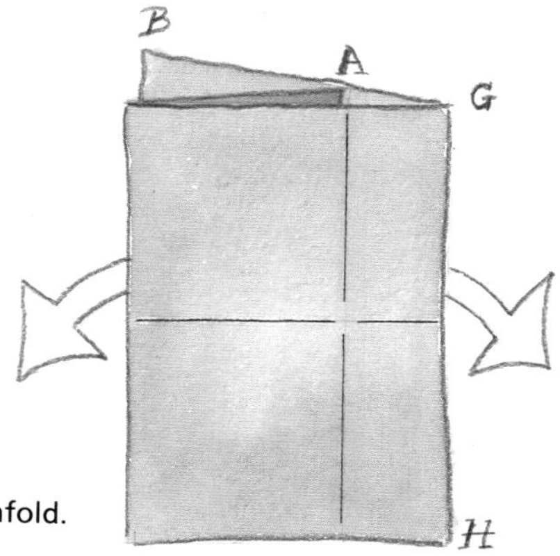

4 Unfold.

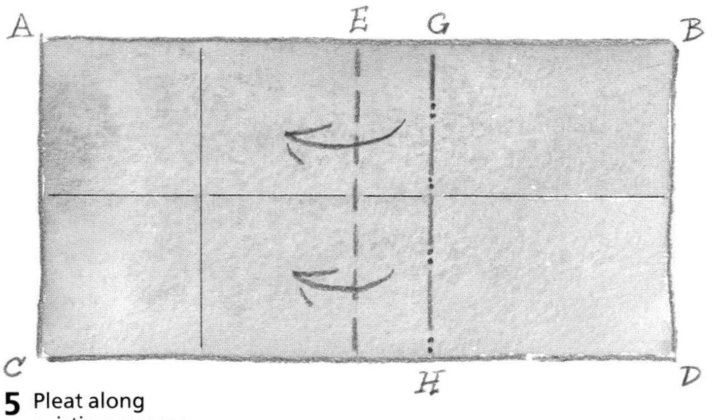

5 Pleat along existing creases EF & GH.

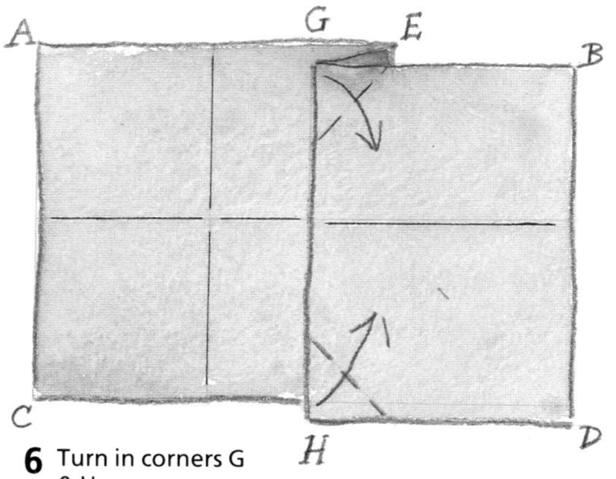

6 Turn in corners G & H.

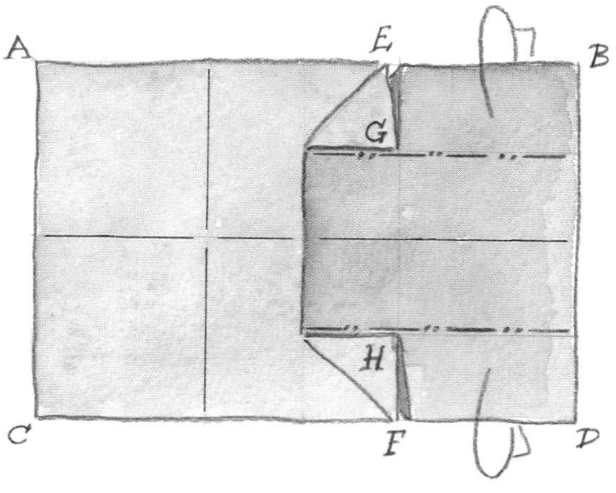

7 Swivel B & D behind, along horizontal mountain creases. Note the shape of Step 8.

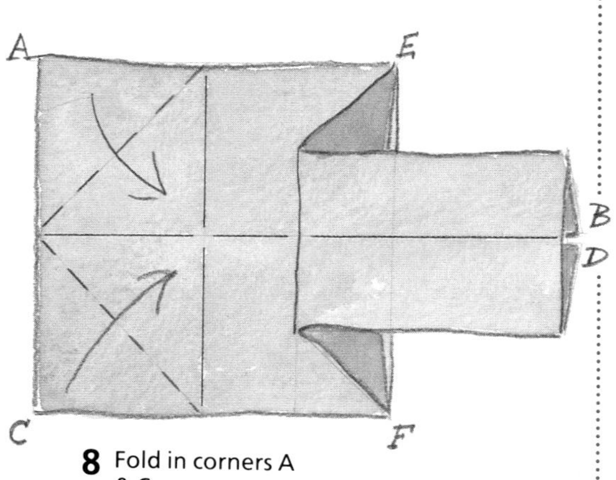

8 Fold in corners A & C.

(continued . . .)

PIG *(continued)*

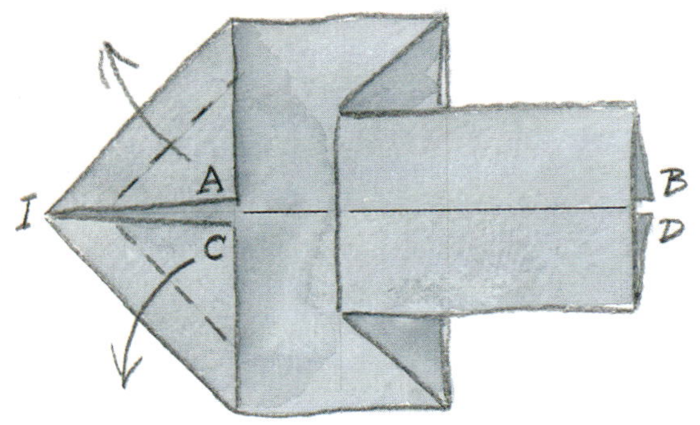

9 Fold A & C back out, the creases tapering towards I.

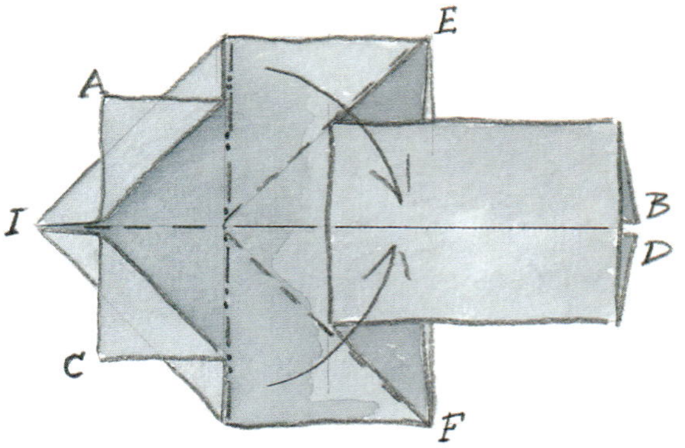

10 Collapse as shown, to make the paper 3D.

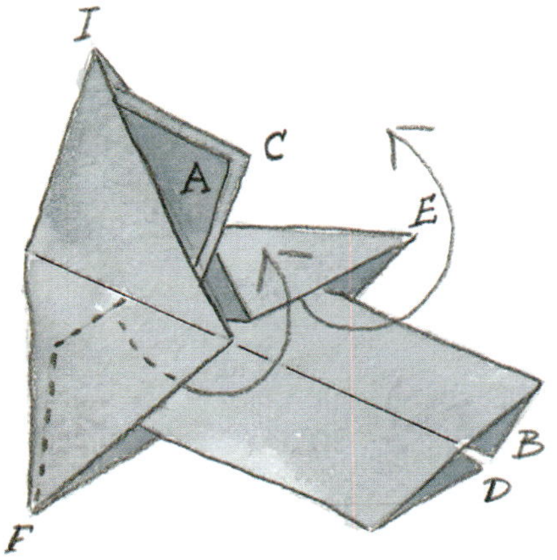

11 Pull out the hidden ledge . . .

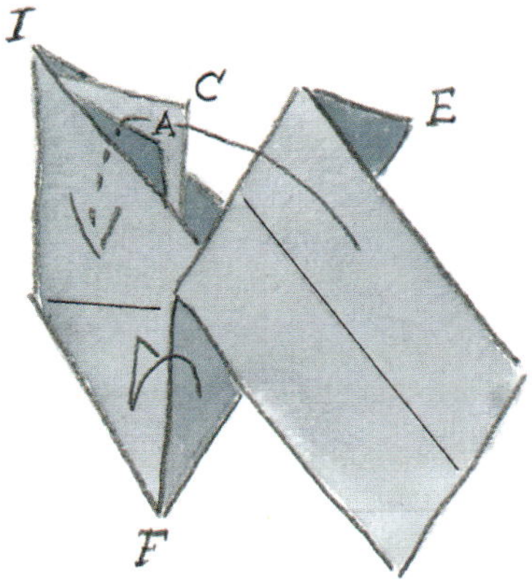

12 . . . and feed it back into the pig between A & C . . .

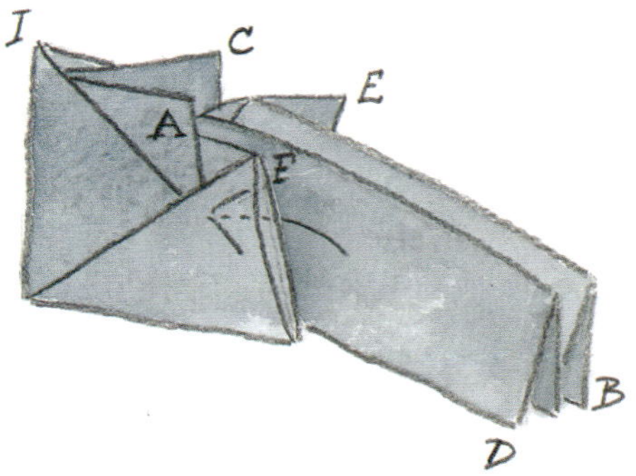

13 . . . like this, bringing F & E back together again.

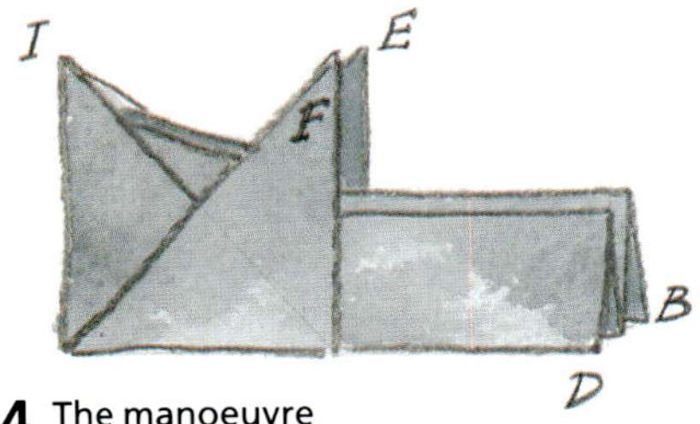

14 The manoeuvre is complete – its purpose is to stop the pig from splaying its front legs. Turn the paper the right way up.

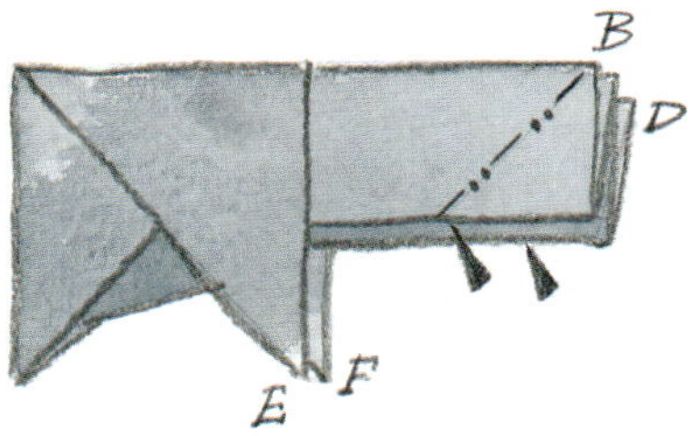

15 Reverse fold at B & D.

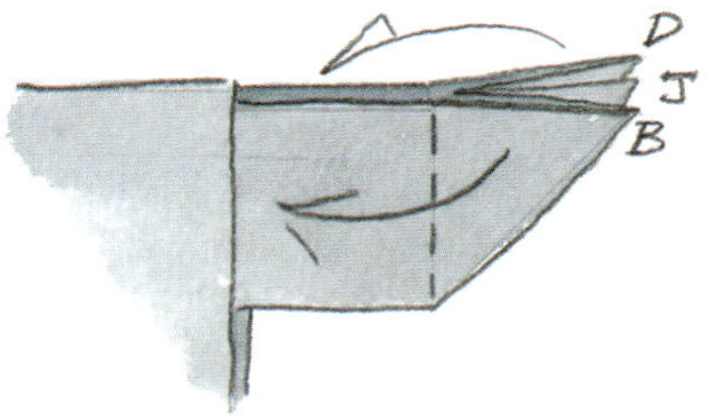

16 Fold B & D towards the neck.

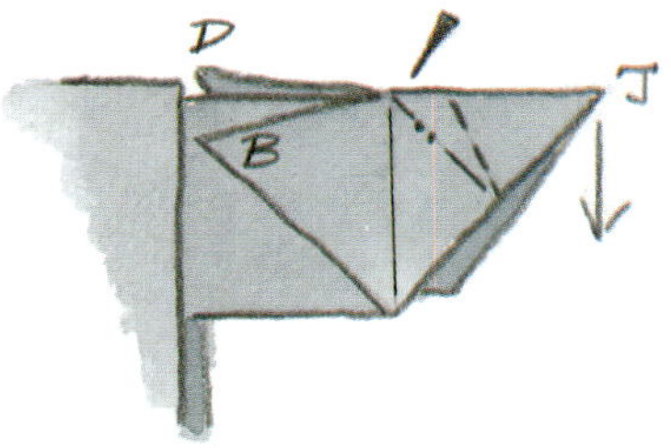

17 Create two reverse folds near the snout, forming a crimp.

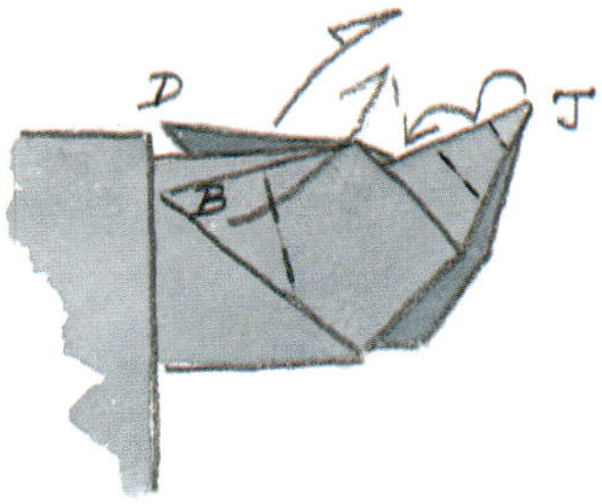

18 Fold the snout over and over. Fold the ears forward.

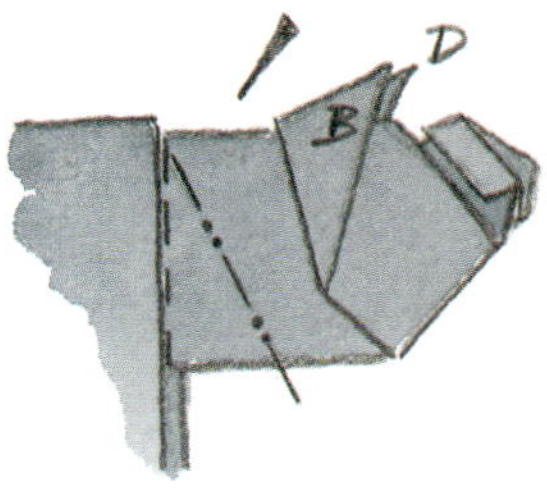

19 Crimp the neck, lowering the head.

20 Pleat the tail.

21 The Pig complete.

STANDING HEART

Hearts are a favourite origami theme, particularly when combined with another element, such as a heart pierced by an arrow, twin hearts or a heart on a finger ring. Here is a conventional single heart, but one which could make an attractive standing ornament for a mantelpiece or desk top. Use a square of red/white origami paper, red side up.

Designed by Paul Jackson.

(Continued . . .)

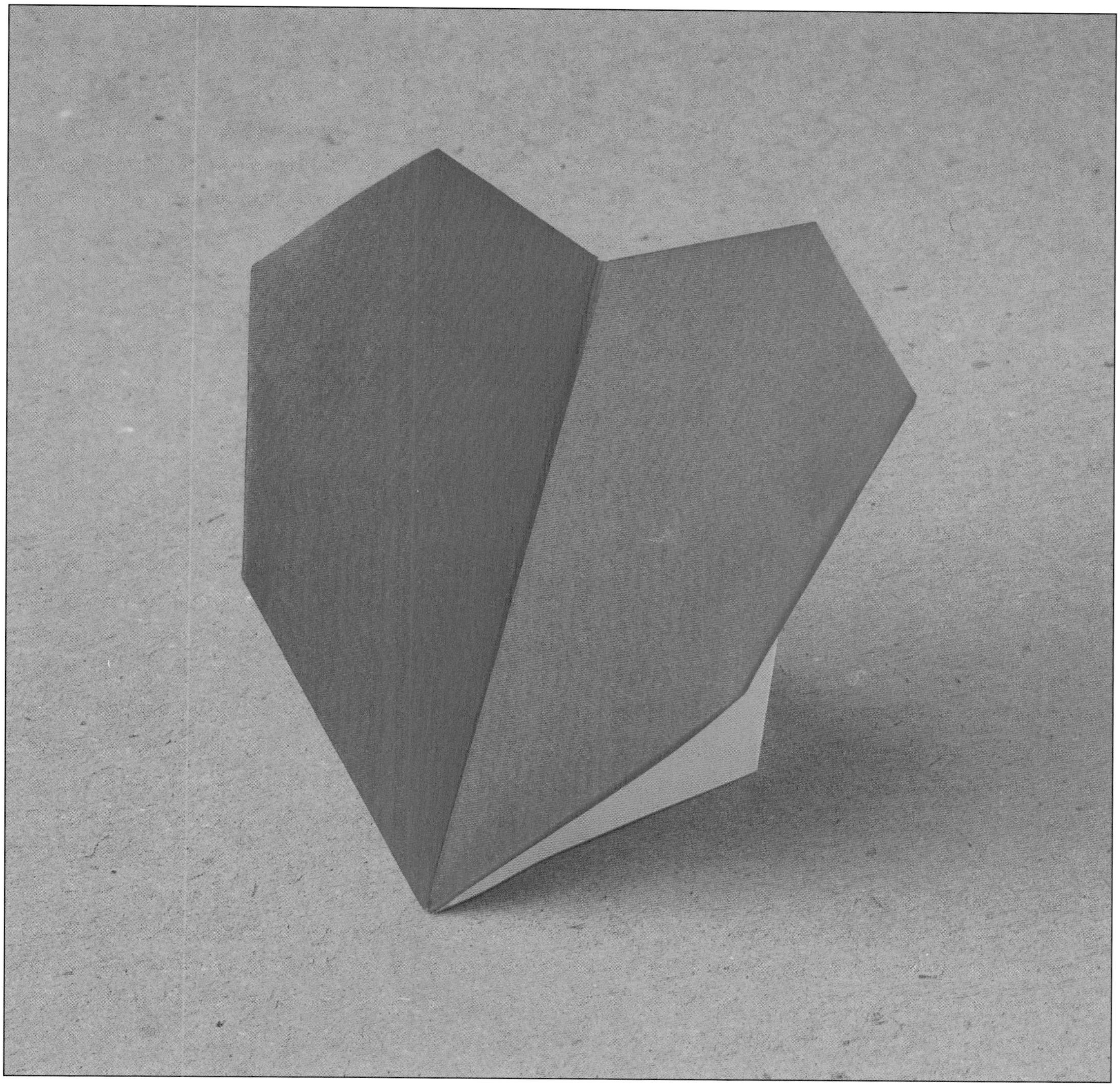

STANDING HEART

(continued)

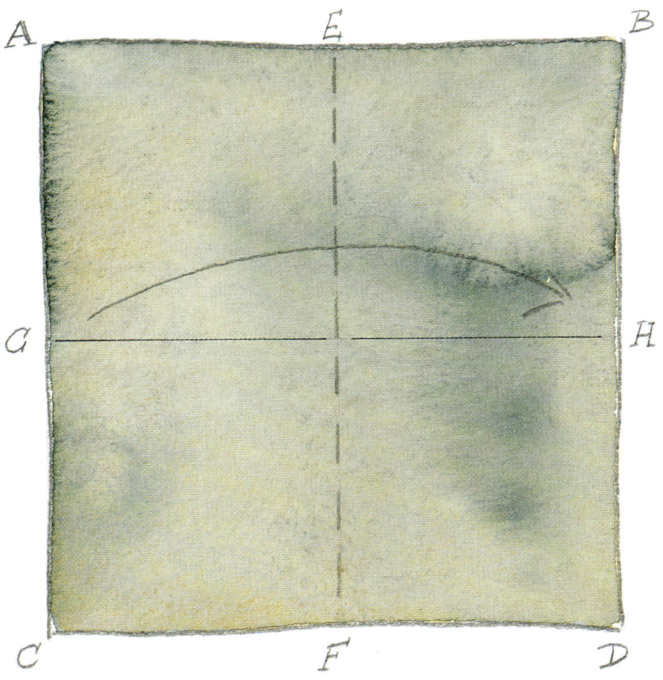

1 Crease and unfold across the middle, then fold AC across to BD.

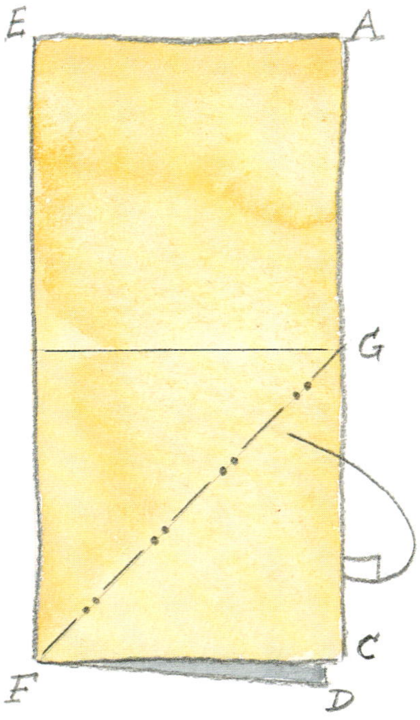

2 Mountain fold corners C & D inside.

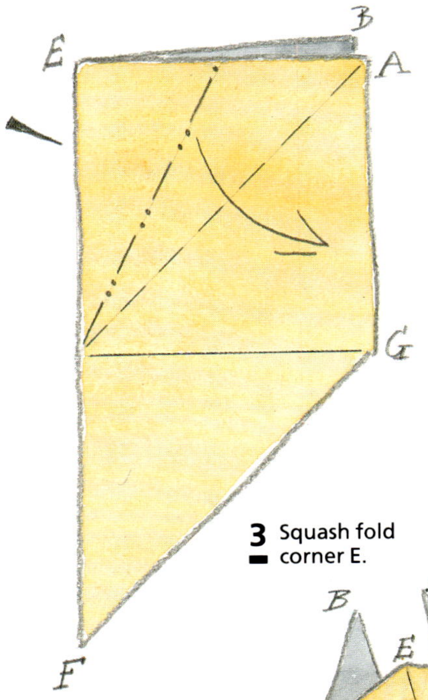

3 Squash fold corner E.

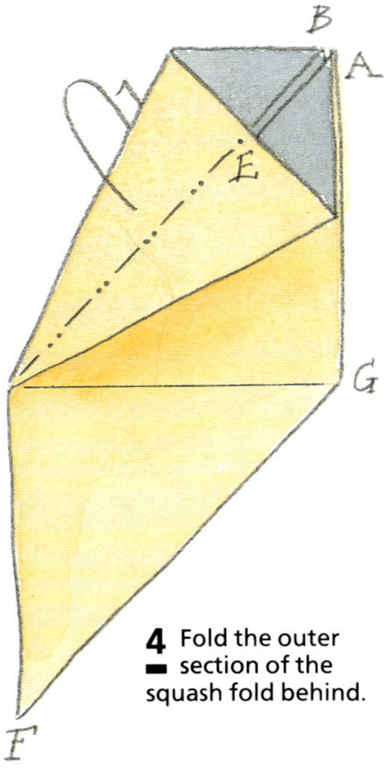

4 Fold the outer section of the squash fold behind.

5 Open the paper between G & H. Turn over to see . . .

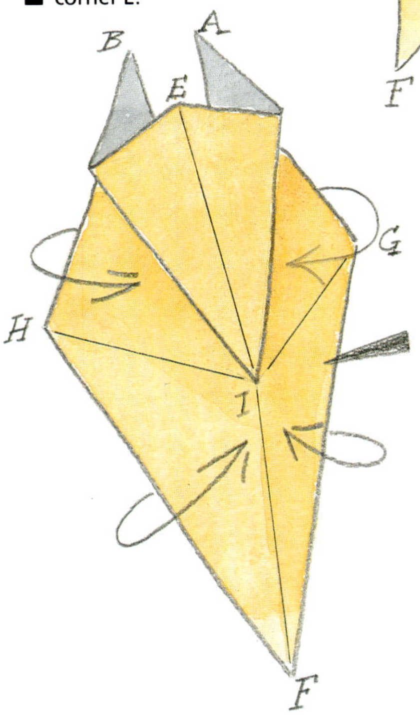

6 . . . a pyramid. Corner I is the apex (the corner nearest to you). Push on I so that it inverts and the paper pops inside out. Corner I is now the furthest point from you, not the nearest.

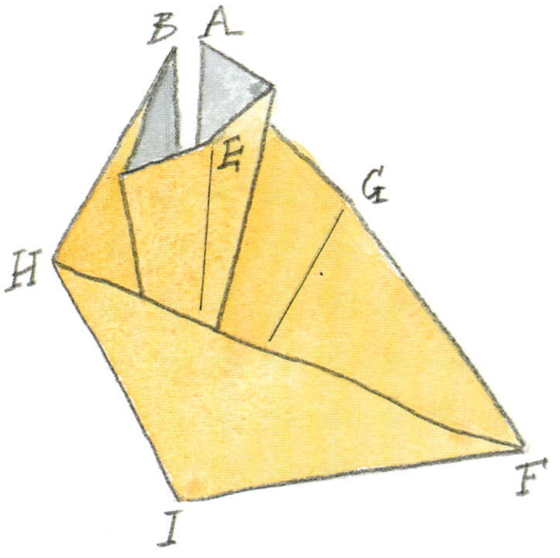

7 This is the shape. Note I.

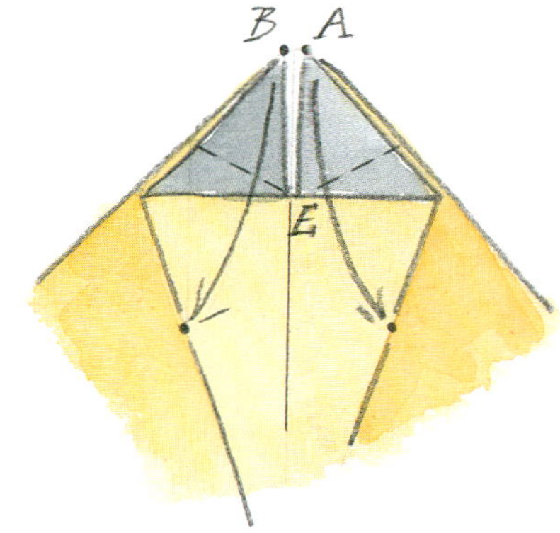

8 Fold down B & A, dot to dot.

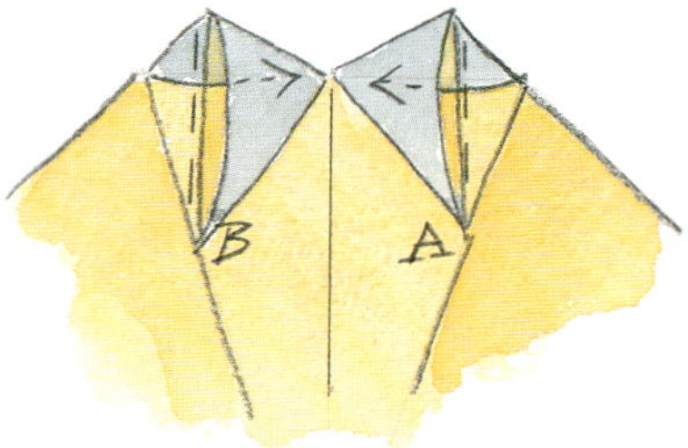

9 Tuck the excess paper into the pockets at B & A.

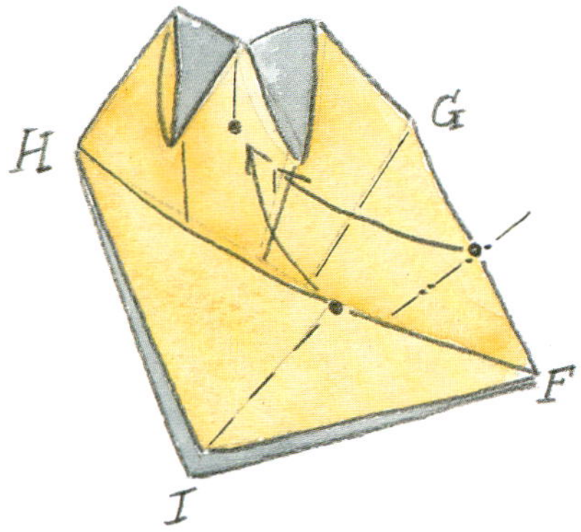

10 Collapse as shown, folding the two outer dots onto the inner one.

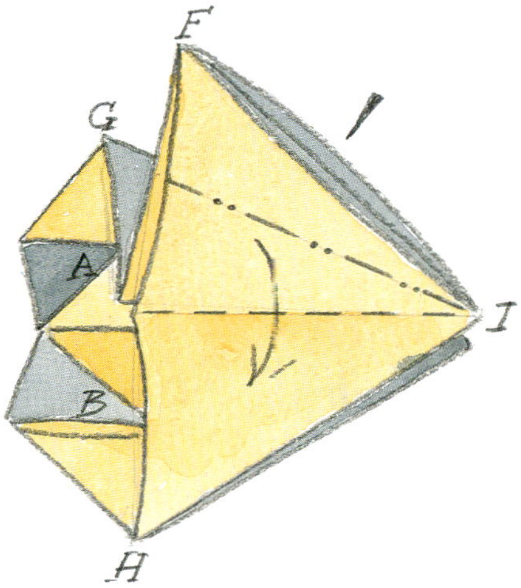

11 Squash F, presently standing upright.

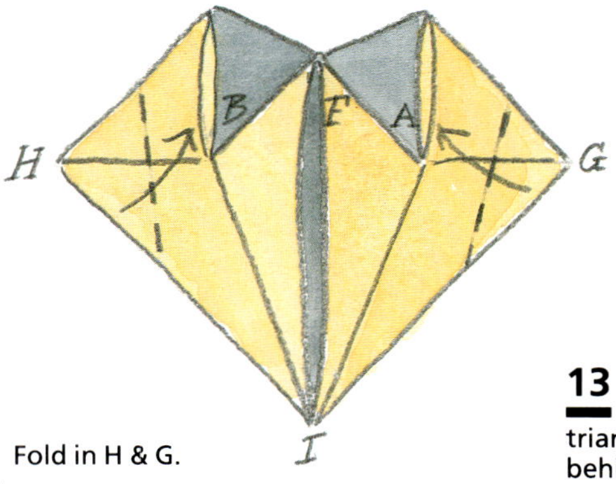

12 Fold in H & G.

13 Fold over G to lock the triangle to the edge behind.

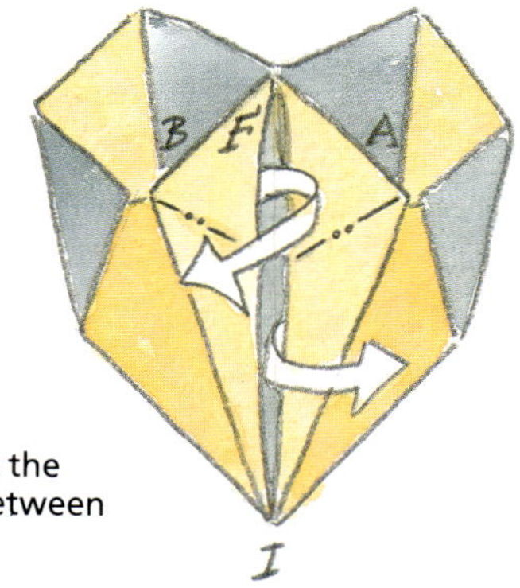

14 Open out the pocket between F & I . . .

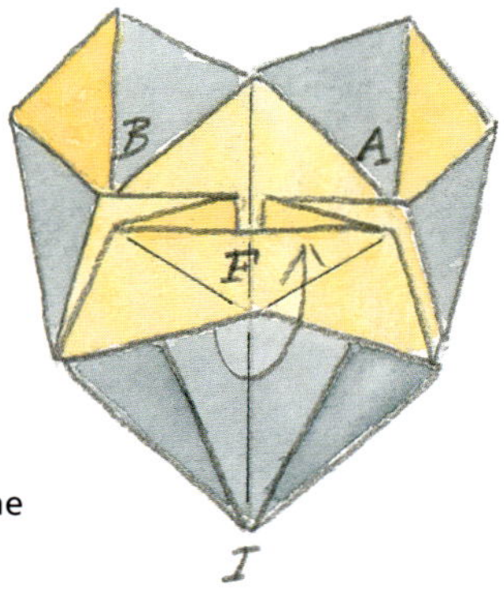

15 . . . like this, flattening the paper.

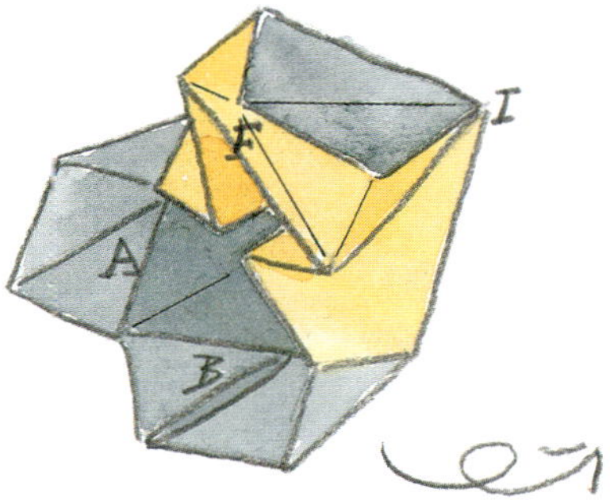

16 Partly close the pocket again. Turn over.

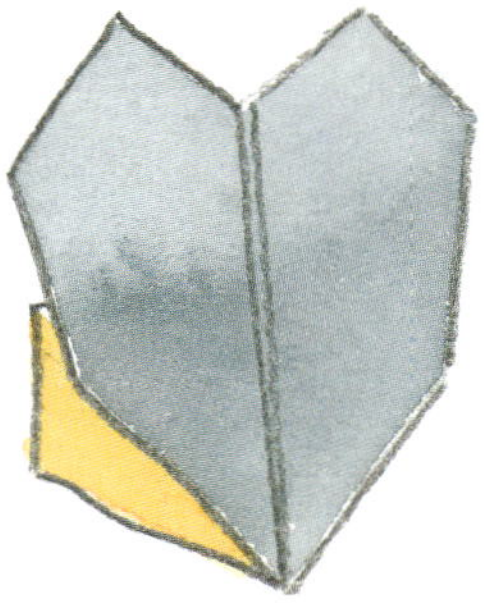

17 The Standing Heart complete.

FIGHTER JET

There are purists who may cry 'cheat' at this design, because it is made from two pieces of paper. A near-identical one-piece version from a 3 × 2 rectangle post-dated this original design, but is messy to make and lacks the simplicity of the original. Use two identical squares of paper of the same size and colour, coloured the same on both sides.

Designed by Paul Jackson.

SHEET 1

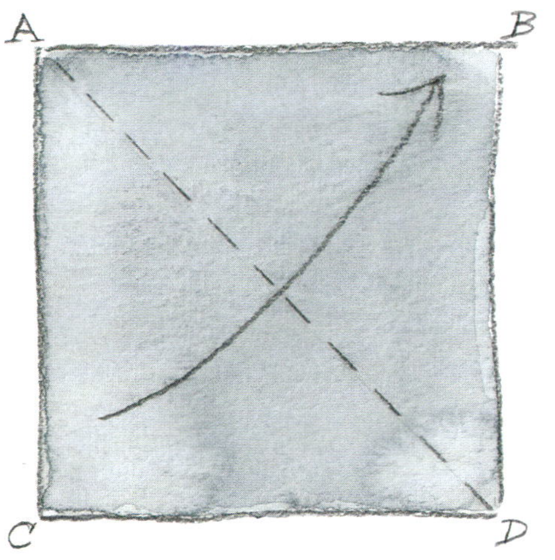

1 Fold C to B.

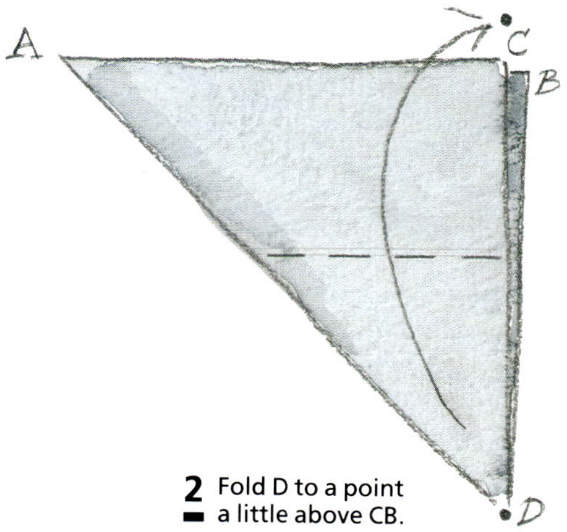

2 Fold D to a point a little above CB.

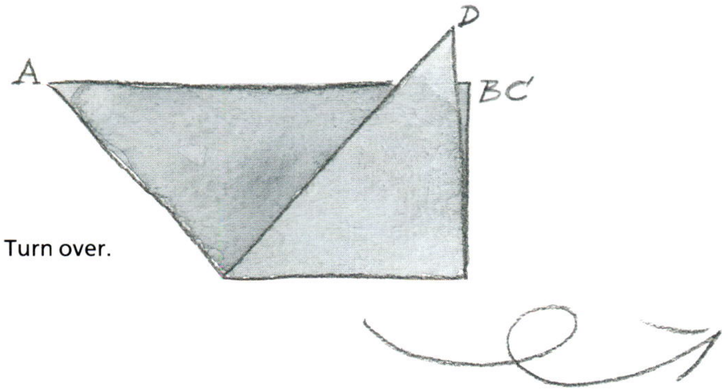

3 Turn over.

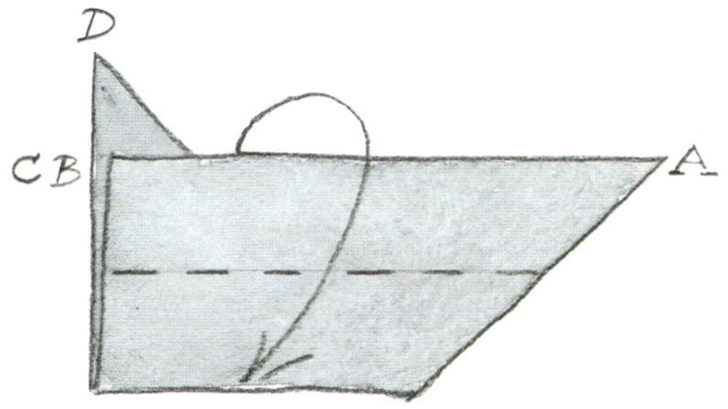

4 Fold edge CB,A down to the bottom edge.

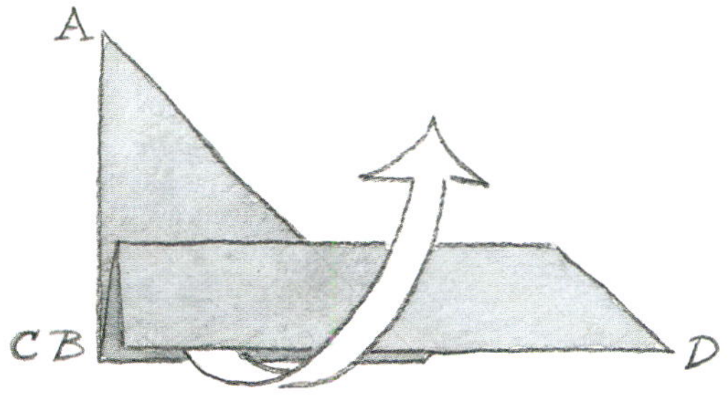

5 Completely unfold.

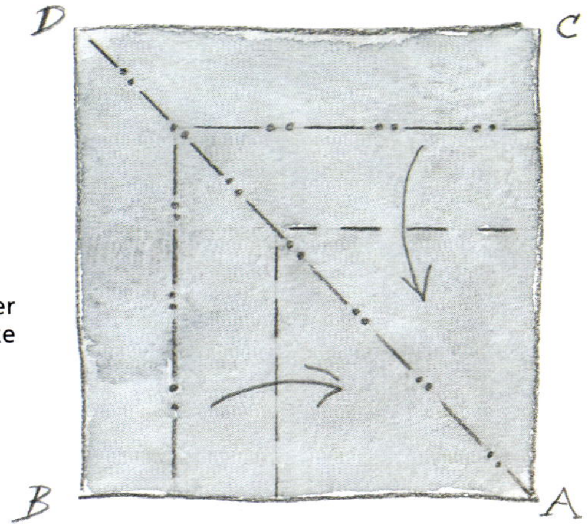

6 Re-crease as shown. The paper will collapse to make Step 7.

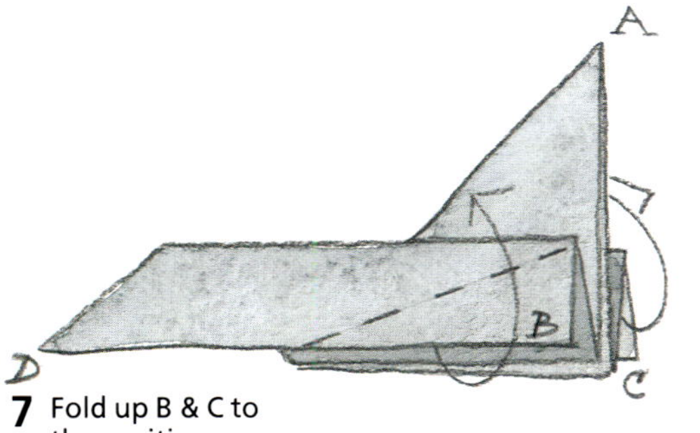

7 Fold up B & C to the position shown in Step 8.

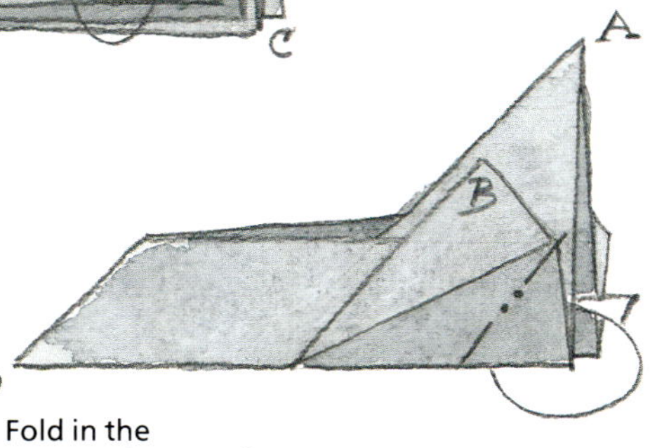

8 Fold in the corners, front and back.

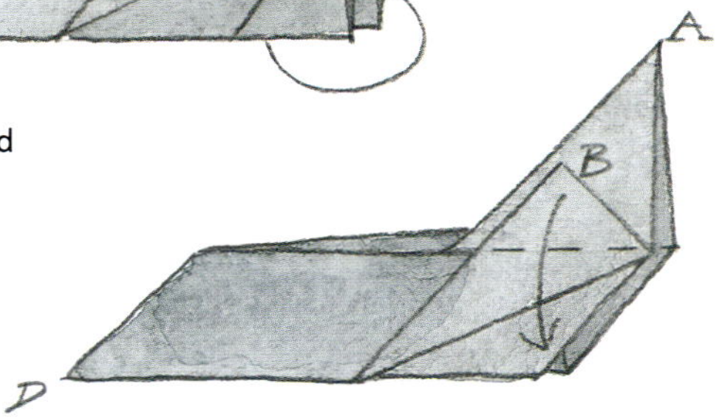

9 Fold down the wings.

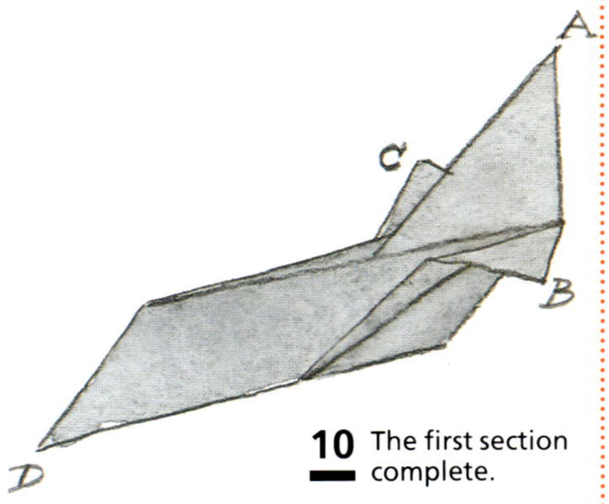

10 The first section complete.

(Continued . . .)

FIGHTER JET *(continued)*

SHEET 2

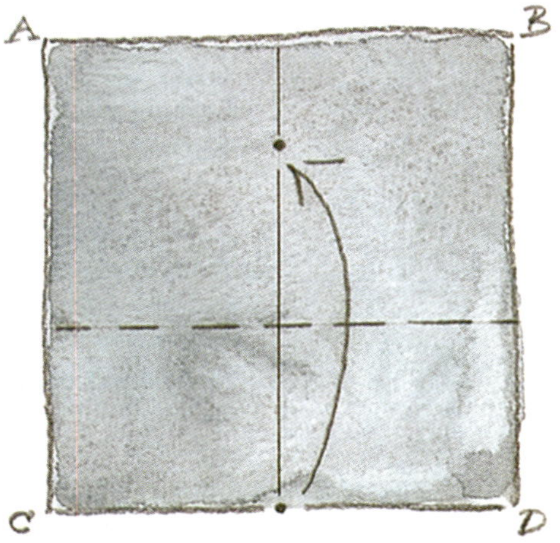

1 Crease and unfold down the centre, then fold up edge CD to the position shown.

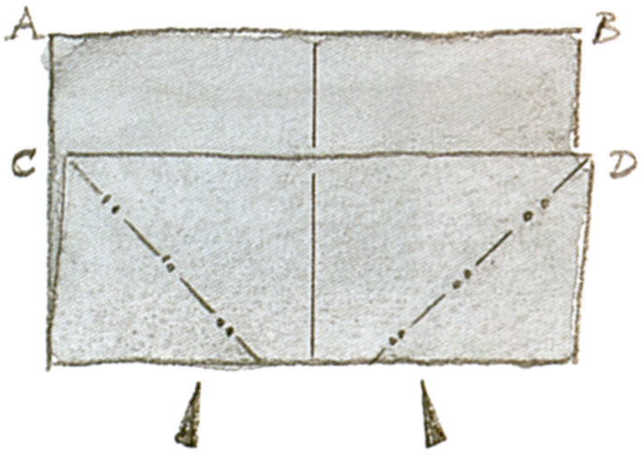

2 Reverse fold the corners.

3 Fold in half.

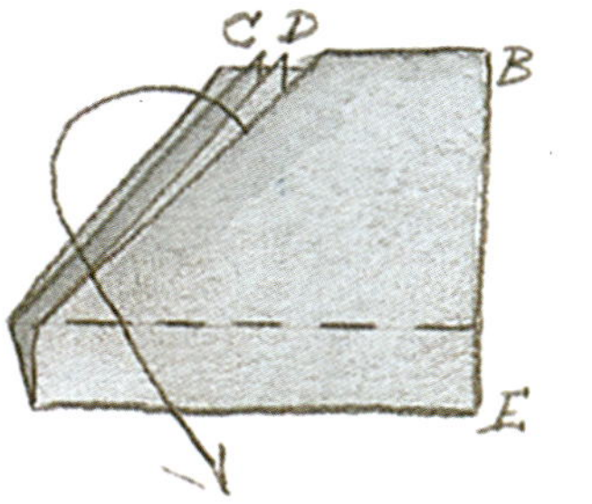

4 Fold down B & A.

5 The second section complete.

ASSEMBLY

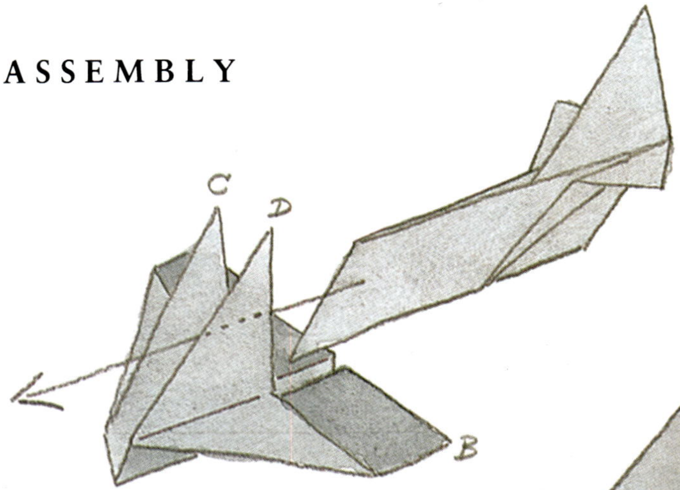

1 Draw the fuselage forward between C & D.

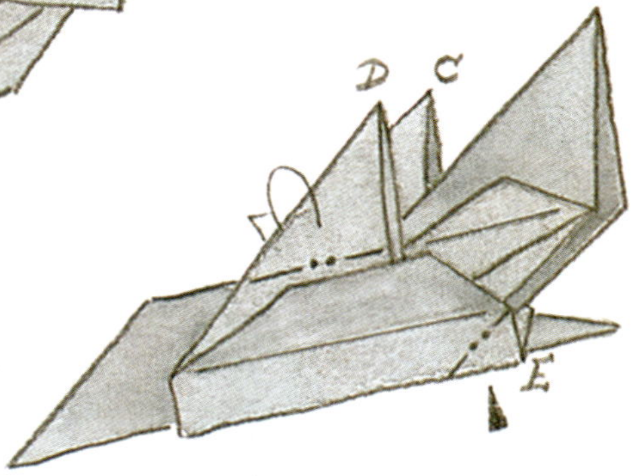

2 Tuck D & C into the top of the fuselage, locking the wing section to it. Reverse fold E into the base of the fuselage.

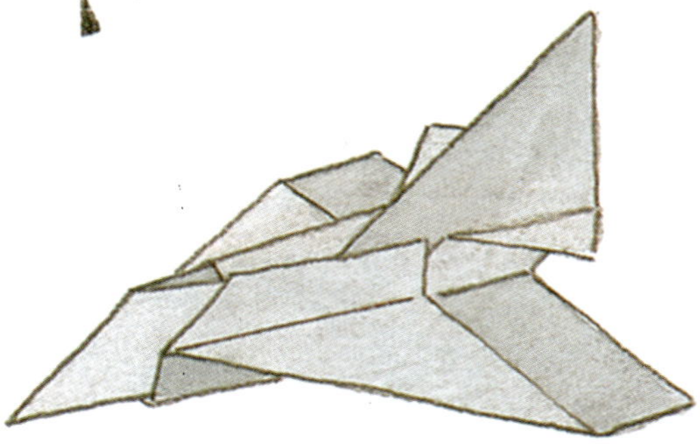

3 The Fighter Jet complete.

ADVANCED PROJECTS

CAMEL

The shape formed in Step 5 is commonly known in origami as the Fish base, and for obvious reasons. Apart from fishes (and a camel), the base at Step 6 is ideally shaped to create many different birds – the blunt points make wings and the sharp points form a head and tail. Use a 15–20 cm (6–8 in) square of paper, same colour both sides.

Designed by Paul Jackson.

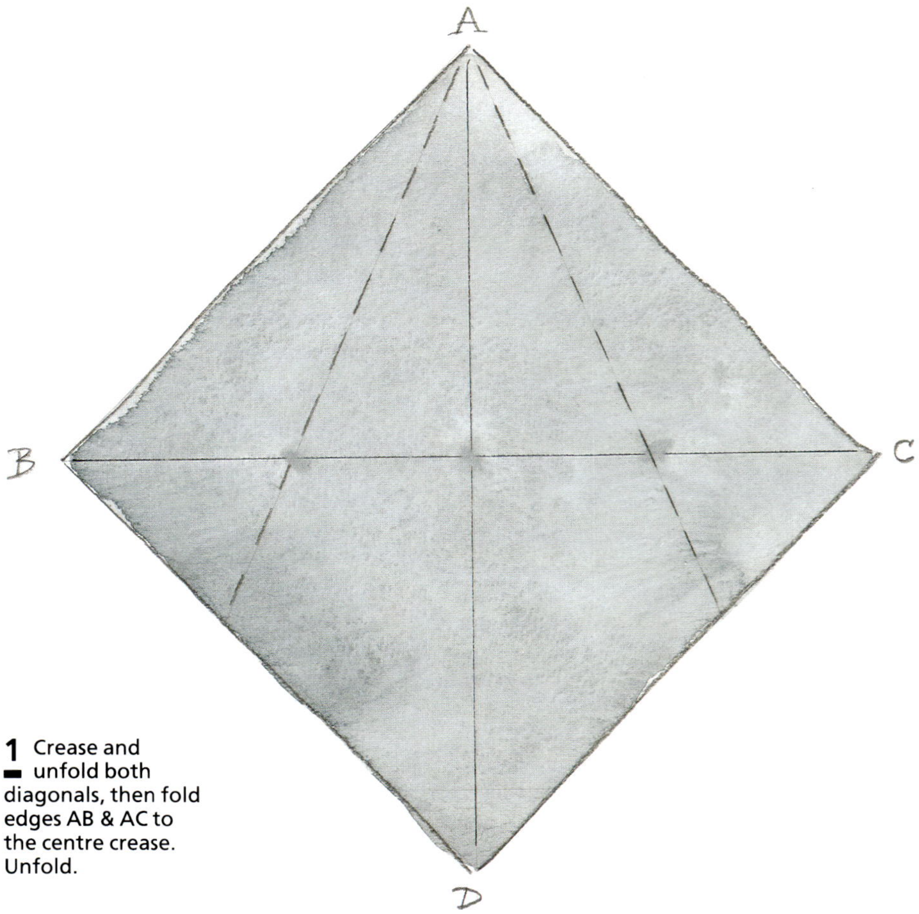

1 Crease and unfold both diagonals, then fold edges AB & AC to the centre crease. Unfold.

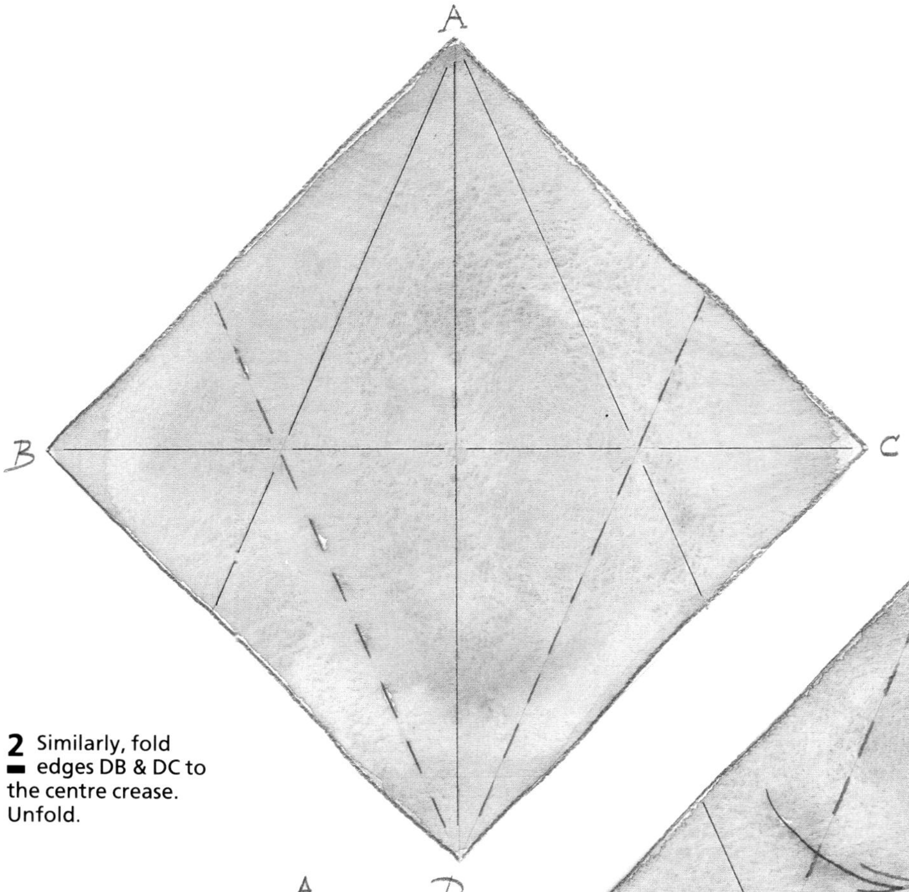

2 Similarly, fold edges DB & DC to the centre crease. Unfold.

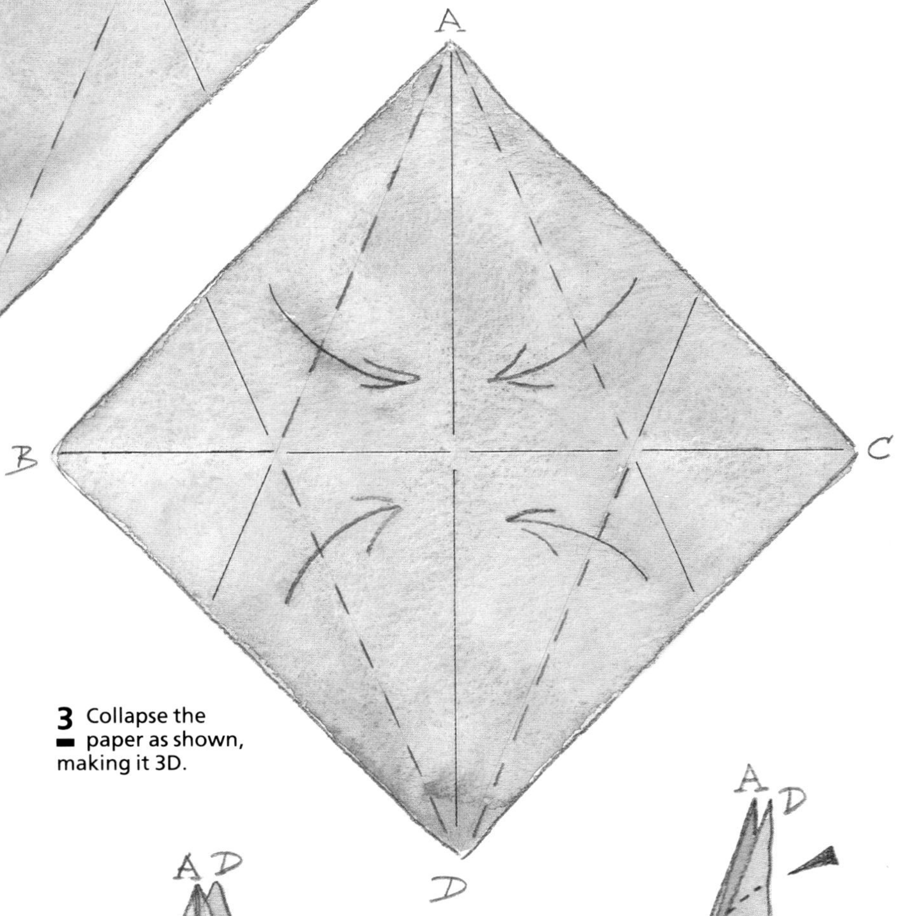

3 Collapse the paper as shown, making it 3D.

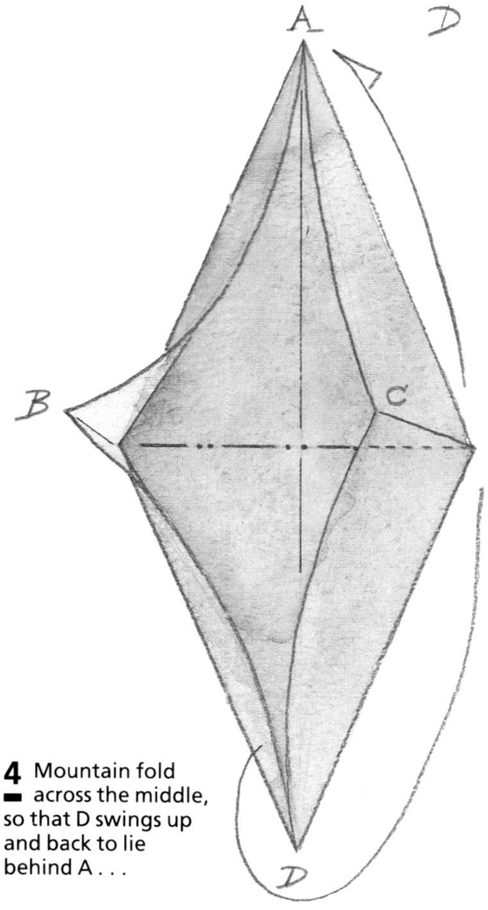

4 Mountain fold across the middle, so that D swings up and back to lie behind A . . .

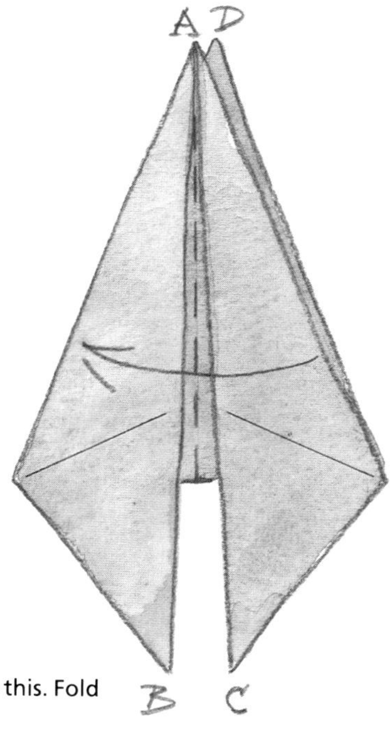

5 . . . like this. Fold in half.

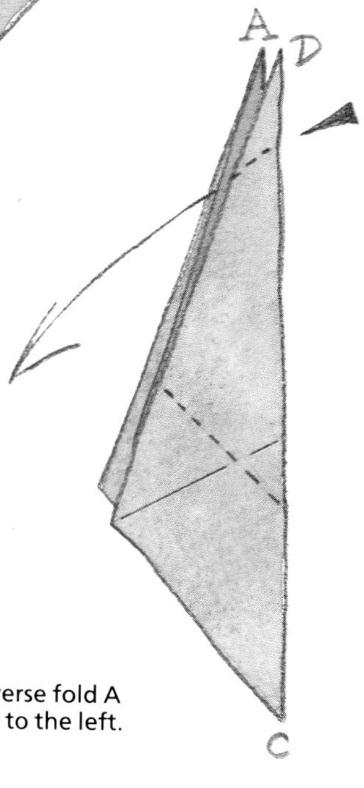

6 Reverse fold A out to the left.

(Continued . . .)

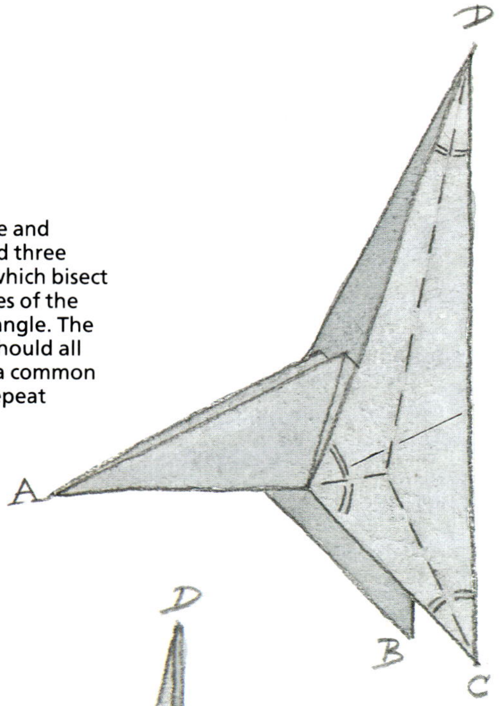

7 Crease and unfold three creases which bisect the angles of the large triangle. The creases should all meet at a common point. Repeat behind.

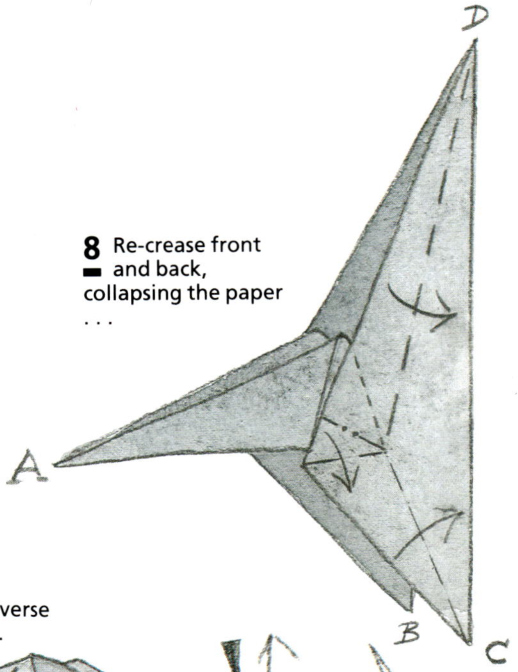

8 Re-crease front and back, collapsing the paper . . .

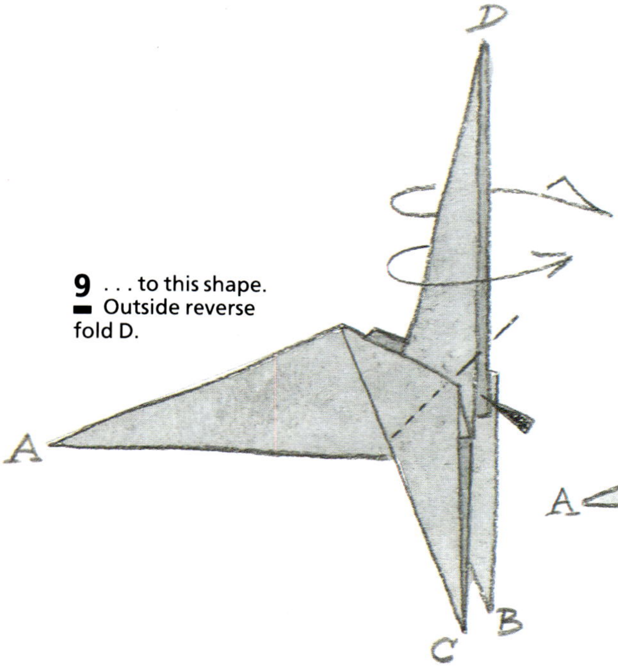

9 . . . to this shape. Outside reverse fold D.

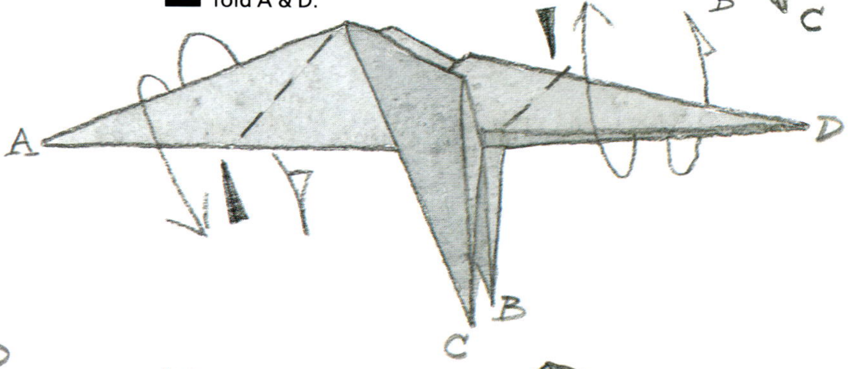

10 Outside reverse fold A & D.

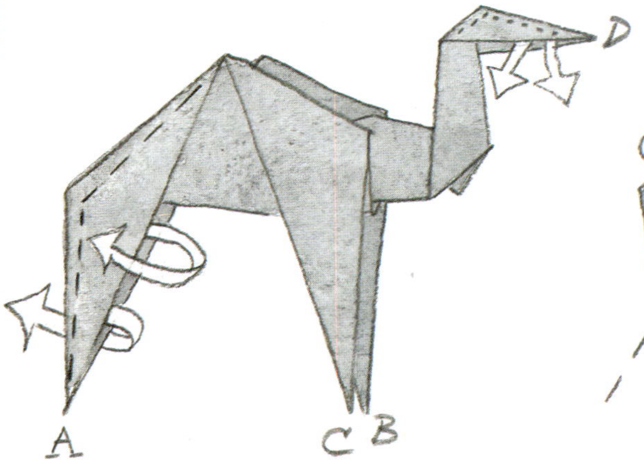

11 Release the layers at A & D. At A, fold the released layers back over the legs. At D, allow the layers to remain visible, increasing the width of the head.

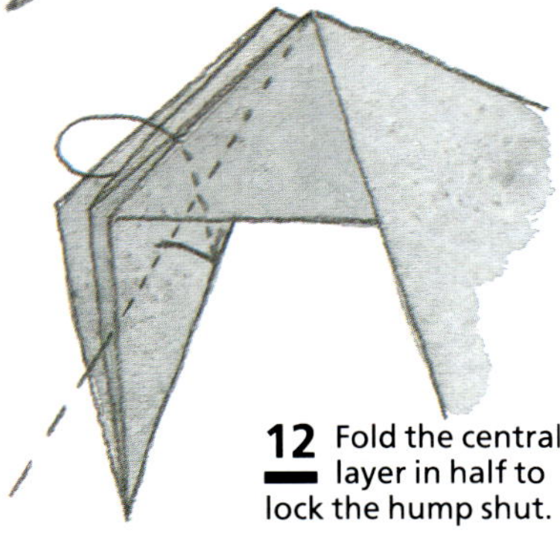

12 Fold the central layer in half to lock the hump shut.

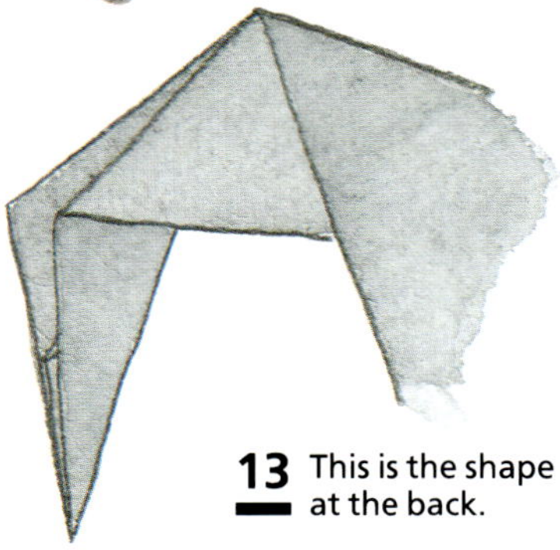

13 This is the shape at the back.

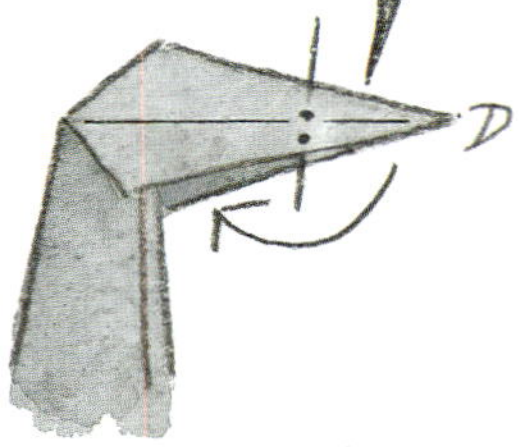

14 Reverse fold D inside.

15 Turn the muzzle inside out.

16 The Camel complete.

CHINESE VASE

This wonderful design was first introduced to the West by Dr Philip Shen (whose bowl appears earlier) and popularized in the USA by the late Verdi Adams. It has a beautifully direct sequence of folds, climaxed by the extraordinary opening out from 2D to 3D. Use a square of paper, not too small. If using origami paper, start white side up.

Traditional design.

(*Continued . . .*)

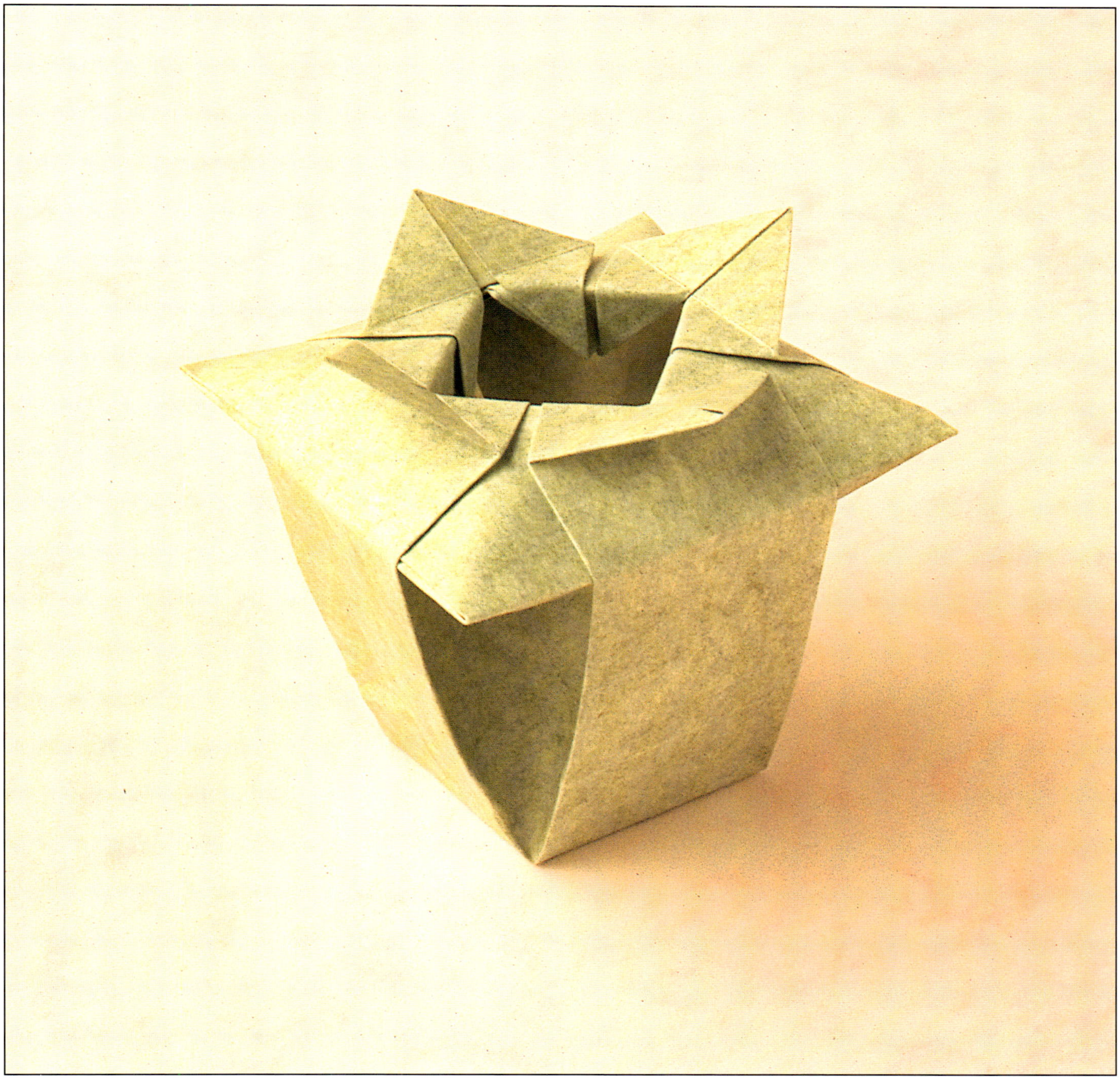

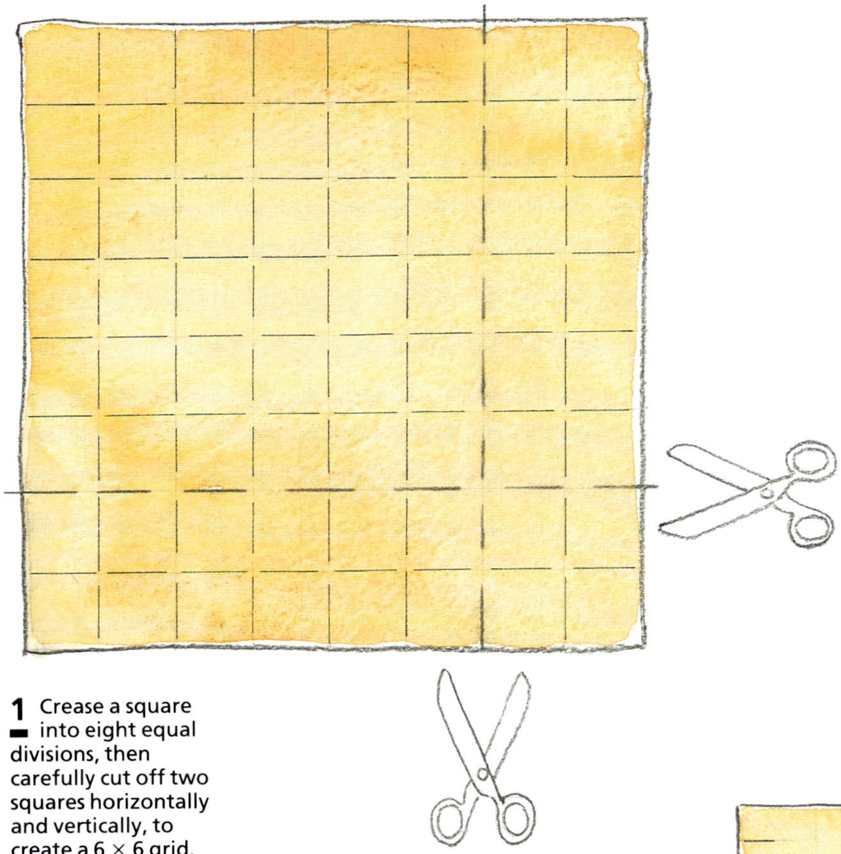

1 Crease a square into eight equal divisions, then carefully cut off two squares horizontally and vertically, to create a 6 × 6 grid.

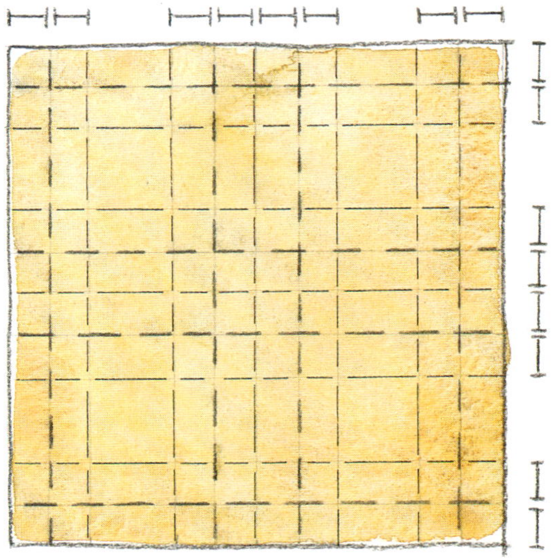

2 Add extra creases where shown.

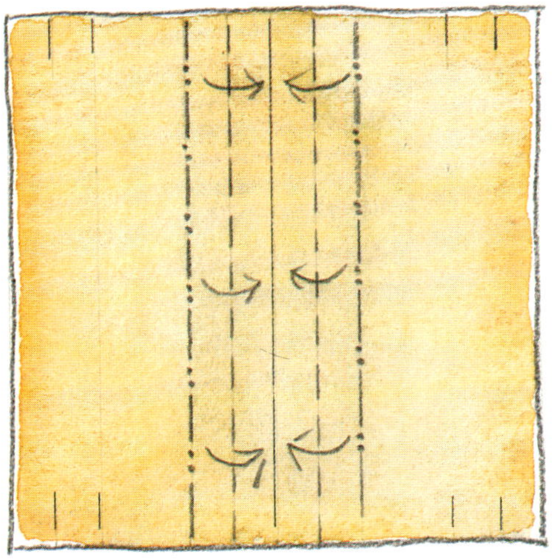

3 Pleat the paper as shown.

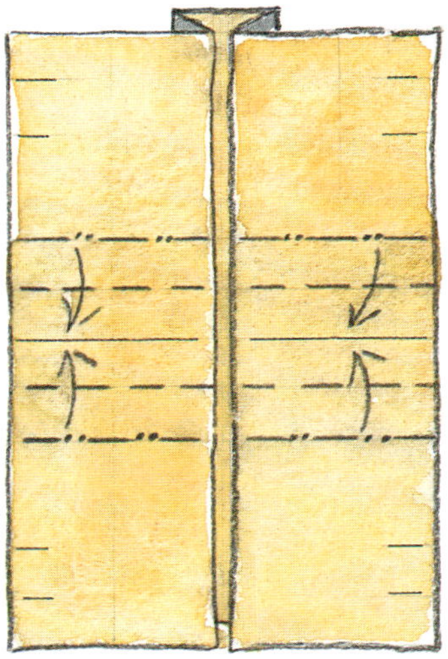

4 Similarly, pleat horizontally.

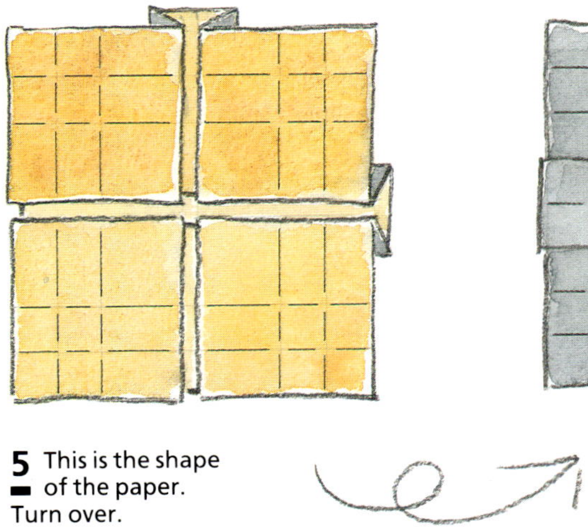

5 This is the shape of the paper. Turn over.

6 This is the shape.

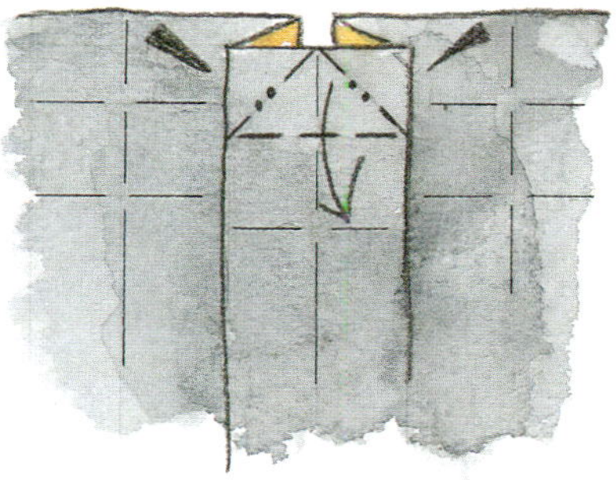

7 Lift and squash the end of each pleat . . .

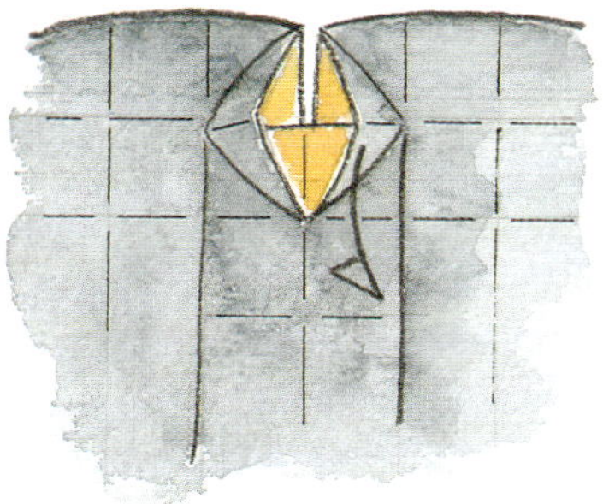

8 . . . like this.

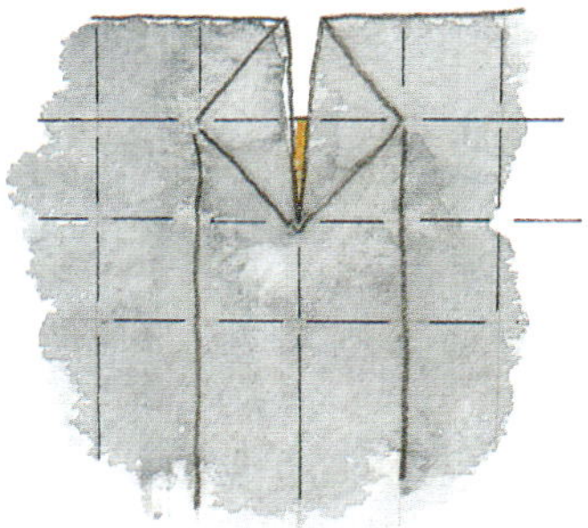

9 Repeat along each edge.

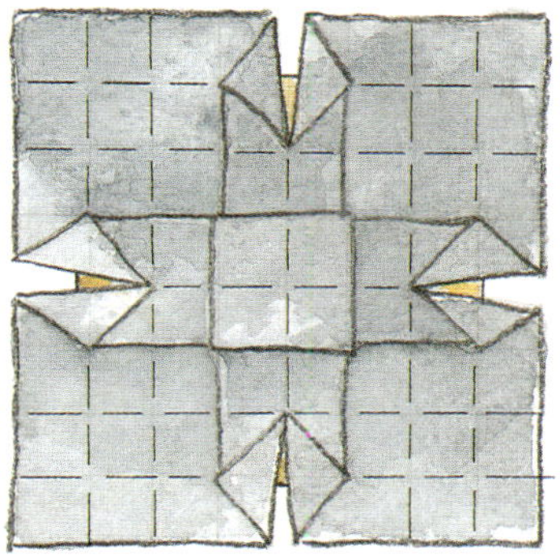

10 Here are the squashed pleats. Turn over.

11 Crease and unfold each loose corner at the pleats. This is to prepare for Step 14.

12 Fold the sides to the middle.

13 Fold the top and bottom edges to the middle, tucking the corners deep into the pockets.

14 Fold the loose corners inside, to create a square opening . . .

15 . . . like this. Turn over.

16 This is the fun part! Carefully tease out the trapped layers inside the pleats to make the vase 3D. Do this by rotating the paper frequently, so that all four sides are developed equally.

17 This is the result. Put a finger into the vase and round out the square, flat corners at the top.

18 The Chinese Vase complete.

SEATED FIGURE

One of the delights of origami is its ability to conjure complex subjects from relatively simple folds, to create not a detailed representation, but a stylized abstraction. When successful, the result is poetic, both in concept and form. Use a square of origami paper, coloured side up.

Designed by Paul Jackson.

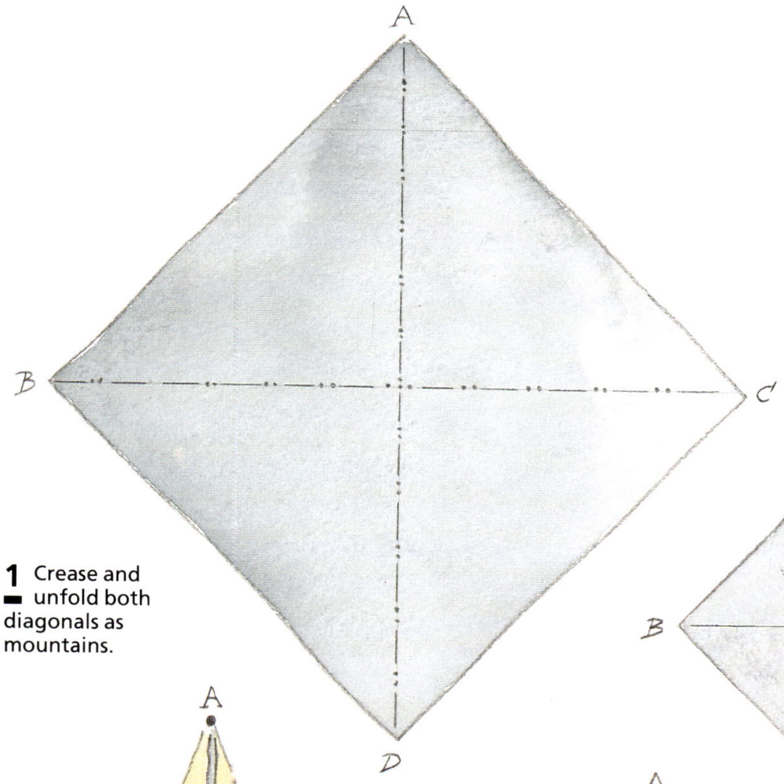

1 Crease and unfold both diagonals as mountains.

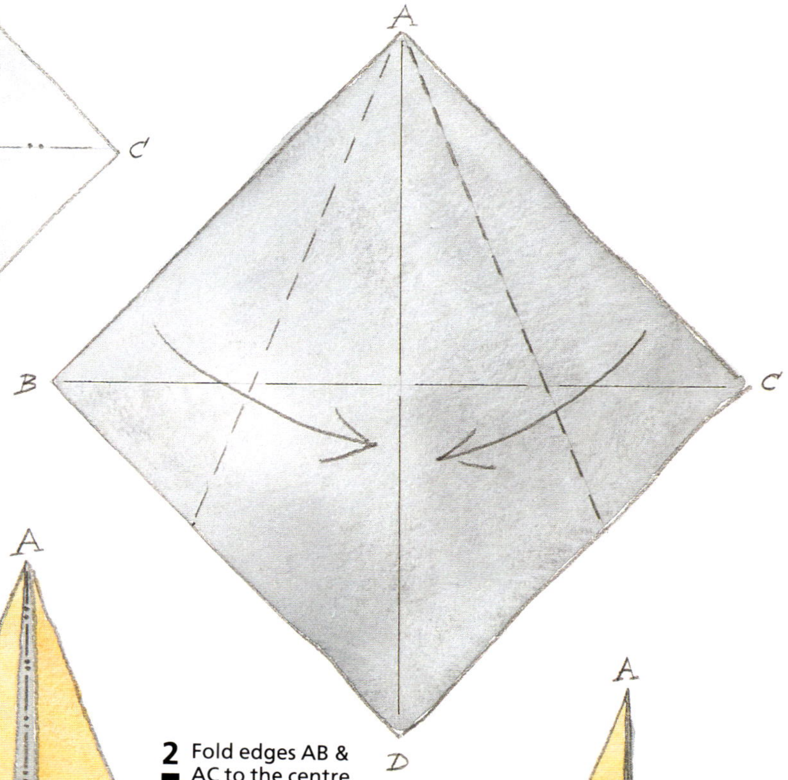

2 Fold edges AB & AC to the centre crease.

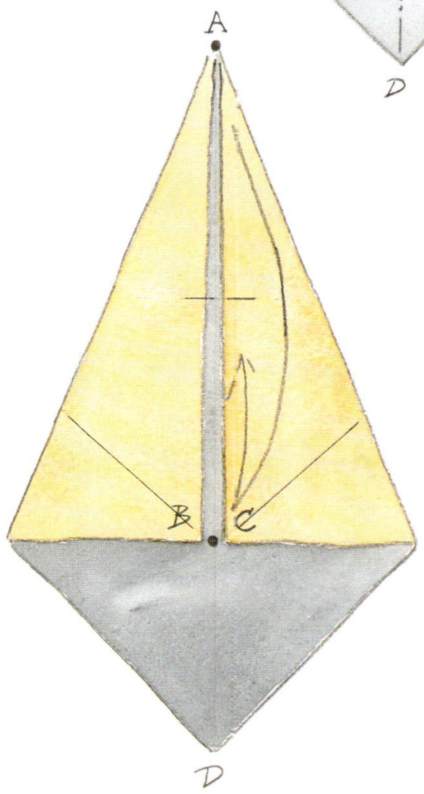

3 Fold A down to BC and pinch across the middle. Unfold.

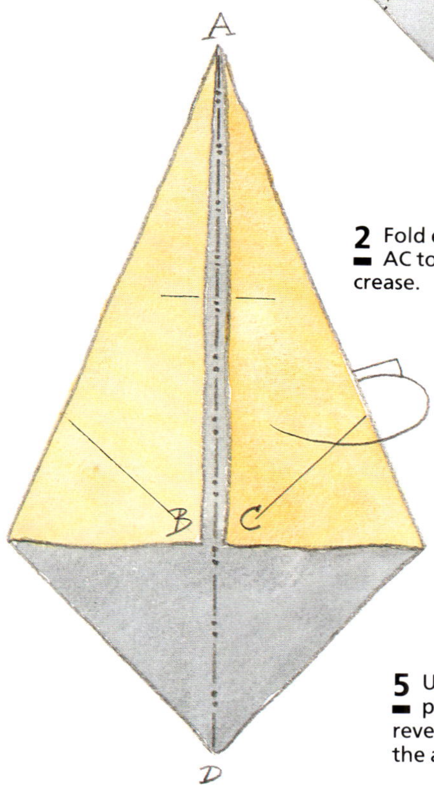

4 Fold C behind.

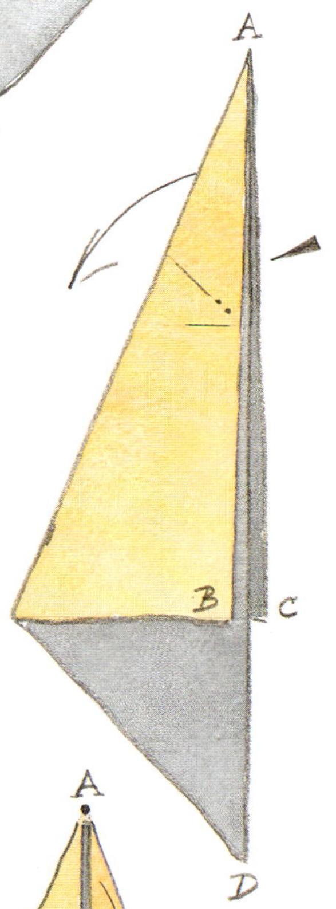

5 Using the Step 3 pinch as a guide, reverse fold A. Note the angle in Step 6.

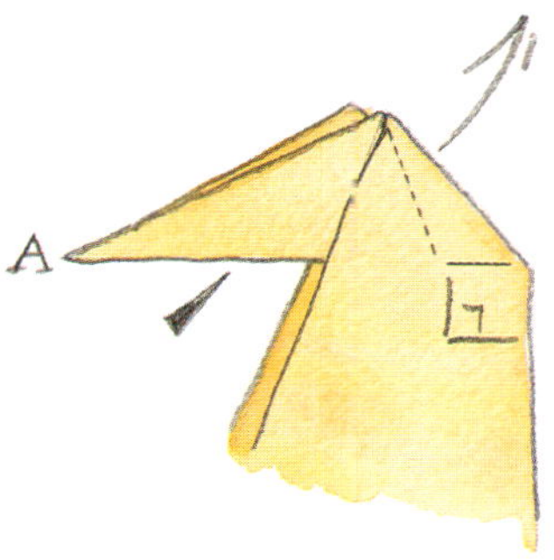

6 Reverse fold A again. Note the angle in Step 7.

7 Unfold back to Step 4.

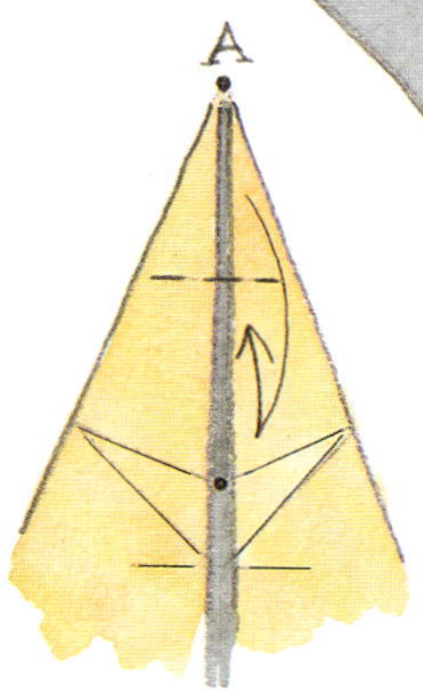

8 Fold A down to the reverse fold made in Step 6. Pinch across the middle. Refold to Step 7.

(Continued . . .)

SEATED FIGURE *(continued)*

9 Reverse fold A, using the Step 8 pinch as a guide. Note the angle in Step 10.

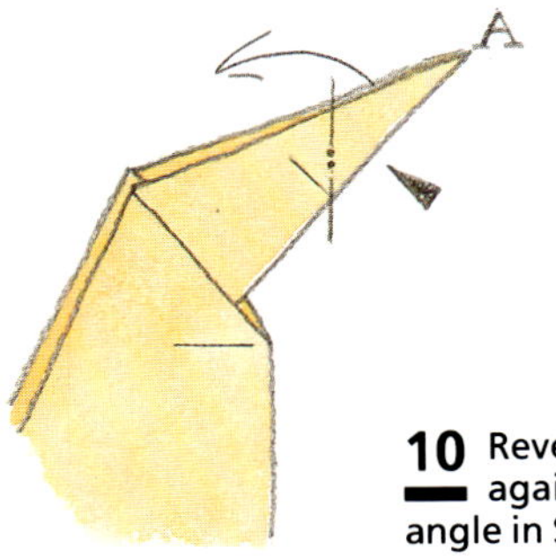

10 Reverse fold A again. Note the angle in Step 11.

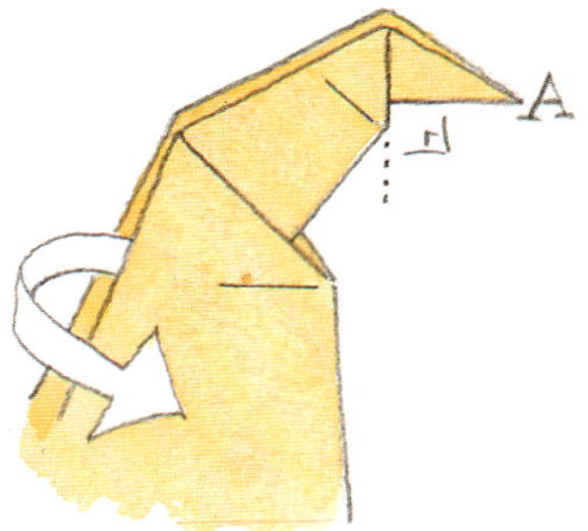

11 Completely unfold.

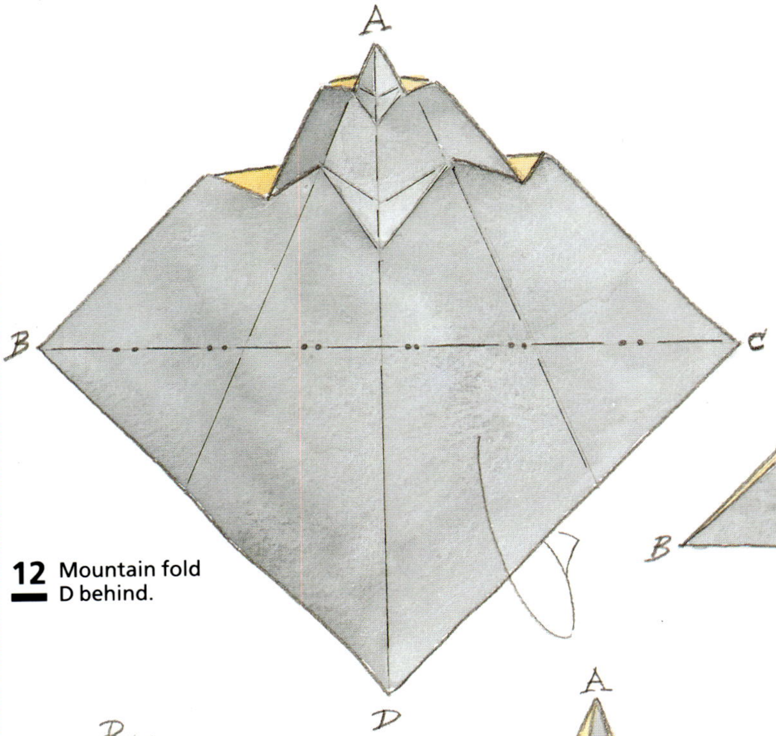

12 Mountain fold D behind.

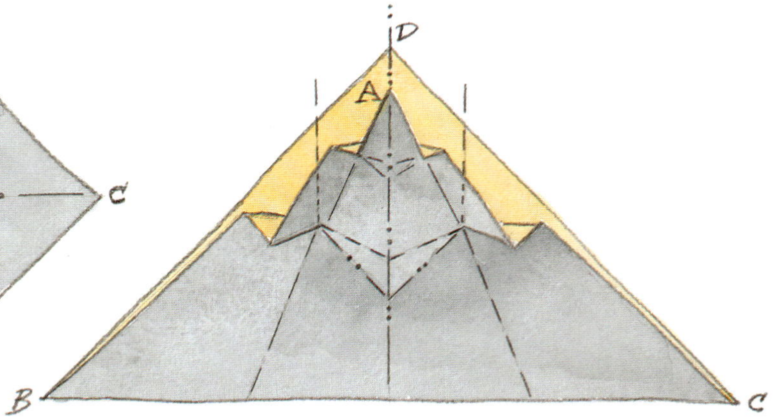

13 Collapse as shown. Note that the reverse folds made in Steps 6 & 7 are here reformed through both layers, but the latter pair of reverse folds are not formed at all.

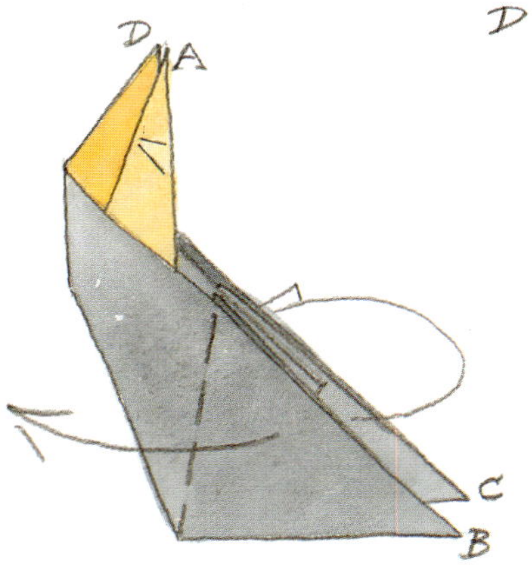

14 Fold back B & C.

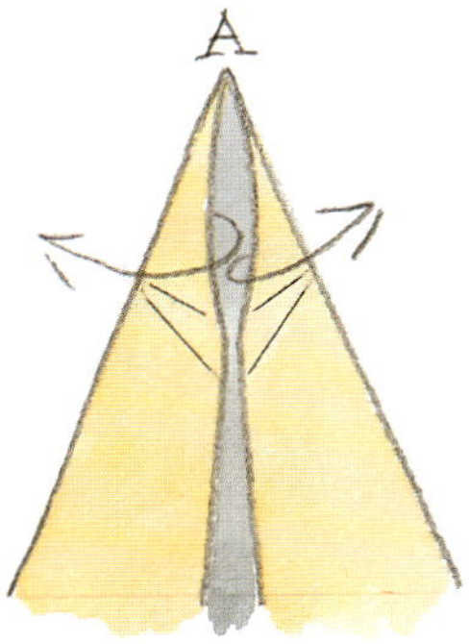

15 Open the head.

16 Fold back the tip.

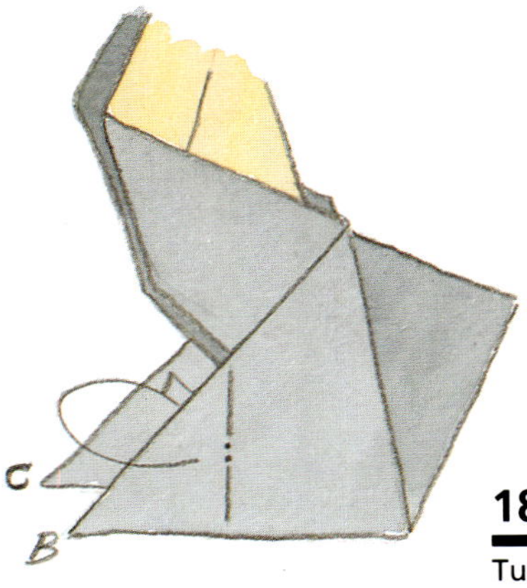

17 Fold in B & C.

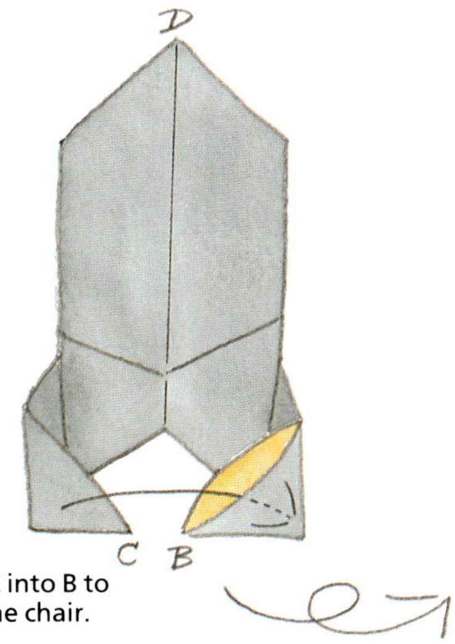

18 Tuck C into B to lock the chair. Turn over.

19 The Seated Figure complete.

ELECTRA

An appeal of modular folding is that spectacular structures can be made from simple units, so that the whole is very much more than the sum of its parts. Thirty modules are needed for this design, which will take about an hour to make. Fold them all very carefully, then slot them together, with diligent regard for the '5 and 3' (pentagons and triangles) interlocking pattern. The result is a pierced structure of great beauty and strength.
Use 30 10 cm (4 in) squares.
If using origami paper, start with the coloured side up.

Designed by David Mitchell, UK.

(Continued . . .)

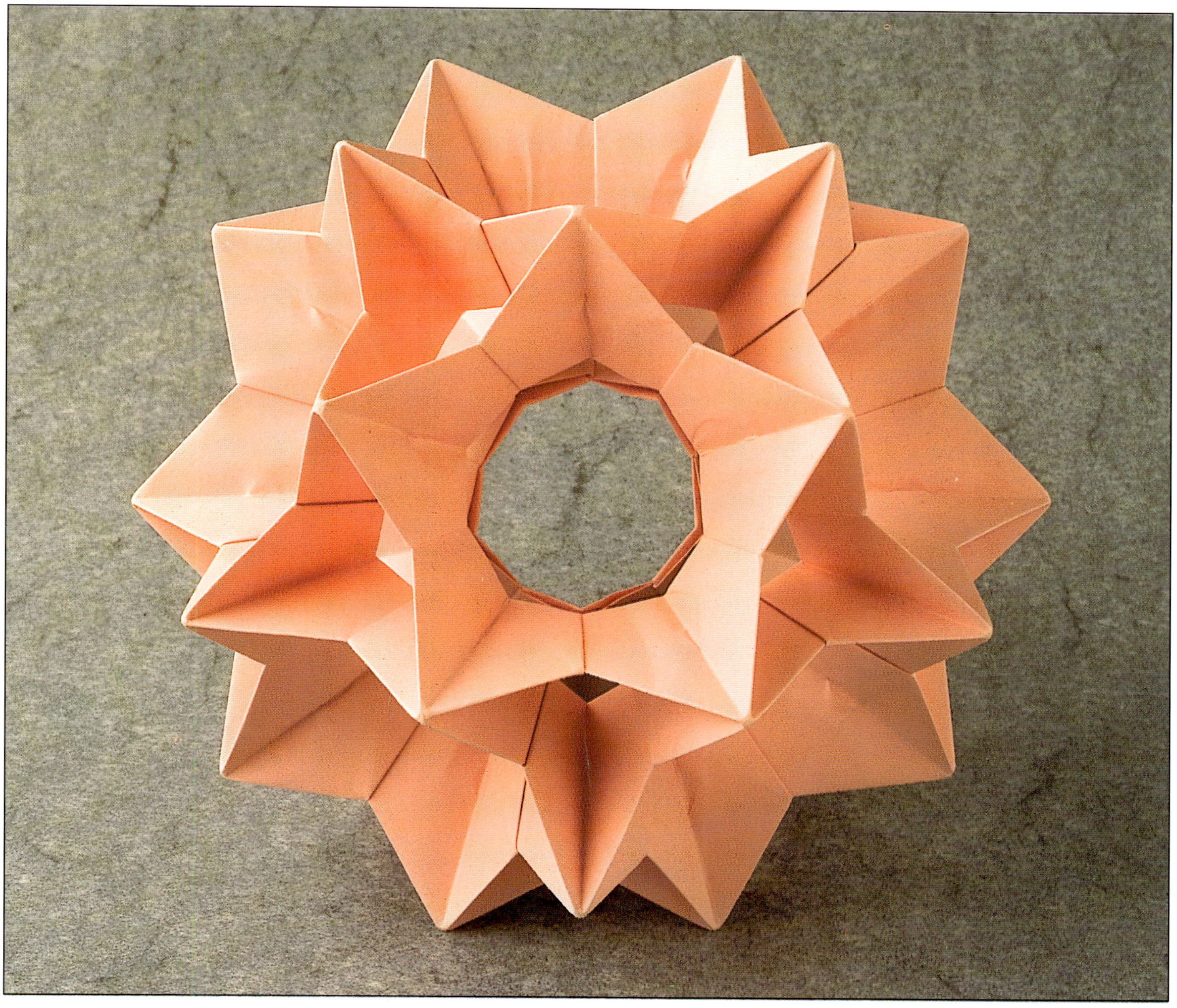

ELECTRA *(continued)*

METHOD

1 Crease and unfold both diagonals as valleys. Turn over.

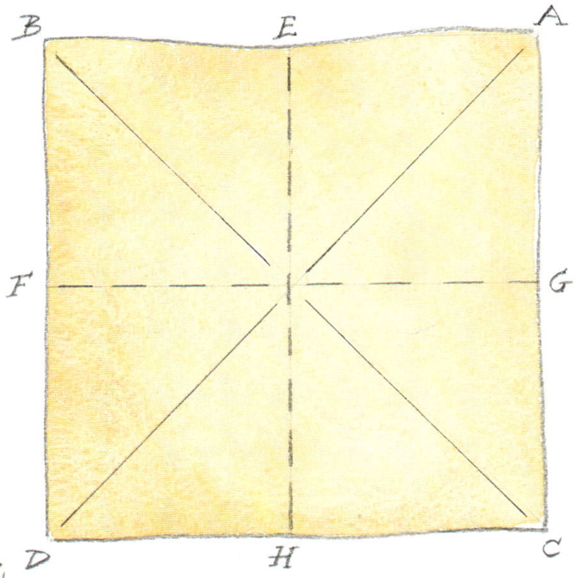

2 Crease and unfold horizontally and vertically. (The diagonals are mountains.)

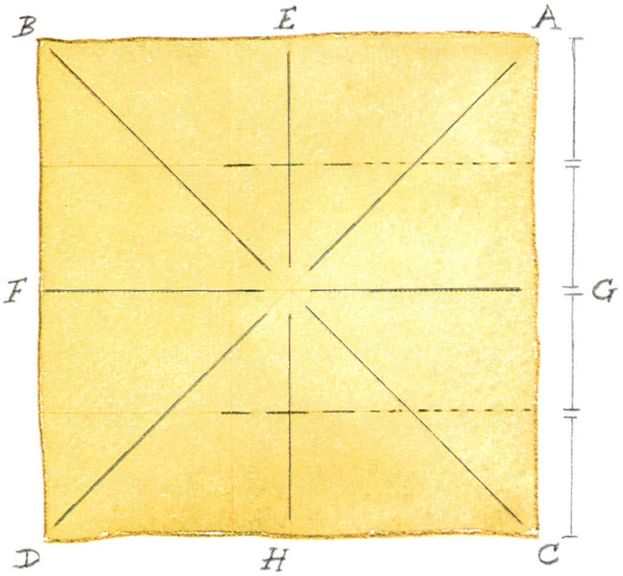

3 Pinch the quarter points along crease EH.

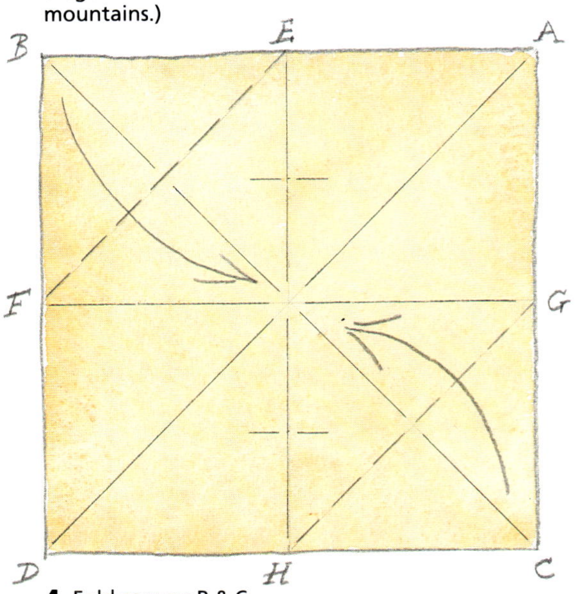

4 Fold corners B & C to the middle.

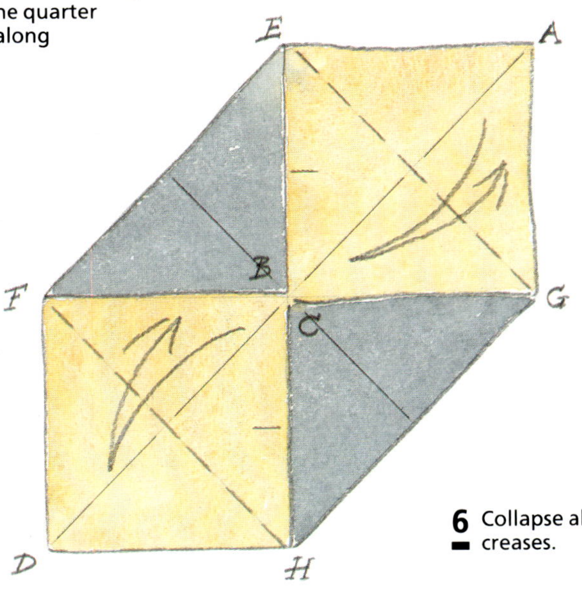

5 Fold and unfold corners A & D.

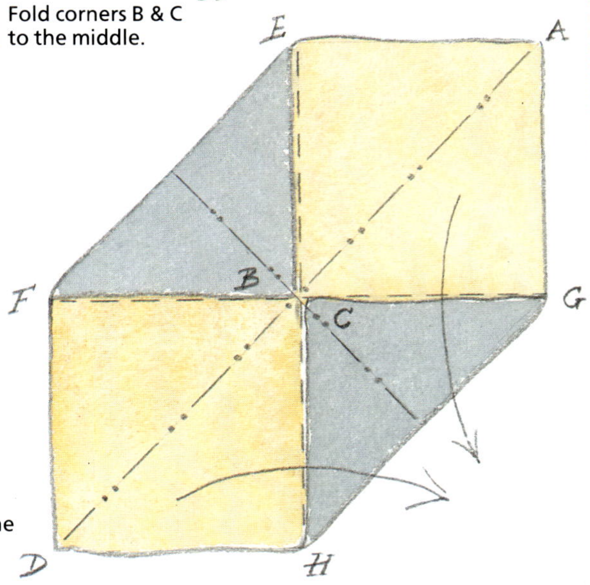

6 Collapse all the creases.

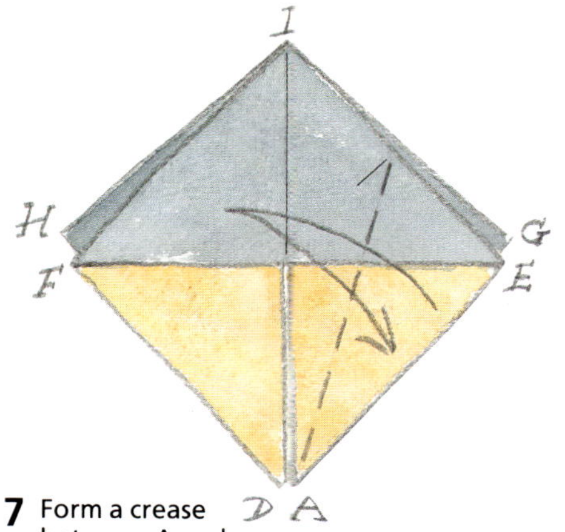

7 Form a crease between A and the pinch made in Step 3, folding E across to the left side. Unfold.

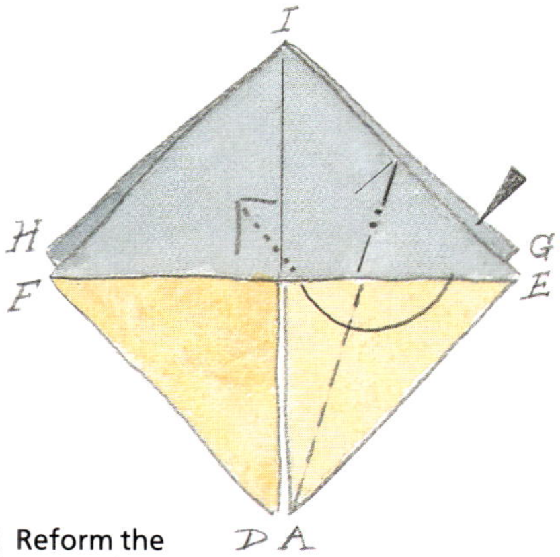

8 Reform the crease, but reverse fold E inside.

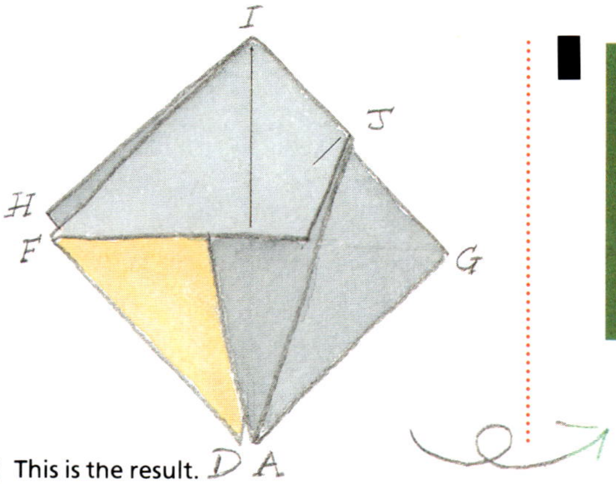

9 This is the result. Turn over.

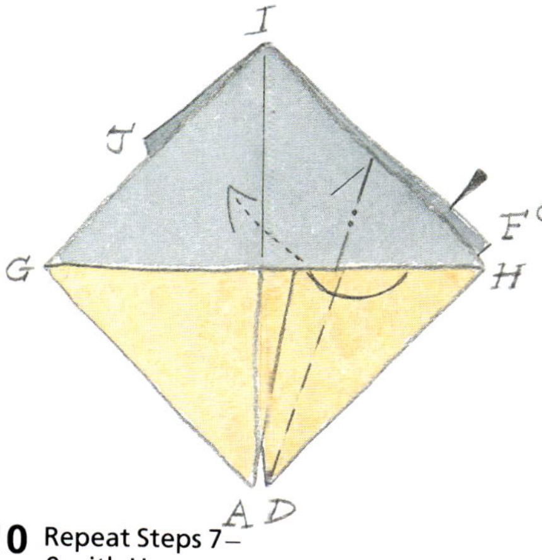

10 Repeat Steps 7–9 with H.

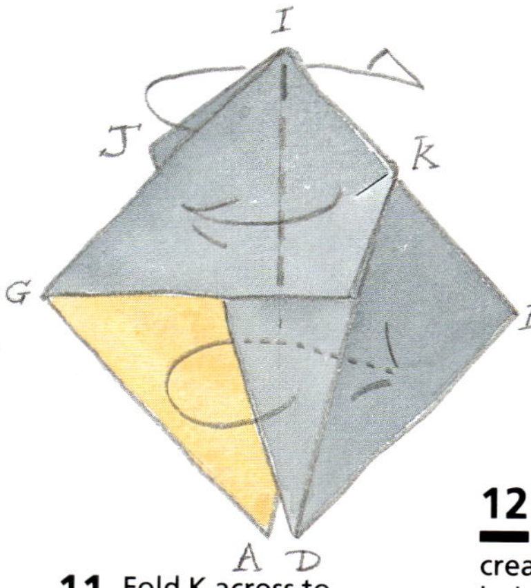

11 Fold K across to the left, allowing the triangle above D to swivel inside and across to the right. Repeat behind with J.

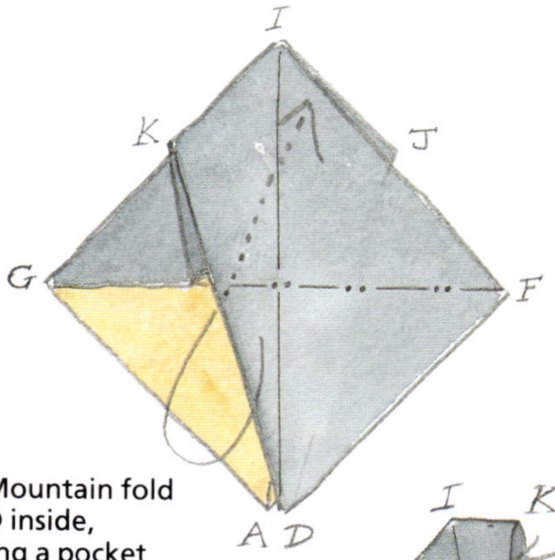

12 Mountain fold D inside, creating a pocket below K. Repeat with A.

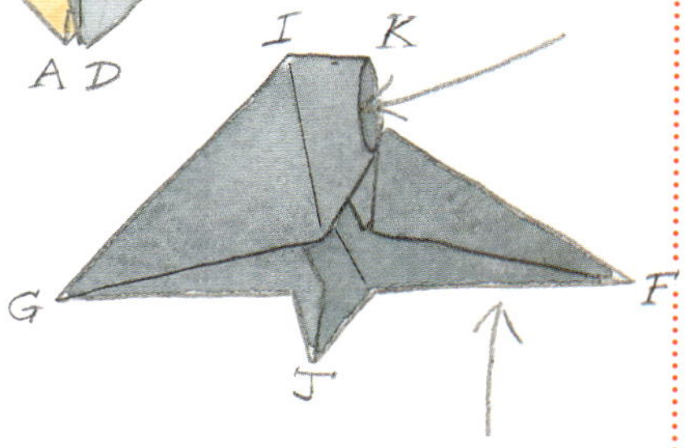

13 This is the completed module. Note the closed pockets below J & K and the extended flaps at F & G.

ASSEMBLY

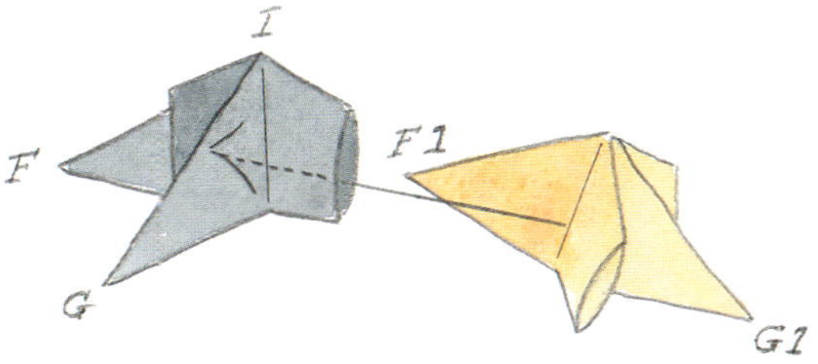

1 Tuck the extended flap on one module (F1), deep inside the pocket of another. To lock them together, fold F or G (depending on which one flap F1 has been tucked into) towards G1.

2 Repeat with the nearside flaps and pockets.

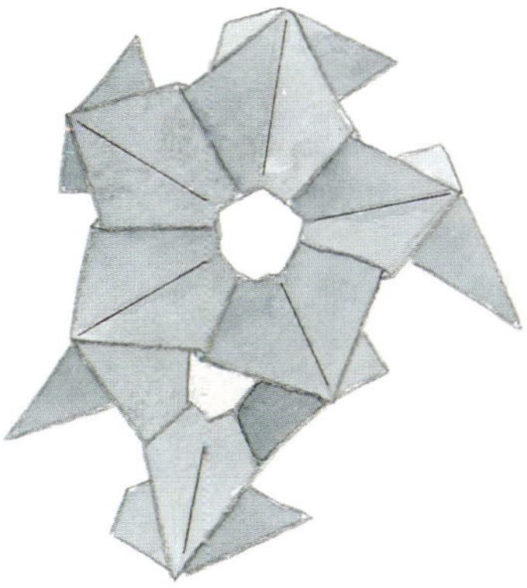

3 Lock 5 modules together, leaving no excess flaps in the centre of the pentagon. A sixth module is shown at the very bottom of the drawing connecting two neighbouring pentagon modules, thereby creating a triangle with no loose flaps in its centre. The completed Electra is thus a combination of pentagons and triangles. Interlock the remaining modules following this pattern.

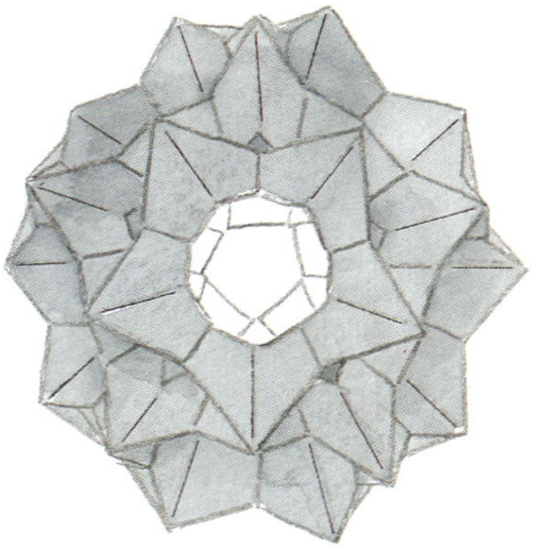

4 The completed Electra.

SEAL ON A ROCK

So called 'double subjects' or 'combination folds' are common in complex origami, where two subjects or objects are folded from a single sheet. Examples might include a mother pushing a pram, a man playing an instrument or, as in this case, a seal basking on a rock. Some creative folders have combined even more subjects, such as several birds in a nest. Use a square of origami paper coloured side up, or for a better effect, two differently coloured or textured sheets folded back to back.

Designed by Dr Martin Wall, UK.

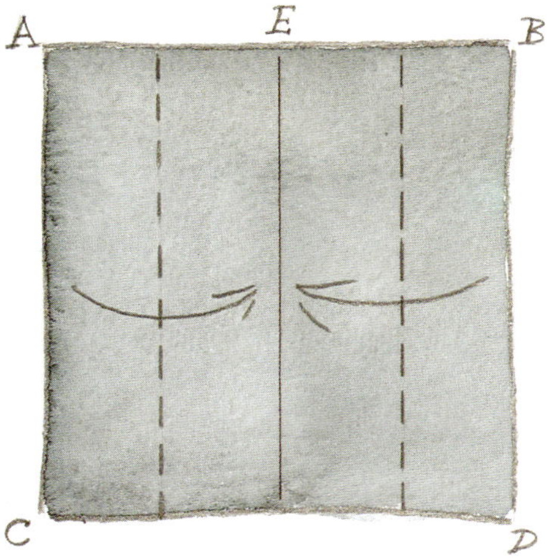

1 Crease and unfold down the centre, then fold the sides to the middle.

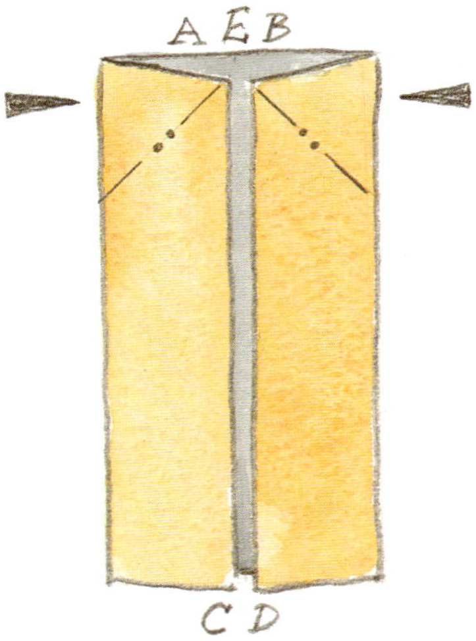

2 Reverse fold the top two corners.

3 Collapse, folding A & B downwards and adding the reverse folds.

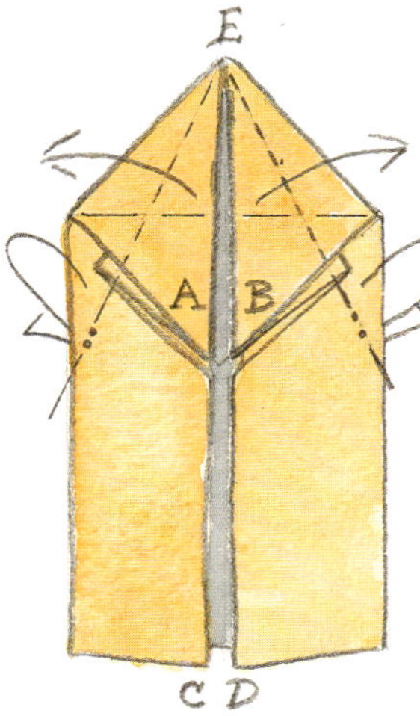

4 Fold as shown, allowing A & B to swivel outwards.

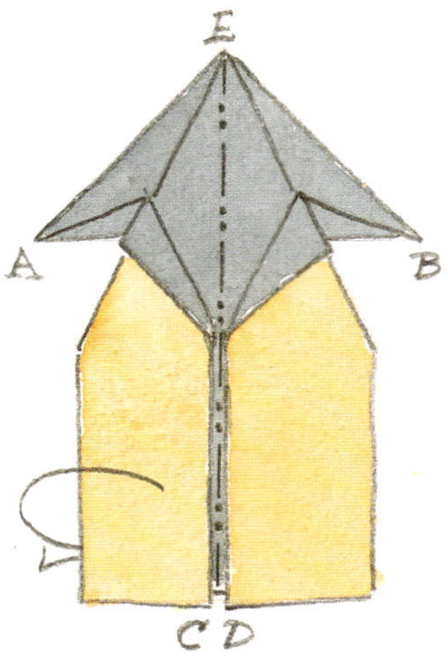

5 Mountain fold A behind.

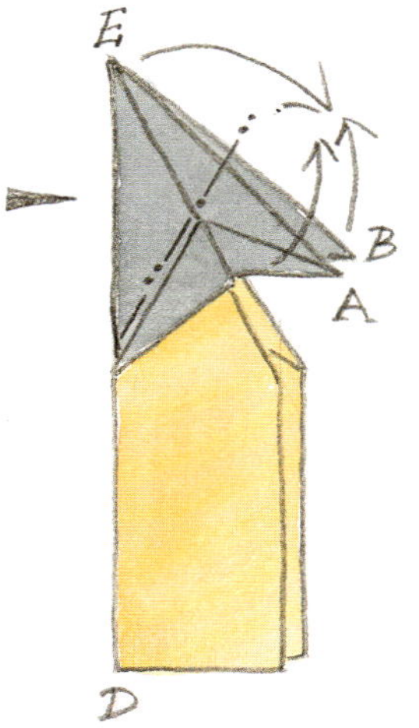

6 Reverse fold E, allowing A & B to pivot upwards to touch E.

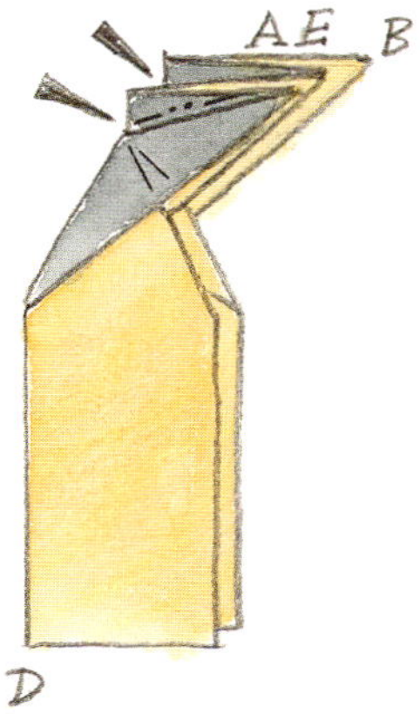

7 Narrow the paper with two reverse folds.

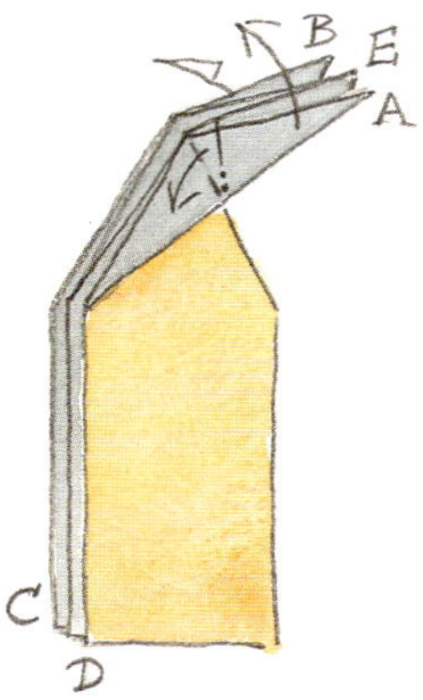

8 Pleat A & B.

9 Turn E inside out, lowering A & B.

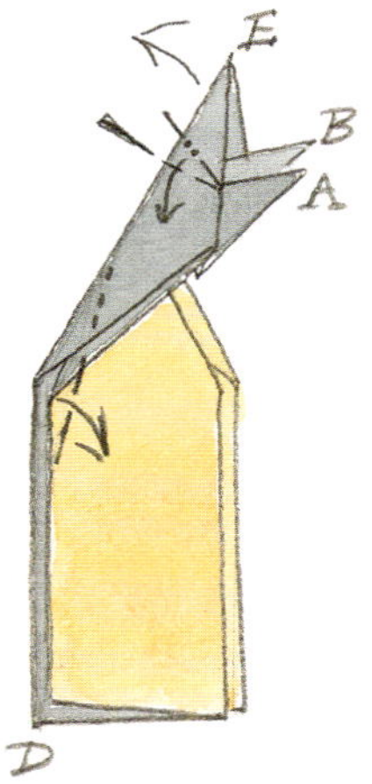

10 Crimp the neck upwards. Release paper for the tail. Repeat behind.

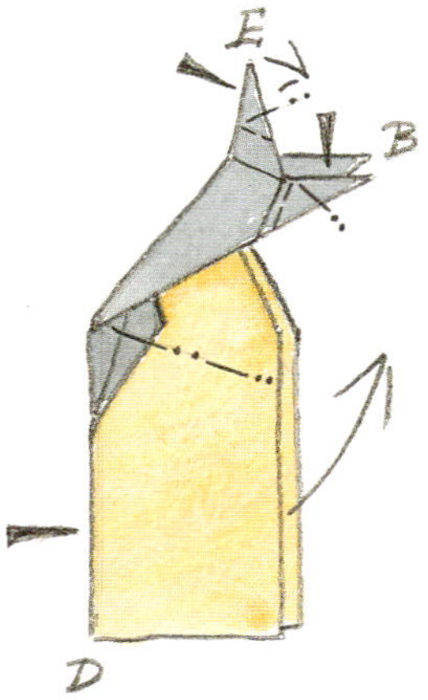

11 Crimp the head. Squash the flippers. Reverse fold the rock.

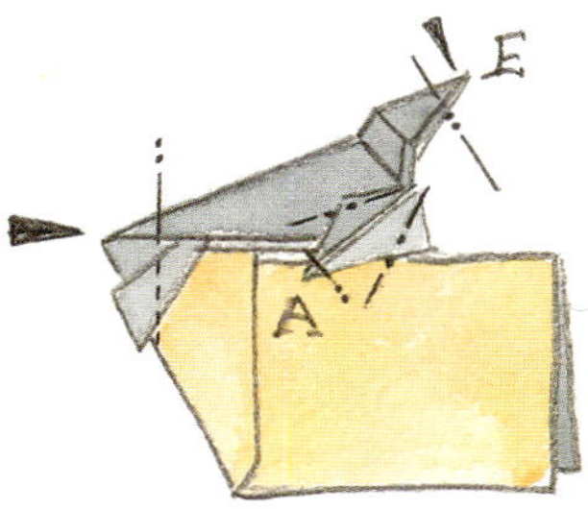

12 Reverse fold the snout. Round off the flippers. Sink the excess paper inside at the tail.

13 Crimp the rock to make it 3D.

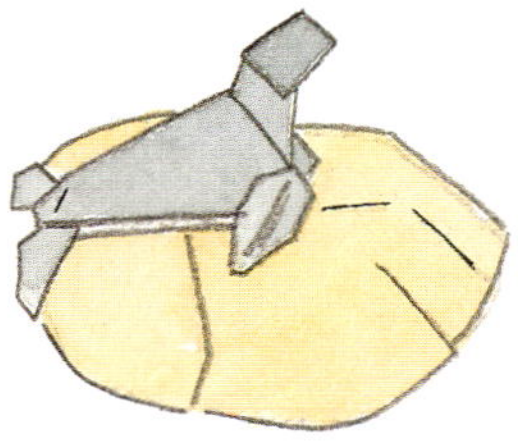

14 The Seal on a Rock complete.

BOWL

Dr Shen is renowned for his geometric and abstract forms which collapse dramatically into shape from an apparently unpromising pattern of pre-creases. In this example, note how the soft, cushion-like base makes an effective contrast to the straight-sided walls. The locking mechanism in Steps 13–14 is also pleasing. Use a square of origami paper, white side up, or paper the same colour both sides.

Designed by Dr Philip Shen, Hong Kong.

1 Crease mountains and valleys as shown.

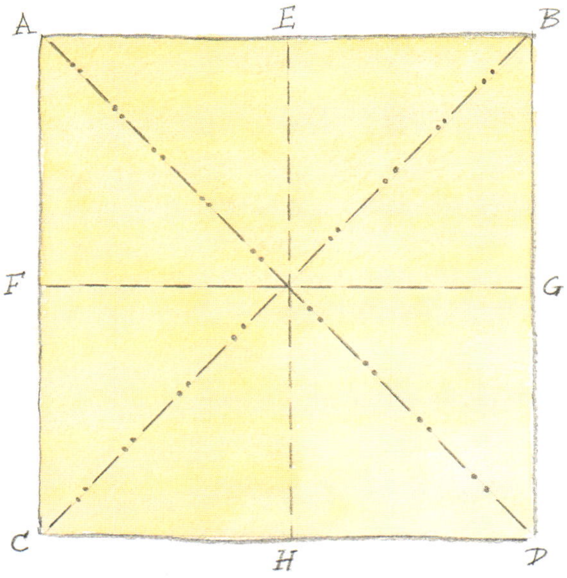

2 Lightly lay corner B onto crease HE, in such a position that if the paper were flattened to make a crease, the crease would run exactly to corner A. However, flatten to make a crease *only* in the two short sections shown. Be precise.

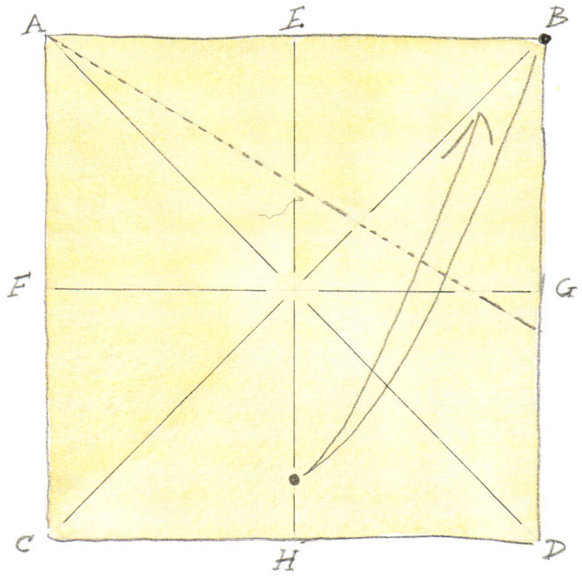

3 Repeat, laying corner C onto crease GF.

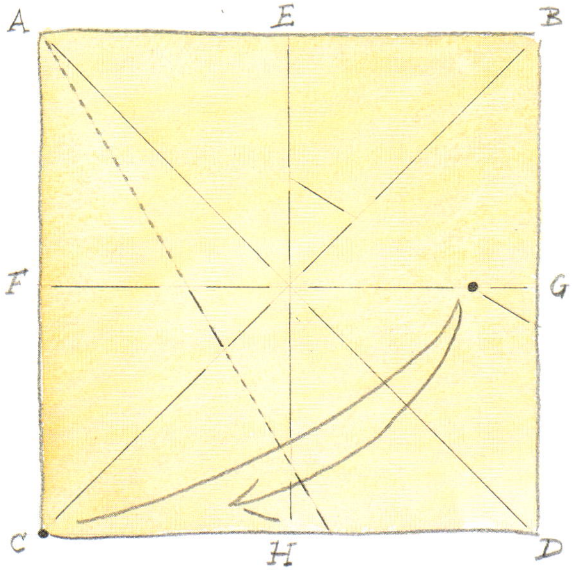

4 Note the crease pattern, both pairs of creases pointing to corner A. Repeat the pattern, so that pairs of creases point to corners B,C, & D.

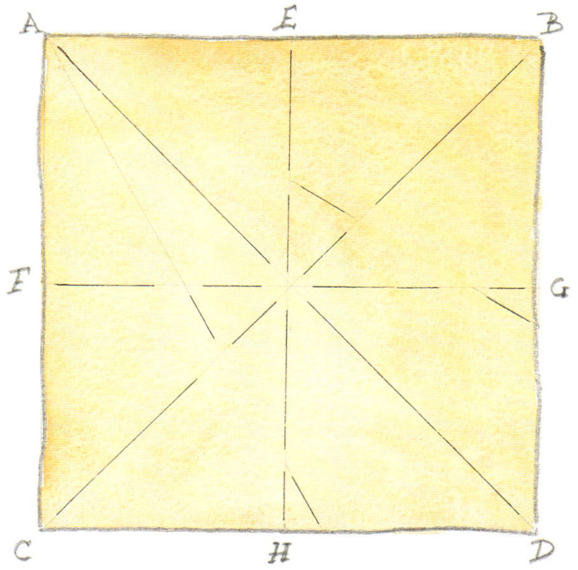

5 Note the octagon of creases in the centre and the 'V's' at E,F,G, & H. Fold B to point I, but crease only where shown. Similarly, fold C to J. Note that if extended, both creases would meet at corner A.

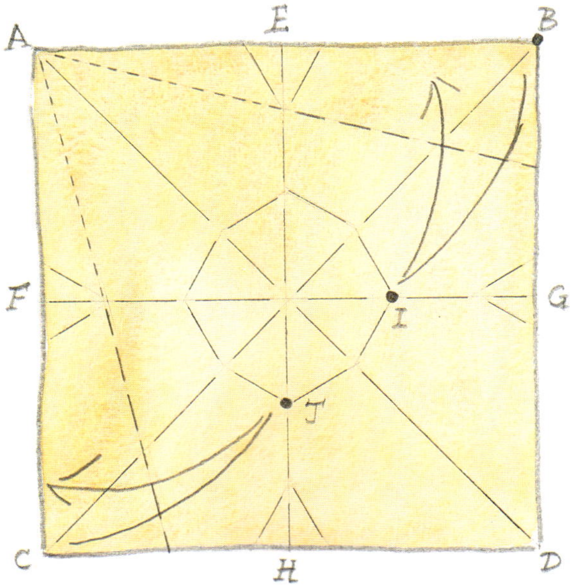

6 This is the crease pattern. Repeat Step 5, creating creases which if extended, would meet at corners B,C, & D.

(Continued . . .)

BOWL

(continued)

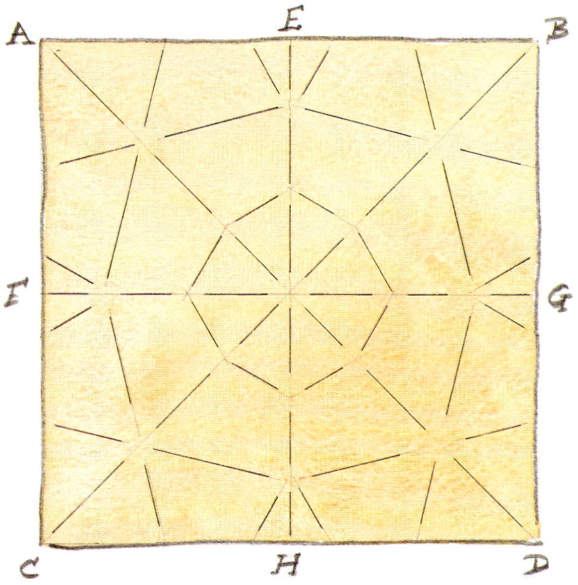

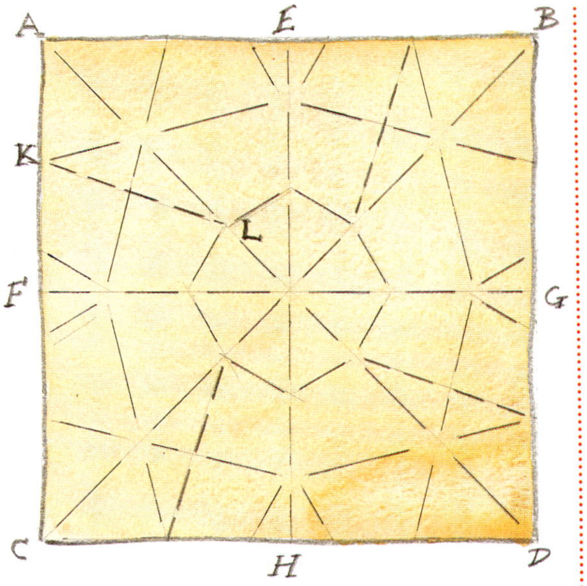

7 This is the present crease pattern.

8 Form crease KL to the left of corner A, then repeat with similar creases to the left of each corner, rotating the square 90° each time.

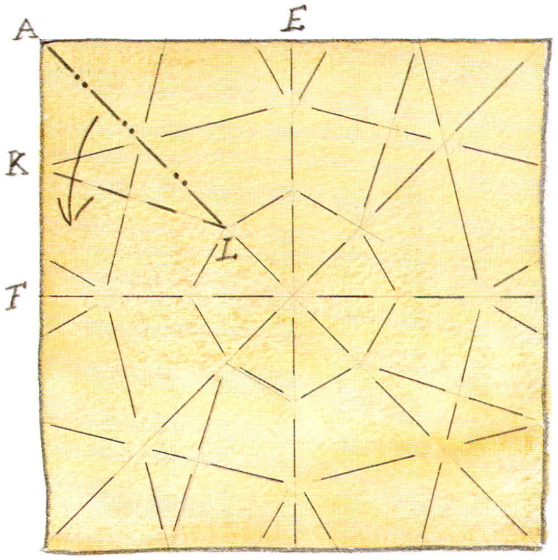

9 Form a pleat along AL & KL, making the paper 3D. Note that L is concave, not convex.

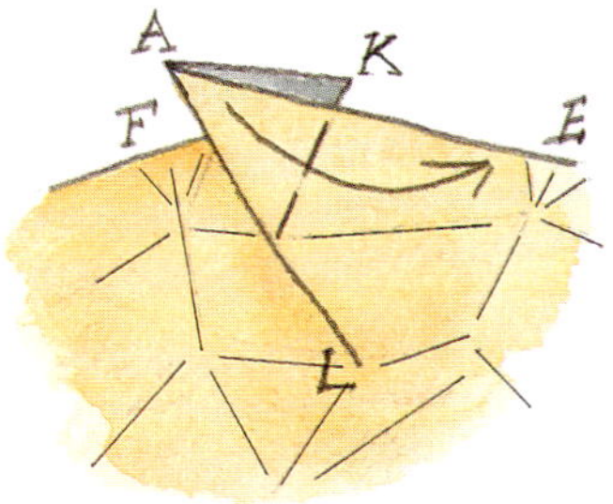

10 Fold A to the right along existing creases. Repeat with B, C & D, folding them also to the right.

13 Form a mountain as shown . . .

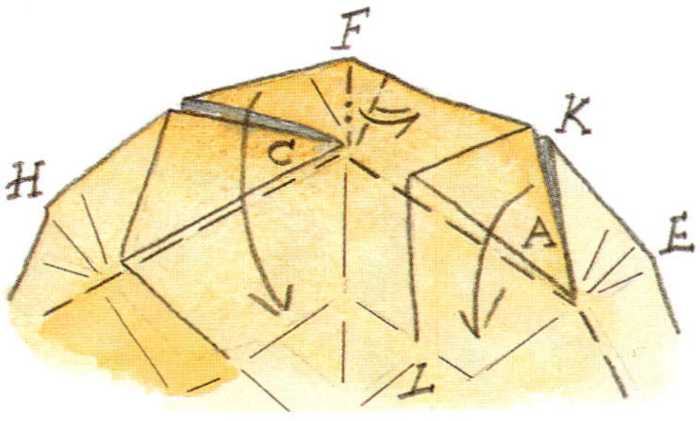

11 Collapse all the way round the bowl. Note the pleat at F, repeated at E, G & H.

12 This is the bowl at present – a loose, badly-locked and rather lumpy form. Turn it upside down.

15 The Bowl complete. Note the soft, cushion-like form of the bottom.

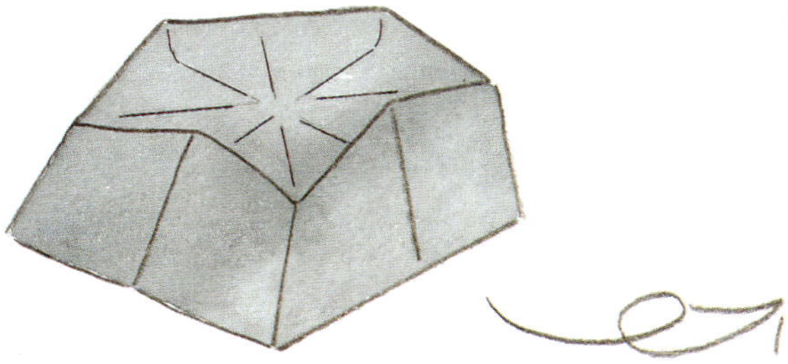

14 . . . to create a flat-bottomed bowl standing on four squat, flat triangles. These flat triangles trap the K corners inside their layers, so neatening the inside of the bowl. Turn over.

ELEPHANT

This final design in the advanced origami section is appropriately the most difficult. Step 7 contains a fiendish closed sink, which will have even the most experienced folders fumbling a little. The Step 11 half-closed sink is little better. It is puzzling to wonder why a design which looks so little like a real elephant should be so immediately recognizable as one! Use a square of paper, same colour both sides. If using origami paper, the coloured side should be outside at Step 1.

Designed by Paul Jackson.

(Continued . . .)

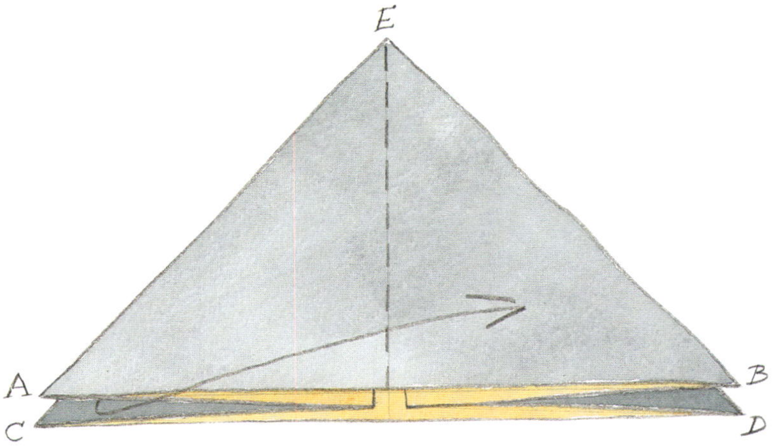

1 Begin with Step 6 of the Waterbomb project. Fold A across to the right.

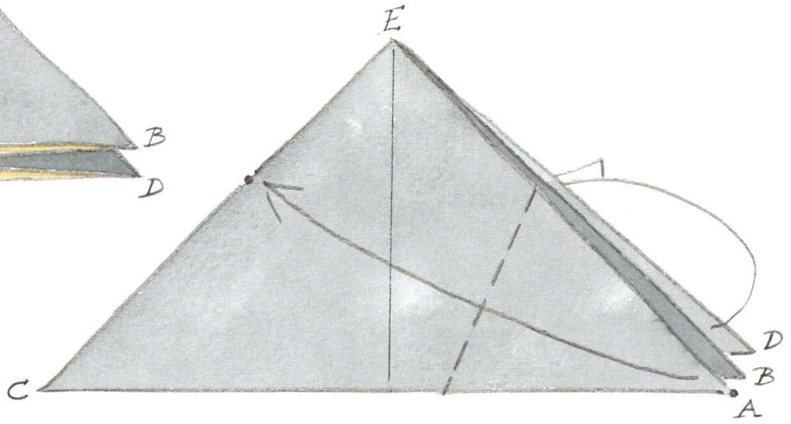

2 Fold A & D across to edge EC . . .

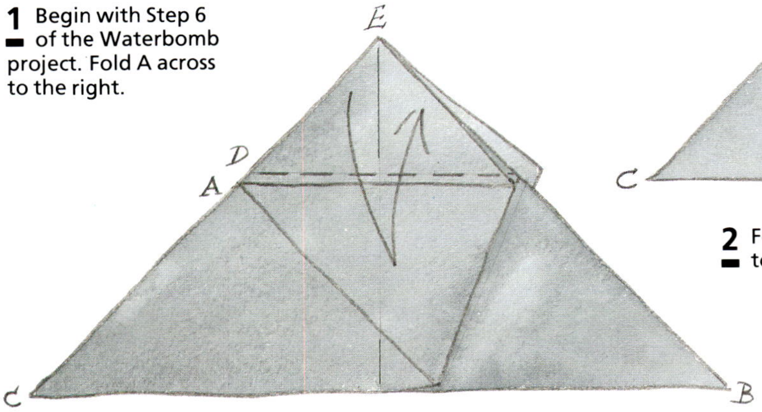

3 . . . like this, so that when the crease is made, it is precisely horizontal. Unfold it.

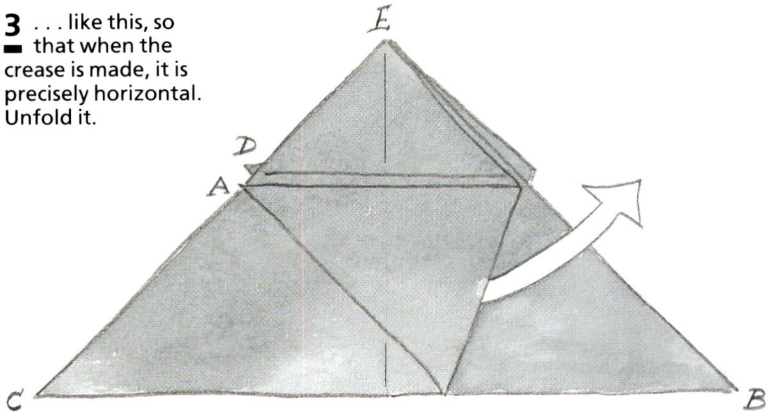

4 Unfold A & D, then swivel B upwards to create the Step 5 shape.

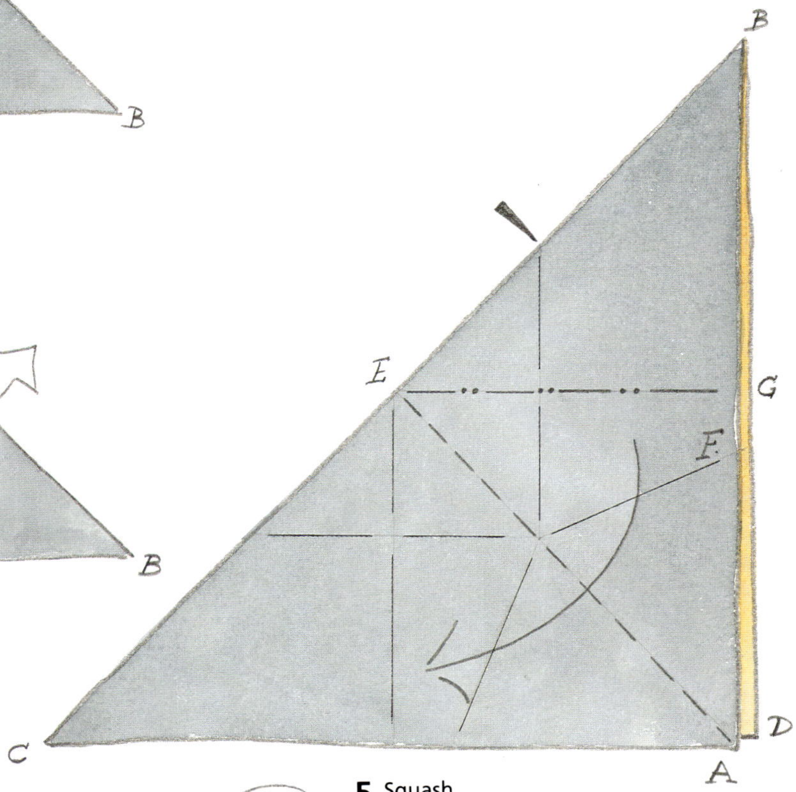

5 Squash, separating F from G.

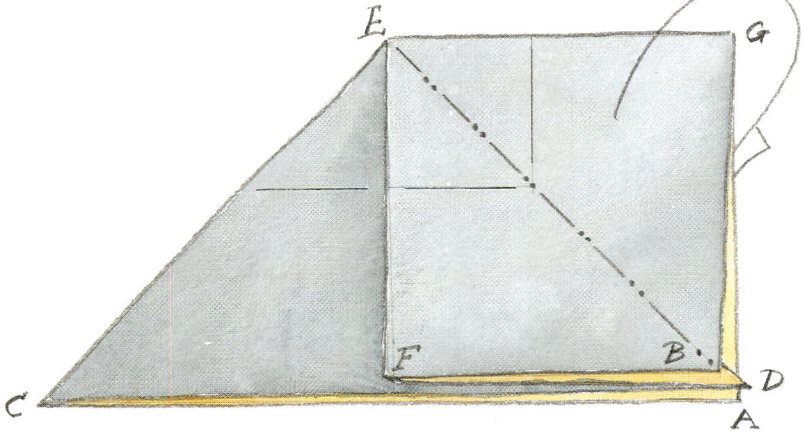

6 Fold G behind.

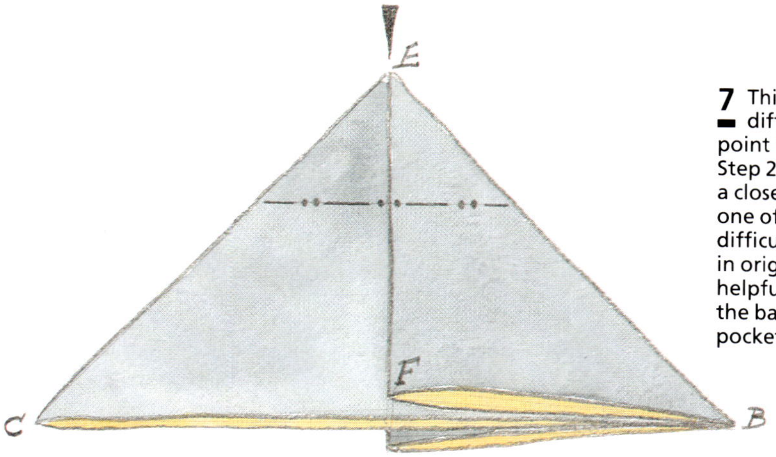

7 This is the difficult step. Sink point E along the Step 2 creases. This is a closed, 2D sink; one of the most difficult procedures in origami. It is helpful to open out the back edge of the pocket to create a large 3-sided pyramid, then invert point E and somehow revert the pyramid back to the 2D shape seen in Step 8. There is no easy way to perform the manoeuvre, but practice will make it more fluent.

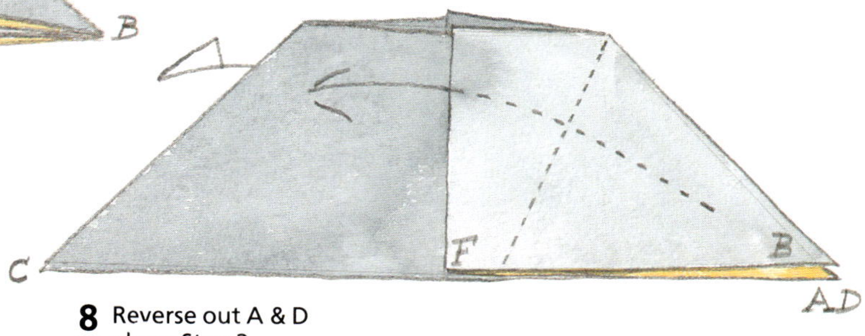

8 Reverse out A & D along Step 2 creases.

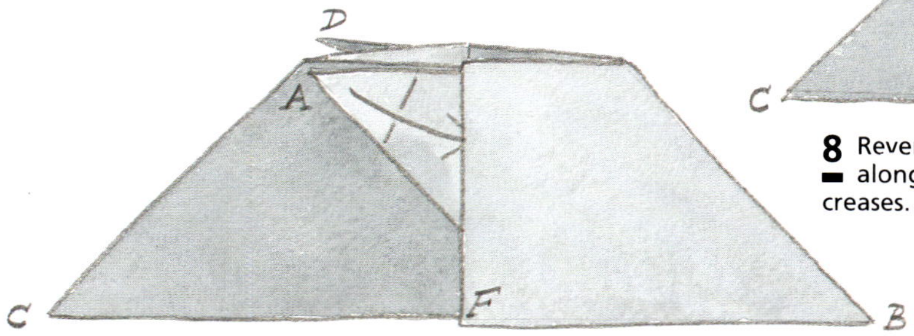

9 Tuck the tip of A just behind the edge. Repeat with D.

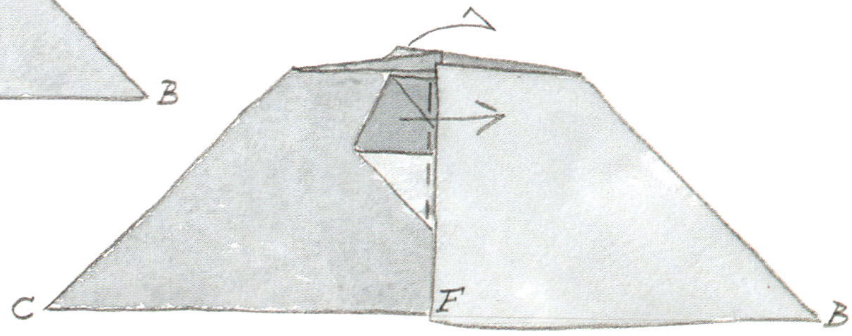

10 Fold the ears across to the right.

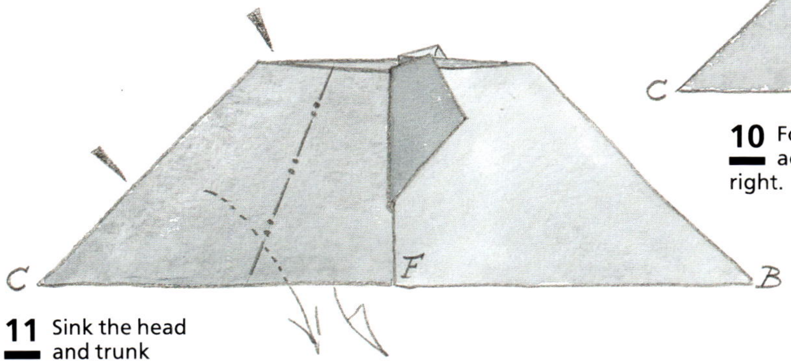

11 Sink the head and trunk (another difficult step!).

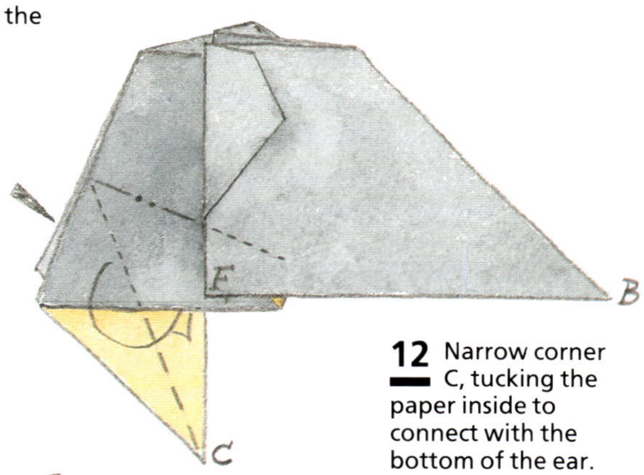

12 Narrow corner C, tucking the paper inside to connect with the bottom of the ear. Repeat behind.

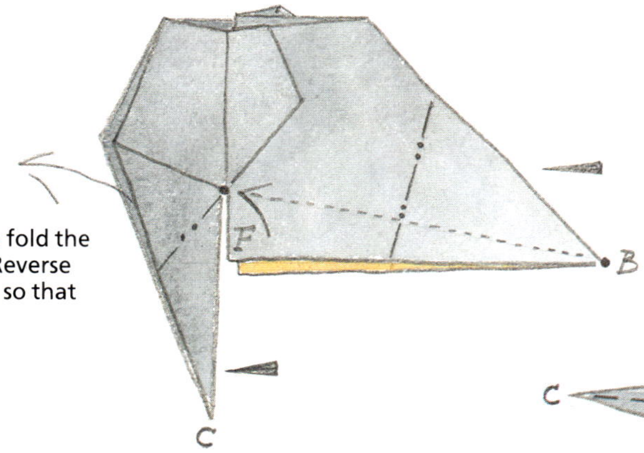

13 Reverse fold the trunk. Reverse fold the tail, so that B touches F.

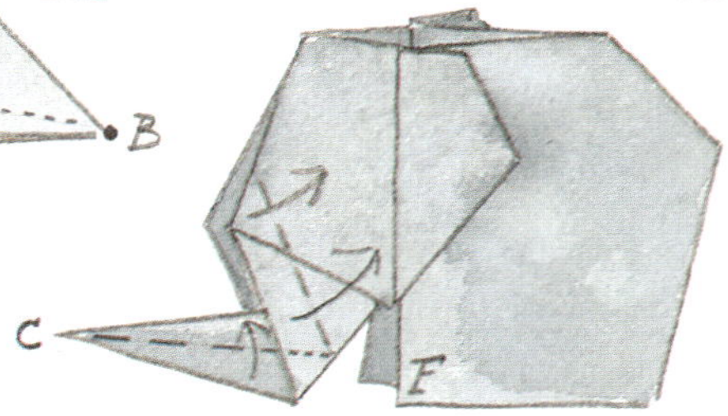

14 Narrow the trunk and head.

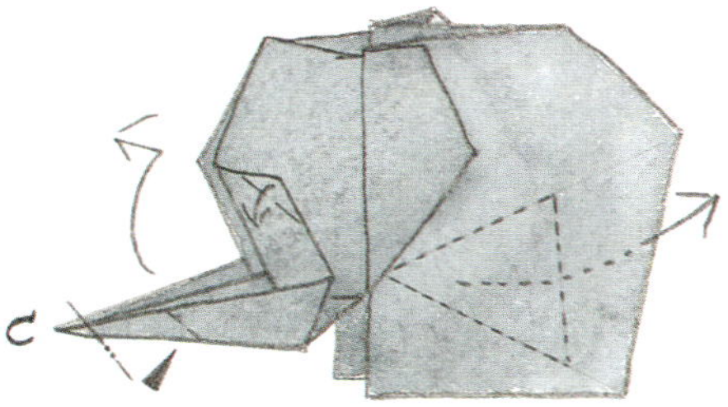

15 Reverse fold the tip of the tail into view. Outside reverse fold the trunk, twice. Fold over the eye. Repeat behind.

16 The Elephant complete. If you managed to make it . . . well done!

INDEX

SUPPLIERS

SUPPLIER S

The author and publishers would like to thank the following suppliers for their generous help and advice in providing materials used to create the projects in this book. These suppliers specialize in selling papers and card direct to the public and can be contacted at the addresses shown below.

UK

Mara Amats
ADAE Associates
c/o 8 Wendover Court
Chiltern Street
London W1M 1PB
(*Specialist in handmade Nepalese papers*)

Falkiner Fine Papers Ltd.
76 Southampton Row
London WC1B 4AR

Robert Horne Paper Company
Huntsman House
Mansion Close
Moulton Park
Northampton NN3 1LA

Neal Street East
5 Neal Street
London WC2H 9PU
(*Stockists of a wide range of origami papers*)

One Four Nine Paper Supplies
PO Box A13
Huddersfield
West Yorkshire HD3 4LW
(*Mail order specialists*)

Paperchase
213 Tottenham Court Road
London W1A 4US

Paperpoint
130 Long Acre
London WC2E 9AL

Paperpoint
26 Calthorpe Road
Edgbaston
Birmingham B15 1RP

USA

Kate's Paperie
8 West 13th Street
New York
NY 10001

Papersource Inc.
730 N Franklin Suite 111
Chicago
Il 60610

Australia

ACT Papers Pty Ltd.
10 McGlone Street
Micham
Victoria 3132